GRAPPLING
WITH THE BOMB
BRITAIN'S PACIFIC H-BOMB TESTS

GRAPPLING WITH THE BOMB

BRITAIN'S PACIFIC H-BOMB TESTS

NIC MACLELLAN

PRESS

PACIFIC SERIES

Published by ANU Press
The Australian National University
Acton ACT 2601, Australia
Email: anupress@anu.edu.au
This title is also available online at press.anu.edu.au

National Library of Australia Cataloguing-in-Publication entry

Creator: Maclellan, Nic, author.

Title: Grappling with the bomb : Britain's Pacific H-bomb tests / Nicholas Maclellan.

ISBN: 9781760461379 (paperback) 9781760461386 (ebook)

Subjects: Operation Grapple, Kiribati, 1956-1958.
Nuclear weapons--Great Britain--Testing.
Hydrogen bomb--Great Britain--Testing.
Nuclear weapons--Testing--Oceania.
Hydrogen bomb--Testing--Oceania.
Nuclear weapons testing victims--Oceania.
Pacific Islanders--Health and hygiene--Oceania.
Nuclear explosions--Environmental aspects--Oceania.
Nuclear weapons--Testing--Environmental aspects--Oceania.
Great Britain--Military policy.

All rights reserved. No part of this publication may be reproduced, stored in a retrieval system or transmitted in any form or by any means, electronic, mechanical, photocopying or otherwise, without the prior permission of the publisher.

Cover design and layout by ANU Press. Cover image: Adapted from photo of Grapple nuclear test. Source: Adi Sivo Ganilau.

This edition © 2017 ANU Press

Contents

List of illustrations vii
Timeline and glossary xi
Maps xxiii
Introduction 1
1. *The leader* — Sir Winston Churchill. .19
2. *The survivors* — Lemeyo Abon and Rinok Riklon 39
3. *The fisherman* — Matashichi Oishi 55
4. *The Task Force Commander* — Wilfred Oulton 69
5. *The businessman* — James Burns 81
6. *The pacifist* — Harold Steele 91
Interlude — On radiation, safety and secrecy 105
7. *The Chief Petty Officer* — Ratu Inoke Bainimarama 125
8. *The sailor* — Paul Ah Poy 135
9. *The high chief* — Ratu Penaia Ganilau 147
10. *The WVS ladies* — Mary and Billie Burgess 157
11. *The pilot* — Geoffrey Dhenin. 167
12. *The Prime Minister* — Harold Macmillan 177
13. *The Foreign Officer* — Gillian Brown .193
14. *The telegraphist* — Roy Sefton 205
15. *The soldiers* — Isireli Qalo 221
16. *The Banaban* — Tekoti Rotan 231
17. *The mothers* — Sui Kiritome 247
18. *The last soldiers* — Josefa Vueti 257

19. *The President*—John F. Kennedy 267

Interlude—Contested illnesses 281

20. *The research scientist*—Al Rowland 291

21. *The litigant*—Pita Rokoratu. 311

22. *The Rear Admiral*—Josaia Voreqe Bainimarama. 323

Aftermath. 339

Acknowledgements 343

Bibliography. 347

Index 375

List of illustrations

Map 1: Pacific Nuclear Test Sites, 1946–96 xxiii
Map 2: Christmas (Kiritimati) Island, 1957–58 xxiv
Sir Winston Churchill, Franklin Delano Roosevelt and Joseph Stalin at the February 1945 Yalta conference 19
Yami Lester, Wallatinna Station, South Australia, 2006 29
Lemeyo Abon and Rinok Riklon, Majuro, Marshall Islands 39
Crew member Matashichi Oishi with the fishing boat Daigo Fukuryu Maru 55
Grapple Task Force Commander Air Vice Marshall Wilfred Oulton . . 69
Postcard of tent city on Christmas Island 75
Former Burns Philp & Company headquarters in Sydney 81
UK security forces tracked the movements of British pacifist Harold Steele from London to Japan 92
Map of Grapple Danger Area 106
Fiji Royal Naval Volunteer Reserve (FRNVR) sailors aboard HMS *Warrior*, off Malden Island, May 1957 125
Paul Ah Poy and sailors from HMS *Warrior* and HMNZS *Rotoiti*, May 1957 135
Paul Ah Poy at the Remembrance Day march, Nausori, Fiji, 11 November 2016 144
Ratu Penaia Ganilau and Fiji Royal Naval Volunteer Reserve (FRNVR) Commander Stan Brown prepare for the second Grapple test 147

FRNVR sailor Amani Tuimalabe carries a memento of his service in Operation Grapple. 152

Mary and Billie Burgess at the Ship Inn in Korea, 1954 157

Geoffrey Dhenin and crew before their flight to gather samples after the 1953 Totem 1 test 167

British Prime Minister Harold Macmillan, 1957 178

Queen Elizabeth meets Commonwealth prime ministers, including Harold Macmillan of the United Kingdom, Jawaharlal Nehru of India, John Diefenbaker of Canada and Robert Menzies of Australia. 185

Churchill, Eisenhower and Macmillan—improving US–UK relations 193

Roy Sefton, aboard HMNZS *Pukaki*, 1957 206

On the quarter deck of HMNZS *Pukaki* preparing for the Grapple 1 test, May 1957. 210

Roy Sefton QSM, Chair of the New Zealand Nuclear Test Veterans Association (NZNTVA). 218

English officers and soldiers from the Royal Fiji Military Forces (RFMF), Christmas Island, 1958 221

Tekoti Rotan in Suva, Fiji, November 2016 232

Sui Kiritome and her daughter Rakieti in Tarawa, Kiribati, 2004 . . . 247

Mushroom cloud from the Grapple Y test, 28 April 1958 250

Royal Fiji Military Forces (RFMF) soldiers deployed to Christmas Island, 1958 257

Captain Viliame 'Bill' Masi and British officers inspect Fijian troops on Christmas Island 262

Harold Macmillan meets US President John F. Kennedy at Key West in Florida to plan US nuclear tests on Christmas Island 267

The first megaton hydrogen bomb test—Grapple X, November 1957. 282

Al Rowland ONZM. 292

LIST OF ILLUSTRATIONS

HMNZS *Pukaki* proceeds towards the mushroom cloud after
 Grapple 1 test at Malden Island, May 1957 297

The Royal Courts of Justice on G.E. Street, The Strand, London . . . 311

Josaia Voreqe Bainimarama, former Republic of Fiji Military Forces
 (RFMF) Commander and current Prime Minister of Fiji 323

New Zealand nuclear veterans receive the New Zealand Special
 Service Medal (Nuclear Testing) 329

Timeline and glossary

Nuclear timeline, 1945–1963

16 July 1945	Alamogordo, New Mexico, USA	United States conducts first-ever nuclear test, codenamed 'Trinity.'
6 August 1945	Hiroshima, Japan	US aircraft *Enola Gay* drops the atomic weapon 'Little Boy' on Hiroshima, killing 80,000 people immediately and an estimated 100,000 people within six months.
9 August 1945	Nagasaki, Japan	US aircraft *Bockscar* drops the atomic weapon 'Fat Man' on Nagasaki, killing 70,000 people immediately and tens of thousands in following months.
30 June 1946	Bikini Atoll, Marshall Islands	Under Operation Crossroads, United States conducts the first of two atomic tests at Bikini Atoll in the Marshall Islands. 'Able' and 'Baker' are the first of 67 atmospheric tests in the Marshall Islands between 1946–1958.
6 August 1948	Hiroshima, Japan	Hiroshima's first Peace Festival.
29 August 1949	Semipalatinsk, Kazakhstan	USSR conducts first atomic test RDS-1 in Operation *Pervaya molniya* (Fast lightning), dubbed 'Joe-1' by United States.
1950–1954	Korean peninsula	United States, Britain and Australia, under a United Nations mandate, join military operations in Korea following clashes between forces from the south and north of Korea. The Democratic People's Republic is backed by the newly created People's Republic of China.
3 October 1952	Monte Bello Islands, Western Australia	Under Operation Hurricane, United Kingdom begins its nuclear testing program in Australia with a 25 kiloton atomic test.

1 November 1952	Bikini Atoll, Marshall Islands	United States conducts its first hydrogen bomb test, codenamed 'Mike' (10.4 megatons) as part of Operation Ivy.
12 August 1953	Semipalatinsk, Kazakhstan	USSR tests first hydrogen bomb RDS-6 ('Joe-4').
15–27 October 1953	Emu Field, South Australia	Under Operation Totem, United Kingdom conducts two atomic tests ('Totem One' with an 8 kiloton yield and 'Totem Two' with 10 kilotons) in the South Australian desert.
1 March 1954	Bikini Atoll, Marshall Islands	United States conducts hydrogen bomb test at Bikini Atoll, codenamed 'Bravo'. The test showers radioactive fallout over the country, especially northern atolls and Japanese fishing vessel *Lucky Dragon* (six H-bomb tests under Operation Castle between February and May).
6–8 August 1955	Hiroshima, Japan	First World Conference against Atomic and Hydrogen Bombs held on anniversary of atomic attacks.
16 May and 19 June 1956	Monte Bello Islands, Western Australia	United Kingdom conducts two atomic tests ('Mosaic One'—15 kilotons and 'Mosaic Two'—60 kilotons) off coast of Western Australia under Operation Mosaic.
June 1956	Christmas Island (Kiritimati), British Gilbert and Ellice Islands Colony	United Kingdom begins construction of airstrip, military encampment and scientific bunkers to prepare for Operation Grapple hydrogen bomb tests.
27 September–22 October 1956	Maralinga, South Australia	United Kingdom conducts four atomic tests ('One Tree', 'Marcoo', 'Kite', 'Breakaway') in South Australian desert under Operation Buffalo.
October–December 1956	Egypt and Hungary	Cold War political tensions rise following United Kingdom, French and Israeli attack on Egypt during Suez crisis, and crushing of Hungarian uprising by Soviet troops.
9 January 1957	London, England	United Kingdom Prime Minister Sir Anthony Eden resigns over Suez crisis; replaced the next day by Harold Macmillan, who restructures UK strategic, colonial and nuclear policy.
15 May 1957	Malden Island, British Gilbert and Ellice Islands Colony	Under Operation Grapple, United Kingdom conducts Grapple 1 'Short Granite' atomic test (0.3 megaton).
31 May 1957	Malden Island, British Gilbert and Ellice Islands Colony	United Kingdom conducts Grapple 2 'Orange Herald' atomic test (0.72 megaton).

TIMELINE AND GLOSSARY

19 June 1957	Malden Island, British Gilbert and Ellice Islands Colony	United Kingdom conducts Grapple 3 'Purple Granite' atomic test (0.2 megaton).
July 1957	London, England	After failure to reach megaton range at Malden Island tests, UK Cabinet agrees to proceed with further hydrogen bomb tests, but relocated to Christmas Island. Further atomic trigger tests to continue in Australia to support H-bomb program.
14 September– 9 October 1957	Maralinga, South Australia	Under Operation Antler, United Kingdom conducts three atomic tests ('Tadje', 'Biak' and 'Taranaki') between 0.9 and 26.6 kilotons in South Australian desert.
4 October 1957	Tyuratam missile range, Kazakhstan	USSR launches Sputnik 1, the first artificial satellite to orbit the earth, highlighting Soviet technological advances and exacerbating Cold War fears in the West.
10 October 1957	Cumberland, United Kingdom	Fire at the Windscale nuclear reactor releases radioactive contamination across the United Kingdom and Europe. Windscale is being used to produce tritium for the UK H-bomb program.
8 November 1957	Christmas Island (Kiritimati), British Gilbert and Ellice Islands Colony	United Kingdom restarts Operation Grapple on Christmas Island, with Grapple X hydrogen bomb test (1.8 megatons).
31 March 1958	Moscow, USSR	USSR suspends its nuclear test program, in lead up to negotiations for a nuclear test ban treaty.
28 April 1958	Christmas Island (Kiritimati), British Gilbert and Ellice Islands Colony	United Kingdom conducts Grapple Y hydrogen bomb test (2.8 megatons), with radioactive fallout over Christmas Island and naval task force.
28 April–18 August 1958	Enewetak Atoll, Marshall Islands and Johnston Atoll	United States begins Operation Hardtack, a series of 35 atomic and hydrogen bomb tests on Bikini and Enewetak atolls, with two high-altitude detonations ('Teak' and 'Orange') from rockets launched from Johnston Atoll.
22 August 1958	London, England	United States and Britain announce one-year moratorium of nuclear tests to commence on 31 October (United Kingdom conducts four more tests before deadline).
22 August 1958	Christmas Island (Kiritimati), British Gilbert and Ellice Islands Colony	United Kingdom conducts Grapple Z atomic test codenamed 'Pennant' (24 kilotons), with the bomb on a tethered balloon.

Date	Location	Event
2 September 1958	Christmas Island (Kiritimati), British Gilbert and Ellice Islands Colony	United Kingdom conducts Grapple Z hydrogen bomb test codenamed 'Flagpole' (1 megaton).
11 September 1958	Christmas Island (Kiritimati), British Gilbert and Ellice Islands Colony	United Kingdom conducts Grapple Z hydrogen bomb test codenamed 'Halliard' (0.8 megaton).
23 September 1958	Christmas Island (Kiritimati), British Gilbert and Ellice Islands Colony	United Kingdom conducts Grapple Z atomic test codenamed 'Burgee' (25 kilotons), with the bomb on a tethered balloon.
October–December 1958	Geneva, Switzerland	United States, United Kingdom and USSR hold talks in Geneva to establish a moratorium for nuclear testing.
13 February 1960– 25 April 1961	Reggane, (French) Algeria	France begins its nuclear weapons program with four atmospheric atomic tests in the Sahara desert, codename 'Gerboise'.
7 May 1960	Nevada, USA	United States announces resumption of underground nuclear testing.
30 August 1961	Moscow, USSR	USSR announces it will end a three-year moratorium on atmospheric nuclear testing, and tests restart the next day.
30 October 1961	Severny Island, Novaya Zemlya	USSR tests the most powerful thermonuclear weapon ever detonated, at 58 megatons. The world's largest hydrogen bomb (RDS-220 code name 'Vanya' or 'Tsar Bomba') is the most powerful man-made explosion in human history.
7 November 1961	In Eker, (French) Algeria	France begins series of 13 underground atomic tests in the Hoggar Massif at In Eker in the Sahara desert, which continue after the Evian peace accords that end Algeria's independence struggle.
January 1962	Washington DC, USA	United States announces resumption of nuclear testing in the Pacific, to begin on Christmas Island in April.
22 April–11 July 1962	Christmas Island (Kiritimati), British Gilbert and Ellice Islands Colony and Johnston Atoll	In Operation Dominic 1, United States conducts 24 atmospheric nuclear tests using United Kingdom infrastructure on Christmas Island, combined with one successful rocket launch from Johnston Atoll (the 'Starfish Prime' high-altitude nuclear test on 9 July under Operation Fishbowl).

TIMELINE AND GLOSSARY

2 October–3 November 1962	Johnston Atoll	United States conducts further nuclear tests in Operation Dominic. Nuclear warheads on rockets are fired from Johnston Island for high-altitude detonation (with several failed launches). Two submarine-launched missiles with nuclear warheads are test-fired. Five nuclear weapons are also dropped from aircraft for air bursts in the vicinity of Johnston Island.
14–28 October 1962	Worldwide	The Cuban Missile Crisis threatens global nuclear warfare, as John F. Kennedy and Nikita Khrushchev face off over nuclear missile deployments in Cuba and Turkey.
5 August 1963	Moscow, USSR	United States, Soviet Union and United Kingdom sign Partial Test Ban Treaty.

Over 50 years, the Western powers used the Pacific region as a laboratory for nuclear testing.

Between 1946 and 1958, the United States conducted 67 atomic and hydrogen bomb tests at Bikini and Enewetak atolls in the Marshall Islands. In 1962, there were 24 further US atmospheric nuclear tests at Christmas (Kiritimati) Island, as well as five atmospheric airbursts and nine high-altitude nuclear tests, with warheads launched on missiles from Johnston (Kalama) Atoll and submarines.

Britain tested nuclear weapons in Oceania between 1952 and 1958. There were 12 atomic tests at the Monte Bello Islands, Maralinga and Emu Field in Australia (1952–57). These were followed by nine hydrogen and atomic bomb tests in 1957–58 at Malden Island and Christmas (Kiritimati) Island in the British Gilbert and Ellice Islands Colony (GEIC)—today the Republic of Kiribati.

France conducted four atmospheric nuclear tests at Reggane and 13 underground tests at In Eker in the Sahara desert in Algeria between 1960 and 1966. France then moved its nuclear test sites to the South Pacific. From 1966 to 1996, France conducted 193 atmospheric and underground tests at Moruroa and Fangataufa atolls in French Polynesia.

Glossary of acronyms and abbreviations

A-bomb	Atomic bomb
AEC	Atomic Energy Commission
AFOAT-1	Air Force Office of Atomic Energy (US)
AMGi	Municipal Archives of Girona
ANU	The Australian National University
ARPANSA	Australian Radiation Protection and Nuclear Safety Agency
AWRE	Atomic Weapons Research Establishment
BBC	British Broadcasting Corporation
BNTVA	British Nuclear Test Veterans Association
BPC	British Phosphate Commission
Bq	Becquerel
CIA	Central Intelligence Agency
CND	Campaign for Nuclear Disarmament
DAC	Direct Action Committee Against Nuclear War
DSC	Distinguished Service Cross
DSO	Distinguished Service Order
DTRIAC	Defense Threat Reduction Information Analysis Center
ED	Efficiency Decoration
FCO	Foreign and Commonwealth Office
FRNVR	Fiji Royal Naval Volunteer Reserve
FRS	Fellow of the Royal Society
GCMG	Knight Grand Cross, Order of St Michael and St George
GEIC	Gilbert and Ellice Islands Colony
H-bomb	Hydrogen bomb
HMAS	Her Majesty's Australian Ship
HMG	Her Majesty's Government
HMNZS	Her Majesty's New Zealand Ship
HMS	Her Majesty's Ship
ICJ	International Court of Justice

TIMELINE AND GLOSSARY

ICRP	International Commission on Radiological Protection
IGY	International Geophysical Year
ISD	Intelligence and Security Department, UK Colonial Office
JARS	*Johnston Atoll Radiological Survey*
JTF7	Joint Task Force 7
KBE	Knight Commander of the Most Excellent Order of the British Empire
KCVO	Knight Commander of the Royal Victorian Order
KStG	Knight of the Order of St John
mFISH	multicolour flourescent in situ hybridsation
MI5	British domestic intelligence agency
MI6	British overseas intelligence agency (also known as SIS)
MINDD	Marshall Islands Nuclear Documentation Database
MN	micronucleus
MoD	Ministry of Defence
MP	Member of Parliament
MSD	Meritorious Service Decoration (Fiji)
mSv	millisievert
MV	Motor Vessel
NAAFI	Navy, Army and Air Forces Institute
NCANWT	National Council for the Abolition of Nuclear Weapons Tests
NCCF	Nuclear Community Charity Fund
NCT	Nuclear Claims Tribunal
NFIP	Nuclear Free and Independent Pacific
NLA	National Library of Australia
NRPB	National Radiological Protection Board
NZ	New Zealand
NZDF	New Zealand Defence Force
NZNTVA	New Zealand Nuclear Test Veterans Association
NZRSA	New Zealand Returned Services Association

OAM	Medal of the Order of Australia
OBE	Order of the British Empire
OM	Order of Merit
ONZM	Officer of the New Zealand Order of Merit
PAMBU	Pacific Manuscripts Bureau
PC	Privy Council of the United Kingdom
PCC	Pacific Conference of Churches
PCRC	Pacific Concerns Resource Centre
PPU	Peace Pledge Union
QFE	Quartz Fibre Electroscope
QSM	Queen's Service Medal
RAAF	Royal Australian Air Force
RAF	Royal Air Force
RFMF	Royal Fiji Military Forces (pre-1987)/Republic of Fiji Military Forces (post-1987)
RMI	Republic of Marshall Islands
RN	Royal Navy
RNZAF	Royal New Zealand Air Force
RNZN	Royal New Zealand Navy
RVS	Royal Voluntary Service
SCAP	Supreme Command for the Allied Powers
SEC	Safety and Ecology Corporation Ltd
SIS	Security Intelligence Service
SPAL	South Pacific Air Lines
SPREP	South Pacific Regional Environmental Program
TT	Troop transport
TTPI	Trust Territory of the Pacific Islands
UK	United Kingdom
UKAEA	United Kingdom Atomic Energy Authority
UN	United Nations
UNESCO	United Nations Educational, Scientific and Cultural Organization

US	United States
USDTRA	United States Defense Threat Reduction Agency
USS	United States Ship
USSR	Union of Soviet Socialist Republics
WRA	Woomera Rocket Area
WVS	Women's Voluntary Service

A note on terminology

As I read archival documents from the 1950s, I had the mental image of some poor British squaddie typing out long lists of Fijian soldiers deployed for Operation Grapple, and cursing when he got to Sapper Silivakadua Naikawakawakawavesi. There are quite a few mistakes in the files, from the days before electric typewriters and correcting fluid.

Beyond obvious errors, the archival documents cited in this book use a variety of spellings, such as Eniwitok instead of Enewetak for the nuclear test site in the Marshall Islands. There are also many examples where Europeans have used different names for atolls than those used by indigenous communities, such as Penrhyn/Tongareva, Fanning/Tabuaeran or Johnston/Kalama. For consistency throughout the book, I have retained the name 'Christmas Island', in spite of local usage. The current name in the i-Kiribati language of the Republic of Kiribati is 'Kiritimati', while Fijians spell Christmas as 'Kirisimasi'.

This book will not go into detailed analysis of the different prototypes for British atomic and hydrogen bombs, nor provide complete data on the types of radiation generated during the Grapple nuclear detonations—the footnotes provide a number of sources for readers interested in greater technical detail.

However, for a general audience, here are a few brief definitions of terms used in the book:

Atomic weapons rely on nuclear fission, where the nucleus of uranium or plutonium splits into lighter elements, instantly releasing massive amounts of energy. A nuclear detonation differs from conventional explosives due to the generated heat, blast and especially radiation.

In contrast to atom bombs, **thermonuclear** or **hydrogen weapons** rely instead on nuclear fusion. Some early hydrogen bombs in the 1950s, using a mixture of tritium and deuterium, relied on **atomic triggers** to generate the massive heat and pressure required start the fusion process.

The explosive **yield** of a nuclear weapon is measured in **kilotons** (**kt**, equivalent to 1,000 tons of TNT explosive) or **megatons** (**mt**, 1,000,000 tons equivalent). The bomb that destroyed Hiroshima was only 12 kt, whereas larger thermonuclear or hydrogen bombs have an explosive power greater than 1 megaton.

Fallout is tiny particles of dirt, weapon debris, fission products or other substances contaminated with radioactivity. These particles are spread into the atmosphere following a nuclear explosion, then return to earth, especially through rainfall. Fallout can be blown for some distance by atmospheric or stratospheric winds.

Some nuclear detonations are fired from a tower or low-level balloon and are defined as a **ground burst**, generating extensive radioactive fallout. Other tests are **air bursts**, detonated at higher altitudes in an attempt to limit the amount of irradiated soil and debris.

Unstable atoms have either an excess of energy or mass (or both). In order to reach a stable state, they release that extra energy or mass in the form of **radiation**. **Ionising radiation** describes the particles and electromagnetic radiations that have sufficient energy to cause ionisation as they interact with matter.

Alpha particles have little penetrating power, and can be blocked by a barrier as thin as a sheet of paper. However, they can cause significant cell damage and potential health risks if ingested or inhaled, because of the large amounts of energy deposited in short distances in tissues. **Beta particles** have slightly more penetrating power, but can be stopped by shielding from metal such as aluminium. In contrast, **gamma radiation** is penetrating electromagnetic radiation that can pass through most shielding (though stopped by dense materials such as lead or thick concrete).

There are different units of measurement for radiation.

First, the activity of radioactive material is the rate at which radioactive decay takes place. It is measured in **Becquerels (Bq)**, an international standard unit where 1 Bq is defined as one disintegration per second.

Second, measurements that reflect the different amounts of radiation energy absorbed by a mass of material are measured in **rad** or **gray** (**Gy**).

Third, other units measure the relative biological damage in the human body. In the 1950s, many countries used the measurement **rem** (**R**), but today, the **sievert** (**Sv**) is the standard unit to measure the health effect of low levels of ionising radiation on the human body. Small doses of radiation are measured in **millisievert** (**mSv**).

As a rough guide, 1 rad = 0.01 Gy = 10 mGy and, similarly, 1 rem = 0.01 Sv = 10 mSv.

There is no accepted threshold below which there is no risk of cancer induction. The risk diminishes with a diminishing dose, but is not eliminated. Risk is cumulative over time with the dose. Regulatory dose limits reflect upper permitted (although not advisable) thresholds of exposures by workers and members of the public. For example, in many countries the legal limit for radiation exposure by nuclear workers is 50 mSv in any one year and 20 mSv per annum averaged over five years (by way of comparison, the average natural background radiation in the United States is 2.6 mSv). An acute radiation dose of 500 mSv or more can begin to cause symptoms of radiation poisoning.

Half-life is the time in which radioactivity will decline to half its initial value through decay. Some radioactive isotopes are long-lasting, such as **plutonium-239** with a half-life of 24,400 years. Other isotopes have relatively short half-lives, but can affect people's health when they are exposed to high-level doses in a short period (such as the way **radioactive iodine-131**, with a half-life of just eight days, which can be rapidly absorbed by the thyroid gland, poses a particular threat to children).

Ionisation in the human body may cause **cellular damage** that leads to the death of a cell, or the cell may be damaged in such a way that it cannot reproduce or fulfil its original function.

Where there is DNA damage in the nucleus of the cell, damaged cells may continue to reproduce and develop into **cancer**, after an interval (latent period) from a few years to many decades.

There is also a documented association between exposure to ionising radiation and adverse impacts including, but not limited to, **reproductive health** including effects on the developing embryo and foetus; **cardiovascular diseases**; **cataracts**; and **immunological diseases**.

Maps

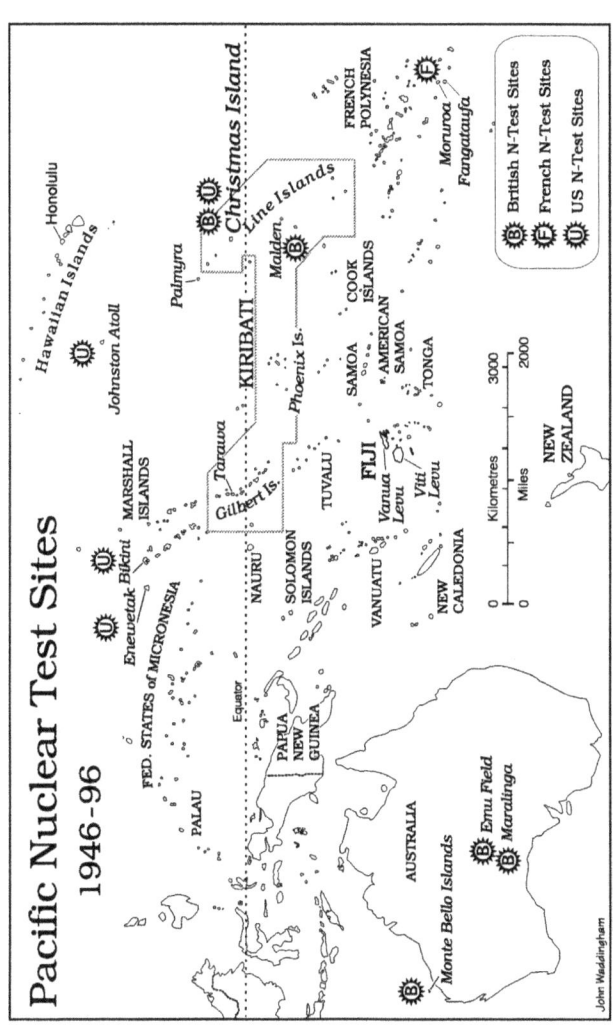

Map 1: Pacific Nuclear Test Sites, 1946–96
Source: Drawn by John Waddingham.

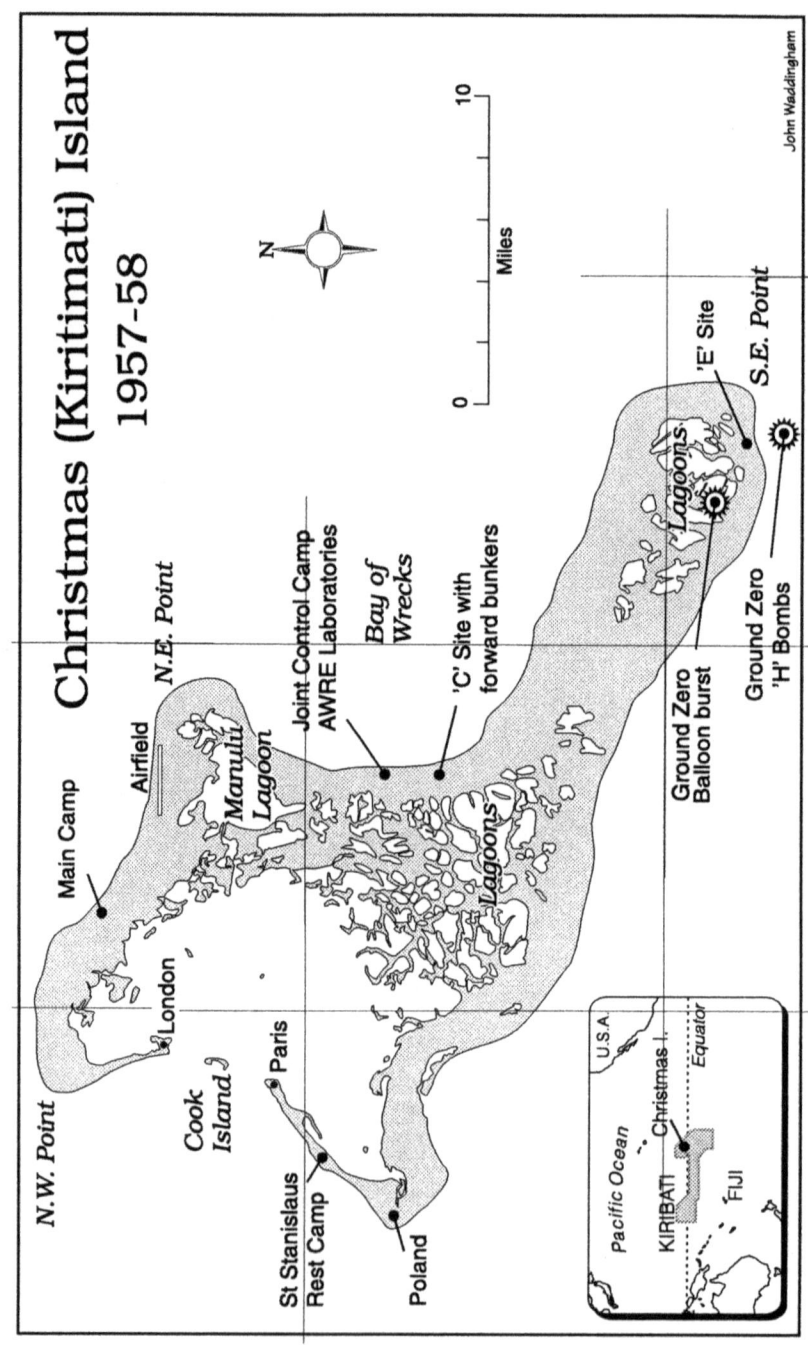

Map 2: Christmas (Kiritimati) Island, 1957–58
Source: Drawn by John Waddingham.

Introduction

From the beginning of the nuclear age, the United States, Britain and France sought distant locations to conduct their Cold War programs of nuclear weapons testing. For 50 years between 1946 and 1996, the islands of the central and south Pacific and the deserts of Australia were used as a 'nuclear playground' to conduct more than 315 atmospheric and underground nuclear tests, at 10 different sites.[1]

These desert and ocean sites were chosen because they seemed to be vast, empty spaces. But they weren't empty. The Western nuclear powers showed little concern for the health and wellbeing of nearby indigenous communities and the civilian and military personnel who staffed the test sites.

In the late 1950s, nearly 14,000 British military personnel and scientific staff travelled to the British Gilbert and Ellice Islands Colony (GEIC) in the central Pacific to support the United Kingdom's hydrogen bomb testing program. In this military deployment, codenamed Operation Grapple, the British personnel were joined by hundreds of NZ sailors, Gilbertese labourers and Fijian troops.[2] Many witnessed the nine atmospheric nuclear tests conducted at Malden Island and Christmas (Kiritimati) Island between May 1957 and September 1958. Today, these islands are part of the independent nation of Kiribati.[3]

---

1   Stewart Firth: *Nuclear Playground* (Allen and Unwin, Sydney, 1987).
2   Between May 1956 and the end of testing in September 1958, 3,908 Royal Navy (RN) sailors, 4,032 British army soldiers and 5,490 Royal Air Force (RAF) aircrew were deployed to Christmas Island, together with 520 scientific and technical staff from the Atomic Weapons Research Establishment (AWRE)—a total of 13,980 personnel. Data from 'Number of men involved in each operation, by service or employer', Table A4.1, Appendix 4 in Lorna Arnold: *Britain and the H-Bomb* (Palgrave Macmillan, London, 2001), p. 241. They were supported by an estimated 551 New Zealand sailors, 276 Fijian soldiers and sailors and nearly 100 Gilbertese labourers.
3   The people of the Ellice Islands, largely Polynesian and Protestant, broke away from the northern atolls in the British Gilbert and Ellice Islands Colony (GEIC) to become the independent Republic of Tuvalu in 1978. The three remaining archipelagos of the Gilbert, Phoenix and Line Islands became

Some British troops remained on Christmas Island until 1962, when the United States conducted 24 further atmospheric nuclear tests at the island.

British scientists had contributed to the US atomic weapons program during the Second World War, but postwar UK governments decided to develop an independent British nuclear weapons capacity. After testing atomic weapons in the deserts and islands of Australia, Britain decided to follow the United States and Soviet Union to develop thermonuclear or hydrogen bombs, vastly more powerful than the atomic weapons that destroyed Hiroshima and Nagasaki.

Under Prime Minister Sir Winston Churchill, the Defence Committee of the British Cabinet held a meeting on 16 June 1954 and secretly decided to construct a hydrogen bomb. Churchill's successor as prime minister, Sir Anthony Eden, only made a statement to the UK House of Commons on 7 June 1956, confirming that thermonuclear weapons would be tested at a remote location in the Pacific Ocean.

By the end of that year, tens of thousands of tons of equipment had been brought from England to establish a military base and upgraded airstrip on Christmas Island in the Line Islands (the eastern archipelago of the British GEIC). A forward base and airstrip was also established on Malden Island, located 636 kilometres to the south.

In May–June 1957, the first three Grapple tests were held at Malden Island, codenamed Grapple 1 (Short Granite), Grapple 2 (Orange Herald), and Grapple 3 (Purple Granite). The nuclear devices were detonated high over the ocean after being dropped from a Valiant bomber. After the three tests, the British Government (falsely) stated that it had achieved a thermonuclear explosion in the megaton range. The *Mid-Pacific News*—a newsletter produced for staff and troops on Christmas Island—reported: 'Bomb Gone! H-Bomb puts Britain on level terms'.[4]

---

the Republic of Kiribati the following year. For details, see W. David McIntyre: 'The Partition of the Gilbert and Ellice Islands', *Island Studies Journal*, Vol. 7, No. 1, 2012, pp. 135–146; Hugh Laracy (ed.): *Tuvalu—a history* (Institute of Pacific Studies, Suva, 1983); Howard Van Trease (ed.): *Atoll politics—the Republic of Kiribati* (Institute of Pacific Studies, Suva, 1993).
4 'Bomb gone! H-Bomb puts Britain on level terms', *The Mid-Pacific News*, special souvenir edition, 15 May 1957, p. 1.

In fact, scientists soon calculated that none of these three detonations had a yield of 1 megaton of explosive power (equivalent to a million tons of TNT explosive). With widespread international protests against the British tests and proposals for a global moratorium on atmospheric nuclear testing in 1958, there was pressure on the Grapple Task Force to speed up efforts to develop a thermonuclear weapon.[5]

Rather than send a naval task force, aircrew and hundreds of support troops back to Malden Island, it was decided to conduct further tests at Christmas Island:

> Because time is so short, it is been decided to carry out the November tests of the south-east tip of Christmas Island; it would have taken too long to set up Malden again.[6]

This decision reduced the enormous logistic problems of conducting the tests so far away from the main base. But it brought the tests closer to the camps where British, NZ and Fijian personnel were stationed and to the village housing Gilbertese workers. From August 1957, there was a major build-up on the island and another six nuclear tests were conducted: Grapple X in November 1957; the massive Grapple Y test in April 1958; and four Grapple Z tests in August–September 1958 (involving two atomic and two hydrogen bombs).

During these tests, service personnel were ordered to line up in the open, face away from the explosions and remain with their backs to the blast, with eyes closed until after the detonation. At sea, crews lined the decks of the naval task force. On land, soldiers and civilian personnel were grouped on the beaches at various points of the island, while scientific staff sheltered in a bunker closer to the test zone. The local Gilbertese population—labourers, plantation workers and their families—were initially taken offshore during the tests or housed aboard British naval vessels to avoid the blast. For the final tests on Christmas Island in 1958, these precautions were abandoned.

---

5   For detailed discussion of how domestic and international public opinion and the looming moratorium on nuclear testing affected the timing of Operation Grapple, see John R. Walker (Foreign and Commonwealth Office, UK): *British nuclear weapons and the Test Ban 1954–73: Britain, the United States, Weapons Policies and Nuclear Testing, Tensions and Contradictions* (Ashgate, 2010), pp. 57–70.
6   Letter from P. Rogers, Secretary of State for the Colonies, 20 September 1957, marked Top Secret. Colonial Office archives CO1036/283.

As this book will detail, the British Government continues to claim that safety preparations and the conduct of the tests minimised radioactive fallout. A 2008 fact sheet released by the UK Ministry of Defence (MoD) argues that:

> Almost all the British servicemen involved in the UK nuclear tests received little or no additional radiation as a result of participation. If personnel who served at Christmas Island at that time had been stationed in the UK in an average location, their dose of naturally-occurring ionising radiation would have been three times greater than it was at Christmas Island.[7]

In contrast, many participants have testified that they were exposed to significant risk. Today, decades later, survivors suffer from serious illnesses that they attribute to exposure to hazardous levels of ionising radiation. The ageing Christmas Island participants are also fearful about the health and wellbeing of their children and grandchildren.

* * *

As a young student, I marched against uranium mining in Australia and boycotted French wines as a protest against nuclear testing on Moruroa Atoll. In 1985, the McClelland Royal Commission published its two-volume report into the 12 British atomic tests in Australia.[8] I was stunned by revelations of the casual racism shown to the indigenous Anangu people of South Australia, as British scientists conducted hundreds of nuclear experiments on Maralinga Tjarutja land, sending plumes of plutonium-contaminated smoke across the desert.

Like most people, however, I knew nothing of the British hydrogen bomb program in the central Pacific. Most histories of Kiribati and Fiji don't mention the Grapple tests. I only really learnt about Operation Grapple when I lived in Fiji in the 1990s, working for the Pacific Concerns Resource Centre (PCRC).

From its founding in 1975, the Nuclear Free and Independent Pacific (NFIP) movement joined with the Pacific Conference of Churches (PCC) and supportive international organisations to campaign against nuclear testing. The signing of the Rarotonga treaty for a South Pacific

---

7 'UK atmospheric nuclear weapons tests: UK programme', Factsheet 5, UK Ministry of Defence, June 2008.
8 Government of Australia: *The Report of the Royal Commission into British Nuclear Tests in Australia* (Australian Government Publishing Service, Canberra, 1985).

Nuclear Free Zone in 1985 was an important milestone in this quest. In contrast to most international peace organisations, which focused on the health and environmental impacts of nuclear testing, NFIP also made the connection to broader Pacific campaigns for indigenous self-determination, decolonisation and political independence. As a network led by Pacific islanders, NFIP stressed that the Western powers could only test nuclear weapons in the Pacific because they were colonial powers in the region.

The slogan went: 'If it's safe, test it in Paris!' While French nuclear testing at Moruroa dominated the headlines in the 1980s and 1990s, the history of British testing in Kiribati was less well known.

As I worked at PCRC in Suva, a number of old men would wander into our library, quietly asking for Mrs Salabula. They were soon closeted with my colleague Losena Salabula, who managed PCRC's disarmament program. I soon realised that they were Fijian veterans of Operation Grapple and were seeking support for their claims: recognition of their military service and health support from the Fiji Government, as well as pensions and compensation for illness and injury from the British Government.

The sense of betrayal from these veterans, who had served God, Queen and Country, was palpable. Fiji was a British colony until 1970 and many ethnic Fijians retain strong emotional ties to the British monarchy. Young Fijian men, imbued by a culture of 'militarism, masculinity and Methodism',[9] maintain a proud tradition of military service in the Republic of Fiji Military Forces (RFMF), through international peacekeeping with the United Nations and also enlistment in the British Army or with private military contractors.

---

9   The phrase comes from the late Teresia Teaiwa: 'Articulated Cultures: Militarism and Masculinities in Fiji during the mid-1990s', *Fijian Studies: A Journal of Contemporary Fiji*, Vol. 3, Issue 2, 2005. For wider discussion of Fiji's military culture, see Winston Halapua: *Tradition, lotu and militarism in Fiji* (Fiji Institute of Applied Studies, Lautoka, 2003); Nic Maclellan: 'From Fiji to Fallujah: the war in Iraq and the privatisation of Pacific security', *Pacific Journalism Review*, Vol. 12, No. 2, September 2006. Teresia Teaiwa also showed that Fijian women too are increasingly joining the British armed forces: 'What Makes Fiji Women Soldiers? Context, Context, Context', *Intersections: Gender and Sexuality in Asia and the Pacific*, Issue 37, March 2015.

As the Christmas Island veterans shared their stories, it was clear that we should record their testimony, which had never been published. Together with researcher Josua Namoce Mudreilagi, Losena and I co-authored the book *Kirisimasi*, published in Fijian and English by PCRC in June 1999.[10] The impact of the book is detailed in Chapter 22.

With the collapse of the Soviet Union in 1991 and the end of French nuclear testing in 1996, many international organisations had diverted their attention and resources to other issues. But for people living near the nuclear sacrifice zones in the Pacific, as well as the civilian and military personnel who had staffed the test sites, the battle for clean-up, remediation and compensation was just beginning.

As subsequent chapters will show, it was only in January 2015 that the government led by coup leader Voreqe Bainimarama—now elected Prime Minister of Fiji—would provide financial support to the surviving Fijian veterans and the families of those who had died. The remaining British, Australian, NZ and Fijian nuclear veterans, now into their 80s, are still campaigning for compensation from the UK Government. Despite their calls, the UK MoD and successive British governments have systematically resisted legal claims from the veterans of the British tests in Australia and Kiribati.

On the 60th anniversary of the British tests in Kiribati, it's important to look back on these events of the 1950s, especially because they influenced Pacific culture in subsequent decades. Occurring in the period before TV and the internet spread across the islands, many stories from this era have been forgotten.

The Grapple tests ended more than a decade before Greenpeace was founded in 1971. Throughout the 1970s and '80s, Greenpeace's *Rainbow Warrior* and other vessels would launch sorties into the waters around Moruroa Atoll, gaining worldwide attention and popularising the campaign against nuclear testing in the international media. But few people recall that, in 1957, an English pacifist named Harold Steele dreamed of sailing a boat into the middle of the Christmas Island test zone and halting the Grapple tests.

---

10   Losena Salabula, Josua Namoce and Nic Maclellan: *Kirisimasi – Na Sotia kei na Lewe ni Mataivalu e Wai ni Viti e na vakatovotovo iyaragi nei Peritania mai Kirisimasi* (Pacific Concerns Resource Centre, Suva, 1999). The book would not have happened without the support of many PCRC staff, as detailed in the acknowledgements.

INTRODUCTION

The 50 years of nuclear testing in the Pacific left economic and social legacies as well as environmental contamination for nations like the Marshall Islands and French Polynesia. Many people welcomed the development of nuclear infrastructure across the region, for the jobs and financial opportunities created by an influx of military personnel. Political leaders, from Prime Minister Robert Menzies in Australia to President Gaston Flosse in French Polynesia, enhanced their political careers through fawning loyalty to Empire. But there was also protest and resistance.

This contrast is a central theme throughout this book. Pacific islanders bore the brunt of the development of nuclear weapons by the United States, Britain and France, but some benefited from employment or seized the opportunity for adventure. Other islanders, facing the loss of land, home and identity, petitioned the newly created United Nations for an end to nuclear testing, even calling for the abolition of nuclear weapons.

One of the earliest indigenous antinuclear protests was in French Polynesia, when the charismatic Tahitian leader Pouvanaa a Oopa—a military veteran in both world wars—collected signatures for the 1950 Stockholm Peace Appeal.[11] Throughout the 1950s, though they were mostly ignored by the nuclear powers, islanders from Fiji, Cook Islands, Marshall Islands, Samoa and other colonial dependencies spoke out against the US and British nuclear programs, petitioning for an end to nuclear testing.

A key element of this story is the many ways that successive British governments have downplayed concern about radioactive fallout from the tests. Today, British authorities continue to argue that the risk of exposure to radiation was minimised throughout the testing program. However, as detailed in subsequent chapters, the archives reveal that elaborate safety precautions on paper were not matched by actual protection on the ground.

Participants in Operation Grapple have reported a range of serious health problems, including many cases of cancer, leukaemia and sterility, which they attribute to their time on Christmas Island. It is clear that for reasons of cost, time pressure and cultural arrogance—even racism—the British

---

11   Interview with Marie-Thérèse Danielsson, Papeete, Tahiti, September 1999. For Danielsson's memories of Pouvanaa, see Nic Maclellan (ed.): *No Te Parau Tia, No Te Parau Mau, No Te Tiamaraa— for justice, truth and independence* (Pacific Concerns Research Centre, Suva, 1999), pp. 18–19. See also Marie-Thérèse and Bengt Danielsson: *Moruroa mon amour* (Stock, Paris, 1974), republished in English as *Poisoned reign* (Penguin, Ringwood, 1986).

authorities constantly cut corners on safety. The Grapple Task Force even set different standards for radiation exposure for 'civilised populations, assumed to wear boots and clothing and to wash' against 'primitive peoples who are assumed not to possess these habits … It is assumed that in the possible regions of fall-out at Grapple there may be scantily clad people in boats to whom the criteria of primitive peoples should apply'.[12]

Some survivors argue that the US and British military planned to use troops and islander populations as guinea pigs, deliberately placing them in harm's way. Later chapters will discuss the sorry history of medical studies on people exposed to high levels of radiation or fallout from nuclear testing, such as Project 4.1 and Project Sunshine.

Unlike the US and France, which have both established compensation schemes for nuclear survivors, the British Government has refused to establish such a scheme for all participants in the Kiribati test program.[13] The US and France also use a presumptive list of diseases, which allows for compensation without extensive proof of causation of the disease. In contrast, the British state still expects Christmas Island veterans to bear the burden of proof when making claims for compensation and war pensions.

* * *

Attempts to hold successive British governments to account have also been hampered by a culture of secrecy.

---

12   Quoted from 'Danger Area' paper from Grapple Task Force Commander Air Vice Marshall Wilfred Oulton, 19 November 1956. See the chapter 'Interlude: On radiation, safety and secrecy', for details of this paper.
13   Praise for the United States and France must be tempered by the reality that they were dragged kicking and screaming to address the issue. Both countries waited far too long to adequately respond to calls for recognition, compensation and clean-up. In the 1986 Compact of Free Association, the United States and the Government of the Republic of the Marshall Islands established a Nuclear Claims Tribunal and a presumptive list of health conditions that could be compensated (although the rulings of the tribunal have not been supplied with adequate funding to pay for the compensation determined in Tribunal rulings). Following the passage of the 2010 Morin law, France established a Compensation Commission for Victims of Nuclear Testing—once again, there are ongoing efforts to strengthen the law to ensure that Pacific islanders can access the pledged compensation.

American researchers and archivists have compiled invaluable databases with un-redacted documents on the US nuclear testing program in the Pacific.[14] The Municipal Archive of Girona (AMGi) in Spain has even digitalised and stored irreplaceable documents, videos and tape recordings from the Marshall Islands Nuclear Claims Tribunal (NCT) to support future nuclear claims.[15]

The UK, with its deep-rooted culture of state secrecy, lacks the same democratic openness and accountability. In a debate still constrained by 'national security' restrictions, access to evidence is still contested terrain. To tell this story, I sought files from the UK National Archives but some key documents are still closed to public access, 60 years after the tests. The full record remains contested ground, with some official reports and data still out of reach. There can be no closure, however, without full disclosure.

Interviewees often pressed copies of documents from the 1950s into my hands, pointing out examples of official perfidy. The importance of proof is a key part of the discussion, as NZ researcher Catherine Trumble argues:

> Ambiguity is what gives archival documents their political potency and dynamism. Test veterans employ this ambiguity when seeking redress for past wrongs. They resist the State's power to control documentary evidence by employing two seemingly contradictory strategies. First, they devalue State documents and contest the truth of military records, instead elevating personal and collective memories based on the idea of witness. Second, veterans believe that if documents trickle out of State files through limited relational and legal routes, then they may be considered legitimate bearers of historical truth … Test veterans thus work both along and against the grain of the archives in order to produce evidence of deservedness and victimhood.[16]

Despite these gaps in the record, much of the story of Operation Grapple has come to light over the last six decades. Before her untimely death, British historian Lorna Arnold used restricted UK government archives

---

14 See, for example, the historic interviews and documents collated by anthropologist Glenn Alcalay at www.atomicatolls.org or the Marshall Islands Nuclear Documentation Database (MINDD) initiated by Alex Wellerstein at data.nuclearsecrecy.com/mindd.
15 Archivist Trudy Peterson, former NCT public advocate Bill Graham and the staff of AMGi deserve special honour for this work, ensuring that future generations can access these materials: www.girona.cat/sgdap/docs/Marshall_NCT_report.pdf.
16 Catherine Trundle: 'Searching for Culpability in the Archives: Commonwealth Nuclear Test Veterans' Claims for Compensation', *History and Anthropology*, Vol. 22, Issue 4, 2011.

to write a series of official histories on the UK nuclear weapons program in Australia and Kiribati.[17] Her books present extensive technical detail of the development of nuclear weapons, and vivid portraits of the scientists who built the British bomb under the leadership of William Penney. Other Foreign Office researchers have documented the sequencing of the UK H-bomb program in the 1950s, to learn how official enemies like Iran and north Korea might go thermonuclear in the 21st century.[18]

This literature, however, makes little reference to the lived experience of the thousands of British troops who staffed the test sites, let alone the NZ, Fijian or Gilbertese personnel. In her official history of the UK H-bomb program, Arnold wrote:

> We should have liked to have written more about these dramatic events and the experiences of the thousands of test participants, many of them young National Service men, most of whom had never been abroad or flown in an aircraft before their long flight to Christmas Island. That would be another book …[19]

Grappling with the Bomb, therefore, hopes to redress the balance in a small way, capturing personal testimonies that are not recorded in the British literature on Operation Grapple or in standard histories of New Zealand, Fiji and Kiribati. I've sought to tell some unfamiliar stories that show the human impact of the Grapple tests, with a particular focus on perspectives from the southern hemisphere.

This book draws on a patchwork of sources: from archival documents to secondary texts and first-hand interviews with the ageing survivors who witnessed the British hydrogen bomb tests. Some historians quibble about the value of personal reminiscences, given the fallibility of memory and our common tendency to exaggeration. But personal testimony and memoir can capture the lived experience of the time and breathe life into

---

17   Lorna Arnold: *A Very Special Relationship—British Atomic Weapons Trials in Australia* (Her Majesty's Stationery Office, London, 1987); Lorna Arnold: *Windscale 1957—Anatomy of a Nuclear Accident* (Palgrave Macmillan, London, 1992); Lorna Arnold: *Britain and the H-Bomb* (Palgrave Macmillan, London, 2001).
18   John R. Walker asks 'whether the UK experience is unique or if it instead offers insights into the potential problems faced by, or facing, other medium or aspiring nuclear weapon states' in 'Potential Proliferation pointers from the past: Lessons from the British Nuclear Weapons Program, 1952–69', *The Nonproliferation Review*, Vol. 19, No. 1, 2012, pp. 109–123.
19   Lorna Arnold: *Britain and the H-Bomb*, op. cit., p. xi.

INTRODUCTION

the archives. On a topic like nuclear strategy, the bureaucratic language of the written record tends to mute the reality of thermonuclear terror that is the essence of nuclear weaponry.[20]

The documentary record still tells tales. The minutes of the Grapple Task Force give insights to official attitudes and the Imperial War Museum in London has an array of photos and film taken by a film crew sent to Christmas Island by the Task Force. To gather information on British colonial policy in the Pacific and the treatment of Gilbertese islanders and Fijian military personnel, I've relied extensively on Colonial Office files.[21]

The Pacific hydrogen bomb tests affected people in many different ways. Chapter 1 starts with Sir Winston Churchill. The British leader's fascination with warfare began in the 19th century as a young soldier and budding author, sent to fight the 'dervishes' in Sudan. It ended with his fateful decision in June 1954 to follow the US and Soviet Union into a nuclear arms race, through the development of a hydrogen bomb after British atomic weapons had already been tested in Australia.

Chapter 2 discusses the impact of the detonation of the US hydrogen bomb, codenamed Bravo, on Bikini Atoll on 1 March 1954. This was not the first test of a US thermonuclear weapon, nor the last, but news of radioactive fallout from Bravo became the focus of international outrage in the mid-1950s. There was extensive mobilisation for disarmament in Japan, after the Bravo test showered fallout on the 23 crew members of the Japanese fishing boat *Daigo Fukuryu Maru* (*No. 5 Lucky Dragon*).

---

20   Historians Anne Curthoys and Joy Damousi argue: 'History and memoir can work together to help later generations understand historic events and experience. While history provides the results of detailed research, using archived documents, oral histories and cultural items like novels, photographs, songs and film, memoir adds to these histories an individual and sometimes highly emotional rendering of personal experience.' Anne Curthoys and Joy Damousi (eds): *What did you do in the Cold War, Daddy? Personal stories from a troubled time* (NewSouth Publishing, Sydney, 2014), pp. 13–14.
21   A list of registered files between 1952 and 1967 from the Pacific and Indian Ocean Department of the Colonial Office and Commonwealth Office (PAC Series CO1036) can be found online at discovery.nationalarchives.gov.uk/details/r/C5225. Copies of these files are available on microfilm, and the author would like to thank the staff at the National Library of Australia (NLA), the Menzies library at The Australian National University (ANU) and the Pacific Manuscripts Bureau (PAMBU). Throughout the footnotes in this book, many documents are sourced to the CO1036 series, followed by the relevant file number. The files of the Colonial Office Intelligence and Security Department (ISD) can be found in the UK National Archives under the code CO1035. For sources of other documents and reports, see Bibliography.

As detailed in Chapter 3, Bravo sparked international protest, popularised the bikini bathing suit and inspired a series of Godzilla movies. Bravo led to more structured national peace organisations, from the creation of the Japan Council against A and H Bombs (Gensuikyo) in 1955 to the formation of the UK Campaign for Nuclear Disarmament in 1958.

After documenting the initial work of the Grapple Task Force under Air Vice Marshall Wilfred Oulton (Chapter 4), the book highlights diverse examples of people who expressed opposition to the looming testing program. These range from businessman James Burns, chair of one of the largest trading houses in the South Pacific (Chapter 5), to British pacifist Harold Steele (Chapter 6). Burns was just one of many business people concerned that Britain's 'hydrogen bomb antics' might threaten their Pacific investments, while Steele travelled from England to India and Japan, attempting to reach the test zone and halt the tests through direct action.

A range of books have gathered testimony from the British, NZ and Australian military personnel who staffed Britain's test sites in Australia and Kiribati.[22] But the stories of Pacific islanders who witnessed the British tests have rarely been recorded (and they are usually presented as victims rather than participants in the operation).

Most histories of the British H-bomb also ignore the contribution of women. Operation Grapple was a largely masculine affair, but the archives of the Royal Voluntary Service (RVS) revealed letters and reports from Mary and Billie Burgess, the only two English women on Christmas Island in 1956–57, living amongst thousands of young servicemen (Chapter 10). The only woman on the first Grapple committee—Foreign Office staffer Gillian Brown – sought to calm diplomatic problems with Japan and the US (Chapter 13).

The official histories also ignore the Gilbertese on Christmas Island, and the colonial administration's debates over employment for islanders and community safety. The personal story of Tekoti Rotan (Chapter 16) reflects the many ways that military conflict, resource extraction, labour

---

22 See, for example, Derek Robinson: *Just testing* (Collins Harvill, London, 1985); Ken McGinley and Eamonn P. O'Neill: *No Risk Involved—the Ken McGinley story—survivor of a nuclear experiment* (Mainstream Publishing, Edinburgh, 1991); Gerry Wright: *We Were There* (Zenith Print, New Plymouth, n.d.); Roger Cross and Avon Hudson: *Beyond Belief—the British bomb tests, Australia's veterans speak out* (Wakefield Press, Kent Town, 2005).

mobility and displacement have reshaped the lives of Pacific islanders. The family of Gilbertese islander Sui Kiritome have captured her memories of the massive Grapple Y test in April 1958 (Chapter 17). Rainfall after this 2.8-megaton atmospheric test sent fallout across Christmas Island and the naval taskforce, affecting sailors, soldiers and civilians.

In other chapters, Fijian soldiers and sailors outline their role in Operation Grapple, drawing on interviews from our book *Kirisimasi* as well as new interviews conducted during recent visits to Fiji. There are reminiscences from Inoke Bainimarama, Paul Ah Poy, Amani Tuimalabe, Pita Rokoratu, Isireli Qalo, Josefa Vueti and many others, as well as the widows and family members of others who have died.

Chapter 9 introduces the story of the late Ratu Sir Penaia Ganilau, a high chief who visited the Fijian naval contingent in mid-1957 and went onto Malden Island straight after the second Grapple nuclear test—with serious consequences for his health. Later serving as Governor General and the President of Fiji, Ratu Sir Penaia's tragic death from leukaemia highlights the hazards of service to the British Empire.

The last of the Grapple tests in September 1958 is not the end of the story. There was ongoing deployment of Fijian military personnel on Christmas Island in 1959–60 (Chapter 18) and further nuclear tests at the island in 1962—this time by the US under Operation Dominic (Chapter 19).

Chair of the New Zealand Nuclear Test Veterans Association (NZNTVA) Roy Sefton (Chapter 14) and NZ geneticist Al Rowland (Chapter 20) also shared their stories. Rowland's pioneering work on the genetic damage affecting NZ sailors highlights the vital contribution of medical research to the wider campaign for recognition and compensation. Chapter 21 outlines the sorry saga of a decade-long legal challenge in the British courts (resisted every step of the way by the UK MoD), through the story of Fijian sailor Pita Rokoratu, who tragically died before a decision in his case.

Finally, Chapter 22 discusses the campaign leading up to the January 2015 ceremony where Fiji Prime Minister Voreqe Bainimarama presented financial support to the surviving Fijian veterans and their families.

While memories fail and some ageing interviewees are not great on dates and details, their vivid testimony provides important additions to the documentary record. The oral history gathered for this book is a small contribution to the growing body of personal testimony by nuclear survivors from other parts of Oceania: women from Yankunytjatjara and Pitjantjatjara indigenous communities in South Australia;[23] Marshall islanders who lived through 67 atmospheric nuclear tests at Bikini and Enewetak atolls;[24] or the Maohi labourers who staffed the nuclear test sites of French Polynesia for 30 years, witnessing 193 nuclear tests.[25]

The veterans' tales also provide important evidence for the ongoing campaign by survivors in Britain, New Zealand and Fiji to obtain recognition and compensation from the British Government for their service during Operation Grapple.

* * *

Another theme that runs through the book is the tension between different arms of the British Government over the costs and consequences of developing thermonuclear weapons.

The four prongs of the Grapple—the Atomic Weapons Research Establishment (AWRE) at Aldermaston and the three UK military services—all focused on the technical and logistical questions of developing weapons within a short time frame. The scientists and military personnel were rushing to develop an independent British nuclear capacity before a testing moratorium in 1958 (and the subsequent Partial Test Ban Treaty of 1963) could halt their atmospheric testing program.

---

23   For the effects of British nuclear testing on indigenous people in South Australia, see Yami Lester: *Yami—the autobiography of Yami Lester* (IAD Press, Alice Springs, 1993); Yalata and Oak Valley communities with Christobel Mattingley: *Maralinga—the Anangu story* (Allen and Unwin, Sydney, 2009); and Christobel Mattingley: *Maralinga's long shadow—Yvonne's story* (Allen and Unwin, Sydney, 2016).
24   For many years, Giff Johnson of the *Marshall Islands Journal* and Jack Niedenthal of the Bikini Atoll Council have recorded Marshallese memories of the US tests. Giff presents a moving portrait of his late wife Darlene in *Don't Ever Whisper—Darlene Keju: Pacific Health Pioneer, Champion for Nuclear Survivors* (CreateSpace Independent Publishing, 2013). Jack Niedenthal records many Bikinian memories in *For the good of mankind—a history of the people of Bikini and their islands* (Micronitor, Majuro, 2001).
25   Pieter Van der Vlies and Han Seur collate Polynesians' testimony during 30 years of nuclear testing in the French Pacific in *Moruroa and Us* (CDRPC, Lyon, 1997), a collection also available in French and Tahitian. The *Moruroa e Tatou* association, which unites Maohi workers who formerly staffed the Moruroa and Fangataufa test sites, collates extensive testimony: www.facebook.com/moruroaetatou/.

Other government departments were constantly seeking to minimise costs, including the Ministry of Supply, which was the lead ministry in the Grapple Task Force, responsible for coordinating the manufacture of nuclear weapons.

In turn, the UK Foreign Office had to deal with complex diplomatic responses to countries like Japan and the US, as public knowledge of the looming test program raised widespread opposition. The Commonwealth Relations Office faced similar concerns in Australia, New Zealand and Canada, even though the three Commonwealth governments were providing political and logistic support for the test program (atomic test sites in Australia, deployment of NZ military forces to assist the Grapple Task Force and use of Canadian air bases, as the hydrogen bomb was flown halfway around the globe from the UK to the central Pacific).

In the 1950s, there were no independent and sovereign island nations in the South Pacific. Public opposition to nuclear testing in New Zealand dependencies like Western Samoa and Cook Islands caused problems for successive NZ governments, as the Commonwealth ally sent two Royal New Zealand Navy (RNZN) frigates to join the British naval flotilla off Christmas Island, and Royal New Zealand Air Force (RNZAF) planes assisted with transport and radiation monitoring around the region.

Finally, the Colonial Office—a more junior partner in the hierarchy—had to address the costs and consequences for the British GEIC.[26] During the Grapple operation, Gilbertese islanders were hired as labourers for the test program, vital shipping was diverted from the Gilbert Islands to the Line Islands and the main copra plantation on Christmas Island ceased operations, losing revenue for the colony.

Western Pacific Commissioner John Gutch (based in Honiara in the British Solomon Islands Protectorate) and Resident Commissioner Michael Bernacchi (located in Tarawa, GEIC) had to deal with a series of orders from London that took little account of the logistic and financial realities of working in the Pacific, given the vast distances across the colony. Bernacchi was looking for financial and employment opportunities for

---

26 Until its dissolution into the Foreign and Commonwealth Office (FCO) in 1966, the Colonial Office had resisted calls from the Treasury, Foreign Office and Commonwealth Relations Office to rapidly give independence to small British dependencies. For discussion of these tensions in the Pacific, see W. David McIntyre: *Winding up the British Empire in the Pacific Islands*, Oxford History of the British Empire Companion Series (Oxford University Press, Oxford, 2014), pp. 32–39.

Gilbertese, while Governor of Fiji Sir Ronald Garvey was also pushing for the employment and training of young Fijians on Christmas Island. This led to the deployment of sailors of the Fiji Royal Naval Volunteer Reserve (FRNVR) and engineers and labourers from the Royal Fiji Military Forces (RFMF) between 1957 and 1960.

* * *

As we mark the 60th anniversary of the Grapple tests in 2017–18, the issues of British nuclear weapons, indigenous rights and a nuclear-free and independent Pacific are still with us.

There are debates in the UK parliament about the cost of renewing Trident, the heart of the UK nuclear arsenal. Post-Brexit, Scottish nationalists are calling for a nuclear-free and independent Scotland as they move towards a second referendum on independence. The Republic of the Marshall Islands—unsuccessfully—has taken Britain and other nuclear weapons states to the International Court of Justice (ICJ) over their failure to meet disarmament obligations under the Nuclear Non-Proliferation Treaty. As a consequence, in February 2017 Britain withdraw from the compulsory jurisdiction of the ICJ on matters of nuclear disarmament, in order to halt further cases that threaten its nuclear arsenal.

Eight Pacific island countries co-sponsored the December 2016 UN General Assembly resolution to establish a treaty banning nuclear weapons, with negotiations amongst 130 governments commencing in March 2017. The South Australian Government is seeking to establish a nuclear waste dump on Aboriginal land, even as the Australian Government exports uranium to fuel nuclear reactors like Daichi Fukushima, which since 2011 has continued to contaminate the land and marine environment. Meanwhile the Tokyo Electric Power Company is wondering who will pay the horrendous price tag—US$160 billion and counting—to clean up the world's latest nuclear sacrifice zone at Fukushima. The list goes on …

Even as some pundits call for an expansion of the nuclear industry to address the challenge of climate change, we have not addressed the costs and consequences of nuclear activities in the 1950s. As we enter a new era of uncertainty, following the Brexit referendum and the election of Donald J. Trump as US President, it is important to remember the tragedy of the nuclear era in the Pacific, so we are never forced to repeat it.

Moreover, it is time for the citizens of the United Kingdom to call on their government to do the right thing and address the legitimate claims of the Grapple survivors.

1
The leader—Sir Winston Churchill

Sir Winston Churchill, Franklin Delano Roosevelt and Joseph Stalin at the February 1945 Yalta conference
Source: US National Archives.

Jock Colville was a worried man. As Principal Private Secretary to Sir Winston Churchill, he could see that the British Prime Minister was a sick man—and burdened by nuclear nightmares. The news that both the United States and the Soviet Union had developed a hydrogen bomb as well as atomic weapons weighed heavily on his boss.

Following the announcement from Moscow that the Soviet Union had tested a hydrogen bomb on 12 August 1953, Colville noted in his diary:

> PM coming round towards resignation in October. Says he no longer has the zest for work and finds the world in an abominable state wherever he looks. Greatly depressed by thoughts on the hydrogen bomb.[1]

After serving as Prime Minister during the Second World War, Sir Winston Churchill had succeeded Clement Attlee for another term of office in October 1951. In his final political years, however, Churchill was ageing and in ill health after suffering a stroke in June 1953.

On 15 August, three days after the Soviet H-bomb test, Churchill told colleagues:

> I was depressed, not only about myself, but about the terrible state of the world. That hydrogen bomb can destroy 2 million people. It is so awful that I have the feeling that it will not happen.[2]

These concerns about the hydrogen bomb were a significant change. As Britain's leader during the Second World War, Churchill had actively supported the US Manhattan project, which developed the first atomic weapon.[3] Following the August 1943 Quebec Agreement on wartime nuclear collaboration between Britain and the United States, British scientists played a key role in translating the theoretical physics of nuclear fission into a practical weapon, which first detonated at Alamogordo in the New Mexico desert in July 1945. Historian Elizabeth Tynan has argued that 'British physics initially powered the US Manhattan project'.[4]

---

1   Sir John Colville: *The Fringes of Power: 10 Downing Street Diaries 1939–1955* (W.W. Norton & Co, London, 1985), p. 675.
2   Martin Gilbert: *Winston S. Churchill, Volume VIII: Never Despair 1945–65* (Heinemann, London, 1988), p. 875.
3   Graham Farmelo: *Churchill's Bomb—a hidden history of science, war and politics* (Faber and Faber, London, 2013).
4   Elisabeth Tynan: *Atomic thunder—the Maralinga story* (NewSouth Publishing, Sydney, 2016), p. 34.

The atom bomb was the horrific weapon deployed by the United States against Japan. US President Harry Truman ordered the atomic bombing of Hiroshima on 6 August 1945. Three days later, another US plane attacked the port city of Nagasaki (the fallback target after the primary target Kokura was obscured by smoke and cloud). No one truly knows how many people died, but estimates range from 90,000–146,000 people in Hiroshima and 39,000–80,000 in Nagasaki, in the initial attack and subsequent weeks. The second attack was directed as much at Moscow as Tokyo, following Stalin's declaration of war against Japan on 8 August.[5]

The two aircraft *Enola Gay* (which carried the atomic weapon 'Little Boy' towards Hiroshima) and *Bockscar* (which dropped 'Fat Man' on Nagasaki) both flew from Tinian Island in the Marianas Islands—highlighting the central role of Micronesia from the very start of the nuclear era.

In July 1945, a month before Japan's surrender, Britain went to national elections. With the population seeking an end to wartime austerity and changes to the political leadership that had dragged the country into disaster, Churchill lost the election to Labour leader Clement Attlee. Britain was facing revolt across the Empire, from India and Ceylon to Palestine and Malaya.

In opposition, however, Churchill was still celebrated as an international statesman. In March 1946, he visited Harry Truman in the US President's home state of Missouri. Welcomed to Westminster College in the small Missouri town of Fulton, Churchill gave a speech entitled 'The Sinews of Peace'.[6] Famous for popularising the term 'the iron curtain', the speech symbolised the end of the wartime partnership between the Western allies and the Soviet Union, which soon collapsed into inter-bloc rivalry.

Throughout this Cold War, nuclear strategy became a central feature of statecraft. Despite calls from many scientists and philosophers for atomic weapons to come under international control through the United Nations, Churchill argued at Fulton:

---

5   For the debate over US motives, see Gar Alperovitz: *The Decision to Use the Atomic Bomb and the Architecture of an American Myth* (Vintage, 1996); Kai Bird and Martin J. Sherwin: 'The Myths of Hiroshima', *LA Times*, 5 August 2005.
6   The speech is published in Martin Gilbert: *Winston S. Churchill*, op. cit., p. 197.

It would nevertheless be wrong and imprudent to entrust the secret knowledge or experience of the atomic bomb, which the United States, Great Britain and Canada now share, to the world organisation while it is still in its infancy. It would be criminal madness to cast adrift in this still agitated and un-united world.[7]

To extend its nuclear monopoly, the United States began a series of atmospheric nuclear tests in 1946, codenamed Operation Crossroads, on Bikini Atoll in the Marshall Islands.[8] The tests were conducted a year before these Micronesian islands were designated as part of the Trust Territory of the Pacific Islands (TTPI)—the only strategic trusteeship created by the United Nations after the Second World War.[9]

In November 1946, the United States' Atomic Energy Act, also known as the McMahon Act, restricted the transfer of nuclear research and technology, even to allies like the United Kingdom.[10] In response, on 8 January 1947, a committee of five ministers led by Britain's postwar Labour Prime Minister Clement Attlee made the decision to commence a British nuclear weapons program.[11] The secretive decision-making process began a tradition of the UK nuclear establishment avoiding accountability—the government had spent nearly £100 million on the project before news of the decision was first announced to the British Parliament in May 1948.

While Attlee carefully weighed the political and moral impacts, some of his ministers were more gung-ho about an 'independent' British nuclear capacity. Fiercely anti-communist, Foreign Secretary Ernest Bevin told Cabinet colleagues:

---

7   Ibid., p. 199.
8   Jonathan Weisgall: *Operation Crossroads—the atomic tests at Bikini Atoll* (Naval Institute Press, Annapolis, 1994).
9   These Micronesian islands had been administered by Japan between the world wars, but became a strategic United Nations trusteeship administered by the US military in 1947, after the defeat of Japanese forces in 1944–45.
10   S.J. Ball: 'Military Nuclear Relations between the United States and Great Britain under the Terms of the McMahon Act, 1946–1958', *The Historical Journal*, Vol. 38, No. 2, 1995.
11   Lorna Arnold details the Labour Party's secretive decision-making in *A Very Special Relationship—British atomic weapons trials in Australia* (Her Majesty's Stationery Office, London, 1987), pp. 8–10. The 'Gen 163' committee included Prime Minister Attlee, Herbert Morrison, Foreign Secretary Ernest Bevin, Minister of Supply John Wilmot, Defence Minister A.V. Alexander and Lord Addison, Secretary of State for the Dominions.

We've got to have this thing over here whatever it costs and we're going to have a bloody Union Jack flying on top of it.[12]

While the roots of the British hydrogen bomb go back to the wartime Manhattan program, UK–US scientific collaboration was hampered by postwar spy scares and political clashes. The United States was seeking to remake international institutions, even as Britain counted the financial cost of the Second World War and the collapse of Empire. Over time, the US nuclear security state became more secretive. As they developed their own operations in the Pacific, British Colonial Office officials complained that the US military was restricting information such as the dates of proposed nuclear tests in the Marshall Islands:

> It will be seen that in 1947, we were given information as to the dates and times of experiments and we handed this on to the High Commissioner [in the Gilbert and Ellice Islands Colony], but I fancy that since then, the US authorities become a great deal more 'cagey' about divulging information of this sort.[13]

The McMahon Act restrictions reinforced the British commitment to create an independent nuclear force. Britain was unable to use US nuclear testing facilities in the Nevada desert or the islands of the central Pacific, requiring other locations with vast space and limited population.

Western leaders were shocked when the Soviet Union announced its first nuclear test on 29 August 1949, in Operation *Pervaya molniya* (Fast lightning). This atomic test, at Semipalatinsk in Kazakhstan, was the first of 456 tests at the site. One witness noted:

> The scene was striking: destruction all around, heavy dead silence, burnt soil, dead burnt birds. An eerie feeling.[14]

Cold War anxiety over Soviet nuclear capacity was amplified by the outbreak of fighting on the Korean peninsula in June 1950. Britain accelerated its nuclear program. On 16 September 1950, Prime Minister Attlee wrote to his Australian counterpart Robert Menzies, asking permission to hold atomic weapons tests in Australia:

---

12   Sir Michael Perrin of the Ministry of Supply reported Bevin's statement in the BBC TV documentary *Britain's Nuclear Bomb: The inside story*, broadcast 3 May 2017.
13   File note in 'Hydrogen bomb experiments—west Pacific', Colonial Office, London. CO1036/236.
14   F.A. Kholin, cited in Togzhan Kassenova: 'Banning nuclear testing: Lessons from the Semipalatinsk nuclear testing site', *The Nonproliferation Review*, Vol. 23, No. 3–4, 2016, pp. 329–344.

> I am telegraphing to you now to ask first whether the Australian government would be prepared in principle to agree that the first United Kingdom atomic weapon should be tested in Australian territory and secondly, if so, whether they would agree to our experts making a detailed reconnaissance of the Monte Bello Islands so that a firm decision can be taken on their suitability.[15]

* * *

Even as Britain began preparing a series of tests of fission weapons in Australia, the US Government was moving to develop a larger thermonuclear or hydrogen bomb. Only a month after the first British atomic test at the Monte Bello Islands, the United States conducted its first test of a thermonuclear device, codenamed Mike, on 1 November 1952. As part of Operation Ivy, the Mike test on Enewetak Atoll was held just three days before the presidential election that saw former allied supreme commander Dwight D. Eisenhower replace Harry Truman as US President.

Well before the construction of sleek warheads, the Mike device was a clumsy beast, larger than a house, weighing 65 tonnes and requiring refrigeration to keep the hydrogen fuel liquid until detonation. Even so, the detonation vaporised the coral islet of Ālokḷap (Elugelap) and left a crater 60 metres deep. At a yield of 10.4 megatons, the explosion created a mushroom cloud more than 100 kilometres wide. It was the first test of a full-scale thermonuclear device and irradiated several US military personnel.[16]

The Soviet Union in turn exploded its own thermonuclear device on the morning of 12 August 1953. The first Soviet hydrogen bomb was much smaller than the American device, but 'the explosion made an awesome impression on all those who witnessed it. As one said, the effects of the first Russian atomic explosion had not inspired such flesh creeping terror'.[17]

---

15 Elizabeth Tynan: *Atomic thunder*, op. cit., p. 3.
16 Only 2,000 of approximately 14,000 participants in Operation Ivy were issued with radiation monitoring badges. Crew of a photographic plane caught in the fallout received up to 11.6 rem (116 mSv) of radiation, far above the 3.9 rem safety limit. The seven-man crew in an amphibious plane that flew to the rescue of a downed pilot received doses between 10 and 17.8 rem (100–178 mSv). In comparison, a standard chest x-ray delivers a radiation dose of about 0.02 rem (0.2 mSv). See 'Operation Ivy', Fact Sheet, US Defense Threat Reduction Agency (USDTRA), May 2015.
17 'The second Superbomb project—the Soviet Union' in Lorna Arnold: *Britain and the H-bomb* (Palgrave Macmillan, Basingstoke, 2001), p. 28.

More than 2,250 people and 40,000 livestock were evacuated 120 kilometres from the Semipalatinsk test site (although the radioactive plume from the test carried over 400 kilometres). Forty people were deliberately left behind at the settlement of Karaul and later used by Soviet scientists as a cohort for medical studies on the effects of radiation.[18] These experiments were an eerie precursor to the Project 4.1 medical studies conducted on Marshall islanders by Brookhaven National Laboratories in the United States, discussed in Chapter 2.[19]

As with the first atomic test by the USSR, the first Soviet H-bomb gave impetus to the British nuclear weapons program. Meeting with US President Eisenhower in December 1953, Churchill expressed 'concern at the cessation of full-scale cooperation between the United States and United Kingdom which had prevailed during the war', and pled for the resumption of nuclear technology transfer that had been limited by the McMahon Act.[20]

Despite this purported ban on nuclear transfers, there was ongoing collaboration between British and US scientists. Physicist William Penney, who had worked with US counterparts during the war, continued to receive information on the latest American scientific and technical advances during the 1950s. Lord Cherwell, the Conservative politician who served as Churchill's chief scientific adviser, wrote to the prime minister describing Penney as 'our chief—indeed our only—real expert on the construction of the bomb and I do not know what we should do without him'.[21]

---

18   Togzhan Kassenova, op. cit., p. 331, drawing on research by Talgat Slyambekov: 'Karaul' in Kanat Kabdrakhmanov: *Odinochestvo—dom bez sten, dusha bez doma—Transtsedentalnoe kocheve, konets puti; 470 bomb v serdtse Kazakhstana* (470 Bombs in the Heart of Kazakhstan), (Kazakhstan, Almaty, 1994), p. 105. After the collapse of the USSR, Kazakh and Russian researchers began to study the effects of Soviet-era testing on local populations and military veterans and to compare the experience of US and Soviet testing. The author was invited to contribute to a 2002 collection contrasting the experience of Pacific islanders, Native Americans and Kazakh farmers—see Nic Maclellan: 'Tikhookeanisky region v yaderny vek: istoriya, problemy, perspective' ('The nuclear age in the Pacific: history, problems, perspectives'), *Yaderny Kontrol*, Moscow, Vol. 8, No. 1, January–February 2002.
19   R.A. Conard, V.P. Bond, J.S. Robertson, E.A. Weden: *Operation Castle Project 4.1a, medical examination of Rongelap people six months after exposure to fallout* (Department of Energy, Washington, March 1954); Robert A. Conard et al.: *March 1957 medical survey of Rongelap and Utirik people three years after exposure to radioactive fallout* (Brookhaven National Laboratories, Upton New York, 1958).
20   Martin Gilbert: *Winston S. Churchill*, op. cit., p. 924.
21   Lorna Arnold: *Britain and the H-Bomb*, op. cit., p. 72. Arnold's history provides a detailed study of Penney's connections with the United States and crucial role in the development of the British bomb. Cherwell was the driving force behind the passage of the July 1954 United Kingdom Atomic Energy Act and sat on the board of the UK Atomic Energy Authority (UKAEA) until his death in 1957.

Penney would go on to serve as the chief scientific coordinator for the British atomic tests in Australia and hydrogen bomb tests in the central Pacific.

Even though the US Mike test was conducted in November 1952, the US Government only publicly announced that it had developed a hydrogen bomb in February 1954.[22] It then conducted the test of a second hydrogen bomb, codenamed Bravo, on 1 March 1954.

Little more than a month after Bravo, on 5 April, Churchill addressed a tumultuous UK House of Commons debate on disarmament.[23] The debate saw him rise to defend the development of the hydrogen bomb by Britain's key Western ally. To the dismay of his own supporters, Churchill fiercely attacked the Labour opposition. He rejected their calls for his government to pressure the United States to abandon its nuclear testing program. He also rejected calls to place nuclear weapons under international controls through the newly formed United Nations:

> The government was not prepared to make any such representations to the United States government or to take any action which might impede American progress in building up their overwhelming strength in nuclear weapons, which provided the greatest possible deterrence against the outbreak of a third world war.[24]

* * *

Just as the United States and Soviet Union had sought isolated locations for nuclear testing, the United Kingdom needed open space. The British atmospheric testing program in Australia was conducted with the agreement and support of Australian Prime Minister Robert Menzies, initially without Cabinet approval. Menzies, however, had added the requirement:

> It will be conducted in conditions which will ensure that there will be no danger whatever from radioactivity to the health of the people or animals in the Commonwealth.[25]

---

22 Ibid., p. 952.
23 Graham Farmelo: *Churchill's Bomb—a hidden history of science, war and politics* (Faber and Faber, London, 2013), p. 423.
24 Lorna Arnold: *Britain and the H-Bomb*, op. cit., p. 963.
25 Adrian Tame and Rob Robotham: *Maralinga: British A-bomb, Australian Legacy* (Fontana/Collins, Melbourne, 1982), p. 66.

1. *THE LEADER*—SIR WINSTON CHURCHILL

Menzies supported the free exchange of scientific and defence data between Australia, Britain and the United States. The prime minister was encouraged by his key collaborator, Minister for Supply Howard Beale. An enthusiastic supporter of the British atomic weapons program, Beale proclaimed:

> England has the bomb and the knowhow; we have the open spaces, much technical skill and great willingness to help the Motherland. Between us, we shall build the defence of the free world, and make historic advances in harnessing the forces of nature.[26]

This book, which will focus on the development of thermonuclear weapons in the British Gilbert and Ellice Islands Colony (GEIC), can only sketch a brief outline of the British atomic weapons program in Australia. Many other authors have comprehensively detailed the Australian experience. For those interested in the technical process of developing Britain's atomic weapons, the UK and Australian governments have both published official histories of the testing program in Australia.[27] More recent studies have woven together official diplomatic history, the testimony of scientists, the memories of the military veterans who staffed the test sites and a more critical appraisal of the lingering effects on health and environment.[28]

Between October 1952 and October 1957, the British Government carried out 12 atomic tests at three sites in Australia. The tests involved thousands of British and Australian military personnel and also affected nearby Indigenous communities. In subsequent decades, both veterans and Indigenous people have campaigned for recognition and compensation for health effects, which they attribute to exposure to hazardous ionising radiation.

The first atomic test on 3 October 1952, codenamed Operation Hurricane, was held at the Monte Bello Islands, off the coast of Western Australia. This was followed by the two Totem atmospheric tests at Emu Field in October 1953.

---

26 Quoted in Government of Australia: *The Report of the Royal Commission into British Nuclear Tests in Australia* (Australian Government Publishing Service, Canberra, 1985), para. 2.1.25, p. 15.
27 The British history is Lorna Arnold: *A Very Special Relationship—British Atomic Weapons Trials in Australia* (Her Majesty's Stationery Office, London, 1987). An Australian history of the tests was published by the Department of Resources and Energy: J.L. Symonds: *A History of British Atomic Tests in Australia* (Australian Government Publishing Service, Canberra, 1985).
28 Roger Cross: *Fallout—Hedley Marston and the British bomb tests in Australia* (Wakefield Press, 2001); Frank Walker: *Maralinga* (Hachette, Sydney, 2014); Elizabeth Tynan: *Atomic thunder*, op. cit.

British testing in Australia was then halted for two years, but resumed in May and June 1956 with Operation Mosaic in the Monte Bello Islands. In September and October that year, four atmospheric tests followed in the South Australian desert at Maralinga, with Operation Buffalo. After the first three Grapple tests on Malden Island in the central Pacific (May and June 1957), testing of atomic triggers continued in Australia in September and October 1957 under Operation Antler.

For 25 years, UK governments and scientists hid documents detailing the full damage that had been cause by the Maralinga tests. After campaigns by veterans groups, Indigenous communities and investigative journalists, the Hawke Labor Government called a Royal Commission into the British tests, headed by Justice James 'Diamond Jim' McClelland. In 1985, the Royal Commission released a scathing, two-volume report that criticised the British Government's failure to adequately address issues of safety.[29]

Beyond the 12 atmospheric nuclear tests, the commission's report highlighted the long-lasting damage caused by a series of over 600 minor trials, assessment tests and experimental programs. These trials near the Maralinga test site—codenamed Kittens, Tims, Rats and Vixen—involved the testing of bomb components and the burning of nuclear materials such as plutonium, uranium and beryllium. These experiments continued until 1963 and sent plumes of contaminated smoke across the desert, causing radioactive contamination that lasts to this day.

* * *

Yami Lester was 10 years old when the Totem 1 test was conducted on 15 October 1953 near his home at Wallatinna. The winds carried dust into his eyes and four years later he lost all sight:

> It was in the morning, around seven. I was just playing with the other kids. That's when the bomb went off. I remember the noise. It was a strange noise, not loud, not like anything I'd ever heard before. The earth shook at the same time; we could feel the whole place move. We didn't see anything, though. Us kids had no idea what it was. I just kept playing.

---

29 Government of Australia: *The Report of the Royal Commission into British Nuclear Tests in Australia*, op. cit. For the political context, see Robert Milliken: *No Conceivable Injury—the story of Britain and Australia's atomic cover-up* (Penguin, Ringwood, 1986).

1. *THE LEADER*—SIR WINSTON CHURCHILL

It wasn't long after that a black smoke came through. A strange black smoke, it was shiny and oily. A few hours later we all got crook, every one of us. We were all vomiting; we had diarrhoea, skin rashes and sore eyes. I had really sore eyes. They were so sore I couldn't open them for two or three weeks. Some of the older people, they died. They were too weak to survive all of the sickness. The closest clinic was 400 miles away.[30]

Yami Lester, Wallatinna Station, South Australia, 2006
Source: Jessie Boylan.

It took years—and the Royal Commission—before the Australian Government would begin to address the full impact of British nuclear testing on the Yankunytjatjara and Pitjantjatjara peoples, whose lands

---

30   For the full history of the black mist and the impact on the community of Wallatinna, see Yami Lester: *Yami—the autobiography of Yami Lester* (IAD Press, Alice Springs, 1993).

in South Australia were taken for the Maralinga test site.³¹ Little thought was given to the reality that the deserts and oceans of the southern hemisphere were not open, empty places, but home to Indigenous peoples.

Aboriginal communities in South Australia had first protested when the Woomera Rocket Area (WRA) was created to test British missiles after the Second World War. From 1947, public meetings, radio broadcasts and information leaflets were organised to campaign against the WRA by the newly formed Council for Aboriginal Rights, supported by groups as diverse as the Aboriginal Advancement League, Quakers, Communist Party of Australia, Women's Christian Temperance Union and Women's International League for Peace and Freedom.³²

By the 1950s, authorities decided to use land within the WRA to test atomic weapons, after the success of the first test at the Monte Bello Islands. Even though everyone was supposed to be evacuated from the Emu Field and Maralinga zones during the 1950s tests, some Aboriginal people remained on their land within the testing range (a fact known to the Australian Government at the time, though covered up until the 1980s). The Anangu people near Maralinga suffered the disruption of their livelihoods and health. The official British historian of the Australian tests, in a rather dismissive manner, notes:

> They had no rights and their interest in the land was not realised or respected, but this was and had been their general situation and was neither new nor particular to the weapons trials.³³

During the tests, some Indigenous people were given one-way train tickets to far-off towns, while others were herded into a camp at Yalata, a church mission station 150 kilometres west of Ceduna. One Aboriginal elder recalled the time:

---

31 For memories of the 1950s and the ongoing effects of nuclear testing on Indigenous women in South Australia, see Yalata and Oak Valley communities with Christobel Mattingley: *Maralinga—the Anangu story* (Allen and Unwin, 2009). For cultural responses to the tests, see Jan Dirk Mittman (ed.): *Black Mist, Black Country* (Burrinja, Upwey, 2016).
32 Bain Attwood: *Rights for Aborigines* (Allen and Unwin, 2003), pp. 149–150. See also Deborah Wilson: *Different white people—radical activism for Aboriginal rights 1946–72* (UWA Publishing, Perth, 2015), pp. 110–113; and Douglas Jordan: *Conflict in the Unions—the Communist Party of Australia, politics and the trade union movement, 1945–60* (Resistance Books, Sydney, 2013). The Communist Party perspective is shown in Alf Watt: *Rocket Range Threatens Australia* (Australian Communist Party South Australian State Committee, Adelaide, 1947).
33 Lorna Arnold: *A Very Special Relationship—British atomic weapons trials in Australia*, op. cit., p. 244.

1. *THE LEADER*—SIR WINSTON CHURCHILL

> Soldiers everywhere. Guns. We all cry, cry, crying. Men, women and children, all afraid.[34]

Sue Coleman-Haseldine is a Kokatha-Mula woman, born at the Koonibba mission near Maralinga:

> I was about three when it happened. The old people used to talk about the Nullarbor dust storm, which really wasn't a dust storm at all. It must have been the fallout from Maralinga. We've had thyroid problems in the family, and it's not just us, it's the whole of the west coast of South Australia.
>
> We've had quite a lot of problems like that, health-wise. When someone says somebody's just died, you ask what from and it's always cancer, cancer, cancer. But as we all know, nobody can prove that the radiation caused the cancer. People have put in for compensation, but because there's no proof that the illnesses stem from the explosions, there is none.[35]

Yvonne Edwards was just six years old when the Buffalo tests began at Maralinga in September 1956 on the land of the Anangu people. Years later, she remembered:

> Grandfather and grandmother telling lots of stories. They had to live at Yalata. Their home was bombed. That was their home when the bomb went off. Really frightened. They thought it was *mamu tjuta*, evil spirits, coming. Everyone was frightened, thinking about people back in the bush. Didn't know what bomb was. Later told it was poison. Parents and grandparents really wanted to go home, used to talk all the time to get their land back.[36]

Aboriginal culture was—and still is—strong in the region. In the 1990s, Aboriginal women in South Australia formed the group *Kupa Piti Kungka Tjuta* and a campaign called *Irati Wanti* (The Poison—Leave It) to oppose further nuclear pollution of their country. Campaigning against government proposals to create a nuclear waste dump on their land, the elders recalled the nuclear tests of the 1950s and expressed their concern about the effects on future generations:

---

34 The late Alice Cox, cited in 'Maralinga's afterlife', *The Age*, 11 May 2003.
35 Speech during the 'Black Mist, White Rain' speaking tour of Australia in April 2016, which united Aboriginal and Marshall Islands nuclear survivors.
36 Christobel Mattingley: *Maralinga's long shadow—Yvonne's story* (Allen and Unwin, Sydney, 2016), pp. 43–44.

All of us were living when the government used the country for the Bomb. Some were living at Twelve Mile, just out of Coober Pedy. The smoke was funny and everything looked hazy. Everybody got sick. Now, again they are coming along and telling us poor blackfellas: 'Oh, there's nothing that's going to happen, nothing is going to kill you.' … And we're worrying for our kids. We've got a lot of kids growing up on the country and still coming more, grandchildren and great grandchildren.[37]

As we'll see in following chapters, the same intergenerational concerns are expressed by men and women in the Pacific islands, including those in the Marshall Islands who bore the brunt of US hydrogen bomb testing at Bikini and Enewetak atolls or the Fijian military personnel who served on Christmas Island during Operation Grapple.

* * *

The Maralinga site was officially closed in 1967, following a brief clean-up operation codenamed Brumby. In the aftermath of the McClelland Royal Commission, the British Government funded a further effort in the late 1990s to remove contaminated soil. Alan Parkinson, a key scientist and the government's representative in the $100 million operation, was later removed from his positions. Parkinson challenged bureaucratic suggestions that the clean-up operation had succeeded, whereas there is extensive contamination to this day. In his forthright account of the failed operation, Parkinson mourns the lingering legacy of plutonium scattered across the desert:

> In less than two decades, British military aspirations turned over 100 km² of pristine Australian bush at Maralinga in South Australia into plutonium-contaminated scrub.[38]

The atomic tests in Australia were a crucial prequel to the development of the British hydrogen bomb, when the UK Government decided to follow the United States and the Soviet Union in the development of thermonuclear weapons. In the 1950s, Churchill's scientific adviser Lord

---

37 From statement by the women of *Kupa Piti Kungka Tjuta* (author's files), opposing the establishment of a nuclear waste dump on their land that was used for the 1950s nuclear tests. Today, the battle continues—the state government of South Australia has again proposed the creation of an international nuclear waste dump on already contaminated land.
38 Alan Parkinson: *Maralinga—Australia's nuclear waste cover up* (ABC Books, Sydney, 2007), p. ix.

Cherwell had argued that the development of hydrogen as well as atomic weapons was central to maintaining Britain's status as an imperial power in the postwar era:

> If we are unable to make the Bomb ourselves and have to rely entirely on the United States for this vital weapon, we shall sink to the rank of a second class nation, only permitted to supply auxiliary troops, like the native levies who were supplied small arms but not artillery.[39]

Churchill's fear of the destruction that a hydrogen bomb could wreak did not last. While contemplating the need for a disarmament summit between the United States, Soviet Union and United Kingdom—similar to the great wartime meetings at Potsdam and Yalta—Churchill recognised that Britain and its allies needed to maintain a monopoly of thermonuclear weapons:

> I wanted America to have a showdown with the Soviet republic before the Russians had the Bomb.[40]

Less than a year before the prime minister left office for the final time, his Defence Policy Committee met on 16 June 1954. The meeting agreed to go ahead with the production of the British hydrogen bomb. This secret decision was not formally communicated to the next meeting of the full British Cabinet on 22 June. Despite this, Churchill privately wrote to US President Eisenhower calling for 'better sharing of information and also perhaps of resources in the thermonuclear sphere'.[41] He then briefed Eisenhower on the H-bomb decision at a meeting in Washington on 25 June and sought supplies of tritium from Canadian Prime Minister Louis St Laurent on 29 June.[42] On 7 July, Churchill argued:

> We could not expect to maintain our influence as a world power unless we possessed the most up-to-date nuclear weapons ... and the thermonuclear bomb would be more economical than atomic bombing.[43]

---

39   Margaret Gowing: *Independence and deterrence*, volume 1 (Macmillan, London, 1974), p. 407.
40   Jonathan Rosenberg: 'Before the bomb and after: Winston Churchill and the use of force', in John Lewis Gaddis (ed.): *Cold War statesman confront the bomb: nuclear diplomacy since 1945* (Oxford University Press, 1999), p. 186.
41   'Message from the Prime Minister', 21 June 1954, Eisenhower Presidential Library: www.eisenhower.archives.gov/.
42   The UK Cabinet was only told about the decision to proceed with the hydrogen bomb in February 1955. Martin Gilbert: *Winston Churchill*, op. cit., pp. 993, 1000, 1094. For Canada, see Lorna Arnold: *Britain and the H-Bomb*, op. cit., pp. 54–55.
43   Jonathan Rosenberg, op. cit., pp. 189–190.

The release of a Defence White Paper in February 1955 saw the public announcement of plans to develop the hydrogen bomb. Even after Churchill's resignation that April, scientific work continued on the weapons prototypes, dubbed 'Blue Danube' and 'Red Beard'. But Britain still needed an area with little population to test their thermonuclear weapons.

Was Australia a possibility? Churchill's successor as prime minister Sir Anthony Eden and Australian Prime Minister Robert Menzies signed a 10-year agreement on 7 March 1956, which approved atomic testing at Maralinga but specified that there would be no explosion of thermonuclear weapons on Australian soil. British scientist William Penney later said the three Antler tests at Maralinga were 'to confirm understanding of the triggering mechanism for high thermonuclear explosions conducted at Christmas Island'.[44]

The Australian Government's need to mollify public opinion over radioactive fallout was not helped when UK authorities announced the final round of tests at Maralinga would be codenamed Operation Volcano.[45] As noted by Elizabeth Tynan:

> The horrified Australians rejected it outright. The name suggested violence and destruction. Antler was chosen after the Australians voiced their concerns.[46]

Given Penney's refusal to share key data with his Australian counterparts, even conservative government ministers were suspicious about British intentions:

> As Operation Grapple was gearing up to test a British H-bomb in the Pacific, the Australian government wondered if the British planned to defy the terms of the Maralinga agreement and test a thermonuclear weapon. In some ways this seemed likely, as thermonuclear weapons were now the main game and Maralinga was the permanent British test site. The terms

---

44   David Leigh and Paul Lashmar: 'Revealed at last: the deadly secrets of Britain's A-Bombs', *The Observer*, 24 March 1985, p. 7.
45   In December 1956, the secretary of the Atomic Weapons Trials Executive issued two memos, the first declaring that there would be a new code word for the 'atomic weapons trials to be carried out at Maralinga in 1957', followed by a second memorandum stating that the code word is 'VOLCANO'! Memos DB/134 and DB/134/01 from C.G. Gray, secretary, Atomic Weapons Trials Executive, 19 December 1956. CO1036/280.
46   For details of the contribution of Operation Antler to the H-bomb program, see Elizabeth Tynan: *Atomic thunder*, op. cit., pp. 110–111.

of the Maralinga agreement had not exactly proved an insurmountable obstacle to the British before. Consequently, approval was slower than usual in coming.[47]

The UK Government then searched the map for another location. The chair of the US Atomic Energy Commission (AEC), Lewis Strauss, informally suggested that the UK could use the US nuclear test site at Enewetak Atoll in the Marshall Islands, but this proposal was quickly overruled by other AEC commissioners.[48]

Before eyes turned to the British GEIC, Sir Anthony Eden made approaches to New Zealand seeking an alternative site. A month after assuming office as prime minister, Eden personally approached his New Zealand counterpart Sidney Holland, seeking use of New Zealand's uninhabited Kermadec Islands for the hydrogen bomb program:

> I am sure that we can count on you for co-operation in a project that is so important to the Commonwealth and the defence of the free world.[49]

Worried that the project would be a 'political H-bomb' for the NZ Government, Holland delayed and later rejected the request to use the isolated South Pacific islands. Attention then turned to the NZ-administered northern Cook Islands and also the Line Islands, which had come under British administration in 1919.[50]

To mend Commonwealth relations after he had turned down the initial UK request, Holland agreed to send the New Zealand warship HMNZS *Lachlan* to investigate potential sites, under the guise of scientific research for the International Geophysical Year (IGY).[51] Royal Navy (RN) Commander John Paton and Royal Engineer Captain P.S. Wadsworth were quietly brought aboard the *Lachlan* to conduct the survey—

---

47 Ibid., p. 111.
48 'Proposal to permit UK to use Eniwetok' [sic], Letter from AEC Commissioner Thomas E. Murray to AEC Chairman Lewis Strauss, 8 March 1955. Marshall Islands Nuclear Documentation Database (MINDD).
49 Rebecca Priestley: *Mad on radium—New Zealand in the atomic age* (Auckland University Press, Auckland, 2013).
50 Following the First World War, the Western Pacific High Commission in Fiji had grouped the Line Islands with the British Gilbert and Ellice Islands Colony (GEIC) for administrative purposes—control over the Line Islands, including Christmas and Malden, was under dispute, however, with the United States still claiming sovereignty in the 1950s.
51 IGY, with activities scheduled between July 1957 and December 1958, was a collaborative international scientific project involving researchers and scientists from both East and West, symbolising a thaw in the Cold War tensions.

both went on to serve as members of the planning team for Operation Grapple.[52] In February and March 1956, Christmas Island and nearby Malden Island were surveyed and identified as potential test sites.

As detailed in later chapters, the New Zealand Government also agreed to Prime Minister Eden's request that two New Zealand frigates join the British naval flotilla off Christmas Island.[53] These vessels would be used as weather ships during the scheduled test series. Weather stations and radiation monitoring would be based on Penrhyn Atoll in the northern Cook Islands, an NZ dependency and one of the closest inhabited locations to the proposed test sites. The Royal New Zealand Air Force (RNZAF) would also provide support services for transport and radiation monitoring. An American offer of a US Air Force monitoring team to be based on Penrhyn was firmly rejected, with New Zealand fearful that this would endorse ongoing US claims of sovereignty over the island.

Despite the restrictions on testing hydrogen bombs on Australian soil, the Australian Government had done its part. The McClelland Royal Commission concluded that the testing of prototypes and atomic triggers in the deserts of Australia provided a crucial step in the development of the British hydrogen bomb:

> Although thermonuclear weapons (H-bombs) were not exploded in Australia either at the Monte Bello Islands or at Maralinga, some of the tests carried out at these sites were associated with the developmental program for Britain's H-bomb program and trials at Christmas Island in the Pacific ... The British tests in Australia only included development tests up to the 'atomic detonator' stage and the test of a British H-bomb was undertaken at Christmas Island in the Pacific in 1957.[54]

---

52 John Crawford: *The involvement of the Royal New Zealand Navy in the British nuclear testing programmes of 1957 and 1958*, research paper for New Zealand Defence Force Headquarters, Wellington, New Zealand, 1989 (declassified 1996), p. 6.
53 The British ambassador in Wellington Sir Geoffrey Scoones relayed the British Prime Minister's request for naval support to the NZ Minister of External Affairs, Mr T.L. MacDonald, in July 1956. Ibid., pp. 7, 9.
54 Government of Australia: *The Report of the Royal Commission into British Nuclear Tests in Australia*, op. cit., volume 1, pp. 21–22.

Without irony, Menzies' Minister for External Affairs Sir Garfield Barwick would later proclaim the government's pride that Australia was one of the first nations in the world to sign and ratify the 1963 Partial Test Ban Treaty.[55]

Sir Winston Churchill too had done his part. The old Cold Warrior paved the way for his successors Sir Anthony Eden and Harold Macmillan to expand the hydrogen bomb program. Churchill publicly acknowledged this legacy just weeks before he retired. Standing before the House of Commons on 1 March 1955, Churchill outlined the contents of a new British Defence White Paper in a formal parliamentary statement. He publicly confirmed that the United Kingdom would follow in the footsteps of the two nuclear superpowers to develop a hydrogen bomb:

> To make our contribution to the deterrent, we must ourselves possess the most up-to-date nuclear weapons, and the means of delivering them.[56]

The date of the UK parliamentary debate was auspicious. It was exactly one year after the United States had conducted its largest-ever nuclear test on Bikini Atoll in the Marshall Islands—codename Bravo.

---

55   'Statement in the House of Representatives on the ratification by the Australian government of the Nuclear Test Ban Treaty, by the Minister for External Affairs Sir Garfield Barwick on 15 August 1963', in *Nuclear Testing*, Select Documents on International Affairs, No. 2 (Department of External Affairs, Canberra, 1963), p. 31.
56   Speech by Prime Minister Sir Winston Churchill, UK House of Commons, Hansard official report, 1 March 1955.

2
The survivors— Lemeyo Abon and Rinok Riklon

Lemeyo Abon and Rinok Riklon, Majuro, Marshall Islands
Source: Nic Maclellan.

On 1 March 1954, Rinok Riklon was a young girl living on Rongelap, one of the northern atolls of the Marshall Islands. Then the bomb went off.

The US Government had exploded a thermonuclear weapon, codenamed Bravo, on Bikini Atoll, 120 kilometres to the west. With an explosive yield of nearly 15 megatons, this was the largest-ever nuclear detonation by the US military. It sent a cloud of radioactive fallout across the Marshall Islands, especially impacting the northern atolls of Rongelap, Utirik, Rongerik and Ailinginae.

In an interview nearly 60 years later, Mrs Riklon said:

> People were playing with the fallout as it fell from the sky. We put it in our hair as if it was soap or shampoo. But later I lost all of my hair.[1]

On the day of the Bravo test, Lemeyo Abon was 14 years old, living on Rongelap:

> We saw the bright light and heard a boom and we were really scared. We had no idea of what was happening. Later on something like powder came from the sky. It was raining when we went home and our parents asked 'what happened to your hair?' The next day our hair fell out. We looked at each other and laughed, saying 'you look like a bald old man!' But in our hearts we were sad.[2]

With the tradition of washing their hair with coconut oil, girls like Rinok Riklon and Lemeyo Abon were at greater risk of exposure to hazardous levels of radiation. A memo from Joint Task Force 7 (JTF7), the military command responsible for the operation, acknowledged that 'the heavy coconut oil hairdressing used by the Marshallese tended to concentrate radioactivity in the hair'.[3]

On the eve of the Bravo test, the US military had received weather reports indicating that atmospheric conditions were getting less favourable. Winds at 20,000 feet were headed towards Rongelap and other atolls to the east.

---

1   Interview with Rinok Riklon, Majuro, Marshall Islands, September 2013, with thanks to interpreter Abacca Anjain-Maddison.
2   Interview with Mrs Lemeyo Abon, Majuro, Marshall Islands, September 2013.
3   'Operation Castle: Radiological Safety Final Report', Vol. 1, Joint Task Force 7 (Technical Branch J-3 Division, Washington DC, 1955). Cited in Holly Barker: *Bravo for the Marshallese—regaining control in a post-nuclear, post-colonial world* (Wadsworth, Belmont, 2004), p. 40.

In spite of these warnings, the test went ahead on the order of Major General Percy W. Clarkson, deputy commander of US Army Forces in the Pacific, who was responsible for the operation as JTF7 commander.[4]

As the winds carried high-level radioactive fallout across inhabited atolls, 28 US Army and Air Force weathermen on Rongerik Atoll were evacuated within hours by plane (even so, some had film badge readings that showed radiation exposure hundreds of times beyond established safety levels).[5] A Navy tanker USS *Patapsco* was sailing east of Bikini when it was also caught in the main path of the Bravo fallout.

In contrast to the rapid response for military personnel on Rongerik, the US task force waited two days to evacuate islanders from Rongelap, Ailinginae and Utirik atolls, despite the hazardous levels of fallout.

As part of Operation Castle, the Bravo hydrogen bomb test was just one of 67 atmospheric nuclear tests between 1946 and 1958. Bikini Atoll hosted many such operations: Crossroads (1946), Castle (1954), Redwing (1956) and Hardtack I (1958). Test series on Enewetak included Sandstone (1948), Greenhouse (1951), Ivy (1952), and some extra tests from Castle (1954), Redwing (1956) and Hardtack I (1958).

In all, 80 per cent of all the nuclear tests conducted by the United States during the Cold War were held in the Marshall Islands. Merril Eisenbud, Director of the US Atomic Energy Commission's (AEC) Health and Safety Laboratory has recalled that the US military would have preferred to test hydrogen bombs in the Nevada desert, but this might have endangered nearby communities:

---

[4] US Government perspectives on the contested debate over weather patterns, fallout and lack of preparation for evacuation can be found in Barton C. Hacker: *Elements of Controversy* (University of California Press, Berkeley, 1994), pp. 134–158; and a 2013 study of Bravo by the US Defense Threat Reduction Agency (USDTRA): Thomas Kunkle and Byron Ristvet: *Castle Bravo: Fifty years of legend and lore*, USDTRA, Defense Threat Reduction Information Analysis Center (DTRIAC) SR-12-001, January 2013.

[5] On Rongerik Atoll, 28 US Army and Air Force personnel had film badge readings of 32 to 52 rem (320–500 mSv). Three members of the US Navy Bikini Boat Pool had heavily exposed badges with readings from 85 to 96 rem (850–950 mSv). As a basis of comparison, a standard diagnostic chest x-ray delivers a radiation dose of about 0.02 rem. See 'Operation Castle', Fact Sheet, USDTRA, May 2015.

> Nevada would be ideal, except that, when you got up above 50 kilotons or so, you made so much bang that you would begin to break windows, crack plaster. Couldn't go much higher than that, and here they wanted to go up to multimegatons. So they had to go out somewhere, and the Marshalls seemed like a reasonable place for them.[6]

In 1947, a year after the US military had begun its testing program, the Marshall Islands were designated as part of the Trust Territory of the Pacific Islands (TTPI). This trust territory was the only one designated as 'strategic' by the United Nations Security Council, so the United States as the Administering Authority was authorised to militarise the territory.[7] At the same time, the Administering Authority was entrusted to protect the land, resources and health of Micronesia's inhabitants.

For many decades, the US Government hid details of the extent of contamination from its testing program, especially when they negotiated a Compact of Free Association with the Republic of the Marshall Islands (RMI)—an agreement that led to self-government and independence for the Micronesian nation in 1986. The RMI Government and people gave away the right to sue in US courts for compensation for damage to person and property from the tests. In return, a fund of US$150 million was established under section 177 of the Compact to deal with the health and environmental legacies of the testing program.

In May 1994, the US Department of Energy released more than 70 boxes of newly declassified documents to the RMI Government. The documents revealed that the spread of fallout from Bravo and other tests was much wider than previously acknowledged by the US Government.[8] For 50 years, the United States had hidden the fact that fallout from the Bravo test had spread over more than 11,000 square kilometres. Other atolls such as Ailuk, Likiep, Wotho, Mejit and Kwajalein had received significant levels of radioactive fallout. Over time, traces of radioactivity from the test were detected in Australia, India, Japan, the United States and Europe.

---

6   Oral History of Merril Eisenbud, United States Department of Energy, Office of Human Radiation Experiments, DOE/EH-0456, May 1995.
7   Gary Smith: *Micronesia—decolonisation and US military interests in the Trust Territory of the Pacific Islands* (Peace Research Centre, The Australian National University, 1991).
8   See, for example, 'Radioactive Debris from Operation Castle—islands of the mid-Pacific', US Atomic Energy Commission (AEC), 18 January 1955. Marshall Islands Nuclear Documentation Database (MINDD).

2. *THE SURVIVORS*—LEMEYO ABON AND RINOK RIKLON

A range of authors have chronicled the sorry history of US nuclear testing in the Pacific and the lingering health and environmental impacts for the Marshallese people.[9] Successive US governments have acknowledged damage to four northern atolls from nuclear testing. But at a March 2017 ceremony to commemorate the 63rd anniversary of the Bravo test, RMI President Hilda Heine stressed that this policy ignores the United States' responsibility for health and environmental impacts across the whole country:

> Studies from the early years that were not known to the RMI government during the Compact negotiation process have now shown that 18 other inhabited atolls or single islands were contaminated by three of the six nuclear bombs tested in Operation Castle, as well as by the Bravo shot in 1954. The myth of only four 'exposed' atolls of Bikini, Enewetak, Rongelap and Utirik has shaped US nuclear policy on the Marshallese people since 1954, which limited medical and scientific follow up and compensation programs.[10]

* * *

The effect of the 1954 Bravo test on British defence policy was profound. Bravo and other thermonuclear tests during Operation Castle were closely studied by British scientists and had both technical and political impact on the British hydrogen bomb program.

In a personal letter to US President Dwight D. Eisenhower immediately after Bravo, British Prime Minister Sir Winston Churchill recognised both the power of the hydrogen bomb and the hazards posed by fallout:

> I am told that several million people would certainly be obliterated by four or five of the latest H-bombs. In a few more years, these could be delivered by rocket without even hazarding the life of a pilot … Another ugly idea has been put in my head, namely, the dropping of an H-bomb in the sea to windward of the island or any other seaborne country in

---

9   Jonathan Weisgall: *Operation Crossroads—the atomic tests at Bikini Atoll* (Naval Institute Press, Annapolis, 1994); Barbara Rose Johnston and Holly Barker: *Consequential Damages of Nuclear War—the Rongelap report* (Left Coast Press, 2008); Jack Niedenthal: *For the good of mankind—a history of the people of Bikini and their islands* (Micronitor, Majuro, 2001); Giff Johnson: *Nuclear past, unclear future* (Micronitor, Majuro, 2009); Giff Johnson: *Don't Ever Whisper—Darlene Keju: Pacific Health Pioneer, Champion for Nuclear Survivors* (CreateSpace Independent Publishing, 2013). For interviews with Marshallese nuclear survivors, see the website established by anthropologist Glenn Alcalay at www.atomicatolls.org.
10   President Hilda C. Heine: Keynote remarks, 63rd Nuclear Victims Remembrance Day, Capitol Building, Majuro, 1 March 2017 (the author was present in Majuro for the ceremony and the Office of the President kindly provided a translation of the speech, which was presented in the Marshallese language).

suitable weather, by rocket or air plane, or perhaps released by submarine. The explosion would generate an enormous radioactive cloud, many square miles in extent, which would drift over the land attacked and extinguish human life over very large areas.[11]

In a speech to the UK parliament on 30 March 1954, just a month after the Bravo test, Churchill defended the US testing program. Under pressure to hold a parliamentary debate, Churchill noted:

> We are all naturally concerned at the prodigious experiments which are being carried out in the Pacific, but I do not think there will be any difference between us, that we would rather have them carried out there than in Siberia.[12]

Many peoples across Asia and the Pacific did not harbour the same sentiments. On 2 April 1954, Indian Prime Minister Jawaharlal Nehru called for a 'standstill agreement' on nuclear testing—launching a process that would culminate in a 1958 moratorium on atmospheric testing. While mass protests about Bravo were concentrated in Pacific Rim nations like Japan and Australia, Marshall islanders also expressed their opposition, despite the US Navy's control of the UN strategic trusteeship.

Just weeks after the Bravo test, Marshall islanders, led by schoolteachers Dwight Heine and Atlan Anien and customary chiefs Kabua Kabua and Dorothy Kabua, lodged a petition with the UN Trusteeship Council. The petition requested that 'all experiments with lethal weapons in this area be immediately ceased', and highlighted the importance of land as a source of culture and identity—land that was being vaporised or contaminated by the nuclear tests:

> the Marshallese people are not only fearful of the danger to their persons from these deadly weapons in case of another miscalculation, but they are also concerned for the increasing number of people removed from their land ... land means a great deal to the Marshallese. It means more than just a place where you can plant your food crops and build your houses or a place where you can bury your dead. It is the very life of the people. Take away their land and their spirits go also.[13]

---

11   'My Dear Friend', letter from Prime Minister Winston Churchill to US President Dwight D Eisenhower, dated March 1954, cited in Martin Gilbert: *Winston S. Churchill, Volume VIII: Never Despair 1945–65*, p. 959.
12   Ibid., p. 965.
13   Petition from the Marshallese People Concerning the Pacific Islands: *Complaint regarding explosions of lethal weapons within our home islands to United Nations Trusteeship Council, 20 April 1954*, circulated as UN Trusteeship Council document T/PET.10/28, 6 May 1954.

Most Marshallese were reluctant to directly challenge the US administration, with the petitioners noting:

> Aside from this complaint, we have found American administration by far the most agreeable one in our memory.[14]

The US Government was suspicious that Americans resident in the TTPI had been involved in drafting the petition, but this was denied by Dwight Heine:

> It taxed me to write it. We worked every day for nearly a month. We would meet with other Marshallese and put down their ideas. Then we would make a rough draft. I thought we had too many 'dangers' in it. So I looked through the dictionary and decided on 'lethal'. I also found the word 'circumvent' as a substitute for 'prevent'.[15]

Even as the Soviet Union conducted its own nuclear tests in Kazakhstan, Russian officials used the UN Trusteeship Council to criticise the United States for using the TTPI as a testing site:

> One of the crimes of American imperialism against the peoples of Oceania is the testing of atomic and hydrogen weapons carried out in Micronesia, on the islands of Bikini and Eniwetok in the Marshalls archipelago. Starting in 1946, the American military gang has carried out a series of experimental explosions of atom and hydrogen bombs six times in this area …
>
> The tests of nuclear weapons carried out by the USA undermined the very basis of existence of the population of the trusteeship territories … The actions of the American 'trustees' aroused the anger of the inhabitants of the trusteeship territories. They submitted petitions to the Trusteeship Council of the United Nations protesting against the American nuclear tests and demanding that they be stopped. The representatives of the USSR in the Trusteeship Council repeatedly spoke in support of these just demands.[16]

---

14 Ibid.
15 Bill Waugh: 'Creation of the N-petition', *Associated Press*, 29 May 1954.
16 A.M. Shilkov: 'The National Liberation Movements in Oceania', pamphlet from All-Union Society for the Dissemination of Political and Scientific Knowledge (translated in *Translations from the Soviet press*, Colonial Office digest no. 365, p. 10). CO1036/859.

In response, the US Ambassador to the United Nations Henry Cabot Lodge Jr pledged that 'the authorities were doing everything humanly possible to take care of everyone who was in the area' and that 'any Marshall islanders removed because of the tests would be re-established without incurring financial loss'.[17]

Despite the assurances, the April 1954 protest to the United Nations—released publicly in early May—sparked international attention and anger. The *Times* of London reported:

> Bikini and Eniwetok were taken away for atomic bomb tests and their inhabitants moved to Kili Island and Ujelang Atoll. Because Rongelab and Uterik [sic] are now radioactive their inhabitants are being on Kwajalein for an indeterminate time. 'Where next?' is the big question in all our minds.[18]

The British Government was well aware of international public concern about radioactive fallout from the Bravo test, but government ministers went out of their way to downplay any need for action.

After publicity about the Marshallese petition to the United Nations, the UK Under-Secretary for Foreign Affairs Sir Douglas Dodds-Parker was questioned in the House of Commons about potential hazards for British dependencies in the Pacific.

Opposition Labour MPs cited media reports 'which say that people on Utirik, which is 511 miles away from the explosion, are now complaining of changes in their bloodstreams, of their hair falling out and of nausea. Oughtn't we not, having a responsibility on the Trusteeship Council, to be in possession of the full facts of the matter?'[19]

Dodds-Parker replied:

> Her Majesty's Government has no responsibility in the matter except as members of the Trusteeship Council. We have no information other than that contained in the petition which was circulated in the United Nations Trusteeship Council document of 6 May.[20]

---

17   'Marshall Islanders urgent pleas—end A-bomb tests', *The Times* (London), 15 May 1954.
18   Ibid. Spelling of Marshallese names as written in original report.
19   'Hydrogen bomb tests Pacific (representation)', UK House of Commons, Hansard official record, 20 May 1954.
20   Ibid.

This parliamentary statement was a lie. Between March and May, under a program known as Aconite, aircraft of the Royal Air Force (RAF) based in Darwin, Australia were used to gather fallout samples from the Operation Castle nuclear tests in the Marshall Islands. After at least six Castle tests, including Bravo, UK Canberra bombers flew missions through the mushroom clouds to gather samples that could help determine the yield of the explosion.[21]

As we'll see in Chapter 19, pilots in Britain's Aconite program suffered augmented doses of radiation during the flights, opening the way for compensation from the US Government, but not the British authorities!

US aircraft flying from Guam, Hawai'i and Kwajalein Atoll monitored the spread of fallout from Bravo over 71 islands and atolls in the central Pacific. This operation included one dedicated US flight over the British Gilbert and Ellice Islands Colony (GEIC):

> One special survey flight, [codename] KING, was flown on 6 March 1954 to monitor the Gilbert Islands for contamination from Bravo. British authorities approved this flight and the results were forwarded to the US Naval attaché, London, to inform the British government.[22]

The US Armed Forces Special Weapons Project also agreed that the Air Force Office of Atomic Energy (AFOAT-1)—which was tracking fallout to determine the yield of US and Soviet thermonuclear weapons—would provide British scientists with long-range detection filters exposed during Operation Castle. This data would provide valuable information about the yield of weapons and the spread of radioactive isotopes from the Marshall Islands tests.[23]

---

21 More than 60 years after the tests, three UK Ministry of Defence (MoD) files entitled 'ACONITE series of American tests: British sampling and analysis' (UK National Archives ES 1/849, ES 1/850 and ES 1/851) are still restricted from public access under section 3.4 of the Public Records Act 1958 'on security or other specified grounds'. In the US archives, there is evidence of UK involvement, such as a February 1954 letter from the US AEC, which 'approved the Joint Chiefs of Staff view that it is now considered practical to grant permission to the United Kingdom for accommodations for two Canberra aircraft during Operation Castle'. Letter from AEC Chairman Lewis L. Strauss to Robert LeBaron, Chairperson, Military Liaison Committee, 15 February 1954. MINDD.
22 'Summary of fallout from shot Bravo' message from Alvin C. Graves, scientific director, JTF7, US AEC SF00 NV0077 7756, 1954, cited in Thomas Kunkle and Byron Ristvet: *Castle Bravo: Fifty years of legend and lore*, op. cit., p. 91.
23 Letter from Captain G.S. Brunson, Armed Forces Special Weapons Project, Department of Defence to Dr Paul McDaniel, US AEC, 26 February 1954 (MINDD). For information on AFOAT-1 and US efforts to track radioactive fallout from the Soviet tests, see Doyle L. Northrup and Donald H. Rock: 'The detection of Joe 1', *Studies in Intelligence*, Central Intelligence Agency (CIA), Vol. 10, Fall 1966 (declassified by the CIA in September 1995).

This data was helpful in the development of the British hydrogen bomb, allowing chief scientist William Penney to draw inferences about the way the United States had constructed its thermonuclear weapon.[24]

Beyond the Aconite program, the UK Government was monitoring whether the Bravo test had caused any contamination in British colonial dependencies in the Pacific. Throughout March and April, there was a flurry of correspondence between UK officials in Honiara, Tarawa, London and Washington, discussing potential hazards from Bravo for the Pacific colonies. The H-bomb test had especially caused anxiety in the British GEIC, as Western Pacific Commissioner Sir Robert Stanley reported to London in late March:

> The United States hydrogen bomb test on 1 March was heard as far south as Arorae and in Tarawa there was sound like gunfire followed by prolonged rumblings.[25]

The Colonial Office queried whether Michael Bernacchi, the GEIC Resident Commissioner in Tarawa, should be advised about potential radiation hazards. According to the Colonial Office:

> [In 1946] our technical advisers were satisfied that there is no likelihood of damage in the Gilbert and Ellice Islands Colony from experiments at Bikini … Since that time, explosions with far greater and more far reaching effects have been carried out and we now hear from the High Commissioner that the recent explosion on 1 March was heard as far south as Arorae (the most southern of the Gilbert Islands) while at Tarawa, the noise was much more severe.

> The Resident Commissioner asks for advice on the exact time of future explosions so that steps can be taken for the security of mental patients etc and also whether there is likely to be any effect on fish, a staple food in the colony.[26]

After the Bravo test, the United States declared a danger zone of 450 nautical miles around Enewetak in the lead up to further tests. The Colonial Office approached the Foreign Office on 29 March about

---

24 Michael S. Goodman: *Spying on the Nuclear Bear: Anglo-American Intelligence and the Soviet Bomb*, Stanford Nuclear Age series (Stanford University Press, 2007), p. 111.
25 Telegram no. 126, marked secret, from Sir Robert Stanley, Western Pacific Commission, to Secretary of State for the Colonies, London, 30 March 1954. CO1036/236.
26 File note dated 30 March 1954, in 'Hydrogen bomb experiments, Western Pacific', PAC 310/4/01, CO1036/236.

potential hazards for the northernmost Line Islands such as Makin, especially as the Bravo cloud did not remain solely within a 450-mile radius around Bikini:

> There were press reports that the last explosion made a ship, or ships, radioactive when they were 1,000 miles from the site. We would, of course, have populated islands and local shipping within that distance. Somewhat further afield is Ocean Island which, like Australia's Nauru, is a phosphate centre and there is an amount of plant and machinery there. No doubt you will tell us if anything should be said to the Gilbert and Ellice authorities.[27]

Foreign officers contacted the UK Embassy in Washington, asking whether Bernacchi:

> could be advised of the times of future explosions which, he understands, will be several times greater in strength, so that he can take measures for the security of mental patients, fragile stores etc. He also enquires whether there is likely to be any effect on fish on which the Colony largely depends for food.[28]

The Foreign Office told the Colonial Office to calm down, downplaying any potential hazards:

> The danger area is 450 miles around Eniwetok [sic]. This has been calculated with all due allowance for chance errors, and you may rest assured that neither Makin Island nor any of the other islands in the Gilbert and Ellice group will be in danger. I suggest that in the circumstances nothing should be said to the Gilbert and Ellice authorities for fear of causing unnecessary alarm.[29]

In the weeks after Bravo, the United States continued with further tests throughout March as part of Operation Castle. These included the 8-megaton Yankee test on Bikini Atoll (22 March) and the 275-kiloton

---

27 Letter from C.J.J.T. Barton, Colonial Office to J.E. Jackson, Foreign Office, 29 March 1954. DEF 103/61/02. CO1036/236.
28 Telegram no. 1340 from Foreign Office, London, to UK Embassy, Washington, 2 April 1954. CO1036/236.
29 Letter, marked Top Secret, from J.E. Johnson, Foreign Office to C.J.J.T. Barton, Colonial Office, 2 April 1954. CO1036/236. Two years later, this policy had been overturned, with Colonial Office officials in the Gilbert and Ellice Islands Colony (GEIC) announcing forthcoming US hydrogen bomb tests. See, for example, a brief item in the GEIC *Headquarters Information Note* in May 1956 stating 'information has been unofficially received that Operation Redwing is the dropping of a thermonuclear weapon by parachute from an aircraft of the US Air Force in the Marshalls area and will take place around 8 May'. *Headquarter Information Note* no. 19, 4 May 1956, p. 2. Gilbert and Ellice Islands Colony. F76/6/32 (1957). PAMBU document AU PMB Doc 493.

Echo test on Enewetak Atoll (29 March). From his headquarters, Resident Commissioner Bernacchi reported to London that the further explosions had been heard on the GEIC islands of Butaritari and Tarawa, though less clearly than the massive Bravo blast.[30]

To calm ongoing concern in Britain's Pacific colonies, Prime Minister Macmillan asked officials whether up-to-date information could be obtained from the US Government about the dates of forthcoming tests on Bikini. Following approaches to the US State Department, the UK Embassy in Washington reported:

> Uncertain meteorological conditions in the Pacific make it impossible for the United States authorities to give us more exact warning of shots than they already do. The Resident Commissioner may be told, however, that the tests will continue at intervals throughout the month and the precautions need not be any more elaborate than warranted by the first two explosions.[31]

With a parliamentary debate likely in early June, the Colonial Office again sought information about effects on people in the GEIC. From Tarawa, Resident Commissioner Bernacchi replied:

> Confirm no (repeat no) harm to British subjects in North Gilberts has been caused by nuclear-fission bomb experiments, although they have caused slight alarm.[32]

The last six words were deleted when the reply was reported to Parliament.

As reports of the Marshall Islands petition to the UN Trusteeship Council spread through the media in the United Kingdom, stories of Bravo's radioactive fallout sparked concern from British companies with operations in the central Pacific.

The British Phosphate Commission (BPC) comprised Australian, British and New Zealand representatives who had managed phosphate mining on Christmas Island, Nauru and Banaba (Ocean Island) since 1920.

---

30   Telegram no. 135 from Assistant High Commissioner, Western Pacific to Secretary of State for the Colonies, 2 April 1954. CO1036/236.
31   Telegram no. 577 from UK Embassy, Washington, to Foreign Office, London, 8 April 1954. CO1036/236.
32   Priority telegram no. 195, from Sir Robert Stanley, Western Pacific Commission, to Secretary of State for the Colonies, London, 25 May 1954. CO1036/236.

BPC's general manager James Bissett wrote to the Australian Department of Territories in May 1954, seeking information about the US nuclear testing program:

> In view of recent press reports concerning hydrogen bomb experiments at Eniwetok, which is approximately the same distance from Nauru as Bikini Atoll, and the fact that some anxiety has been expressed by members of our Nauru and Ocean Island staff, the commissioners would appreciate any information obtainable in the United States authorities and Australian nuclear research experts as to possible effects, if any, at Nauru and Ocean Island.[33]

Tipped off from Canberra, a Foreign Office official sent a personal message to the BPC's UK representative, in an effort to short-circuit any public protest. Enclosing copies of a statement by UK Secretary of State for the Colonies Oliver Lyttelton to the House of Commons, the Foreign Officer argued that there was no danger to the Gilbert Islands and 'as some of these islands are considerably closer to Eniwetok than is Ocean Island, I thought that Mr. Lyttelton's answer in the House of Commons would be of interest to you'.[34]

* * *

For the Marshallese, the aftermath of Bravo led to tragic consequences. The US military and medical staff from Brookhaven National Laboratory, led by Dr Robert Conard, saw an opportunity to research the effect of radiation on people living on contaminated land. Under Project 4.1, medical studies were undertaken on at least 539 men, women and children—often without informed consent—including experimental surgery and injections of chromium-51, radioactive iodine, iron, zinc and carbon-14.[35]

---

33 Letter, marked confidential, from Jas. A. Bissett, general manager BPC, for British Phosphate Commissioners, to the Secretary, Australian Department of Territories, 15 May 1954. CO1036/237.
34 Letter from J.B. Sidebottom, Foreign Office, London to G. Calder, British Phosphate Commissioners, 23 June 1954. CO1036/237.
35 In the first 15 years after Bravo, 54 medical studies were published by Project 4.1 researchers. Documents from Project 4.1, which continued until the 1970s, can be found in the MINDD. A short history of the project by some of its key staff can be found in E.P. Cronkite, R.A. Conard and V.P. Bond: 'Historical events associated with fallout from Bravo shot—Operation Castle and 25 years of medical findings', *Journal of Health Physics*, Vol. 73, No. 1, 1997, pp. 176–186.

Merril Eisenbud of the US AEC's Advisory Committee on Biology and Medicine noted in 1956:

> It will be very interesting to go back and get good environmental data, how many per square mile, what isotopes are involved and a sample of food changes in many humans through their urines, so as to get a measure of the human uptake when people live in a contaminated environment. Now, data of this type has never been available. While it is true that these people do not live, I would say, the way Westerners do, civilised people, it is nevertheless also true that these people are more like us than mice.[36]

Dr Thomas Shipman, health division leader at the Los Alamos nuclear weapons laboratory, wrote to Dr Robert Conard of Project 4.1 stating:

> Many thanks for the copy of the most recent survey of the Rongelap natives ... The development defects in the small children are also of considerable interest, and I presume an attempt will be made to correlate these findings with what has been reported in Japan.[37]

With little irony, Shipman recalled the dangers of sunburn while visiting the Micronesian islands:

> Maybe one of these days I can get back out when your survey team goes and sees the natives again. I will, however, be very careful about getting a sunburn comparable to the one I got on my previous visit to Rongelap.[38]

Reluctant to be used as mice or guinea pigs, Marshall islanders again petitioned the Trusteeship Council in 1958.[39] US Ambassador Lodge formally requested UN Secretary General Dag Hammarskjöld to delay introducing the Marshallese petition until after the US military had completed Operation Hardtack, a new series of 35 atomic and hydrogen bomb tests on Bikini and Enewetak atolls.[40] Hammarskjöld agreed and the second petition was not formally considered by the United Nations.

---

36 AEC: *Minutes of the Advisory Committee on Biology and Medicine, 13–14 January 1956* (AEC, New York, 1956), cited in Holly Barker: *Bravo for the Marshallese*, op. cit., p. 45. See Eisenbud's January 1995 oral history for his role in human experiments—Merril Eisenbud : 'Human radiation studies, remembering the early years', United States Department of Energy, Office of Human Radiation Experiments, DOE/EH-0456, May 1995.

37 Letter from Thomas L. Shipman M.D., Los Alamos, New Mexico to Dr Robert Conard, Brookhaven National Laboratory, New York, 13 March 1961. MINDD.

38 Ibid.

39 Interview with Ambassador Tony de Brum, Majuro, Marshall Islands, March 2017.

40 Ambassador Lodge: *Memorandum to the Secretary General of the United Nations regarding the delay of submission over Marshallese petition to the Security Council*, 1958, cited in Holly Barker, *Bravo for the Marshallese*, op. cit., p. 24. For details of the tests, see 'Operation Hardtack', Fact Sheet, USDTRA, May 2015.

The adverse effects of Bravo continue to this day. Marshallese from the northern atolls are still displaced from their home islands. Food plants like breadfruit and coconut take up radioactive caesium-137 from the soil and this hazard has persisted on Bikini, Rongelap and other contaminated islands to this day.[41] Although the US Congress has allocated funding to finance a partial clean-up, only a small part of Rongelap, Rongerik and Ailinginae atolls have been remediated. Exiled residents are calling for more comprehensive efforts before they return home.

The presence of radioactive isotopes that can accumulate in the food chain pose particular hazards for women and children, as detailed by UN Special Rapporteur Calin Georgescu:

> Because of cultural differences and language barriers, Marshallese dietary customs were either unknown or ignored during the testing period. For example, the difference in dietary and other eating habits of men, women and children may have led to higher exposure of some members of the population, especially women. Women eat different parts of the fish to those eaten by men, especially bones and organ meat, in which certain radioactive isotopes tend to accumulate.
>
> The differences in the retention of radionuclides by coconut and land crabs were not recognised by the medical profession in the United States. Apparently, women were more exposed to radiation levels in coconut and other foods owing to their role in processing foods and weaving fibre to make sitting and sleeping mats, and handling materials used in housing construction, water collection, hygiene and food preparation, as well as in handicrafts.[42]

After Bravo, Lemeyo Abon was one of the children relocated from Rongelap—an evacuation that began a decades-long odyssey, which has left many people still living in exile. After returning to live on the contaminated atoll for 30 years, she was again evacuated to Mejatto Island

---

41 For current contamination levels on Bikini, Enewetak and Rongelap, see recent research from a Columbia University team led by Professor Emlyn Hughes. Autumn S. Bordnera et al.: 'Measurement of background gamma radiation in the northern Marshall Islands', *Proceedings of the National Academy of Sciences of the United States of America*, Vol. 113, No. 25, 2016, pp. 6833–6838. DOI: 10.1073/pnas.1605535113.
42 Report of Calin Georgescu, UN Special Rapporteur on the implications for human rights of the environmentally sound management and disposal of hazardous substances and wastes, on his mission to the Marshall Islands (27–30 March 2012) and the United States of America (24–27 April 2012), UN Human Rights Council, Twenty-first session, 3 September 2012, A/HRC/21/48/Add.1.

in 1985 aboard the Greenpeace vessel *Rainbow Warrior*.[43] She later moved to the Marshall Islands capital Majuro—still far away from her home island. Speaking to Mrs Abon in Majuro in 2013, her loss was clear:

> We are still living in this place in exile from our homeland, like a coconut floating in the sea. The United States has to live up to their responsibility and make sure our children and grandchildren will be cared for.[44]

As we'll see in later chapters, women who were living on Christmas Island during the British hydrogen bomb tests express similar concerns for their spouses, children and grandchildren.

The nuclear test site on Bikini Atoll is now considered a world heritage site, symbolising a significant stage in human history. As the United Nations Educational, Scientific and Cultural Organization (UNESCO) notes:

> Through its history, the atoll symbolises the dawn of the nuclear age, despite its paradoxical image of peace and of earthly paradise.[45]

---

43 Just weeks later, this Greenpeace vessel was sunk in Auckland Harbour by French intelligence agents who had been sent halfway around the world to sabotage protests over French nuclear testing at Moruroa and Fangataufa atolls. For the Marshallese relocation, see David Robie: *Eyes of Fire—the Last Voyage of the Rainbow Warrior* (Little Island Books, Auckland, 2015) and testimony from participants at eyes-of-fire.littleisland.co.nz/.
44 Interview with Lemeyo Abon, Majuro, September 2013.
45 UNESCO: *World Heritage List: Bikini Atoll Nuclear Test Site*: whc.unesco.org/en/list/1339.

3
The fisherman—Matashichi Oishi

Crew member Matashichi Oishi with the fishing boat Daigo Fukuryu Maru
Source: Tatsuya Hagiwara, Kyodo.

The fallout from Bravo was political, as well as radioactive.

After the 1 March 1954 test, the greatest international outcry came from Japan. Public opinion was already raw from the atomic bombing of Hiroshima and Nagasaki, but was inflamed when the United States' largest hydrogen bomb test irradiated the 23 crew members of a Japanese fishing boat *Daigo Fukuryu Maru* (*No. 5 Lucky Dragon*).

Crew member Matashichi Oishi was just seven years old when Japanese military forces attacked Pearl Harbor, Hawai'i, in December 1941, extending the Pacific War, which had been raging in Manchuria and China since 1931. With his family impoverished by wartime privation, he was forced to leave school at age 11, becoming a sailor:

> I was the oldest of the four brothers. School was wholly out of the question. If I didn't support the whole family, if I didn't start working immediately, we'd starve. I quit school when I was in eighth grade, and at fourteen, out of harsh necessity, I became a fisherman. I was plunged into a world full of veterans back from the war and all kinds of rough fellows.[1]

On 22 January 1954—the day before his 20th birthday—Oishi was aboard the 140-ton wooden vessel *Lucky Dragon* as it set off from its home port of Yaizu in Shizuoka Prefecture. As they sailed towards fishing grounds in Micronesia, the crew members had an average age of 25 (Captain Tsutsui Hisakichi was just 22 years old).

After losing nets as they fished near Midway Island, the crew sailed on towards the Marshall Islands. Weeks later, on the morning of 1 March 1954, the crew were fishing for tuna in waters to the east of Bikini Atoll, north of Rongelap.

At 6.45 am, the western sky lit up with a flash as a 7-kilometre-wide fireball shot up from Bikini Atoll. Minutes later, the fishing boat was rocked by the blast of the detonation. Bemused by the glow in the sky, the captain and crew continued fishing, unaware they were close to the testing site on Bikini, although they were aware of the prescribed danger zone around Enewetak Atoll.

In August 1952, the US State Department had notified the Japanese Maritime Safety Agency that a danger zone had been created around Enewetak, restricting movement by fishing vessels and other craft. In October the following year, the US Hydrographic Office announced that the zone had been expanded eastwards, incorporating waters around Bikini Atoll. However, Captain Hisakichi was unaware of the 1953 extension of the zone, and thought his crew were safe as long as they stayed away from Enewetak.

---

1   Matashichi Oishi: *The day the sun rose in the west—Bikini, the Lucky Dragon and I* (University of Hawaii Press, Honolulu, 2011), translated from Japanese by Richard H. Minear, p. 11.

3. THE FISHERMAN — MATASHICHI OISHI

Even if they had been outside the extended danger zone, the crew would still have been in danger—winds carried fallout well outside the prescribed danger area. By 10 am on 1 March, prevailing winds carried radioactive particles of pulverised coral dust over vast areas, which showered over the vessel. The fishing boat and its catch of tuna were contaminated by the fallout, with the crew suffering symptoms of acute radiation poisoning. Decades later, Oishi recalled:

> I noticed that the rain contained white particles. 'What's this?' Even as I wondered, the rain stopped, and only the white particles were falling on us. It was just like sleet. As it accumulated on deck, our feet left footprints. This silent white stuff that stole up on us as we worked was the devil incarnate, born of science.
>
> The white particles penetrated mercilessly—eyes, nose, ears, mouth; it turned the heads of those wearing headbands white. We had no sense that it was dangerous. It wasn't hot; it had no odour. I took a lick; it was gritty but had no taste. We had turned into the wind to pull in the lines, so a lot got down our necks into our underwear and into our eyes, and it prickled and stung; rubbing our inflamed eyes, we kept at our tough task.[2]

After they returned to Yaizu, the US Government initially denied that the crew had been exposed to radioactive fallout (although specialist Japanese doctors were well aware of the symptoms of radiation after the bombing of Hiroshima and Nagasaki). Six months after arriving back in port, the oldest crew member—40-year-old radio operator Aikichi Kuboyama—died of secondary infection after acute radiation exposure, leaving a wife and three daughters. Sadly, Kuboyama's dying wish was not to be fulfilled:

> *Gensuibaku no higaisha wa, watashi wo saigo ni shite hoshii.* [I pray that I am the last victim of an atomic or hydrogen bomb.][3]

After months of hospitalisation and unending battles with the bureaucracy to gain financial support, Oishi abandoned the sea and moved to Tokyo to open a laundry. His first child was stillborn and deformed:

---

2 Ibid., pp. 19–20.
3 Mark Schreiber: 'Lucky Dragon's lethal catch', *The Japan Times*, 18 March 2012.

Suffering from prejudice and discrimination for being a nuclear victim, I fled my hometown and tried to hide in the crowded city of Tokyo. But I couldn't outrun the devil—the radiation that had penetrated deep into my body. It haunted all of us, robbed me of my first child, and took the lives of my fellow fishermen, one after another.[4]

* * *

More than America's first thermonuclear test in 1952 or the Soviet Union's first hydrogen bomb test in 1953, the 1954 Bravo disaster truly catalysed international public opinion against atmospheric nuclear testing. The fate of the Japanese seafarers aboard the *Lucky Dragon* reinforced anti-testing sentiment at home and abroad, increasing calls for the abolition of all nuclear weapons.

In Australia, favourable media treatment of the UK Totem test in 1953 was transformed into negative coverage after Bravo. An Australian Government briefing note on 'Press reaction to atomic trials' noted that public opinion was changing 'partly due to the death of a Japanese fisherman injured by radioactive fallout from American H-bomb explosion in the Pacific'.[5]

Antinuclear sentiment had slowly been growing in Japan, as more information became available about the effects of the atomic bombings at Hiroshima and Nagasaki. This popular sentiment expanded during the mid-1950s, after the end of the postwar military occupation that lasted from August 1945 until April 1952. The Supreme Command for the Allied Powers (SCAP) had censored information about the effects of the atomic bombing of Japanese cities, even supressing visual images of the devastation:

> Documentary footage filmed in Hiroshima and Nagasaki between August and December 1945 by a team of some thirty Japanese cameramen was confiscated by the Americans in February 1946 and sent to Washington, with orders that not a single copy was to remain in Japan.[6]

---

4   Matashichi Oishi: *The day the sun rose in the west.* op. cit.
5   'Press reaction to atomic tests', National Archives of Australia: A6456, R047/011, cited by Elizabeth Tynan: *Atomic Thunder—the Maralinga story* (NewSouth Publishing, Sydney, 2016), p. 109.
6   John Dower: *Embracing defeat—Japan in the wake of World War Two* (W.W. Norton, New York, 1999), pp. 413–415.

Even as war raged in Korea and Cold War paranoia over spies and subversion made protest difficult, many Japanese began to speak out against nuclear weapons. A growing peace movement sparked a massive cultural transformation in Japan, reinforcing the notion of the country as a victim of the nuclear age and undercutting the memory of Japanese militarism and war crimes throughout Asia and the Pacific islands during the Second World War.[7]

The development of hydrogen bombs—first by the United States, then by the Soviet Union and United Kingdom—gave a focus to inchoate fear and catalysed this public concern.

Soon after the war, under military occupation, the threat of nuclear weapons had been explored in Japanese cinema. *Bells of Nagasaki* (1950) was based on the book *Nagasaki no Kane* by scientist Takashi Nagai, whose wife died in the Nagasaki bombing and who died himself from radiation sickness in 1951. This was followed by other reflective, sombre films such as *I'll never forget the song of Nagasaki* (1952), *Children of the Atom Bomb* (1952) and *Hiroshima* (1952).[8]

For many Japanese, the visceral cultural fear of nuclear testing was best captured by the *Gojira* (Godzilla) movies. Godzilla is a monstrous creature from the deep, which rampages across urban centres in Japan. The first of an ongoing series of Godzilla films began production in 1954, soon after the Bravo test, directed by Ishirō Honda and produced by Toho studios. Through many remakes, the monster has continued as an icon of nuclear horror, a metaphor for the devastation created by US nuclear testing in the Pacific.[9]

---

7   For details of Japanese militarism, see Yuki Tanaka: *Hidden Horrors—Japanese war crimes in World War II* (Westview Press, Colorado, 1996); Yuki Tanaka: *Japan's comfort women—Sexual slavery and prostitution during World War Two and the US Occupation* (Routledge, London, 2002); and Gavan McCormack and Hank Nelson: *The Burma-Thailand Railway* (Allen and Unwin, Sydney, 1993).
8   For discussion of postwar antinuclear cinema, see Michael Broderick (ed.): *Hibakusha Cinema: Hiroshima, Nagasaki and the Nuclear Image in Japanese Film* (2nd printing: Routledge, London, 2014; Japanese language edition: Gendai Shokan, Tokyo, 1999); and Tony Barrell and Rick Tanaka: *Higher then Heaven—Japan, war and everything* (Private Guy International, 1995), pp. 151–152.
9   Ironically, the rather tacky US remake in 1998—the first Godzilla film to be produced by a major Hollywood studio—relocates the nuclear testing site from the Marshall Islands to French Polynesia. According to Hollywood, France rather than the United States is responsible for the nuclear tests that spawn Godzilla!

This cultural mobilisation extended across the region. In Australia, media reports about Bravo and stories about nuclear testing in *Time* magazine inspired the book *On the Beach* by British-born Australian author Nevil Shute.[10] The book, published in 1957, sold over 4 million copies. The subsequent 1959 Hollywood film by director Stanley Kramer, starring Ava Gardner, Gregory Peck and Fred Astaire, reached a huge audience and reinforced despair over the dystopian threat of thermonuclear weapons.[11]

Bravo also served as a symbol of life and death for generations of Pacific poets. In 1959, the Māori poet Hone Tuwhare first published 'No Ordinary Sun'. Tuwhare had visited Hiroshima to witness the devastation of the 1945 atomic bombing, but his poem was written in the aftermath of the Bravo test, contrasting the tree as a symbol of life against the devastation of the hydrogen bomb:

> Tree let your naked arms fall
> nor extend vain entreaties to the radiant ball.
> This is no gallant monsoon's flash,
> no dashing trade wind's blast.
> The fading green of your magic
> emanations shall not make pure again
> these polluted skies ... for this
> is no ordinary sun.[12]

Tuwhare noted that his allegory of 'atomic apocalypse' had a central theme of 'the horror and desolation that an H-bomb would bring, something I feel very strongly ... I am aware all the time of the threat that is hanging over our world'.[13]

After Bravo, the term 'bikini' entered popular consciousness, as both a nuclear sacrifice zone and as a bathing suit. The poet and scholar Teresia Teaiwa wryly noted that 'the Bomb and the bikini are colonial military and neo-colonial technologies respectively'.[14]

---

10   Nevil Shute: *On the Beach* (Heinemman, Sydney, 1957). *On the Beach* is set in Melbourne, Australia, following a nuclear war that has devastated the northern hemisphere, and tracks the moral dilemmas facing the survivors, even as radioactive fallout heads towards the southern redoubt of Oceania.
11   For the cultural and political context around the book and film, see Gideon Haigh: 'Shute the messenger—How the end of the world came to Melbourne', *The Monthly*, June 2007.
12   Excerpt from Hone Tuwhare: *No Ordinary Sun* (Blackwood and Janet Paul, Auckland, 1964).
13   Cited in Elizabeth DeLoughrey: 'Solar Metaphors: "No Ordinary Sun"', *Ka mate ka ora: A New Zealand journal of poetry and poetics*, Issue 6, September 2008, p. 52. Thanks to Michelle Keown for introducing me to Tuwhare's work.
14   Teresia Teaiwa: 'bikinis and other s/pacific n/oceans', *The Contemporary Pacific*, Vol. 6, No. 1, 1994, p. 96.

In her performance poem 'Bad coconuts', Teaiwa—a Fiji islander of i-Kiribati and Afro-American heritage—echoed Tuwhare to capture the contrast between the irradiated coconut palm as a source of life and death in the Pacific:

> An apple a day, keeps the doctor away
> but a coconut a day will kill you
> if you live on Moruroa
> if you visit Fangataufa
> return to Enewetak
> resettle Bikini
> a coconut a day
> will kill you.[15]

Marshallese poet Kathy Jetnil-Kijiner also contrasts local memory and colonial militarism in 'History Project', a striking performance on the devastation affecting Bikini and Enewetak:

> I flip through snapshots
> of american marines and nurses branded white with bloated grins
> sucking beers and tossing beach balls along
> our shores
> and my Islander ancestors, cross-legged
> before a general listening
> to his fairy tale
> about how it's
>   *for the good of mankind*
> to hand over our islands
> let them blast
> radioactive energy
> into our sleepy coconut trees
> our sagging breadfruit trees
> our busy fishes that sparkle like new sun
> into our coral reefs[16]

* * *

---

[15] 'Bad coconuts' (featuring Teresia Teaiwa, H. Doug Matsuoka and Richard Hamasaki) in *Terenesia*, spoken word recording by Teresia Teaiwa and Sia Fiegel: itunes.apple.com/us/album/terenesia/id386191157. Teresia died in March 2017, sadly missed by the many Pacific scholars, students and poets she has mentored.

[16] Excerpt from 'History Project' in Kathy Jetnil-Kijiner: *Iep Jaltok—Poems from a Marshallese Daughter* (University of Arizona Press, Phoenix, 2017), pp. 20–23. For a live performance of 'History Project' at the 2012 Poetry Parnassus at Southbank Centre, London, see www.youtube.com/watch?v=DIIrrPyK0eU.

The cultural mobilisation sparked by Bravo and the *Lucky Dragon* translated into political action across Japan in the mid-1950s. Following the Bravo test, a nationwide signature campaign against nuclear testing was initiated across Japan. Launched in Tokyo on Hiroshima Day 1954, the campaign gathered more than 32 million signatures. In August the following year, the first World Conference against A and H Bombs was held in Hiroshima, beginning a series of peace and disarmament conferences that continue to this day. Inspired by the first world conference, Japanese activists founded Gensuikyo (the Japan Council against A and H Bombs) on 19 September 1955, as a national umbrella body for local peace and disarmament groups. Matashichi Oishi joined *hibakusha* (nuclear survivors) from Hiroshima and Nagasaki to become an advocate for disarmament.[17]

While public opinion in the early 1950s was largely focused on the US and Soviet nuclear programs, there was new protest after the public announcement by the Macmillan Government that Britain would test a hydrogen bomb in the Pacific. Given public awareness of the 1954 Bravo test and the fate of the *Lucky Dragon,* the news about Britain's looming test program in the Gilbert and Ellice Islands Colony (GEIC) mobilised widespread public concern.

In the first half of 1957, diplomats from the British Embassy in Tokyo sent regular reports to London, detailing their concern over rising protests against the proposed Christmas Island tests.[18] On 14 February, Japanese Ambassador to the United Kingdom Haruhiko Nishi lodged a formal diplomatic note with the British Foreign Office, stating that:

> It is considered unavoidable that … the Japanese people will suffer psychologically and materially as a result of the tests. The carrying out of the tests will be extremely distressing to the Japanese people, who have been subjected to the calamity of nuclear weapons more than any other nation in the world and are devoted to the peace and happiness of mankind.[19]

---

17   In later years, Japanese *hibakusha* were joined by Marshall islanders, Fijians and other nuclear survivors who attended antinuclear conferences in Hiroshima and Nagasaki each August. Oishi, well into his 80s, is still campaigning for the abolition of nuclear weapons.
18   Detailed reports of Japanese protests are included in Telegram No. 75 (5 March 1957) and Telegram No. 79 (7 March 1957) from British Embassy, Tokyo to Sir Esler Dening, Foreign Office, London. CO1036/281. Dening previously served as UK Ambassador to Japan between 1952 and 1957.
19   Diplomatic note presented by to Selwyn Lloyd, Secretary of State for Foreign Affairs, 14 February 1957. CO1036/281.

Popular protest increased. In early 1957, the General Council of Trade Unions (*Sohyo*) and the student network *Zengakuren* both delivered protest notes to the UK Embassy condemning the UK tests (*Zengakuren* was criticised by embassy officials as 'the noisy, fellow-travelling students' organisation').[20]

The Japan Council against A and H Bombs organised a major protest rally in Tokyo on 1 March 1957. The date was chosen as the third anniversary of the Bravo test but, in a message to London, British Embassy officials complained 'the whole emphasis was on the forthcoming British tests, which were condemned as an act of violence against the whole world'.[21]

The 1 March rally featured the reading of telegrams from Japanese Prime Minister Nobusuke Kishi, Sri Lankan Prime Minister Bandarenaike and the USSR's Marshall Bulganin. Once again, embassy officials complained about the perceived double standard of protests against US and UK tests rather than Russian ones. Their reports railed against a speech to the rally from an Egyptian diplomat, coming soon after the Suez crisis where Britain, France and Israel had tried and failed to invade Egypt: 'the Egyptian can only have been invited to speak because Egypt is hostile to Britain'.[22]

The British Ambassador was convinced that the Japanese Government was encouraging the protests:

> I have a conviction, though it is difficult to prove, that the Japanese Prime Minister and Foreign Minister, far from damping down agitation (which is the official Japanese Foreign Office line) are quietly stimulating it in order to achieve popularity ... That communists and fellow-travellers should exploit it to the full is only natural. But the press and radio are giving full publicity to all the arguments against us, ignoring any arguments in favour ...

---

20   Telegram from British Embassy Tokyo to Sir Esler Dening, Foreign Office, London, 5 February 1957. CO1036/281.
21   Telegram No. 75 from British Embassy, Tokyo to Sir Esler Dening, Foreign Office, London, 5 March 1957. CO1036/281.
22   Ibid.

> Buddhist priests have continued to bang drums around this [embassy] compound since 1 March and may well go on indefinitely. I am advised that the authorities have the power to stop this nuisance (which is what it is intended to be) if they want to and since they do not use them, one must assume their willingness that the noise should continue.[23]

Two days later, on 3 March, the Japan Council announced plans to send a ship into the danger zone to protest against the first UK test.

On 4 March, the Japanese Ambassador to the United Kingdom again met with Foreign Office officials in London to formally call for an end to the tests. That very day, Prime Minister Kishi responded to questions in the Diet in Tokyo, saying the proposals to send a protest fleet to the test zone deserved 'a cautious study' as 'it might have powerful appeal to world public opinion'.[24] The Japanese Prime Minister noted:

> The British government might not suspend its hydrogen bomb tests even though the Japanese protest fleet carried out a sit down movement. Unless public opinion in Britain makes the British government leaders reconsider atomic bomb experimentation, there will be no way of suspending the nuclear bomb test.[25]

Facing growing international publicity, British Prime Minister Harold Macmillan went before the House of Commons in London to downplay concerns over radioactive fallout, arguing:

> The present and foreseeable hazards, including genetic effects, from external radiation due to fall-out from the test explosions of nuclear weapons, fired at the present rate and in the present proportion of the different kinds, are considered to be negligible.[26]

Kishi continued to lobby publicly for a change of policy. He announced that he was encouraging a delegation of religious leaders to travel to London to call for a halt to the tests on moral grounds. The British

---

[23] Ibid. Kishi—grandfather of Japan's current Prime Minister Shinzo Abe—was certainly no pacifist. As a Cabinet member in 1941, Kishi had signed the declaration of war against the United States. After the Second World War, he was jailed as a suspected Class A war criminal, because of his role in conscripting forced labour in the puppet state of Manchukuo. In 1948, he was released and rehabilitated by the US occupation forces as a good anti-communist leader. He served as Foreign Minister until his elevation to become the 57th Prime Minister of Japan from 25 February 1957 to 12 June 1958, with a second term from that date until 19 July 1960.

[24] Telegram No. 75 from British Embassy, Tokyo to Sir Esler Dening, Foreign Office, London, 5 March 1957. CO1036/281.

[25] Ibid.

[26] UK House of Commons, Hansard official report, 5 March 1957, Vol. 566, col. 178.

Embassy in Tokyo closely monitored preparations by this delegation, led by Bishop Yashiro of the Japanese Anglican Episcopal Church, with Bishop Makita of the Episcopal Church, Generals Segawa and Uemura of the Salvation Army and Sekitani, the secretary of the non-conformist Protestant churches.[27]

The Japanese Red Cross also appealed to the International Committee of the Red Cross and national Red Cross societies in Russia, the United States and the United Kingdom to campaign against the H-bomb tests.[28]

The pressure began to tell on the UK Government. Fearful that Japan might take the United Kingdom to the International Court of Justice (ICJ) to stop the Christmas Island tests, the UK Government temporarily withdrew its 1955 declaration accepting compulsory ICJ jurisdiction.[29]

Grassroots campaigners began direct, public protests against the British. On 25 March 1957, Kiyoshi Kikkawa, Shoichi Minami, Ontetsu Kobayashi and Ichiro Kawamoto began a sit-in in front of the Cenotaph for A-bomb victims in Hiroshima to call for a halt of the first UK hydrogen bomb test. In later years, Ichiro Kawamoto recalled that:

> Sitting with our backs against the Cenotaph expressed Hiroshima's message of protest, alongside the A-bomb victims.[30]

The proposal to send a peace fleet into the danger zone inspired the young Hiroshima protesters, with Ichiro Kawamoto volunteering to board a vessel to travel towards Christmas Island. He later explained:

---

27   Telegram No. 80 from British Embassy, Tokyo to Sir Esler Dening, Foreign Office, London, 7 March 1957. CO1036/281.
28   'Our H-bomb tests will be "so small"', *News Chronicle*, 28 March 1957.
29   John R. Walker (Foreign and Commonwealth Office UK): *British nuclear weapons and the Test Ban 1954–73—Britain, the United States, Weapons Policies and Nuclear Testing, Tensions and Contradictions* (Ashgate, 2010), p. 22. Sixty years later in February 2017, the United Kingdom again withdrew from the ICJ's compulsory jurisdiction on matters relating to nuclear disarmament. This contemporary display of arrogance followed the unsuccessful case lodged in 2014 by the Marshall Islands to press all the nuclear weapons powers to fulfil their obligations under the Nuclear Non-Proliferation Treaty. See International Court of Justice: *Declarations Recognising the Jurisdiction of the Court as Compulsory, United Kingdom of Great Britain and Northern Island*, 27 February 2017. For discussion, Sebastian Brixey-Williams: 'UK revokes ICJ jurisdiction over its nuclear weapons', BASIC (British American Security Information Council), 27 March 2017.
30   Tetsuya Okahata: 'Protests against nuclear tests', *Chugoku Shimbun* (Hiroshima), 25 June 1995 (thanks to Akira Kawasaki for translation of this reference).

Mr. Kikkawa invited me to take part, suggesting that we first do what we could in Hiroshima, then saying I could give my life for this cause while on the voyage, if that's what I wanted.[31]

The sit-in by young people sparked wider popular support in Hiroshima and 20 April was designated 'the National Action Day against Christmas Island Nuclear Tests'. The protest that day saw thousands of people rallying in Hiroshima to call for an end to UK atomic and hydrogen bomb tests. In Tokyo, a protest rally was held in Shimizudani Park, addressed by international delegates including William Morrow of the Australian Peace Committee.[32]

* * *

As news of these protests filtered back to the United Kingdom, British newspapers reported that Japanese opinion was sceptical about official UK statements that the tests would not cause radioactive fallout. British officials tried to counter public concern about health impacts, but the *Birmingham Post* noted:

> Since 1945, the Japanese have been in no mood or condition to listen to official assurances or scientific reasonableness about atomic bombs. They are quite simply frightened of them and remind themselves more frequently about Hiroshima and Nagasaki than about any incident that the Japanese armed forces were involved in.[33]

UK reporters also complained that Japan was more focused on the British bomb than Russia's arsenal:

> The British program produced frequent mass meetings, protest processions, a succession of diplomatic notes to London and the dispatch of a world tour of Dr. Masatoshi Matsushita as personal envoy of Mr. Nobusuke Kishi, the Japanese Prime Minister.[34]

---

31   Ibid. The pledge to give up one's life for disarmament was no idle boast. In 1959, Ontetsu Kobayashi—one of the four sit-in protesters from Hiroshima—committed *seppuku* (ritual suicide by disembowelment), standing before the Japanese prime minister's residence in Tokyo, as a protest against proposals for Japanese rearmament!
32   *No More Hiroshimas, the news of the Japan Council against A and H-bombs*, Vol. 4, No. 9, 30 May 1957, p. 6.
33   'H-bomb tests alarm Japan', *Birmingham Post*, 9 May 1957.
34   Ibid.

3. THE FISHERMAN—MATASHICHI OISHI

British officials had difficulty accepting that there was widespread popular opposition to nuclear testing. After the horrors of the Second World War, marked by Japanese war crimes and the torture of allied prisoners, British representatives to SCAP were openly hostile to emerging democratic forces in Japan. In 1946, one official wrote to London that the Japanese were 'as little fitted for self-government in a modern world as any African tribe, though much more dangerous'.[35]

A decade later, as protests over the looming Christmas Island tests increased, UK Embassy officials in Tokyo continued to regard Japanese as both 'hysterical' and 'callous', as shown in a letter by one diplomat to Sir Oscar Moreland at the Foreign Office in London:

> When we first notified the Japanese government on 7 January about the megaton tests, I had a shrewd suspicion that they would exploit the situation—and they have done so. They can, of course, whip up more agitation if they want to, and as the Japanese are a hysterical people, it is never hard to do. But I do not believe that the Japanese people are in the least spontaneously agitated by these tests, nor do I believe them to be any less callous than they were in the past. As for compensation, I think it is a pure racket …
>
> It is the American guilt complex over the original atom bombs at Hiroshima and Nagasaki which I consider responsible for the whole Japanese attitude on this question. They found that the Americans were vulnerable on the issue and they have pressed hard ever since.
>
> When I went to Hiroshima early in 1952, I was asked to give a press conference. The first question invariably was what I thought of the atom bomb damage. When I replied—deliberately—that having been in two wars it looked like any other war damage, there was dead silence and the conference fizzled out.[36]

The problem, however, was that the protests were not limited to Japan. On 15 March, the Foreign Office sent a draft statement about the tests to British High Commissions in Australia, New Zealand and Canada,

---

35 Historian John Dower cites this and other examples of Western 'expert opinion' about Japan in *Embracing defeat*, op. cit., pp. 217–220.
36 Letter from Bill Waring, British Embassy, Tokyo, to Sir Oscar Moreland, Foreign Office, London, 15 February 1957. CO1036/281. Moreland would later serve as Ambassador in Tokyo from 1959 to 1963.

as well as embassies in Djakarta, Peking, Bangkok, Rangoon, Manila and Singapore. The anodyne statement gave little information about what was developing, with London officials noting:

> We do not wish to stimulate publicity about these tests, but if there are signs of local misunderstanding and rumours on the subject … you should draw on the following paragraphs, adhering strictly to the wording given.[37]

Protests from larger Pacific Rim countries were hardly surprising. There was growing anti-colonial sentiment across Asia—symbolised by the 1955 conference on non-alignment in Bandung, Indonesia, which explicitly called for a moratorium on nuclear testing. At the same time, the postwar strength of Labor and communist parties in Australia and New Zealand had not completely dissipated despite the Cold War, and they joined trade unions and religious and women's organisations to mobilise against the nuclear threat.

---

37 Telegram from Foreign Office to British Embassies in Djakarta, Peking, Bangkok, Rangoon, Manila, Singapore and Tokyo (copied to all UK High Commissions in Commonwealth countries), Intel No. 48, marked 'Confidential', 15 March 1957. CO1036/281.

4
The Task Force Commander— Wilfred Oulton

Grapple Task Force Commander Air Vice Marshall Wilfred Oulton
Source: UK Government.

In February 1956, Air Vice Marshall Wilfred Oulton was appointed as Task Force Commander for Britain's hydrogen bomb testing program. His commanding officer, Air Vice Marshall Lees, told him 'to go out and drop a bomb somewhere in the Pacific and take a picture of it with a Brownie camera'.[1]

As they prepared for the operation, the British military were well aware of the environmental and political fallout of the Bravo test and US testing in the Marshall Islands. On the very day that he found out about his job, Oulton was told 'we can't have another incident like the American trouble at Bikini' and presented with a bundle of documents to browse in preparation for the task:

> Extracts from American journals, notes on visits and so on, including reports on the US test in which Japanese fishermen were injured by fallout and on the wave of shrill criticism which ensued.[2]

For Oulton, who had joined the Royal Air Force (RAF) in 1929 and gained rapid promotion during the Second World War, the timeline to prepare for Britain's hydrogen bomb test was daunting. At the time of his appointment, he had no staff or offices and an uncertain budget. Within a year, however, he had to establish a military base and scientific facilities on an atoll thousands of kilometres away in the central Pacific.

The Task Force chose the name 'Grapple' for the operation. The image of a cormorant mounting a four-pronged grappling hook was used as a logo, decorating specially made ties that were distributed to headquarters staff. Each prong of the grapple symbolised one of the four key institutions involved in the deployment to Christmas Island: the British Army, the RAF, Royal Navy (RN) and the Atomic Weapons Research Establishment (AWRE) at Aldermaston.

Christmas Island—known today as Kiritimati—lies 232 kilometres north of the Equator, and 2,160 kilometres south of Honolulu, Hawai'i. With 388 square kilometres of land and a lagoon shoreline extending for nearly 50 kilometres, it has the largest land area of any coral atoll in the world.

---

1   Wilfred Oulton: *Christmas Island Cracker—an account of the planning and execution of the British thermonuclear bomb tests 1957* (Thomas Harmsworth, London, 1987), p. 7.
2   Ibid., pp. 8, 24.

A small airstrip—known as Casady Field—was built on Christmas Island during the Second World War, with a US military contingent deployed to hold the island against Japanese forces. Allied governments were concerned that the Japanese, advancing eastwards across Micronesia, might construct their own airstrip on the atoll to attack vital transport routes between Hawai'i and Australia.

In 1956, the island was an isolated outpost of the British Gilbert and Ellice Islands Colony (GEIC), which spread over a vast distance in the central Pacific. Britain had declared a protectorate over the Gilbert and Ellice Islands in 1892, but with the discovery of valuable phosphate on Banaba (Ocean Island) in 1900, the government transferred its administrative headquarters from the Gilbert Islands to Banaba. During the First World War, British, Australian and New Zealand troops clashed with German forces in the Pacific territories, and London soon began to combine a range of Pacific dependencies in one jurisdiction. W. David McIntyre, in his history of the collapse of British power in the Pacific, notes:

> This process started on 10 November 1915 when, by Order in Council, the protectorate became the Gilbert and Ellice Islands Colony. To this was added Ocean Island on 27 January 1916, along with the northern Line Islands that had been annexed in 1888, which included Washington (Teraina) and Fanning (Tabuaeran), where a trans-Pacific cable station was to be built. Later in 1916, the Tokelau group was added; Christmas Island (Kiritimati) followed in 1919. The new Crown Colony, known in Whitehallspeak as GEIC, then sprawled over 5,000,000 km² of ocean.[3]

Before the massive military build-up in the mid-1950s, the Line Islands had a very small population. As one of three archipelagos in the GEIC, the Line Islands are nearly 3,300 kilometres from Tarawa, the administrative capital of the colony, where Resident Commissioner Michael Louis Bernacchi was based.[4] Some of the Line Islands hosted Gilbertese plantation workers transferred from the Gilbert Islands (the easternmost archipelago of the colony). Christmas, Jarvis, Washington and Fanning

---

3   W. David McIntyre: *Winding up the British Empire in the Pacific Islands*, Oxford History of the British Empire Companion Series (Oxford University Press, Oxford, 2014), p. 15.
4   Michael Louis Bernacchi CMG OBE (1911–1983) had previously served as a Lieutenant Commander in the Royal Navy (RN) and as a Colonial Office district officer in Malaya. During the war, as a young naval officer, he was engaged to Elaine Chapman of Navua, Fiji (Engagement notices, *The Argus*, Melbourne, 4 May 1943, p. 6). Chapman encouraged Bernacchi to consider the Pacific islands as the site for his postwar career—she was the granddaughter of Sir Maynard Hedstrom, founder of Morris Hedstrom and Company (the largest trading corporation in Fiji, with subsidiaries in Samoa and Tonga).

islands all hosted plantations managed by Burns Philp & Company or other smaller firms, under the occasional supervision of Colonial Office staff.

The plantation on Christmas Island was first established by French priest Emmanuel Rougier, who leased the island from 1913. Rougier planted more than 800,000 coconut palms on the island, which formed the basis of the copra plantation staffed by Gilbertese workers. However, during the Second World War, his nephew Paul, who managed the plantation, was a collaborator with the Vichy regime in occupied France.[5] In response, the United States and United Kingdom assumed joint control of the island in 1940. By the mid-1950s, the Gilbertese plantation workers were monitored by a New Zealander, Percy Roberts, the only official of European heritage on the island until thousands of British personnel arrived.

The Micronesian atolls were alien terrain for the English and even for the Fiji islanders deployed to support the British operation. Fijian soldier Josefa Vueti later described the low-lying islands as starkly different from the fertile hills and river valleys of his homeland:

> This island had no hills. It was flat all around, and the only trees there were coconut palms. There was just a small area that was the highest point a few feet high. In the middle of the island were some bushes where there was a small pool of water. There were *via* [a variety of wild bush taro] growing there. Our staple foods like *tavioka* [cassava] and *dalo* [taro]—there are none there, although we once tried to plant some vegetables there.
>
> Despite this, the place had lot of seafood. There was fish, *lairo* [land crabs] and *urau* [crayfish]. Every week, we always used to eat these. There were *lairo* crawling everywhere, all the time. Even though the dining place had food and lots of it, we Fijian soldiers always went to the sea to fish. It was really easy getting fish from the sea. Everything was there: *urau*, *kawakawa*. Name whatever fish you wanted—you got it. It was very easy. You really did not need a proper spear—you could use a piece of iron. We never worried about food there, there was so much of it.[6]

---

5   For portraits of Emmanuel and Paul Rougier, see Eric Bailey: *The Christmas Island Story* (Stacey International, London, 1977), pp. 43–52.
6   Interview with Josefa Vueti, Suva, Fiji, 1998. For full interview see Losena Salabula, Josua Namoce and Nic Maclellan: *Kirisimasi—Na Sotia kei na Lewe ni Mataivalu e Wai ni Viti e na vakatovotovo iyaragi nei Peritania mai Kirisimasi* (Pacific Concerns Resource Centre, Suva, 1999), pp. 44–47.

4. THE TASK FORCE COMMANDER—WILFRED OULTON

* * *

In his 1987 memoir *Christmas Island Cracker*, Oulton presents a boy's own view of the challenges facing his Task Force: establishing a weather forecasting service over extensive areas of ocean; building navigation, radio and communication systems on neighbouring islands; constructing fuel tanks and a water distillation system; establishing a radiation monitoring system across thousands of kilometres from Australia to Hawai'i and Tahiti; setting up a network of airport transit stops from the United Kingdom through Canada and west coast USA, then on to Hickam Air Force Base in Hawai'i and Christmas Island.

Oulton was under pressure to get the test program underway as soon as possible, because of growing international pressure for a moratorium on the testing of nuclear weapons in the atmosphere.[7] In mid-1956, the Task Force prioritised the rapid upgrade of facilities on Christmas Island. But this posed logistic nightmares: could engineers be deployed halfway around the world to build an army base and airstrip before the global testing moratorium could be finalised?

Naval staff on the Grapple Task Force began to assemble a flotilla of Navy and civilian vessels to transport equipment from the United Kingdom: graders, bulldozers, fire engines, concrete laying plant and more. The light aircraft carrier HMS *Warrior* left Portsmouth on 2 February 1957 to serve as flagship for the operation, supported by other ships from Britain and New Zealand.

To get started, Oulton looked for military troops already deployed in the Asia-Pacific region. The 55 Field Squadron of 28 Royal Engineers Regiment had remained in Korea after the Korean War, when the rest of the regiment returned to England. These engineers had hoped for some leave at home after wartime service, but Oulton decided to give them bad news—they must travel from Korea directly to the central Pacific:

> The timescale is very tight and I think we could save some time by sending 55 Field Squadron and some supporting units direct from Korea to Christmas Island—except possibly for a few compassionate cases. They could get cracking building a camp in the port area, ready for the main

---

7   This debate culminated in a moratorium on testing between 1958 and 1961 and, ultimately, the 1963 United Nations Partial Test Ban Treaty: *Treaty Banning Nuclear Weapons Tests in the Atmosphere, in Outer Space and Underwater*, 5 August 1963.

force to move in and start work without delay. Of course, they have as yet no idea that they will not be coming home on leave. I think it would be sensible and prudent to go to Korea to break the news and sell them the idea that it would be fun to try out the charms of a coral island![8]

The engineers were not impressed, as they had just been given permission to purchase overcoats and warmer clothing to cope with the Korean winter!

The first Grapple team reached Christmas Island on 19 June 1956. Cargo ships from the Royal Fleet Auxiliary arrived a few days after, and the troop ship *Devenish* arrived with the Royal Engineers from Korea. More vessels arrived in July and the following month HMS *Messina* arrived to serve as the Task Force headquarters (the ship was also equipped with desalination equipment and freezers to provide fresh water and food for the troops ashore).

By the end of the year, work was progressing on the core infrastructure, according to a December 1956 report from the colony's Resident Commissioner Michael Bernacchi:

> Rapid progress is being made in the preparation of the base at Christmas Island for Britain's nuclear test next year. Men of the Royal Engineers, helped by Gilbertese workers of Christmas Island Plantation, have already completed 25 miles of good roads, an auxiliary airstrip and a 7,000 foot runway for bombing aircraft.
>
> With the cooperation of the Royal and merchant Navies, many thousands of tons of heavy equipment and stores have been landed at Christmas. Transport Command of the Royal Air Force are maintaining a regular service between Christmas Island and Honolulu with Hastings aircraft, flying in mail and fresh food. The Royal Navy has also landed parties at Malden Island, 400 miles to the south of Christmas, where a forward airstrip will be constructed.[9]

---

8   Wilfred Oulton: *Christmas Island Cracker*, op. cit., p. 66.
9   Office of the Resident Commissioner: *Headquarters Information Note*, No. 52, 14 December 1956, Gilbert and Ellice Islands Colony. F76/6/32 (1957) p. 3. PAMBU document AU PMB Doc 493.

4. THE TASK FORCE COMMANDER—WILFRED OULTON

THE MAIN CAMP, CHRISTMAS ISLAND, PACIFIC

Postcard of tent city on Christmas Island
Source: Reprinted from *Kirisimasi* (courtesy Pacific Concerns Resource Centre, Suva).

Malden is uninhabited, low-lying and arid, with sparse vegetation. It lacked even basic infrastructure until the Royal Engineers landed ashore in 1956 to construct a small airstrip and fly in equipment for the nuclear testing program.

The decision to conduct the Grapple tests at Malden Island was kept secret from the public for many months. The description of Malden as 'a forward base and instrumentation site' was declassified in January 1957, but the Ministry of Supply decreed that 'Malden should not, in classified or unclassified material, be referred to as a target island'.[10]

* * *

Despite the attempts at secrecy, public concern was sparked by the growing activity on Christmas Island and related Air Force and scientific visits to other Pacific territories. For the Colonial Office, it was important to notify key authorities as soon as possible, in order to dampen down protest. The official British historian of the tests acknowledged:

---

10   'Atomic Weapons Trials Executive—Operation Grapple', Memo from D.A. Lovelock, Ministry of Supply, marked 'Confidential/UK eyes only', 22 January 1957. Grapex (57)/P.1.

Since Castle Bravo, international protests against testing were an ever present political factor and American experience showed that some local opposition to testing in the Pacific and the use of certain islands was likely.[11]

The growing public awareness of the British hydrogen bomb program was causing problems for Commonwealth allies like New Zealand, which administered the Polynesian territories of Western Samoa, Cook Islands, Tokelau and Niue.

After the formal announcement of the tests by UK Prime Minister Sir Anthony Eden, Western Samoa petitioned the United Nations Trusteeship Council to halt the operation (at the time, Samoa was still a dependent trust territory of New Zealand).[12]

Vigorous interventions by Sir Leslie Monroe, New Zealand's representative on the Trusteeship Council, rejected claims by the Soviet delegate that the tests threatened the health of the people of Western Samoa. After debate, the Trusteeship Council rejected the petition by a vote of 9–1, with only Russia voting in favour. The resolution did, however, assure the people of Western Samoa that the United Kingdom would take the necessary precautions 'to guard against possible danger to persons or property'.[13]

In late 1956, New Zealand newspapers carried short items suggesting that the tests would not actually take place on Christmas Island, but over another atoll. During a session of the Cook Islands Legislative Council in late October 1956, the visiting representative of the NZ Government George Walsh MP stated that the test area would be situated many miles north of Christmas Island.

This sparked widespread commentary in the Pacific media, given that the only British-controlled atolls north or west of Christmas Island were inhabited. Gilbertese were working on a Washington Island plantation run by Burns Philp & Company. Fanning had an important trans-Pacific

---

11 Lorna Arnold: *Britain and the H-bomb* (Palgrave Macmillan, London, 2001), p. 101.
12 Telegram from High Commissioner for Western Samoa to Minister of External Affairs, 8 and 12 May 1956, cited in John Crawford, op. cit.
13 The UN Trusteeship Council debate was widely reported in the Pacific: 'UN will not stop Pacific H-bomb test', *Fiji Times*, 23 July 1956, p. 1; *NZ Evening Post*, 21 June 1956; *Dominion*, 21 July 1956; *Pacific Islands Monthly*, March 1957.

telegraph cable station run by Cable & Wireless Ltd, managed by Tong Ting Hai (a Chinese refugee who was father of a future President of the Republic of Kiribati).[14]

For this reason, there was (accurate) media speculation that the tests would be held to the south, not the north, of Christmas Island. In December 1956, the regional news magazine *Pacific Islands Monthly* reported:

> An air of mystery surrounds the exact point of the intended British atom bomb tests next year. It is, of course, well known that the base of operations and the place from which the bomb dropping aircraft will take off is Christmas atoll, in the northern Line Islands. But some time ago, a senior boffin associated with the tests let drop, while visiting New Zealand on high-level talks, that the actual explosion would take place over another atoll. This being the case, the only possible other atolls are Jarvis, Malden or Starbuck, as being of sufficient distance from inhabited islands.[15]

The speculation increased concern in the Cook Islands, as the main inhabited atoll to the south of Christmas Island was Tongareva (Penrhyn Island), located 550 kilometres to the south of Malden. At the time, about 1,600 people were living on the islands of Rakahanga, Manihiki and Penrhyn in the northern Cook Islands. *Pacific Islands Monthly* reported that 'a section of public opinion in the Cook Islands was campaigning against the possible dangers to the inhabitants of the northern Cooks'.[16]

Customary leaders on the Rarotonga Island Council soon submitted a report to the Cook Islands Legislative Council, expressing concern about the proposed British tests on Christmas Island and asking 'that the testing area be situated at some greater distance than the Cook Islands'.[17]

---

14   Tong Ting Hai arrived in the British Gilbert and Ellice Islands as a refugee from Hong Kong after the Second World War. Tong married an i-Kiribati woman, Nei Keke Randolph, and fathered six children. His third child, Anote Tong, went on to serve for three terms as President of the Republic of Kiribati between 2003 and 2016 (personal communication to author from President Anote Tong, November 2015). For a vivid description of the Cable & Wireless station and its 'Chinese headman Tong Ting Hai', see Des Kinnersley: 'Life on a remote Telegraph Cable Station in the early 1960s', *Overseas Telecommunications Veterans Association newsletter*, Vol. 7, Issue 1, June 2002, pp. 93–95.
15   'H-bomb tests—North, South, East or West of Christmas Island?', *Pacific Islands Monthly*, volume XXVII, No. 5, December 1956, p. 55.
16   Ibid.
17   *Proceedings of the Legislative Council of the Cook Islands*, paper number 3, 1956. See David Stone: 'The awesome glow in the sky: the Cook Islands and the French nuclear tests', *Journal of Pacific History*, Vol. 2, Issue 1, 1967, pp. 154–155.

Before the first test on Malden, RN and Royal New Zealand Navy (RNZN) vessels visited Rakahanga and warned inhabitants not to drink water from wells and roof tanks or to eat fish and crops. British naval vessels later transited through Penrhyn where a weather station was established and reefs were blasted for shipping access (leading to reports of the disease ciguatera at the time of the tests).

Today, some Cook islanders are concerned that they may have been exposed to fallout. As a 10-year-old girl, Tauariki Meyer was on the beach at Rakahanga in 1957 when she saw a brilliant flash across the sky. Tau later reported that the ground shook, the lagoon changed colour and fish floated up dead. Decades later, Tau Meyer is confined to a wheelchair with a diagnosis of spinocerebellar ataxia, a genetic condition that causes immobility and progressive degeneration.[18]

* * *

The official response to debate in the colonies was to clamp down on information that might cause public alarm. A meeting of the Atomic Weapons Trials Executive in December 1956 noted: 'A large build-up of publicity was not wanted and material for release to the press had to be spread as evenly as possible.' The chairman of the meeting agreed: 'publicity must be kept under strict control.'[19]

To feed the press with the official line, the Ministry of Supply pushed other government departments to generate 'innocuous' stories for Christmas 1956, featuring military personnel serving on Christmas Island. Brigadier Ivor Jehu, the Ministry's head of public relations, wrote to the Colonial Office stating:

> In order to enable normal service publicity about troops in overseas stations, and particularly Christmas fare material, to be issued without playing up H-bomb activities, and also to discourage speculative stories arising from the press possibly contacting personnel returning from Christmas Island, we consider it urgently necessary to get out innocuous material about the area.[20]

---

18   'Fallout from nuclear tests in the Pacific continues', *Cook Islands Herald*, cited in *Britain's Pacific Nukes*: pacificnukes.wordpress.com/cook-is/.
19   Minutes of the December 1956 meeting, Atomic Weapons Trials Executive, St Giles Court, 12 December 1956, p. 2. CO1036/280.
20   Letter from Brigadier Ivor Jehu, Ministry of Supply, London to H. Hall, Colonial Office, London, 7 December 1956. CO1036/280.

Jehu created a range of propaganda initiatives to influence public opinion in Britain, at a time when there was growing debate about government proposals for civil defence measures to protect the population against Russian hydrogen bomb attacks.

Staff at the Grapple Task Force headquarters organised for toy manufacturers to donate a large number of toys, and troops deployed on Christmas Island were ordered to write out individual labels with Christmas greetings for children. Nearly 2,000 toys were then distributed to hospitals on Christmas Day 1956, bearing the troops' messages from the central Pacific. The exercise was widely publicised through the British Broadcasting Corporation (BBC), newsreel films for cinemas and articles in the *Daily Telegraph*, *Daily Mirror* and *Daily Sketch*.[21]

When a copy of the December 1956 *Pacific Islands Monthly* article was forwarded to London, the Ministry of Supply called on the Foreign Office and the Commonwealth Relations Office to monitor the media in Fiji, Australia, New Zealand and the United States. Ministry officials urgently requested that copies of any press reports about the hydrogen bomb tests in the Pacific be sent to London.[22]

Despite efforts to spin the media, journalists began to comment about potential hazards from the looming tests. This was even true in the South Pacific colonies, where the press began to reflect the significant popular opposition to the proposed testing program to the north. In February 1957, the Indo-Fijian newspaper *Jagriti* editorialised:

> People living in the vicinity of the islands where the atom and hydrogen bombs have been tested are afflicted with hazardous diseases. Full information has not been given so far about them. Nations engaged in testing these bombs in the Pacific should realise the value of the lives of the people settled in this part of the world. They too are human beings, not 'guinea pigs'.[23]

---

21   Joan Smith: *Clouds of Deceit—the deadly legacy of Britain's bomb tests* (Faber and Faber, London, 1985), p. 84.
22   File note, 9 January 1957. CO1036/280.
23   Editorial, *Jagriti*, 20 February 1957. Cited in Brij V. Lal: *Broken waves—a history of the Fiji islands in the 20th century*, Pacific Islands Monograph Series, No. 11 (University of Hawaii Press, Honolulu, 1992), p. 158.

The *Fiji Times*, the main English-language newspaper in the British colony, gave front page coverage to international protests against the nuclear tests. An April 1957 editorial in the *Fiji Times* noted:

> Nobody knows how many people will die or how many children will be born mentally or physically deformed because of atomic or hydrogen bomb tests, past or future. That is why there is so much disquiet in so many countries and among so many peoples of varying political beliefs about the continuation of such tests by the United States and Russia and about the forthcoming tests on Christmas Island …
>
> The free nations should seek foreign agreement with Russia to curtail or suspend completely all tests until their effects on the future of mankind can be more accurately assessed. To continue with indiscriminate and unrestricted tests in the present state of uncertain knowledge will be irresponsible folly indeed.[24]

The preparations for the testing program were also raising concern amongst leading businessmen with interests in the Pacific islands, who were worried about their properties and workforce—like James Burns of Burns Philp & Company.

---

24 Editorial: 'Bomb tests', *Fiji Times*, 4 April 1957.

5
The businessman—James Burns

Former Burns Philp & Company headquarters in Sydney
Source: Clytemnestra (commons.wikimedia.org/wiki/File:BurnsPhilp.JPG).

In December 1956, just a few days before Christmas, James Burns was reading his morning newspaper. A short item in Sydney's *Daily Telegraph* caught his eye.

According to the story, technicians at Edinburgh Airfield in Adelaide (the capital of South Australia) were fitting 10 Royal Air Force (RAF) Canberra jets with recording instruments. The jets were preparing to relocate to Christmas Island to participate in Britain's hydrogen bomb tests. As noted in the story, 'the jets will fly through radioactive cloud'.[1]

Burns was worried because his company had extensive plantations in the Line Islands, the easternmost archipelago of the British Gilbert and Ellice Islands Colony (GEIC).

Burns Philp & Company was created by Scottish merchant Sir James Burns (1846–1923). His son—also named James—joined the family firm in 1898 and was appointed a director in 1919. Following his father's death in 1923, Burns took over as chair and managing director. In the first half of the 20th century, the company expanded operations throughout Melanesia, the central Pacific and parts of South-East Asia, with shipping, insurance and copra plantations.[2] Burns developed a reputation as a buccaneer, as reported by his biographer Ken Buckley:

> Although conservative-minded, modest and cheerful, Burns was regarded by the administration in Papua-New Guinea as a commercial pirate who sought to use political influence to gain monopolies.[3]

This political influence came to the fore as Burns sought to protect his investments from Britain's nuclear test program. As one of the leading businessman in the Pacific, he could express his concerns straight to the top. The same day as the *Daily Telegraph* story, Burns wrote to Australia's Minister for Defence Sir Philip McBride, with a copy to Alan Lennox-Boyd, the UK Secretary of State for the Colonies in London. Burns enclosed the clipping from the *Daily Telegraph* and asked for reassurance about his property near the nuclear test site:

> In connection with the British government's decision to carry out hydrogen bomb tests at and around Christmas Island, I would like to draw attention to the fact that we have very large plantation interests in Fanning and Washington islands, under 200 miles away from Christmas Island …

---

1   'Preparing for H-blast', *Daily Telegraph*, 20 December 1956.
2   Ken Buckley and Kris Klugman: *The Australian presence in the Pacific—Burns Philp 1914—1946* (George Allen and Unwin, Sydney, 1983).
3   Ken Buckley: 'Burns, James (1881–1969)', *Australian Dictionary of Biography*, Vol. 13 (Melbourne University Press, Melbourne, 1993).

We would like to point out that there seems to be a difference of opinion as to how far the effect of the hydrogen bombs will be experienced and we would like to have the assurance of the Australian government—if it is participating by fitting Canberra jets with recording instruments for the hydrogen bomb tests—that the employees of our plantations or the plantations themselves will not suffer any ill effects.[4]

In another letter to Australia's Minister for Supply Howard Beale in January 1957, Burns complained that his company had suffered losses during the Second World War. The company had large plantations in the British Solomon Islands Protectorate at Gavaga (Tetere), Mberande and Muvia on Guadalcanal Island.[5] But Burns Philp's plantations were devastated during the war—the company was ordered to destroy 1,000 tonnes of copra and burn plantation houses so they could not be used by advancing Japanese troops during the 1942 battle of Guadalcanal.

Noting that his company suffered losses 'in the vicinity of £250,000', Burns complained to Beale that Burns Philp & Company received 'no post-war compensation from the British Government for the damage in the Solomon Islands or other Pacific locations'.[6]

Burns then pressed Beale for guarantees about potential damage from the British nuclear test series on Christmas Island:

> I do hope, if there are any hydrogen bomb 'antics' in the Pacific and our property is damaged, that we will not find ourselves in the same position. I sincerely trust that nothing like this will occur, but there seems to be some diversity of opinion by well-known scientists as to the effect of the hydrogen bomb. I do think we should be assured by the British government, if any damage does occur to our properties in the Pacific from these tests, the payment for such damage will be sympathetically considered.[7]

---

4   Letter from James Burns to Sir Philip McBride, Australian Minister for Defence, 20 December 1956. CO1036/513.
5   'Burns Philp and Company', *Solomon Islands Historical Encyclopaedia 1893–1978*. www.solomonencyclopaedia.net/.
6   Letter from James Burns to Howard Beale, Australian Minister for Supply, 9 January 1957. CO1036/513.
7   Ibid., p. 2.

Beale had been the key minister responsible for the British tests in Australia at Monte Bello and Maralinga. But facing questions over legal liability from a leading Australian businessman, Beale preferred to handball the problem to London. In his reply, Beale explained that:

> The proposed H-bomb test in the Pacific is a British test. The decision to conduct it was made by the British government, the Australian government not being a party to it.[8]

James Burns' private lobbying prompted extensive discussions amongst British officials on arrangements to take care of the Gilbertese workers on Christmas and neighbouring islands—a topic discussed in Chapter 16.

* * *

As Britain continued preparations for the testing program, Burns Philp & Company was not the only company with operations in the Line Islands that faced disruption. British archives reveal that a major problem for UK officials were the US and Japanese businesses that might be affected by the declaration of a danger zone and the subsequent tests—especially as the United States and United Kingdom had an ongoing dispute about sovereignty of the islands.

After the Second World War, the United States reopened discussions of its claims of sovereignty to Christmas Island and other locations in the Line Islands. The British Government counter-posed with a proposal to grant a 99-year lease of the Casady Field airstrip on Christmas Island, but these proposals were rejected by the US Government in November 1948.

The government led by Prime Minister Harold Macmillan was sensitive to public criticism that the use of Christmas and Malden islands as nuclear test bases might inflame the ongoing dispute with United States over control and sovereignty. London repeatedly assured Washington that the test program would go ahead without prejudice to the claim of either government over sovereignty.

On 16 April 1957, Macmillan was questioned in the UK House of Commons about US claims over the ownership of Christmas Island. He told parliament that:

---

8   Letter from Howard Beale, Australian Minister for Supply to James Burns, 14 January 1957. CO1036/513.

The United States government claims sovereignty over Christmas Island, which has been under British administration for many years as part of the Gilbert and Ellice Islands Colony. Her Majesty's government have informed the United States government that the action which they are now taking does not in any way prejudice the claims of either government.[9]

A Labour MP asked whether 'it is not rather reprehensible that we should be exploding this weapon over territory the ownership of which is in some dispute?', with Macmillan replying:

In the first place, I do not think that this difficulty is likely to be serious. In the second place, the bomb is not being exploded over that territory.[10]

As debate grew over the looming Grapple X test, British officials were eager to hose down any possible dispute with Washington. Following articles in the communist *Daily Worker* and Labour-aligned newspapers, the Foreign Office wrote to the British Embassy in Washington encouraging them to avoid public discussion of the issue:

You may have seen some tiresome articles in the *News Chronicle* and the *Daily Worker* of 13 August, which suggest that the maintenance of troops on Christmas Island is connected with the problem of disputed sovereignty. We did not mention the sovereignty aspect to Mister Dulles and I do not think that there would be any advantage in doing so at the moment. If, however the State Department comment on these articles you should of course assure them that they are nonsense. We had no thought of influencing the sovereignty issue by our action.[11]

Despite its reluctance to raise the sovereignty issue publicly, the US State Department believed that Britain should bear the cost of any disruption to US commercial activities in the central Pacific. They were concerned about air and sea transportation, fishery resources outside the territorial waters, and other matters of interest that affected US businesses using facilities on Christmas Island.

In 1953, for example, the US military had granted a lease to an American company South Pacific Air Lines (SPAL), incorporating landing rights on the Casady Field airstrip on Christmas Island (which the United States

---

9   Question to Prime Minister Harold Macmillan, UK House of Commons, Hansard official report, 16 April 1957.
10 Question to Prime Minister Harold Macmillan, ibid.
11 Letter from P. Dean, Foreign Office, London to J.E. Coulson, British Embassy, Washington, 14 August 1957. CO1036/282.

still regarded as its territory). The Fish and Wildlife Service of the US Department of the Interior had also signed a contract with a West Coast fishing company. This allowed two fishing vessels operating along the Equator to use Christmas Island as a harbour to obtain fresh water and stockpile fuel and supplies.

British plans to ban civilian air and maritime traffic from the testing danger area was causing debate within the US Congress, because SPAL were threatening to sue the US Government if the lease to use the airfield was terminated.

A diplomatic note from the US State Department to the British Embassy in Washington outlined US government support for SPAL:

> It is noted that permission previously granted by the British authorities for this airline to operate at Christmas Island has, for security and other reasons, been withdrawn because the use of the island is required as a result of what the British government regards as the overriding military necessity of conducting the testing in question. As the ambassador is aware, the South Pacific Air Lines claims that this enforced change in its plans will result, and indeed is already resulting, in a considerable financial loss.
>
> Furthermore, the US government considers that inability to use Christmas Island may prevent the development of an air route between Honolulu and the Society Islands; it may also impede the development of efficient air routes between the United States and the South Pacific. The British government will appreciate that the US government must reserve its rights in these respects.[12]

The Matson Navigation Company also operated shipping services between Hawai'i, Australia and the Society Islands. British officials quickly realised that the proposed danger zone in the Line Islands would block their normal navigation routes, and called on the British Embassy in Washington to lobby US officials:

> They may decide that the simplest course would be to make a small diversion in order to avoid the danger area throughout the period of its existence. Alternatively, it should be possible to come to an arrangement with the company enabling them to send their ships through the danger

---

12   Draft text of diplomatic note from the US State Department to the British Embassy, Washington, n.d. CO1036/280.

area on days when firing is not taking place. I suggest that the State Department should inform the shipping line in confidence that the danger area will now fall across the probable route.[13]

While officials were willing to make concessions to Matson and its Oceanic Steamship Company, they were not willing to grant the same rights to Japanese shipping interests, which transported phosphate to Japan from mines on Makatea in French Polynesia. The Mitsui Shipping Company chartered vessels through the Anglo/French Phosphates Company to transport the phosphate, with vessels passing through the prescribed danger area in the Line Islands on average three times a month.

Foreign Office official Gillian Brown argued in favour of the US company, at a time that Japanese diplomats were harassing the British Government over the looming test program:

> There is of course a possibility of our offering the vessels facilities to pass across a tip of the danger area on days when firing is not taking place. Such an arrangement may be suitable for the few voyages to be made by the Oceanic Steamship Company, but I do not think it follows that we should add to the difficulties of the Task Force by permitting vessels under Japanese control to enter the area … In any case they would probably not accept such an offer for fear that Japanese organisations would claim that the phosphates had been contaminated. If we are accused of discrimination in favour of the Oceanic Steamship Company, I have no doubt that we can argue that the size of the vessels and the circumstances were very different.[14]

The angry public reaction to fallout from the 1954 Bravo test on Bikini meant that US politicians were particularly sensitive to any public debate about radioactive contamination from the British tests. The US diplomatic note also highlights:

> the apprehension of the people of Hawai'i and Palmyra with respect to the possible effects of this testing, and the apprehension of the United States Pacific Coast canners with respect to a possible widespread adverse psychological reaction of the US public to fish, particularly tuna, coming from the Western Pacific which might later be sold in the United States. This would have a drastic effect on the market.[15]

---

13   Letter from Foreign Office, London to British ambassador Sir Harold Caccia, Washington, 22 December 1956. CO1036/280.
14   Letter from Gillian Brown, Foreign Office, London to J.A. Lovelock, Ministry of Supply, London, 1 March 1957. CO1036/281.
15   Draft text of diplomatic note from the US State Department to the British Embassy, Washington, n.d. CO1036/280.

Privately, British officials acknowledged that US businesses had legitimate legal claims over Christmas Island, even as formal negotiations over sovereignty continued:

> The United States government seem to be within their rights in requesting the return of property which they gave the government of the Gilbert and Ellice Islands Colony the right to use in 1950, but of which they specifically retained ownership at the time.[16]

By late 1956, British Embassy officials in Washington were pressing London to respond to US concerns:

> We should do all we can do hasten a decision on the diplomatic note, as he considers that it is becoming increasingly embarrassing for the State Department not to have anything on paper. This is apparently led them into difficulties already with the Governor in Honolulu, and Washington considers that when our danger area is published they may come under additional fire.[17]

The UK Embassy pressed their Foreign Office colleagues to take note of US complaints before any public announcement of restricted areas around the test zone:

> If our publication of the danger area attracts the attention of the US Congress, the State Department may have to stand by its terms and so lose the opportunity of replacing it by something more acceptable to us. They could not tell the Congress that, when we had reached the stage of making public announcements, the protection of United States interests in the area still rested on an informal understanding.[18]

After negotiation with the US State Department, the British Foreign Office came to a suitable wording about compensation for SPAL, noting:

> Her Majesty's government cannot, as at presently advised, accept legal liability. They are, however, prepared ... to consider any claim by SPAL for compensation on its merits and indeed discussions and exchanges

---

16 Letter from British Embassy, Washington to Japan and Pacific Department, Foreign Office, London, 30 October 1953. CO1036/280.
17 Letter from Foreign Office to R.G. Elkington, Ministry of Supply, London, 4 January 1957. CO1036/280.
18 Telegram no. 23 from UK Ambassador to the United States, Sir Harold Caccia to Foreign Office, London, 4 January 1957. CO1036/280.

of information are taking place with representatives of SPAL as a result of which it is hoped that a decision will be risk reached acceptable to all concerned.[19]

After months of negotiation, SPAL relocated operations, using an airstrip at Bora Bora in French Polynesia. At the same time, the company sought compensation from the UK Government and by September 1957 was granted £500,000 compensation and a pledge that the Grapple Task Force would relocate its supplies from Christmas Island.[20]

* * *

Facing these pressures, London ordered Colonial Office officials in the Pacific to pass legislation to ban foreign vessels from waters around the Line Islands.

On 22 March 1957, High Commissioner John Gutch proclaimed the *Prohibited Areas Ordinance 1957 no.1* and the *Prohibited Areas Regulation 1957* (Queens Regulation no. 5 of 1957). The ordinance gave the High Commissioner power to proclaim that any island within the GEIC, and also territorial waters within 3 miles of that island, could be declared a prohibited area. After proclamation, no person could remain, enter or attempt to enter any prohibited area without the authority of the Resident Commissioner of the GEIC. The ordinance and regulations gave powers to 'any administrative officer, Constabulary officer or an officer holding a commission in the Navy, Army or Air Force' to remove or detain people entering the prohibited area without authority.[21]

Five days later, Gutch declared both Christmas Island and Malden Island to be prohibited areas, under the provisions of the newly legislated ordinance.[22] This allowed officials to act on their concern about the potential for Japanese vessels to operate inside or near the Grapple danger zone.

---

19 Telegram no.42 from UK Ambassador to the United States, Sir Harold Caccia to Foreign Office, London, 8 January 1957. CO1036/280.
20 Letter from D.A. Lovelock to Gillian Brown, Foreign Office, London, 9 September 1957. DB/133/08. CO1036/282.
21 'Prohibited Areas Ordinance 1957', *Headquarters Information Note*, No. 15, 5 April 1957, Office of the Resident Commissioner, Gilbert and Ellice Islands Colony, F 76/6/32 (1957), p. 2. PAMBU document AU PMB 493.
22 'Proclamation under Prohibited Areas Ordinance and Prohibited Areas Regulation', ibid., p. 3.

The Japanese Government claimed that Japanese fishing interests would be adversely affected by the closure of waters around the test sites. But British officials regarded these diplomatic claims as a political ploy to bolster Japan's call for an end to testing. In a March 1957 diplomatic note prepared for the Japanese Ambassador in London, the Foreign Office argued:

> HMG [Her Majesty's Government] takes note of the statement that 'a regular route of cargo vessels' would normally pass through what is part of the 'danger area.' It is also desirable to make it clear now that HMG does not accept the contention in your Note that the area around the Line Islands is a 'traditional' fishing ground for Japanese fishermen.[23]

Given the irradiation of the crew of the *Lucky Dragon* by the US Bravo test, however, UK authorities were unwilling to simply ignore the fate of fishing boats when the issue was raised by Japanese diplomats.

In May 1957, less than two weeks before the first Grapple test, the British Government was aware that nine Japanese boats from the Muroto Fishing Cooperative were fishing in the area designated as a danger zone. The final solution was to remain silent about potential hazards to the fishing vessels. Indeed, both the UK and Japanese governments were reluctant to publicise the presence of these vessels, with the British Embassy in Tokyo reporting that:

> It is difficult to avoid the impression that the order has gone out that no mention should be made of the subject ... One can well visualise that the Japanese know very well that they cannot accept the responsibility for doing nothing to pull these vessels out of danger, but the publicity for any action taken to this end would be embarrassing for the cause.[24]

Their other concern was the possibility that peace protesters would deliberately sail vessels into the area to disrupt the tests. Many years before Greenpeace perfected the technique, British pacifist Harold Steele had the idea of sailing a boat into the middle of the danger zone.

---

23   H.C. Hainsworth, Foreign Office, London: *Draft note to Japanese ambassador*, 20 March 1957. CO1036/281.
24   Letter from R. W. Selby, British Embassy, Tokyo, to H. C. Hainsworth, Foreign Office, London, 3 May 1957, 1242/296/57, marked Confidential. CO1056/513. References to the boats are also found in Telegram no. 221, marked Confidential, from British Embassy, Tokyo to Foreign Office, London, 3 May 1957.

6
The pacifist—Harold Steele

In March 1957, a six-paragraph article in the communist newspaper *Daily Worker* sparked the interest of Britain's security service MI5. The newspaper reported that Harold Steele, a 63-year-old 'white-haired and keen eyed' ex-poultry farmer from Great Malvern, Worcestershire, intended to 'go out to the Pacific and sail into the H-blast area'.[1]

Steele had a long history of pacifist protest. While studying at Exeter University during the First World War, he refused the offer of an officer's commission if he enlisted. As a conscientious objector and member of the No Conscription Fellowship, believing that 'Christianity and socialism forbade any resort to war', he was court-martialled five times and sentenced to seven years' hard labour.[2] After three years in prison, he was only released in April 1919, months after the war was over.

Decades later, despite poor health, limited income and three children to feed, he was still campaigning for peace. Steele's protest against the British nuclear tests in the Pacific, which took him to Japan in 1957, symbolised the growing passion in the United Kingdom against nuclear weapons testing.

---

1   'Will sail to H-test area', *Daily Worker*, 19 March 1957, annotated and filed in CO1036/513.
2   Biography in commemorative program, *International Conscientious Objectors Day ceremony*, London, 15 May 2014. Available at: www.ppu.org.uk/nomorewar/download/May15 commemorativev2.pdf.

CONFIDENTIAL

OUTWARD TELEGRAM
FROM THE SECRETARY OF STATE FOR THE COLONIES

70

TO FIJI (Sir R. Garvey)

Code   PAC/AU 3

Sent 26th April, 1957.   10. 15 hrs.

PRIORITY
CONFIDENTIAL
No. 105.

Your telegram No. 105.

Harold Steele.

    Aged 63 years, retired poultry farmer said to have been imprisoned for 3 years during first World War for refusal to serve in Forces. Was member of Peace Pledge Union in last war and appears to be bona fide pacifist but not subversive.

    2. Reuters correspondence confirms he was informed by person named that he proposed to fly to Fiji. No mention of this has appeared in U.K. press and neither B.O.A.C. nor QANTAS can trace any passage booking for him. Latest press reports say he now plans to travel to India to see if he can obtain a boat there to sail to Pacific but attempts to raise money have so far been unsuccessful.

    3. His resources seem very limited and unless he could obtain local backing in Fiji it is doubtful whether he could do much harm. As it seems unlikely he will come to Fiji it would only create unnecessary publicity to declare him a prohibited immigrant at this stage. In any case it would seem preferable to take action against him under section 8(5)(b) of Immigration Ordinance if necessity arises. Final decision is a matter for you but please consult me before taking action against him.

    4. I will inform you if I obtain any definite information about his intention to visit Fiji.

UK security forces tracked the movements of British pacifist Harold Steele from London to Japan
Source: Colonial Office file CO1036/513.

Steele's protest also highlights the role of Britain's intelligence agencies as the 'missing dimension' in the history of Britain's postwar imperial decline.[3] In the 1950s, Britain's intelligence agencies—MI5, the Secret

---

3   Calder Walton and Christopher Andrew: 'Still the missing dimension: British intelligence and the historiography of British decolonisation' in Patrick Major and Christopher Moran (eds): *Spooked—Britain, Empire and intelligence since 1945* (Cambridge Scholars Publishing, Cambridge, 2009).

Intelligence Service (SIS) and the Government Communications Headquarters—played a central role in Empire management. They helped create intelligence services in Commonwealth nations like Australia, monitored dissident forces across the British Empire and sought to counter Soviet active measures in British dependencies. At the same time as they were spying on anti-colonial nationalists, MI5 posted Security Liaison Officers to all the British dependencies that were moving towards political independence, and offered to set up intelligence services for the newly independent nations. The Colonial Office maintained its own Intelligence and Security Department (ISD), led by a former MI5 officer.[4]

While lacking the rigour of today's cyber monitoring, the UK National Archives holds files from the 1950s related to protests by Steele and other activists against the Grapple nuclear tests. These include newspaper clippings, letters, telegrams and diplomatic cables sent between London, the Secretary of State for the Colonies, the Governor's office in Fiji, the British Embassy in Tokyo and Foreign Office bureaus in Honolulu and Tahiti.[5]

With thousands of UK military personnel involved in preparations for Operation Grapple, there was growing public awareness of the looming tests. Opinion polls showed that nearly half the British population were opposed to the tests, echoing the concern shown in Australia, New Zealand, Japan and the Pacific islands. The National Council for the Abolition of Nuclear Weapons Tests (NCANWT)—the forerunner of the Campaign for Nuclear Disarmament (CND)—soon had 100 branches around the United Kingdom. NCANWT launched a series of public appeals, campaigning in the Labour Party to halt the tests.[6]

---

4 The files of the Colonial Office Intelligence and Security Department (ISD) can be found in the UK National Archives under the code CO1035. For a recent study on the role of UK intelligence services in Britain's withdrawal from Empire between 1945 and 1965, see Calder Walton: *Empire of secrets—British intelligence, the Cold War and the twilight of Empire* (Harper Press, London, 2013).
5 Some of the newspaper clippings, telegrams and letters cited in this chapter are collated in 'Protests against the H-bomb tests in the Pacific', Colonial Office archives CO1036/513.
6 CND was only founded in January 1958, spurred by public awareness of Britain's nuclear contribution to the Cold War and the United States' deployment of nuclear forces to UK air bases and submarine bases in Scotland. See Richard Taylor: *Against the bomb—the British peace movement, 1958–1965* (Clarendon, Oxford, 1988).

The cautious advocacy of the NCANWT, however, was not militant enough for small socialist and pacifist groups. Surveying the British disarmament movement and 'the new pacifism' in 1962, radical activist Nicolas Walter explained:

> The British unilateralist movement sprang not from the formation of the Campaign for Nuclear Disarmament in January 1958, nor even from that of its parent, the National Council for the Abolition of Nuclear Weapons Tests, in February 1957. It was really brought to life by Harold Steele's proposal to enter the Christmas Island tests zone early in 1957, which led to the formation of an Emergency Committee for Direct Action against Nuclear War and which followed years of grinding work by dedicated pacifists.[7]

* * *

Harold Steele's idea to travel to Christmas Island was inspired by a circular letter from Takeko Kowai of the 'Peace Protection Association of Toyohashi Citizens' in Japan. Kowai, the wife of the president of Aichi University, circulated a call for direct action to peace activists in the United States, France and Britain, seeking international support to oppose the British nuclear program in the Pacific. This followed earlier protests by her Peace Protection Association against US and Russian atmospheric testing.

With support from other pacifists linked to the Peace Pledge Union (PPU), Harold Steele and his wife Sheila announced in March 1957 that they would travel to Tokyo. Their aim was to join a protest fleet to sail to the central Pacific and halt the Grapple hydrogen bomb tests. In London, the Emergency Committee for Direct Action Against Nuclear War was formed the following month to raise funds to support the planned direct action, with sponsors including philosopher Lord Bertrand Russell, playwright Laurence Houseman and comedian Spike Milligan.

At a press conference organised by the PPU, Steele told journalists:

> The time has come when someone must make a real move to stop the H-bomb tests. My wife and I will willingly sacrifice ourselves to prove to the world the horror of this devilish device. Personal considerations are

---

7   Nicolas Walter: 'Direct action and the new pacifism', *Anarchy: A Journal of Anarchist Ideas*, No. 13 (special edition on Direct Action), Freedom Press, March 1962, p. 89. For discussion of the Emergency Committee, see Lawrence Wittner: *Resisting the bomb—a history of the world disarmament movement, 1954–70*, Vol. 2 (Stanford University Press, 1997), pp. 44–45.

secondary. My three children—much as I love them—are not important. If I should die, I commend them to the care of my Quaker friends. I believe this demonstration will shake the conscience of man out of its lazy acceptance of the H-bomb and all its horrors.[8]

By the time of their public declaration, however, the Japanese Government had not yet given a visa for the Steeles to travel to Japan. Harold Steele told reporters:

> The Japanese government is formally opposed to anything like our plan, but I believe that privately officials support us and are touched by our intentions. My wife and I are prepared to end our days in pain to prove how horrible effects of nuclear radiation can be. The time has come for someone to make a real move to stop the tests.[9]

In late April, noting publicity about the planned protest, the Foreign Office directed the British consulates in Hawai'i and Tahiti to report if either Steele or his wife 'come to notice in your territory'.[10] But with the start of the test series looming and the trip to Japan uncertain, Harold Steele began to look at other options, such as travelling alone to the Pacific via India or Fiji.

After Steele sought permission to travel to the region via Fiji, the Governor in Suva requested advice from London as to whether he should forbid entry to the peace activist. Internal discussions within the Foreign Office noted that the Governor 'is likely to be advised that he should grant Steele a visa, but advised that the latter's continued stay in the island should be contingent on his not disturbing the peace'.[11]

The other option of India had many attractions. As a peace activist who campaigned alongside Quakers and other pacifists influenced by Gandhian traditions of non-violence, Steele noted that 'my feeling is that I shall find in India, which owes its existence to Gandhi and his principles, a sympathetic orientation of mind'.[12]

---

8   'We will risk our lives to prove the bomb is evil', *Sunday Pictorial*, 24 March 1957.
9   'Malvern couple refused visas for "suicide" plan', *Birmingham Post*, 27 March 1957. Sheila Steele did not accompany her husband to the Pacific and fades from the public record after this initial publicity.
10 Restricted telegram from Foreign Office, London to UK consulate, Honolulu, 26 April 1957. CO1036/513.
11 Letter, marked Confidential, from H. C. Hainsworth, Foreign Office, London, to R.W. Selby, British Embassy, Tokyo, 27 April 1957, 1242/318/57. CO1036/513.
12 'Prepared to die on a Pacific atoll—pacifist's H-bomb protest', *The Scotsman*, 9 May 1957.

The other attraction of India was the potential to link up with two young British war resisters, 25-year-old David Graham and 21-year-old Ian Dickson, who were already in New Delhi. Both men had refused to be conscripted for UK national service, and had hitchhiked to India with hopes to travel on to Japan or to Fiji to join the nuclear testing protest. The British Embassy in Tokyo reported to London:

> According to the *Times of India*, Graham has already spent a term in jail for refusing to be conscripted. I do not know whether this might give the authorities in Fiji an excuse to frustrate their efforts should this be thought desirable or necessary.[13]

Embassy officials also expressed concern that Jawaharlal Nehru, the Prime Minister of newly independent India, had given his 'blessings and good will' to the young protesters.[14]

Graham and Dixon were also eager to meet with Steele in New Delhi to obtain funds before travelling to Japan to mobilise a protest fleet. However, with only £500 of the proposed £5,000 originally pledged in England, funds were tight and it was clear that the protest fleet would be difficult to organise at short notice.

The British state was deeply interested in the peace activists' possible subversive (i.e. communist) connections.[15] After the *News Chronicle* reported that Steele's travel itinerary might include India, an annotation on the newspaper clipping in his intelligence file asks: 'Any news?' The handwritten response:

> Only that he is assessed as a bona-fide pacifist and as a member of the Peace Pledge Union in the past. If he has otherwise subversive links, it would be known. I suggest we write him off.[16]

---

13   Letter from T.W. Aston, British Embassy, Tokyo, to H.C. Hainsworth, Permanent Under-secretary's Department, Foreign Office, London, 10 May 1957 (marked 'Restricted Def.55/66/50'). CO1036/513.
14   'Protests to sail into or near the danger area', Telegram no. 137 from R.W. Selby, British Embassy, Tokyo to Foreign Office, London, 12 April 1957. CO1036/513.
15   UK Government concern that communists in the Pacific would support Soviet 'anti-colonial' propaganda is documented in 'Communism—Pacific' PAC 182/777/01, CO1036/859 and 'Australian and New Zealand interest in communism in the Pacific', PAC 182/777/02, CO1036/860.
16   Handwritten note in Colonial Office file 'Protests against the H-bomb tests in the Pacific', CO1036/513.

6. THE PACIFIST—HAROLD STEELE

Throughout April and early May 1957, UK diplomats and intelligence officers were closely monitoring whether Steele, Graham and Dixon would manage to travel to the Asia-Pacific region. The archives contain a long series of letters and telegrams between London, Tokyo, Suva, Honolulu and Tahiti trying to track the protesters' movements. A confidential letter from the Foreign Office in London to the British Embassy in Tokyo notes:

> In view of the conditions which the Japanese government has imposed for any visit by Steele to Japan, it seemed remotely possible that, if he can raise the necessary funds, this man will try to approach the danger area from some other jumping off point. For this reason we have telegraphed Honolulu and Tahiti asking for news as it comes to notice, since we must take all reasonable measures to prevent Steele from obstructing the tests.[17]

An article in the *Fiji Times* on 17 April reported that Steele had booked an air passage to Fiji on 5 May. In a telegram from the Governor's office in Fiji to the Foreign Office on 18 April, marked 'immediate and confidential', the Deputy Governor in Suva reported that:

> Steele is alleged to have told reporters that he hopes to arouse some kind of protest among the Fijian population against proposed nuclear test in the Pacific area … I should be grateful if you would make appropriate enquiries and inform me whether you consider Steele should be declared to be a prohibited immigrant under section 7(c) of Immigration Ordinance 1947.[18]

The reply from Secretary of State for the Colonies Alex Lennox-Boyd to Governor of Fiji Sir Ronald Garvey noted:

> His resources seem very limited and unless he could obtain local backing in Fiji, it is doubtful whether he could do much harm. As it seems unlikely he will come to Fiji it would only create unnecessary publicity to declare him a prohibited immigrant at this stage. In any case it would seem preferable to take action against him under section 8 (5) (b) of Immigration Ordinance if necessity arises.[19]

---

17   Letter from H.C. Hainsworth, Permanent Under-secretary's Department, Foreign Office, London to R.W. Selby, British Embassy, Tokyo, 27 April 1957 (marked 'Confidential 212/244'). CO1036/513.
18   Inward telegram from Fiji to Secretary of State for the Colonies Alex Lennox-Boyd: 'Immediate confidential number 105', 18 April 1957, registered in London 20 April 1957. CO1036/513.
19   Outward telegram from Secretary of State for the Colonies Alex Lennox-Boyd to Governor Sir Ronald Garvey, Fiji, 'Priority/confidential number 105', 26 April 1957, (marked 'Confidential Pac/Au 3'). CO1036/513.

The wonders of the bureaucratic mind at work! Article 7(c) of Fiji's *Immigration Ordinance 1947* allowed a person to be declared a prohibited immigrant to a British colony if 'the entry of the said person into the Colony is likely to be prejudicial to the peace and good order of the Colony and should be prohibited'.[20] In contrast, Article 8(5)(b) of the Act allowed entry to the colony, but then granted powers to the Principal Immigration Officer to 'order a person forthwith to leave the Colony' if he or she 'behaves in a manner prejudicial to the peace or good order of the colony'.[21]

This Cold War concern over 'subversion' in Fiji followed a 1956 visit by Alex MacDonald of the Colonial Office ISD, who travelled to Suva to advise the Governor on the organisation of intelligence services in the British colony.[22] MacDonald, who had served as a British police officer in India and Malaya and then returned home to become an MI5 officer, was seconded from MI5 in June 1954 to work as the Security Intelligence Adviser to the Colonial Office. This led to the establishment of the ISD the following year. Between 1954 and 1957, MacDonald made 57 trips to 27 different British overseas dependencies, including visits to Fiji and the Western Pacific Commission, to train a new generation of intelligence officers in the British colonies.[23]

Uncertain of his own travel plans, Steele remained eager to highlight opposition to the Pacific tests:

> Perhaps I can persuade other people to persuade the authorities to change their minds. If not, then I feel I must make my own personal protest in the area of detonation, whether the result is mutilation or death.[24]

---

20 Colony of Fiji: *An ordinance to make better provision of control of immigration*, 3 December 1947, Article 7.
21 Ibid., Article 8. See also 'Deportation of UK subjects or protected persons from colonial territories': replies to circular from Alan Lennox-Boyd, Secretary of State for the Colonies. Colonial Office ISD file 121/01. CO1035/113.
22 A.M. MacDonald: 'Report on organisation of intelligence in Fiji', reports by Security Intelligence Advisers, January–December 1956, Colonial Office ISD file 118/49/01. CO1035/107. See also 'Organisation of Intelligence Services in the Colonies: Fiji', 1 January 1956–31 December 1957, Colonial Office ISD file 65/49/01. CO1035/48.
23 For details of Alex MacDonald's career in MI5, the Colonial Office ISD, Kenya and Cyprus, see Calder Walton: *Empire of secrets*, op. cit., pp. 140–145.
24 'Prepared to die on a Pacific atoll—pacifist's H-bomb protest', *The Scotsman*, 9 May 1957.

6. THE PACIFIST—HAROLD STEELE

The Japanese Government finally granted a visa to Steele on condition that he would not undertake any actions that would endanger human life. But too late: he was unable to reach Japan before the first Grapple test, conducted on Malden Island on 15 May. Steele flew first to New Delhi, where he met with Prime Minister Jawaharlal Nehru, noting:

> Mr. Nehru wished me well and his whole bearing and attitude of speech showed he was not opposed to my mission.[25]

He then flew on to Tokyo on 16 May, still hoping to mobilise support from the Japanese peace movement. Graham and Dixon could not find a way to join him for the Pacific protests. The Commonwealth Relations Office reported to the Foreign Office:

> They are thought to have left Delhi on 28 May taking a devious route hitchhiking from port to port in an attempt to get a cheap passage, since their funds are very low. In view of this, it is difficult to predict when they will turn up here, but it is certainly now seems that Tokyo and Fiji need no longer have any fear of their turning up there.[26]

* * *

On 17 May, two days after the first British test on Malden Island, there were protests across Japan involving an estimated 350,000 people. In Tokyo, 20,000 students held a demonstration against the test, surrounding the British Embassy. That night, 3,000 school students also held a lantern procession.

A delegation of four peace activists met with embassy officials, delivering a copy of a message for Prime Minister Macmillan and calling for the immediate halt of any further tests at Christmas Island. The delegates also asked for Britain to join an agreement between the United States and Soviet Union prohibiting nuclear testing. However, British officials reportedly told the delegation:

> We think that the influence of the last nuclear test on mankind is negligible. We have heard enough of the demand for the agreement of prohibition of the tests, and we are in no mood for answer to you [sic].[27]

---

25 'Pacifist seeks to demonstrate against H-tests', *Florence Times* (US), 16 May 1957.
26 Letter from T.W. Aston, Commonwealth Relations Office to G.A.C. Witheridge, Ministry of Supply, 5 June 1957. CO1056/513.
27 *No More Hiroshimas, the news of the Japan Council against A and H-bombs*, Vol. 4, No. 9, May 1957, pp. 3–6.

One of Steele's first acts in Tokyo was to meet with diplomats at the British Embassy to argue his case for a halt to further tests. Reporting to London after the meeting on 18 May, diplomat R. W. Selby noted: 'Steele was at pains to point out that his mission was in no way political. It was essentially humanitarian and, he supposed, religious.' Ending his report, Selby noted that 'naturally for his sake and everyone else's sake, I hoped that his mission would be a flop and that he would have a happy journey home'.[28]

Over subsequent days, however, the British activist engaged in a series of meetings and newspaper interviews. Steele visited a dozen Japanese students who were conducting a hunger strike in a park opposite the British Embassy, telling them that he 'came here in good hope and with a firm determination to join in protesting nuclear tests'.[29]

On 22 May, as the Executive Council of the Japan Council Against A and H Bombs debated the pros and cons of deploying a protest fleet into the danger zone, Steele told the meeting that direct action was the only way to halt the tests.[30]

But with funds running short, Steele was increasingly frustrated by the difficulties of gaining firm commitments for action. A proposed meeting with the Deputy Prime Minister Mitsujiro Ishii was repeatedly delayed. Organising a vessel for the protest fleet was much harder than expected. There were also significant differences between affiliates of the Japan Council, with some urging direct action, but others arguing the protest boat proposal was 'adventurous' and likely to damage public opinion. Some Gensuikyo executive members sought alternatives 'drawn up so as carefully to give no ground to the opposition that this was something of a suicidal nature, like kamikaze attack by Japanese forces had resorted to during the Pacific war'.[31]

Steele's frustration boiled over, as the Japanese debate on direct action echoed his own experience in the British disarmament movement. He told a reporter from Reuters that the Japan Council 'had let the side down. They had gone into this thing with plenty of steam but had fizzled out'. As with peace movements in Britain, 'the societies are constantly

---

28 Letter from R.W. Selby, British Embassy, Tokyo, to H.C. Hainsworth, Foreign Office, London, 24 May 1957, 1242/338/57, marked Confidential. CO1056/513.
29 Reuters report published in *Milwaukee Journal*, 18 May 1957.
30 Reuters Tokyo press cable, 22 May 1957. CO1036/513.
31 Detailed reporting of the internal debates within the peace movement is found in *No More Hiroshimas*, op. cit., pp. 3–6.

arguing, splitting hairs and going around corners. I fear that Japan's peace movement, which is very young, is in danger of developing the same weakness'.[32]

Without the capacity to mobilise an extensive protest flotilla, the Japan Council still organised other protests. Regular reports from Reuters' Tokyo office carried news to Europe, the United States and Australia, while the Pacific islands media gave coverage to protests in Japan, such as a front-page report in the *Fiji Times* of another 15,000-strong rally in Tokyo.[33]

The British Embassy in Tokyo sent daily reports to London on the efforts by Japanese peace activists to organise ships to travel to the test site—with barely suppressed glee that these efforts were unsuccessful.

From Kochi, on the south-east coast of Shikoku Island, activists continued to mobilise for the protest. The Kochi Prefectural Committee for the Prevention of Nuclear Tests on Christmas Island had planned to send a steamer with 27 crew and eight demonstrators on board to the area near the danger zone for 100 days, for both a symbolic protest and to collect samples of radioactive fallout. Soon after the first test on Malden Island, the British Embassy reported that the Japan Council was supporting the Kochi Prefectural Committee with ¥3.5 million, as a contribution towards the ¥8.5 million cost to hire and outfit fishing boats to travel to the test zone.[34]

However, on 19 May, four days after the first test on Malden Island, the British Embassy noted that the Kochi committee 'announced cancellation of its plan to send vessel to the testing grounds in view of danger of contamination from first test'.[35]

Hundreds of letters condemning the tests were then given to the captains of two Japanese fishing boats *No. 3 Koho Maru* and *No. 5 Ryoi Maru* to throw into the sea near the test site. These ships sailed on 30 May, carrying journalist Takei Hajima from the Communist-aligned *Akahata* newspaper, displaying banners that said 'Stop the H-Bomb Tests' and

---

32   Reuters Tokyo press cable, 22 May 1957. CO1036/513.
33   'Tokyo H-bomb protest', *Fiji Times*, 31 May 1957, p. 1. Beyond the Asia-Pacific region, Steele's visit received coverage in papers as diverse as the *Sydney Morning Herald* (Australia), *Manchester Guardian* (UK), *Milwaukee Journal* (USA) and even the *Florence Times* (Alabama, USA).
34   Letter from R.W. Selby, British Embassy, Tokyo, to H.C. Hainsworth, Foreign Office, London, 17 May 1957, 1242/318/57, marked Confidential. CO1056/513.
35   Telegram from British Embassy in Tokyo to Foreign Office, London, 19 May 1957. CO1056/513.

'Japanese fishermen are not laboratory rabbits!'[36] The British Embassy in Tokyo confidently reported that the fishing boats 'would not go anywhere near the danger zone'.[37]

* * *

The protests in Japan and the Pacific islands were amplified by actions in Australia and New Zealand, as churches, unions and peace groups began to criticise the British tests.[38]

On 27 May 1957, following the first test on Malden Island, the President-General of the Methodist Church of Australasia, Reverend Harold Wood, wrote to the British Secretary of State for the Colonies expressing concern about the nuclear test on Christmas Island. Conveying a resolution of the General Conference of the Methodist Church, Reverend Wood called 'for the abandonment of the tests that have begun in the Pacific' and urged the British Government:

> to consider the most unfortunate position of the inhabitants of the various Pacific island groups in many of which the Methodist Church is conducting its overseas mission work … We are prompted to respectfully remind you of the very great danger of radioactive fallout on the scattered islands of the Pacific and also the deplorable psychological effect on primitive people because of the nuclear tests. We remind you that most of the native people concerned are, directly or indirectly, under the administration of the British Colonial office.[39]

In June, Steele returned to England, his dream of sailing to Christmas Island still out of reach. But the whole experience drove him on, to focus public opinion in Britain on the UK testing program. Under his enthusiastic gaze, the Emergency Committee for Direct Action Against Nuclear War was transformed into the Direct Action Committee Against Nuclear War (DAC) in April 1958 'to assist the conducting of non-violent direct action to obtain the total renunciation of nuclear war and its weapons by Britain and all other countries as a first step in disarmament'.[40]

---

36   *No More Hiroshimas*, op. cit, p. 6.
37   Confidential telegram No. 191, British Embassy, Tokyo, to Foreign Office, 27 May 1957. CO1056/513.
38   Barbara Carter: 'The peace movements in the 1950s' in Ann Curthoys and John Merritt: *Better Dead than Red—Australia's first Cold War 1945–59* (Allen and Unwin, Sydney, 1986), p. 67.
39   Letter from Reverend Harold Wood, President-General of the Methodist Church of Australasia, 27 May 1957, with covering letter by D.J. Derx to D.A. Lovelock, 11 June 1957. CO1056/513.
40   Direct Action Committee (DAC): *Policy Statement*, 10 April 1958.

More militant than CND, the DAC launched a new campaign of civil disobedience against nuclear weapons, with protests and sit-ins against the Atomic Weapons Research Establishment (AWRE) at Aldermaston, US Polaris submarine bases in Scotland and Britain's own nuclear missile force.[41]

A failed quest? Harold Steele's dream of sailing a boat into the middle of the Pacific nuclear test zone went unfulfilled, but his vision inspired many others. In 1958, US pacifist Albert Bigelow planned to sail the *Golden Rule* from California to Enewetak Atoll in the Marshall Islands, to disrupt the US military's test series codenamed Operation Hardtack.[42] When Bigelow's yacht was seized by the US Coast Guard off Hawai'i, a former US naval officer Earle Reynolds took up his voyage, and sailed the yacht *Phoenix* to waters off Bikini Atoll. Reynolds, his wife Barbara and children later sailed to the USSR to protest against Soviet nuclear testing.[43]

More than a decade later, the rusting fishing trawler *Phyllis Cormack* was renamed the *Greenpeace*, and sailed from Vancouver in 1971 attempting to halt US nuclear tests in the northern Pacific. Greenpeace activists and other mariners aboard the *Vega*, *Fri*, *Rainbow Warrior* and other vessels bedevilled the French state in the waters off Moruroa Atoll until France's nuclear testing program ended in 1996.[44] In the 1980s, Bill and Lorraine Ethell mortgaged their home in Australia and took three children aboard the *Pacific Peacemaker*, sailing across the Pacific to challenge the regional deployment of nuclear-armed US Trident submarines.[45]

Harold Steele's tradition of moral witness and 'bodies on the line' had taken root in the Pacific—a lesson learnt by a new generation of climate activists.[46]

---

41   'Two protests against the hydrogen bomb 1957', Appendix XI in Andrew Bone (ed.): *Détente or destruction 1955–57, collected papers of Bertrand Russell*, Vol. 29 (Routledge, New York, 2005). See also 'From Operation Gandhi to the Direct Action Committee Against Nuclear War (DAC)', *Nonviolent Resistance*, 22 March 2015. After a series of protests, the DAC later merged with the Committee of 100, led by the philosopher Bertrand Russell, to continue its tradition of militant protest.
42   Albert Bigelow: *The Voyage of the Golden Rule* (Doubleday & Company, Garden City, NY, 1959). Thanks to Dale Hess for introducing me to this tradition of Quaker protest.
43   Earle Reynolds: *The Forbidden Voyage* (David McKay Company, New York, 1961).
44   Michael Brown and John May: *The Greenpeace Story* (Dorling Kindersley, London and New York, 1991).
45   Win Olive: *Voyage of the Pacific Peacemaker* (Wild & Woolley, Glebe, 1999).
46   For the connection with a new generation of environmental campaigners, see Nic Maclellan: 'Young Pacific islanders are not climate change victims—they're fighting', *The Guardian*, 22 September 2014.

Interlude — On radiation, safety and secrecy

The British authorities have an ongoing duty of care for the civilian and military personnel who staffed the test sites and the population of neighbouring atolls. This is based on the core principle that the prime responsibility for management of radiation risks rests with the organisation responsible for activities that gave rise to the risks.

This duty was recognised at the time, in the commitments made by the Ministry of Supply for Fijian troops deployed on Christmas Island:

> The Ministry of Supply has undertaken to indemnify the Government of Fiji against claims for pensions to which men of the Fijian Military Forces or their dependants may become entitled to as a result of death or injury sustained by them during their service on the Nuclear Weapons Testing Base at Christmas Island in the Pacific.[1]

In the lead-up to the tests in early 1957, UK Prime Minister Harold Macmillan publicly dismissed any concern about extensive radioactive fallout, noting:

> We will make our tests so small and on such a scale that they cannot really add to anything that would be dangerous in the world.[2]

In March 1957, Macmillan told the House of Commons:

> The present and foreseeable hazards, including genetic effects, from external radiation due to fall-out from the test explosions of nuclear weapons, fired at the present rate and in the present proportion of the different kinds, are considered to be negligible.[3]

---

1 Letter from G.M.P. Myers, Ministry of Supply, to D.J. Derx, Colonial Office, London, 17 June 1958. CO1036/514.
2 'Our H-bomb tests will be "so small"', *News Chronicle*, 28 March 1957.
3 Statement by Prime Minister Harold Macmillan, UK House of Commons, Hansard official report, 5 March 1957; Vol. 566, col. 178.

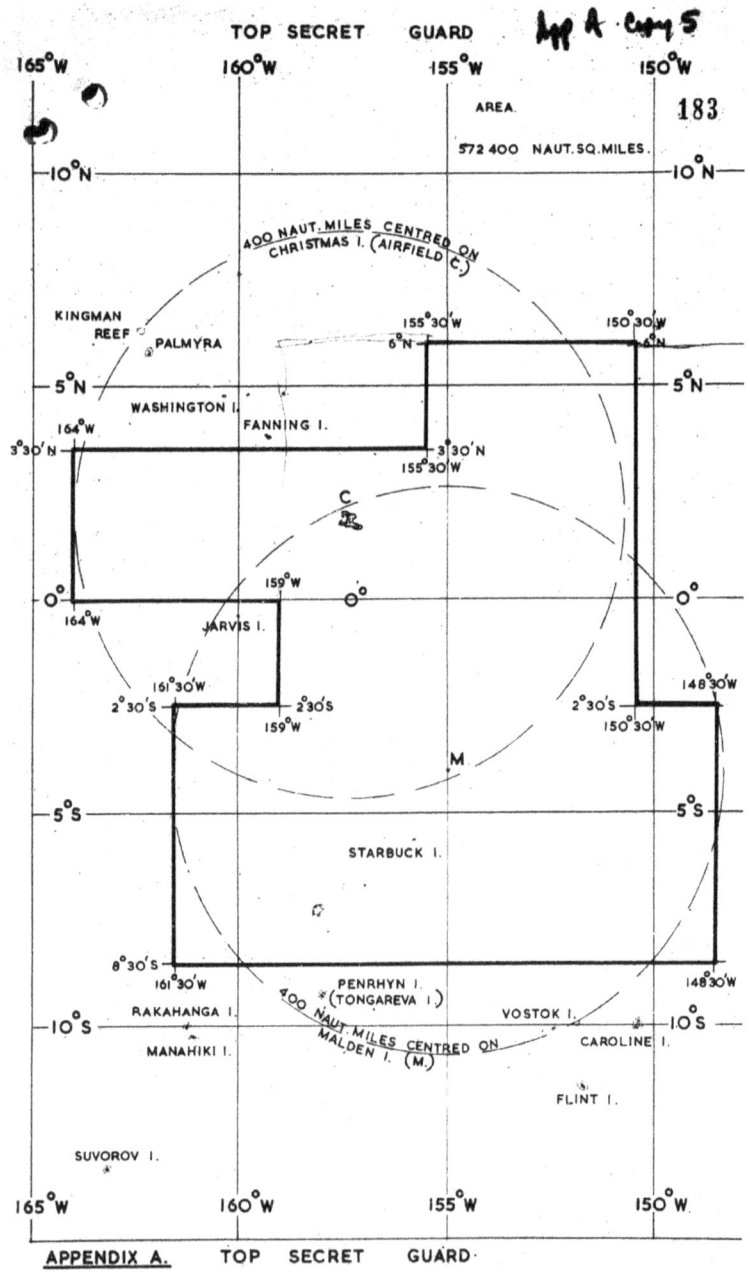

Map of Grapple Danger Area
Note the way that radioactive fallout will move within neat squares, avoiding inhabited islands like Penrhyn, Jarvis and Fanning.
Source: Colonial Office file CO1036/280.

To this day, the official position of the UK Government is that the Grapple nuclear tests involved rigorous safety standards, which protected service personnel and civilian staff from exposure to radiation. The government has argued that—with the exception of some aircrew—those present on Christmas Island were too far from the actual detonation point to be at risk from direct exposure and the 'prompt radiation' effect. Successive government ministers have stated:

> The mass of evidence shows that the health and safety of the trial participants were regarded very seriously, and that a great deal of trouble was taken over radiological protection.[4]

On paper, the Grapple Task Force had established elaborate radiation monitoring systems. In reality, these were not always implemented. For example, before the early tests, sailors were issued with film badges to measure the total dose of radiation received, similar to those used in hospital radiotherapy departments. But not everyone was given the badge, a fact acknowledged by the UK Ministry of Defence (MoD) in 2008:

> Badges were not issued to all personnel: the Ministry of Defence estimates that 21 per cent of total participants [in Australia and Kiribati] had badges. In general, more badges were issued for the earlier tests (96 per cent of those present at Operation Hurricane had a badge while only 20 per cent of those at Operation Grapple).[5]

A New Zealand Defence Force (NZDF) study of the operation, declassified in 1996, revealed that many of these badges were not processed to provide evidence of radiation exposure:

> Before each nuclear test the crewmen were issued with a new film badge and after the test they would be collected and sent for processing on *HMS Narvik*. However, during Operation Grapple most film badges—including those from the New Zealand frigates—were not processed, principally because of problems with storing the chemicals needed for processing.[6]

---

4 'Nuclear Test Veterans', Statement by Secretary of Defence John Spellar MP, UK House of Commons, Hansard official report, 4 February 1998, col. 1009.
5 'UK atmospheric nuclear weapons tests: UK programme', Factsheet 5, UK Ministry of Defence, June 2008.
6 John Crawford: *The involvement of the Royal New Zealand Navy in the British nuclear testing programmes of 1957 and 1958*, research paper for New Zealand Defence Force Headquarters, Wellington, New Zealand, 1989 (declassified 1996), pp. 23–24.

The Christmas Island veterans argue that they were often placed in the path of radioactive fallout, that existing records don't document the realities on the ground and that there were many pathways for them to ingest or inhale hazardous particles of fallout.

In the aftermath of the tests, the British Government eventually conducted studies of the health of nearly 14,000 military personnel, run by the UK National Radiological Protection Board (NRPB). These studies dismissed the claims of many veterans that they had been exposed to hazardous levels of radiation. The official report reveals 'no detectable effort on the participants' expectation of life, nor on their risk of developing cancer or other fatal diseases'.[7]

These claims are still vigorously contested by veterans' associations in Britain, Australia, New Zealand and Fiji. They have critiqued the official health reports and have campaigned for independent medical studies to investigate the documented health effects that they attribute to exposure to ionising radiation rather than other causes. As detailed in Chapter 20, independent studies like the genetic survey conducted at Massey University in New Zealand have shown significant adverse impacts.

Some veterans go further, claiming they were deliberately used as guinea pigs or 'lambs to the slaughter'.[8] They argue that, well before the nuclear tests, senior members of the British military bureaucracy clearly saw that personnel would be exposed to radiation as part of the nuclear test program.

Documentary evidence from the UK archives suggests that one of the purposes of the tests was to study the effects of nuclear detonations on personnel as well as equipment. For example, the British Chiefs of Staff had a Defence Research Policy Committee on the Atomic Weapons Trials, looking at the military applications of atomic energy. A memo from the committee, dated 20 May 1953, states that a series of 'tests' needed to be included in future atomic weapons trials:

---

7   Lorna Arnold: *Britain and the H-bomb*, (Palgrave Macmillan, London, 2001), p. 243.
8   Statement by Avon Hudson, in Roger Cross and Avon Hudson: *Beyond Belief—the British bomb tests, Australia's veterans speak out* (Wakefield Press, Kent town, 2005), p. 171.

The Navy requires information on the effects of various types of atomic explosions on ships and their contents and equipment ... The Army must discover the detailed effects of various types of explosion on equipment, stores *and men, with and without various types of protection.*[9]

A memo from the Royal Air Force (RAF), dated 29 November 1955, states:

During the 1957 trials, the RAF will gain invaluable experience in handling the weapons and demonstrating at first hand the effects of nuclear explosions *on personnel* and equipment.[10]

A meeting was held at the Atomic Weapons Research Establishment (AWRE) at Aldermaston on 15 July 1958. At the meeting, attended by Task Force Commander Air Vice Marshall John Grandy and Grapple scientific director Roy Pilgrim, service and medical representatives discussed whether, in the aftermath of Grapple Y, to revise radiological safety precautions for Christmas Island issued the previous March.[11]

Arguing against medical advice that blood tests should be carried out before the next round of Grapple Z tests, Air Commodore W.R. Stamm of the Princess Mary RAF Hospital objected to blood sampling being carried out on individual servicemen:

If the person was examined and found to be normal before posting to Christmas Island and who later developed leukaemia, it might be difficult to refute the allegations that this is due to radiation received at Christmas Island.[12]

The meeting finally agreed that men in the forward areas would be given blood counts, while a decision on the rest of the servicemen would be taken at a later date.

---

9   'Chief of Staff Committee—Atomic Weapons Trials: Reports by the Defence Research Policy Committee', memo labelled Top Secret, 20 May 1953, UK National Archives COS53/257. (Emphasis added.)
10 'Atomic weapons trials and training—Joint Operations', memo by Group Captain S.W.B. Menault, Royal Air Force, 29 November 1955. UK National Archives CMS.2680/55/DD Ops (AWT). (Emphasis added.)
11 Atomic Weapons Research Establishment (AWRE) Trials Planning Branch: *Radiological safety regulations for Christmas Island*, RSRC/58(1), March 1958. UK National Archives, item ES 12/360 (copy in author's files).
12 Cited in Catherine Trundle: 'Searching for Culpability in the Archives: Commonwealth Nuclear Test Veterans' Claims for Compensation', *History and Anthropology*, Vol. 22, No. 4, 2011, pp. 497–512.

The veterans' concern that they were being used as guinea pigs is not simply paranoia. During the Cold War, the United States conducted a number of human radiation experiments. Many of these activities were only revealed after the Clinton administration ordered a review in 1994 of human radiation studies conducted by the United States between 1944 and 1974. The review revealed 'the perhaps surprising finding that officials and experts in the highest reaches of the Atomic Energy Commission (AEC) and Department of Defence (DOD) discussed requirements for human experiments in the first years of the Cold War'.[13]

The review by the Advisory Committee on Human Radiation Experiments found that Cold War practices included experiments on prisoners and invalids, including plutonium injections during the Manhattan project:

> Sick patients were used in sometimes secret experimentation to develop data needed to protect the health and safety of nuclear weapons workers. The experiments raise questions of the use of sick patients for purposes that are not of benefit to them, the role of national security in permitting conduct that might not otherwise be justified, and the use of secrecy for the purpose of protecting the government from embarrassment and potential liability.[14]

During Operation Grapple, UK politicians and senior officers were reluctant to talk openly about radiation, fallout or potential hazards from the tests, cloaking their lack of accountability under the mantra of 'national security'. One example came just days before the first Grapple test on 15 May 1957. UK Minister for Supply Aubrey Jones drafted a brief statement for public release after the test, but sought approval of the text from the prime minister and other relevant ministers. The Cabinet agreed that the first paragraph was uncontroversial:

> The Minister of Supply, the Right Honourable Aubrey Jones has received a report from Air Vice Marshall W. E. Oulton, commander of the Task Force, and Mister W. R. J. Cook, scientific director of the trials, that the first explosion of a nuclear device in the present series took place today at altitude in the central Pacific.[15]

---

13 Advisory Committee on Human Radiation Experiments: *Executive summary and Guide to final report* (Department of Energy, Washington, 1995), p. 24. DOE/EH–96001171.
14 Ibid., p. 26. Not surprisingly, the review found that: 'Current policies do not adequately safeguard against the recurrence of the kinds of events we studied that fostered distrust.'
15 'Draft press announcement by the Ministry of Supply after round one', memo from Minister of Supply Aubrey Jones, 9 May 1957. CO1036/282.

However, the second sentence was more controversial and was eventually deleted:

> The order to proceed with firing was given only when the meteorological conditions had proved suitable and reconnaissance had confirmed that no ships or aircraft were in the position of danger.

Foreign Secretary Selwyn Lloyd argued in a memo:

> I do not consider that the second sentence is necessary. If by any chance an intruder has got in the way or there has been some accident, we had much better say afterwards that we took all reasonable steps. If no one had got in the way, it will be self-evident that we have taken all necessary precautions.[16]

Lloyd also amended the final sentence of the release, arguing that:

> I see no reason why in a communiqué of this sort we should get involved in statements about fallout.[17]

With the endorsement of Prime Minister Macmillan, one sentence in the draft statement was amended: 'scientific records are being collected for accurate evaluation to confirm previous estimates of fallout effects and weapons performance'. The final version, issued publicly the day after the test, simply read: 'Scientific records are being collected for accurate evaluation of the tests.'[18]

* * *

One common defence of the British authorities is that they were operating to standards of radiation safety known at the time. In the 1950s, guidelines for radiation exposure were set by the International Commission on Radiological Protection (ICRP), with the British Medical Research Council approving slightly different standards for the nuclear trials in 1952.

---

16 Memo from Foreign Secretary Selwyn Lloyd to Prime Minister Harold Macmillan, 11 May 1957. CO1036/282.
17 Ibid.
18 Memo from Prime Minister Harold Macmillan (signed P. de Zulueta), 14 May 1957. CO1036/282.

The levels of exposure that were regarded as acceptable in the 1950s are higher than those that are regarded as safe today. A common unit of measurement for exposure was the 'rad', though today the standards are measured in millisievert (mSv). In 1956, as the Grapple Task Force began its work, the ICRP's occupational limit was 3 mSv a week. In 1958, this was amended to 30 mSv a quarter and an annual average of 50 mSv (in comparison, today's occupational limits average 20 mSv per year and 1 mSv per year for the public).

As leading nuclear weapons campaigner Dr Tilman Ruff has noted:

> There has been a consistent trend over time that the more we know about radiation effects, the greater the evidence indicates those effects to be. Maximum permitted radiation dose limits have never been raised over time; they have always been lowered. For example, from 1950 to 1991, the maximum recommended whole-body radiation annual dose limits for radiation industry workers declined from approximately 250 to 20 mSv.[19]

In the 1950s, however, there was already extensive knowledge about the hazards of radiation amongst the scientific community who worked at the AWRE at Aldermaston. The understanding of risk was based on the work of British physicists and biologists over decades, studies conducted on Japanese people affected by the bombing of Hiroshima and Nagasaki and more recent information from US nuclear testing in the Marshall Islands, which was shared with Britain.

This information was also transmitted to British politicians and officials, who nonetheless went out of their way to minimise public knowledge of the risks, and adopted policies that deliberately reduced the safety margins for affected groups.

Later chapters will document the lived experience of service personnel and Gilbertese workers from Christmas Island, which shows they were placed in situations that increased the risk from hazardous ionising radiation.

For the moment, however, let us look at the many ways that the Grapple Task Force and the UK authorities in London deliberately changed proposed safety standards in order to maintain operational secrecy, increasing the risk for people living on Christmas Island and neighbouring atolls. These policy decisions included:

---

19   Tilman A. Ruff: 'Health implications of ionising radiation' in Peter van Ness and Mel Gustov (ed.): *Learning from Fukushima: Nuclear power in East Asia* (ANU Press, Canberra, 2017).

- setting standards for radiation protection with different safety limits for 'civilised' and 'primitive' peoples
- changing the boundaries of the danger area to exclude inhabited islands that came within the original zone
- maintaining a culture of secrecy that put mariners and flight crews at risk by hiding relevant safety information until the last minute.

* * *

In November 1956, Grapple Task Force Commander Air Vice Marshall Wilfred Oulton circulated a study to senior members of the Task Force outlining the 'Danger Area' to be promulgated for the Grapple tests. The purpose of the top secret document—issued to just 14 people—was to define an area to warn off shipping, aircraft or fishing vessels that might intrude in the test zone. The study sets 'several definitions of levels of radioactivity resulting from fall-out' and looks at the danger of an 'accidental surface burst'.[20]

The document reveals that the acceptable dosage of radiation was different for British personnel than for the islanders who lived on Christmas Island and on neighbouring inhabited atolls such as Fanning, Jarvis and Washington in the Line Islands or Tongareva (Penrhyn) in the Cook Islands. The dosage for so-called 'primitive peoples' exceeded safety levels set by international standards:

> For civilised populations, assumed to wear boots and clothing and to wash, the amount of activity necessary to produce this dosage is more than is necessary to give an equivalent dosage to primitive peoples who are assumed not to possess these habits. For such peoples the corresponding level of activity is called level B'. It is assumed that in the possible regions of fall-out at Grapple there may be scantily clad people in boats to whom the criteria of primitive peoples should apply.

---

20 'Danger Area', paper from Air Vice Marshall W.E Oulton, 19 November 1956, GRA/TS.1008/1/Air. Only 14 copies of the paper, marked 'Top Secret—Guard', were prepared for the British Army and Navy, the Colonial Office, Commonwealth Relations Office and other authorities. CO1036/280.

> It is desirable that the Declared Danger Area should at least enclose the whole region in which there is a possibility that level B' may be produced. The dosage at this level is about 15 times higher (for primitive peoples) than that which would be permitted by the International Commission on Radiological Protection.[21]

A meeting of officials held a week later to discuss the study agreed 'that the levels recommended by the ICRP would necessarily be exceeded' and that 'the proposed Grapple Danger Area is considerably larger than that prescribed for similar American tests'. Officials agreed to inform the minister, however, that:

> Independent authorities agree that … only very slight health hazard to people would arise, and that only to primitive peoples.[22]

The UK Government was well aware that the atmospheric testing of nuclear weapons would contribute to the spread of strontium-90. This radioactive isotope, with a half-life of 28.8 years, is produced by nuclear fission, and can be carried around the globe as the mushroom cloud extends to the stratosphere and high-level winds.

By the mid-1950s, UK authorities were aware of the role of nuclear testing in the spread of strontium-90. British researchers were involved in Project Sunshine, an initiative started by the US AEC in 1953 to measure the amount of strontium-90 in the bones and tissue of human beings.[23] More than 19 countries were involved in this gruesome project, which involved the use of cadavers—often babies and children—for testing, often without the knowledge or consent of their families. US doctors and scientists in the Marshall Islands also removed both decayed and healthy teeth from Rongelap children and sent them to New York for testing.[24]

From 1954, the US AEC, the UK Atomic Energy Authority (UKAEA) and the UK Ministry of Agriculture, Fisheries and Food began testing for strontium-90 in food, animals and plants. This was soon extended to human testing and the UKAEA tested bones from thousands of dead

---

21   Ibid., pp. 2–3.
22   Minutes of meeting on 27 November 1956, marked 'Top Secret—UK Eyes Only'. XY/181/024. CO1036/280.
23   RAND Corporation: *Project Sunshine—worldwide effects of Atomic Weapons* (RAND, Santa Monica, 6 August 1953). The RAND Corporation coordinated Project Sunshine across 19 countries, especially in Europe, North America and Oceania but extending as far as Chile, Brazil and Iran.
24   Barbara Rose Johnston and Holly Barker: *Consequential Damages of Nuclear War—the Rongelap report* (Left Coast Press, 2008), p. 158.

children. Samples from more than 6,000 people who died in Britain were tested between 1955 and 1970.[25] In Australia, the Atomic Weapons Tests Safety Committee began a program in 1957 to collect samples in Australia and the Australian-administered Territory of Papua and New Guinea. Bones and samples from more than 21,000 corpses—mainly babies— were incinerated and the ash sent to the United Kingdom for testing.[26]

On 18 January 1955, the US AEC held a conference to discuss how they could obtain more human material for analysis of strontium-90. US AEC commissioner Dr Willard Libby told the meeting:

> Human samples are of prime importance and if anybody knows how to do a good job of body snatching they will really be serving their country ... In 1953 we hired an expensive law firm to look up the law of body snatching. This compendium is available to you. It is not very encouraging. It shows you how very difficult it is going to be to do it legally.[27]

By 1957, however, the main concern of British officials was whether any public statements should acknowledge the reality that strontium-90 from nuclear testing was being spread over vast distances.[28] For example, when the Foreign Office had to develop a statement to reply to Japanese concerns over atmospheric testing, Foreign Office official H.C. Hainsworth noted that the statement should be edited to remove claims that there would be no effects from 'radioactive material':

---

25 The history of Project Sunshine in the United Kingdom and subsequent UKAEA strontium testing programs is documented in the *Redfern Inquiry into human tissue analysis in UK nuclear facilities* (Her Majesty's Stationery Office, London, 10 November 2010), Vol. 1, pp. 405–449. See also Sue Rabbitt Roff: 'Project Sunshine and the slippery slope: The ethics of tissue sampling for strontium-90', *Medicine, Conflict and Survival*, Vol. 18, Issue 3, 2002, pp. 299–310.

26 A report from the Australian Radiation Protection and Nuclear Safety Agency (ARPANSA) confirms that the agency has 21,830 records of people in Australia and Papua New Guinea from whom bone samples were taken—*Australian Strontium-90 Testing program 1957–78* (ARPANSA, Sydney, n.d.), p. 11.

27 The 1955 conference and the legality of sampling is discussed in the *Redfern Inquiry into human tissue analysis in UK nuclear facilities*, op. cit., pp. 410–411.

28 UK officials were well aware of the dangers of long-distance contamination, as the United States had conducted extensive weather and wind mapping during the Operation Castle series. See Thomas Kunkle and Byron Ristvet: *Castle Bravo: Fifty years of legend and lore*, US Defense Threat Reduction Agency (USDTRA) Defense Threat Reduction Information Analysis Center (DTRIAC) SR-12-001, January 2013, pp. 36–88.

The Lord President's Office have expressed some doubt about the phrase used in our Intel. and other public statements that 'firing will not take place under any conditions in which inhabited islands might be affected by radioactive material.' They point to the fact that there will be some increased deposit of strontium-90 in bone as a result of these tests.

We have argued that the sentence in context means that there will be no harmful effect and point to the fact that the Medical Research Council have said that strontium-90 have not yet reached a potentially dangerous level. In view of their doubts, we are trying to avoid using the phrase too frequently, until this point has been resolved.[29]

* * *

In December 1956, British officials prepared a guidance note with information about the safety precautions for Operation Grapple. This guideline states that 'no individual will be within a circle of 35 nautical miles radius of ground zero, i.e., the point immediately below the burst. Since the burst will take place at a considerable height there will be, assuming all goes as planned, no area of intense fallout'.[30]

As shown in the map above, the original version of the danger area was a 400-nautical-mile circle around the drop zone, the estimated area for a surface burst equivalent to 150 kilotons.[31] In reality, even this danger area was too limited. Many of the actual Grapple explosions were much larger than 150 kilotons (three of the tests had yields greater than 1 megaton, and the April 1958 Grapple Y test measured at nearly 3 megatons). Beyond this, prevailing winds tend to carry fallout in long plumes rather than neat circles. The British Government knew this very well, having studied data from recent US hydrogen bomb testing at Bikini and Enewetak atolls, which travelled far beyond 450 miles.

Despite these flaws in safety protection, London-based officials worked to further reduce the size of the danger zone to avoid potential political problems. Some officials argued that 'such an area is patently too large and has been reduced' according to some 'basic principles'. On this basis, the

---

29   Letter from H.C. Hainsworth, Foreign Office, London, to R.G. Elkington, 20 March 1957. CO1036/281.
30   'Safety precautions at Operation Grapple', memo from Ministry of Supply, marked 'Top Secret/ UK eyes only', 14 December 1956. CO1036/280.
31   The 1956 Grapple Task Force 'danger area' study (GRA/TS.1008/1/Air) and the draft of the map of the danger area can be found in the archives at Colonial Office CO1036/280.

400-mile circular boundaries of the danger area around Christmas Island and Malden Island were artificially redrawn with square boundaries—excluding neighbouring inhabited islands from the danger area.[32]

The Gilbert and Ellice Islands Colony (GEIC) Resident Commissioner then published a version of the map with rectangular rather than circular boundaries that were neatly drawn to exclude Washington, Fanning, Palmyra and Jarvis Island, all of which had small islander populations. The protests of businessman James Burns, detailed in Chapter 5, seem to have had a perverse effect, because islands artificially excluded from the danger area include all those where Burns Philp plantations were located.[33]

The archives also reveal extensive debate between the Grapple Task Force and officials from the Foreign Office, Colonial Office and Commonwealth Relations Office about the wording of the statement announcing the danger area. A key concern was the need to avoid any reference guaranteeing safety within the danger zone, given the potential for legal liability.

One example was a debate over whether to retain the same warnings as those issued before Operation Mosaic (the two atomic tests conducted in May–June 1956 off the Monte Bello Islands in Western Australia).

The Mosaic warning to mariners included the sentence: 'All possible precautions will be taken to ensure that no hazard to life or property will occur within the danger area.' Foreign Office officials argued for its inclusion in the Grapple danger area warning, 'on the basis that, while such a promise might be difficult to keep and might induce a false sense of security, its omission might be noticed by a legalistically inclined nation'.

In response, the Grapple Task Force Commander called for the deletion of the sentence in any leaflets distributed to mariners near Christmas Island. Oulton wrote to the British Admiralty that:

---

32 Thanks to Professor Wadan Narsey for this insight. See Wadan Narsey: 'Raw deal for nuke test Guinea Pigs', *Sunday Times* (Fiji), 13 June 1999.
33 A version of the final map, with rectangular boundaries and not 400-mile circles, is published in *Headquarters Information Note* No. 4, 18 January 1957. Gilbert and Ellice Islands Colony. F76/6/32 (1957). PAMBU document AU PMB Doc 493.

I feel it unwise to include the final sentence as was done in MOSAIC because it might lull intruders into a false sense of security and they might place too much reliance on my force for both observing them and guiding them out of harm's way.[34]

Given the 'slight chance of a mishap whereby one of the weapons does not burst until it hits the surface of the sea', the government agreed to declare a danger area on 1 January 1957, to come into force on 1 March.[35] Officials later postponed the announcement until 7 January, arguing that 'psychologically, it would be best to avoid such an announcement on New Year's Day'.[36]

The debate over warnings to mariners and aircraft was more than academic. Oulton's 1987 book *Christmas Island Cracker* opens with the story of the Liberian freighter *Effie*, which sailed into the danger zone around Malden Island and was on course to be near ground zero at the time of detonation. Oulton describes how he was dragged from his bed to the Joint Operations Centre to deal with the crisis:

> For a few seconds, he permitted himself the luxury of raging against that stupid bloody man the Secretary of State, who—despite a careful and logical explanation of the vital need for it—had refused to let the international warning notice to mariners be sent out in time to keep shipping clear of the designated danger area. Now, in consequence, they were all in this frightful and very dangerous situation. Blast the man![37]

Discussion of the danger area also involved analysis of the hazard to troops on Christmas Island if a plane carrying a hydrogen bomb were to crash on take-off. The AWRE joined with the Admiralty and the National Institute for Oceanography to model what would happen if there was a surface burst, rather than the expected air burst, of a weapon just off Christmas Island. The comforting outcome was that troops housed near the airfield would not need to worry about drowning in a tidal wave. They would already be dead from the heat and blast:

---

34   Letter from Air Vice Marshall W.E. Oulton, Task Force Grapple, to Admiral W.J. Yendell, Royal Navy, London 17 December 1956, GRA/TS.1008/1/Air.
35   Ibid.
36   Letter from D.V. Bendall, Foreign Office, London, to G.A.C. Witheridge, Ministry of Supply, 21 December 1956. CO1036/280.
37   Wilfred Oulton: *Christmas Island Cracker—an account of the planning and execution of the British thermonuclear bomb tests 1957* (Thomas Harmsworth, London, 1987), pp. 3–4.

INTERLUDE—ON RADIATION, SAFETY AND SECRECY

The conclusion reached is that, with the maximum yield to be expected under the conditions visualised, there is a danger of serious flooding for several miles along the coast near the explosion that would affect the air field in particular, but that this danger would be overwhelmed by the thermal dose received over the same area … this additional risk of flooding adds little to the other risks.[38]

* * *

In the early 1950s, the United States maintained an elaborate program for monitoring Soviet nuclear weapons trials, run by the US Air Force Office of Atomic Energy (AFOAT-1).[39] US officials soon realised that this system could also be extended to monitor the Grapple tests.

In early 1957, US AEC and military officials were privately debating how to evade the restrictions of the 1946 McMahon Act to allow collaboration between US and UK scientists on weapons development. One proposal was to use AFOAT-1 monitoring systems to share data:

> AFOAT-l proposes to give the UK copies of the recordings obtained on the UK weapons trials in the spring of 1957, as well as additional information concerning the equipment on which this data was obtained … The proposed exchange of information will permit acquisition by the US of important information relating to design and fabrication of UK nuclear weapons. AFOAT-l believes that the proposed exchange of information would not reveal important information or, in fact, any information concerning the design or fabrication of the nuclear components of US atomic weapons.[40]

At the same time, British authorities made preparations to establish their own independent radiation monitoring stations across the Pacific. A confidential briefing paper sent to the US Government noted:

> When the tests have taken place, samples of air will be taken, by arrangement with the authorities concerned, at Christmas Island, Canton Island, Penrhyn Island, Samoa, Tahiti, Fiji, New Caledonia, Adelaide,

---

38 'Christmas Island—effect of a tidal wave in the event of a crash in the sea and explosion on take-off', Ministry of Supply memo, marked 'Secret', 20 February 1957. CO1036/281.
39 For information on AFOAT-1 and US efforts to track radioactive fallout from Soviet tests, see Doyle L. Northrup and Donald H. Rock: 'The detection of Joe 1', *Studies in Intelligence*, Central Intelligence Agency (CIA), Vol. 10, Fall 1966 (declassified by the CIA in September 1995).
40 'Exchange of Information with the British in Connection with its Megaton Weapons Trials Scheduled for the Spring of 1957', Memorandum for the Chairman, Military Liaison Committee, AFOAT-l/SWTD, 11 January 1957. Marshall Islands Nuclear Documentation Database (MINDD).

Brisbane and it is hoped the Tuamotu group, to confirm that no contamination has in fact taken place. Samples of seawater will be taken with the same purpose.[41]

From February 1957, Hastings aircraft flew each week from Edinburgh Field in Salisbury, South Australia, to Christmas Island, stopping at Canton, Nadi and Amberley. After April 1957, the returning flights called 'in addition eastbound at [the airports of] Tontouta, New Caledonia and Faleolo, Western Samoa, to collect radiation measurement samples'.[42]

One complication for long-range monitoring of radiation was the secrecy surrounding the actual date of the next hydrogen bomb test. The UK MoD was reluctant to allow discussion of radiation protection outside protected, classified channels for fear that the date of the next test would be compromised.

UK officials were anxious that the logistics required in setting up these stations should receive no publicity. In response to possible public concern in Hawai'i, French Polynesia and New Caledonia about radioactive fallout, British officials prepared calming announcements that could be used if there were any questions:

> When announcing last June Her Majesty's Government's intention to hold trials of megaton weapons in 1957, Sir Anthony Eden said that the explosions would take place far from any inhabited island and that the tests would be so arranged as to avoid dangers to persons or property. The tests would be high airbursts, which would not involve heavy fallout.
>
> All safety precautions would be taken in the light of the Government's knowledge and of experience gained from the tests of other countries. Since then, detailed plans for the operation had been made with this as their basis and these assurances can be categorically reaffirmed. There is no question of Hawai'i being in the slightest danger. Firing will not take place under any conditions in which inhabited islands might be affected by radioactive material.[43]

---

41 'UK nuclear tests', advance copy of circular note to all heads of missions, from Foreign Office, London, to British Embassy, Washington, marked Confidential, 21 December 1956. CO1036/280.
42 Telegram no. 45 from Secretary of State for the Colonies to Mr John Gutch, Western Pacific Commissioner, 27 January 1957. CO1036/281.
43 Telegram from Foreign Office, London to British consulate, Honolulu, 7 January 1957. CO1036/280. The same telegram was sent to the British consulate in New Caledonia, substituting the relevant island for 'Hawaii'.

INTERLUDE — ON RADIATION, SAFETY AND SECRECY

After the first three tests, as the Grapple Task Force prepared to relocate the testing site from Malden Island to Christmas Island, they decided that there was a need to reconfirm approval for the network of radiation monitoring stations.

For Grapple X, Task Force Commander Wilfred Oulton sought the approval of the United States, Australia and New Zealand to establish a network of radiation measurement stations at various locations on their territory across the Pacific. These stations were proposed for Aitutaki and Penrhyn (Cook Islands), Nadi (Fiji), Brisbane (Australia), Canton Island, Kwajalein Atoll (Marshall Islands), Honolulu (Hawai'i), Malden Island and Fanning Island (GEIC), and Apia (Western Samoa).[44]

On 21 August, Squadron Leader R.J. Wilson, the RAF officer responsible for air operations, wrote to Foreign Office and Commonwealth Relations Office officials, seeking their support to negotiate the establishment of radiation monitoring equipment on US, British and Commonwealth soil:

> There is a requirement to take radiation measurements at various locations in the Pacific during the above operation. The equipment to be used and services required will be almost identical to those in Operation Grapple and the period of operation is expected to be from about mid-October until mid-December 1957. The locations concerned are as follows: Honolulu, Kwajalen [sic], Fanning Island, Canton Island, Penrhyn Island, Brisbane, Western Samoa, Fiji.[45]

For the first round of tests on Malden Island, the Task Force had set up radiation monitoring instruments in Fiji, at the Royal New Zealand Air Force (RNZAF) base at Nadi airport. As the second round of tests on Christmas Island was being prepared, London officials wrote to the Governor's office in Suva, seeking practical support from the local administration:

> In connection with the new operation, it is required to take radiation measurements, as before, in Fiji. The equipment to be used and the services required will be almost identical to those for Grapple and the period of operation is expected to be from about mid-October until mid-

---

44 'Outlying recording stations', letter from Air Vice Marshall Wilfred Oulton, Grapple Headquarters Task Force, London, 20 September 1957. GX/TS.3015/4/AIR. CO1036/283.
45 'Operation Grapple X—Long Distance Radiation Measurements' letter from RAF Squadron Leader R.J. Wilson, Headquarters, Task Force Grapple, to Foreign Office and Commonwealth Relations Office, 21 August 1957. GX/TS.3010/S/air. CO1036/282.

December 1957. Permission is requested to set up the equipment in Fiji and it is hoped that the persons who kindly gave the equipment a few minutes attention daily during Grapple will be willing to do so again.[46]

Fiji Governor Sir Ronald Garvey replied to London confirming that:

> We will willingly assist, but facilities for both radiation and microbarograph measurements were provided at Nadi airport from previous tests. Assume you will again make direct approach to New Zealand authorities.[47]

Once again, however, the demand for secrecy helped override the practicalities of establishing this network. The radiation monitoring station in Nadi would require the cooperation of RNZAF personnel, but London was reluctant to inform the colonials! A letter to the Governor of Fiji noted:

> In view of desire to maintain secrecy about forthcoming nuclear test to last moment, may be decided undesirable approach to New Zealand personnel at Nandi [sic] about operating this equipment. In that event only alternative will be to ask if district officer in area Nandi will operate the equipment.[48]

London's paranoia about operational secrecy was somewhat undercut by the realities of the coconut wireless in small island states, where information passes freely outside official channels. Locals were clearly aware that an operation was looming, given the constant stream of aircraft flying between Nadi and Christmas Island. As the Governor of Fiji informed London:

> You should know that the build-up of traffic through Nadi from Christmas Island is naturally causing some speculation.[49]

---

46 Telegram no. 209, marked 'Secret and personal' from the Secretary of State for the Colonies to Sir Ronald Garvey, Governor of Fiji, 23 August 1957. CO1036/282.
47 Telegram no. 224, from Sir Ronald Garvey, Governor of Fiji to Secretary of State for the Colonies, marked 'Immediate, secret and personal', 29 August 1957. CO1036/282.
48 Telegram no. 231 from Secretary of State for the Colonies to Sir Ronald Garvey, Governor of Fiji, 30 September 1957. CO1036/283. The constant travel of the district officers meant that the New Zealanders were eventually asked to fulfil this role.
49 Telegram no. 252 from Sir Ronald Garvey, Governor of Fiji to Secretary of State for the Colonies, 4 October 1957. CO1036/283.

INTERLUDE—ON RADIATION, SAFETY AND SECRECY

Similar requests were sent to the Western Pacific Commission to re-establish radiation monitoring systems on Canton Island, without telling the technicians who would use the equipment:[50]

> In view of instruction to keep fact and date of new operation secret as long as possible, not desirable for you to inform Cable & Wireless and civil aeronautics administration on Canton. Not necessary to do so in relation to Fanning, since now understood that meteorological station task force proposed to set up on Fanning will look after radiation measurement equipment installed there.[51]

Even though effective radiation monitoring would require extensive preparation and training of staff, secrecy overruled practicality. A letter from the MoD in September 1957 noted that:

> Discussions could take place with persons who are not covered by any security acts, either British or American. It has been ruled on the highest level of the fact that further megaton trials are also to take place and the date of the trial, and anything that might reveal this, is TOP SECRET. Consequently it is necessary to ensure that no breach of security occurs during these discussions, which could obviously have been avoided. I therefore suggest you should follow the Foreign Office suggestion and clear the necessary arrangements through channels which can handle classified information.[52]

---

50 Telegram no. 391 from the Secretary of State for the Colonies to Assistant High Commissioner, Western Pacific, 22 August 1957. CO1036/282.
51 Telegram no. 93 from Secretary of State for the Colonies to Resident Commissioner, Gilbert and Ellice Islands Colony, 2 September 1957. CO1036/282.
52 Letter from H.B. Macklen, Ministry of Defence to G.A.C. Witheridge, Ministry of Supply, 9 September 1957. CO1036/282.

7
The Chief Petty Officer—
Ratu Inoke Bainimarama

Fiji Royal Naval Volunteer Reserve (FRNVR) sailors aboard HMS *Warrior*, off Malden Island, May 1957

Chief Petty Officer Inoke Bainimarama is second from the left in the middle row, Acting Petty Officer Viliame Raikuna is second from the right. Viliame Cagilaba stands second from the left in the back row.

Source: Courtesy Cagicmudre Lewenilovo.

Ratu Inoke Bainimarama served in the Fiji Royal Naval Volunteer Reserve (FRNVR) during the Second World War, then joined the prison service in the 1950s. With rumours circulating among senior military personnel about the proposed tests on Christmas Island, he was recalled to duty.

With two NZ frigates scheduled to visit Suva en route to take part in Operation Grapple, there was an opportunity to provide training for young Fijian naval recruits. Needing a Fijian NCO to lead the personnel, Commander Stan Brown of the Fiji Royal Naval Volunteer Reserve (FRNVR) asked Bainimarama to act as an instructor to lead a contingent of 40 sailors on the training exercise.

It was agreed the sailors would travel to Christmas Island on the NZ frigates HMNZS *Pukaki* and HMNZS *Rotoiti*, before transferring to the British aircraft carrier HMS *Warrior* for further training. The Fijians would then return to Fiji aboard the NZ warships after the first series of Grapple tests.

Inoke Bainimarama soon realised why no one else was volunteering to lead the contingent:

> I was aware of what was going on and what the trip was about. I had to think deeply about this. I was already married with children and working. If something went wrong, my family would suffer. There was no insurance cover or anything for them. I knew all this. However, if I never volunteered, it would not do any good either. I would be made to look small and ridiculed for not accepting the challenge.[1]

In early 1957, the group of 40 sailors prepared for travel. With one sailor dropping out before departure, the final contingent of 39 men left Suva in March 1957, two months before the first nuclear test on Malden Island. The FRNVR contingent was split into two, with 19 men led by Chief Petty Officer Bainimarama on HMNZS *Pukaki*, and the other 20 on HMNZS *Rotoiti* led by Acting Petty Officer Viliame Raikuna.[2]

---

1   Interview with Ratu Inoke Bainimarama, Suva, Fiji, 1998, published in Losena Salabula, Josua Namoce and Nic Maclellan: *Kirisimasi—Na Sotia kei na Lewe ni Mataivalu e Wai ni Viti e na vakatovotovo iyaragi nei Peritania mai Kirisimasi* (Pacific Concerns Resource Centre, Suva, 1999), pp. 22–25.
2   Full details of the group can be found in Ministry of Fijian Affairs: 'Names of Fiji naval personnel who took part in the British nuclear testing at Christmas Island, in 1957 aboard *HMS Warrior*', 23 March 1990 (copy in author's files).

One NZ sailor recalled the sombre atmosphere for the departure from Suva:

> There were some sad scenes on the jetty, as friends and family bade the Fijian volunteers farewell. The Fiji military band did its best to raise the spirits of all and provide a cheerful atmosphere, but with little success.[3]

According to Bainimarama, most of the Fijian contingent had no knowledge that the operation involved the testing of nuclear weapons:

> One thing to note about the men we took with us on this trip was that the majority had just left school. There were not enough jobs around, and they would take whatever job came their way. When it was said that they would get the chance to go overseas and travel on a British navy ship, they were very eager and excited to go. They had no idea of what lay ahead …
>
> While the training was going on, the boys began to realise that there was going to be a nuclear test. Some came to me asking questions. I said: 'Weren't you told in Fiji?' They replied: 'No! We were just told that we were going on the ship for exercises.'
>
> I said: 'This is the military. Whatever order is given, no matter what happens to you, it's an order. I am sorry.' Some of the boys cried. You know many of them were just kids. Many were under 19 years of age. Think of it—they just finished high school, and this was the first job ever for them to do. They were very innocent.[4]

Other members of this contingent have confirmed that they were unaware of the purpose of Operation Grapple. Viliame Cagilaba had left a government job to join the Navy for the training exercise. As an Able Seaman (FRNVR 1189), he travelled to Christmas Island on HMNZS *Rotoiti*:

> I did not know that this trip to Christmas Island was to do with the testing of the hydrogen bombs. When we went there, all we knew was that it was for naval training—learning everything about sailing and navigation; training on the use of guns, all different kinds of weapons. We got to like this training trip very much, because we saw and experienced new things. However, when we reached Christmas Island and boarded *HMS Warrior*, we came to hear of a different story altogether. We were taken there just for the testing of the hydrogen bomb.

---

3   Gerry Wright: *We Were There* (Zenith Print, New Plymouth, n.d.), p. 45.
4   Interview with Ratu Inoke Bainimarama, Suva, Fiji, 1998, for *Kirisimasi*, op. cit.

> We were lectured on the hydrogen bomb and how dangerous it was to human life. We continued to be told about the bomb—how it was conceptualised, planned and made, and the possible effects of the bomb on our bodies if it was detonated on Christmas Island. We then realised there the dangers that we were facing. After the training, we were not sure if we would have to face this terrible thing.
>
> Before going, we were never told anything, because it was the army. Whenever one becomes a soldier, one signs away his life and everything to the army. If there was an order that was not right, you just obeyed first. You follow the order and you then complain later. You don't disobey orders straight on, or you will suffer, because you will be court-martialled. If an order came to do something, you follow and do it, even if you think it's not right.[5]

Susitino Lasagavibau (FRNVR 1221) also travelled to Christmas Island with the first naval contingent, working in the sickbay:

> I believe if we were told about this terrible weapon, none of us would have gone. We had not experienced or done anything like this before. All we had learnt and had knowledge about was to do with the navy— how to use basic weapons. But not this. We were never told about this very dangerous weapon.[6]

* * *

In total, from June 1956 until June 1957, 3,515 British personnel were deployed for the initial three Grapple tests on Malden Island. This included 1,722 sailors from the Royal Navy (RN); 638 soldiers from the British army; 1,038 aircrew from the Royal Air Force (RAF); and 117 scientific and technical personnel from the Atomic Weapons Research Establishment (AWRE). These UK forces were complemented by personnel from the Royal New Zealand Navy (RNZN) and Royal New Zealand Air Force (RNZAF), the RFMF and the FRNVR.[7]

During their deployment, the Fijian contingent witnessed the first three nuclear tests, conducted above Malden Island: the Grapple 1 'Short Granite' atomic test on 15 May 1957, Grapple 2 'Orange Herald' on 31 May and Grapple 3 'Purple Granite' on 19 June.

---

5   Interview with Viliame Cagilaba, Suva, Fiji, 1998, for *Kirisimasi*, op. cit., pp. 29–32.
6   Interview with Susitino Lasagavibau, Suva, Fiji, 1998, for *Kirisimasi*, op. cit. pp. 34–35.
7   Data from 'Number of men involved in each operation, by service or employer', Table A4.1, Appendix 4 in Lorna Arnold: *Britain and the H-Bomb* (Palgrave Macmillan, London, 2001), p. 241.

For each test, elements of the naval task force would sail south from Christmas Island to monitor the test off Malden Island. The NZ frigates were deployed to monitor the weather and gather radiation samples. The Fijian sailors were allocated a range of tasks aboard HMS *Warrior*, which served as Forward Area Control Ship for the trials and the Task Force flagship for the vessels stationed off Malden Island during the first series.

As detailed in Chapter 9, the Fijian contingent were visited by FRNVR Commander Stan Brown and high chief Ratu Penaia Ganilau, to witness the 'Orange Herald' test on Malden Island in June 1957.

Viliame Cagilaba recalled the routine on D-day for each test:

> We sailed towards Malden Island about 160 miles from Christmas Island where this bomb was to be dropped. When the day of the test came, no one knew beforehand. There was only a day left before we knew. The daily routine orders came and 'Today is D-Day' was written on it. That meant the bomb was to explode on that day.
>
> Three planes brought in the bomb, coming all the way from Christmas Island. They circled the target area where the bomb was to be dropped three times. On the third run we were told to sit with our backs to the area where the bomb was to be dropped. The scientists were also there: those scientists closest to the bomb were about 15 to 16 miles from the target area.
>
> We were all dressed up and ready. No part of your body was to be seen or any clothing to be torn, because you might burn your skin from the heat of the bomb. You wore goggles because of the light given off by the bomb. We then sat down with our backs towards the target area. We were also facing the wind. They called out for us to shut our eyes. We then pressed the palms of our hands against our closed eyes. You should not open your eyes or see any bit of light.
>
> When the bomb dropped, it was being dropped behind us. It took about one minute for the bomb to drop from the sky and reach ground level. Then just before it blew, they called out 10, 9, 8, 7, 6, 5, 4, 3, 2, 1. They called out 'The bomb has exploded!' At that instant we were not able to hear anything. We only felt the heat brush past our backs.[8]

---

8   Interview with Viliame Cagilaba, Suva, Fiji, 1998, for *Kirisimasi*, op. cit.

Able Seaman Filipe Rogoyawa (FRNVR 1178) also recalled the fierce heat, even miles from the detonation:

> We could feel the heat on our backs when the bomb exploded. I knew how hot the sun feels, but the heat given off by the bomb was different. The colour of the explosion was really terrifying. What if this bomb had dropped on land? None of us who went there would have survived.[9]

The sailors aboard HMS *Warrior* were issued with white overalls and protective gear to avoid flash burns from the heat of the detonation, as Inoke Bainimarama recalled:

> We had this thing on called flash gear. You know, it covered our whole bodies. It covered our whole face. There were goggles provided, hand gloves, boots, there was nothing left out. We wore this thing, then they gave us a badge each. They said if anything happened to us this badge will be useful. If our bodies were to vaporise, this badge would not. You know after they said this, who would not be unsettled. I was already mature, so if something happened to one of the boys, or if one of them died, then I would be responsible.

Viliame Cagilaba also reported that he was issued with overalls, gloves and goggles and given a safety briefing:

> Not any part of your body was to be exposed. The goggles were so weak because we could see the sun with them. It was like looking at the moon at night. When you are wearing all these things, you don't know where the other Fijians are, which one was a white man or Englishman. You could not see anyone's skin. If someone spoke to you in Fijian, you could then know that that person was Fijian. However, you still couldn't tell who you were speaking to. Not a single part of your body was visible.

> Included in the clothing we wore was a gas mask, cup and your lunch pack. This was a precaution in case they mistimed the bomb. If it exploded too close to us, then we would have to escape below deck. This aircraft carrier had nine decks and you were supposed to run to the 9th deck.[10]

Later Fijian naval contingents deployed on Christmas Island were not given the same protective gear. Electrical Mechanic Epi Ratu (FRNVR 1257), who witnessed the Grapple Z tests when he served on Christmas Island in late 1958, noted:

---

9   Interview with Felipe Rogoyawa, Suva, Fiji, 1998, for *Kirisimasi*, op. cit., p. 32.
10 Interview with Viliame Cagilaba, Suva, Fiji, 1998, for *Kirisimasi*, op. cit.

We who were together between '58 and '59 did not really have any protective clothing. In the navy we wore long sleeved blue shirts and dark blue long trousers. That was all. There was nothing else to protect us like a safety helmet or something to protect our ears. We wore the ordinary clothes that we wore every day while on Christmas Island.[11]

* * *

Interviewed decades after the event, the Fijian naval veterans had vivid memories of the day of the Malden Island tests. Even the older leader of the contingent, Inoke Bainimarama, acknowledged the stress of sitting on the deck of the warship, backs to the blast, waiting for the detonation:

Every time I recall this moment, I feel afraid. You know, when you go to war, you fight. You prepare yourself and then you fight. If you are shot, you die. Here you do nothing. You go there and sit down waiting to die.

Then they called that the bomb had been dropped. Ten seconds, think of it. We had our backs to the bomb, our eyes pressed by our palms and we bowed down. No part of our body was exposed. This person called out the numbers. Counting started from 10, 9, 8, 7 … If the count went a bit longer, a person could have fainted. This is the truth.[12]

Susitino Lasagavibau echoed the same feeling of suspense as the minutes ticked down to the detonation:

I used to joke a lot with one guy from Rewa. We used to joke and tease each other a lot. However, on that morning when I spoke to him, he was wide eyed and never spoke back. I had the same kind of scared feeling he had. We were not sure of what really was going to happen …

The plane that was carrying the bomb was listening for instructions and orders from another plane that was leading it. Then the orders came, about one minute before the explosion. They counted the seconds from 60 to 5, 4, 3, 2, 1. Then they announced that this dangerous thing had gone off.

We were all silent, listening. After a little while, we heard the loud bang. Then the order came allowing us to take our goggles off and turn back to look towards the bomb. After the bomb went off, there was a blackish red

---

11   Interview with Epi Ratu, Suva, Fiji, 1998, for *Kirisimasi*, op.cit., pp. 42–43.
12   Interview with Ratu Inoke Bainimarama, Suva, Fiji, 1998, for *Kirisimasi*, op. cit.

cloud like the flames from burning firewood. Our backs were now turned towards the land. At this stage, a British plane flew through the cloud then on towards Britain.

After the explosion we sailed away, but after about 20 hours, we came back to the site on the orders of those in charge. I can remember seeing some dead fish on the sea's surface. If the distance were a bit closer, we would have suffered the same fate as the fish.[13]

Following the three tests on Malden Island, the Fijian contingent performed a traditional *veiqaravi vakavanua* (ceremony of thanks) for Commodore Hicks and the ship's company of HMS *Warrior*, then returned to Suva aboard the *Pukaki*.

Later in the year, more Fijian sailors were based onshore at HMS *Resolution*, the name used for the military encampment situated at Port London, on the north-west side of the island, approximately 43 kilometres from the point of detonation.

Another small contingent of Fijian sailors spent five weeks at HMS *Resolution* in late 1957, without witnessing a nuclear test. Captain Stan Brown and Chief Petty Officer Sakaraia Tabua led the contingent of a dozen men, who were sent to Christmas Island en route to Singapore 'to collect and effect delivery of the Fiji governor's new yacht, an 85-foot, twin screw vessel'.[14]

Peni Kolikata (FRNVR 1267) was just 17 years old:

> Our group was not there for the tests. You see, the government was going to get a new ship for the Governor of Fiji. A ship had been ordered from Singapore called the *Ramarama*. The navy was given the job of delivering the ship to Fiji. We were picked for this task. We left Fiji on a plane destined for Singapore. However, we had to stop over at the military base on Christmas Island. Unfortunately there was a delay in the building of the ship *Ramarama*. We had to stay on Christmas Island until the ship was ready. We ended up staying on the island for two months.[15]

---

13 Interview with Susitino Lasagavibau, Suva, Fiji, 1998, for *Kirisimasi*, op. cit.
14 *Headquarters Information Note*, No. 2, 3 January 1958, Gilbert and Ellice Islands Colony. F 76/6/32 (1958). PAMBU document AU PMB DOC 493. The full list of participants in this jaunt can be found in Ministry of Fijian Affairs: 'Names of naval personnel of the Fiji Royal Naval Volunteer Reserve (FRNVR) who served ashore at Christmas Island from 23/12/57 to 23/2/58 before being transferred to Singapore to take MV Ramarama back to Fiji', Appendix 2, 23 March 1990 (copy in author's files).
15 Interview with Peni Kolikata, Suva, Fiji, 1998, for *Kirisimasi*, op. cit., pp. 38–40.

The group was based at the Port Camp between 23 December 1957 and 3 February 1958, while waiting for the next available ship to carry them to Singapore. Excused from standard duties, Kolikata recalls spending many days fishing in the waters of Christmas Island:

> Fish, there was plenty of fish. While we were there, we ate a lot of fish. There were a lot of *lairo* [land crabs] which we caught and ate. Those of us who ate the fish got poisoned once. I think it was to do with the contaminated sea, but it could have been due to our greediness as we caught and ate too much fish.
>
> Other than fish poisoning, we did not suffer from any illness. The only exception was Tevita Matakitoga. After some time on the island, Tevita began to have an unusual behaviour. He got sick. It was not clear what kind of sickness he had. His medical report could not clearly say what he suffering from. He was like brain dead. In his room he used to be seen sitting and staring. All he did was sitting down and staring ahead. He never said a word. He later died when we returned to Fiji.[16]

In the end, the contingent was transported back to Suva on the only available transport:

> We ended up coming back to Fiji after spending two months there. We went from Christmas Island to Fiji, then to Hong Kong and then to Singapore. We still had to finish our job—which was delivering the Governor's boat, the *Ramarama*.

Viliame Cagilaba witnessed three nuclear tests during his deployment in 1957, but recognised his service to Empire was part of a much larger project:

> In 1957, I witnessed three explosions. I understand that during that time, there were tensions, disagreements and disputes between the big nations over nuclear weapons. At that time Russia did not want to reduce its weapons and the size of its army. I still remember that when the first bomb on Christmas Island exploded, within days Russia agreed to reduce its military and nuclear weapons. The same with the other big nations. This enabled a reduction of weapons. This is one area where the British tests were good.

---

16   Ibid.

However, there is one area where the British government failed. Since Britain used people this way when their lives were at risk, it should give compensation for the damage done to the soldiers and servicemen. It was a time of colonial rule with Fiji under British protection. The British government should provide monetary compensation to all servicemen who served on Christmas Island during the hydrogen bomb tests.[17]

Decades later, however, it became clear that the British Government had kept little information that could be used for ongoing monitoring of the health of the Fijians who'd joined the British naval operations. For example, Cagilaba reported that there had been radiation monitoring of the initial Fijian contingent on board the HMS *Warrior*:

> We wore a film badge that would be returned to the scientists after a bomb was tested. This would help the scientists find out if we had been exposed to radiation or not. We always returned this to the scientists.[18]

The British Government, however, did not retain any documentation that could confirm whether any Fijian personnel were exposed to hazardous levels of radiation. Years later, responding to parliamentary questions in the House of Commons in 2007, the Under-Secretary for Defence Derek Twigg confirmed:

> The Ministry of Defence holds limited information on Fijian nationals who were present at the British nuclear tests in the Pacific. Records held by the Atomic Weapons Establishment (AWE) contain four pages listing the names of Fijian nationals involved, and the tests for which they were present. No radiation doses were recorded for any Fijian national.[19]

The UK authorities claim that only a small number of service personnel received small doses of radiation and the vast majority of troops deployed on Christmas Island were not exposed to hazardous levels of radiation. Despite this, many veterans who witnessed nuclear tests in the Line Islands developed significant illnesses and have had to live with this uncertainty for decades.

---

17 Interview with Viliame Cagilaba, Suva, Fiji, 1998, for *Kirisimasi*, op. cit.
18 Ibid.
19 UK House of Commons Hansard official report, 29 October 2007, col. 979W.

8
The sailor—Paul Ah Poy

Paul Ah Poy (standing left) and sailors from HMS *Warrior* and HMNZS *Rotoiti*, May 1957
Source: Courtesy Paul Ah Poy.

Today, Paul Ah Poy often wears sunglasses to ward off the glare of the sun and bright lights. They also hide the terrible sadness in his eyes that comes from seeing his contemporaries slowly dying off, one by one, while waiting for the British Government to address their claims.

Paul was born on 1 June 1936 at Namatakula on the Coral Coast of Fiji's main island, Viti Levu. His father came from Canton (Guangdong), China, while his mother was born in Nawaisomo village on the island of Beqa. A veteran of the Fiji Royal Naval Volunteer Reserve (FRNVR) and a merchant seafarer for most of his life, Paul spent many years on the ocean. Today, he is a landlubber, living in retirement with his wife in Suva, the capital of Fiji.

Still active at 81, he is President of the Fiji Nuclear Veterans Association and one of the leading campaigners seeking justice for the survivors of the British nuclear testing program. He speaks quietly, but with understated passion, about the legacy of his service on Christmas Island, which began months before the first British personnel arrived.

Paul's life as a sailor began in 1955, when he joined the navy at age 18:

> I had just come out of school. There was not much jobs around and they were recruiting at that time for the Malayan campaign. We were excited to be able to travel overseas, so quite a few of us came up and joined the Navy—that was back in 1955.
>
> In 1956, the New Zealand survey ship HMNZS *Lachlan* called into Suva to pick up a couple of scientists who'd flown in from Britain. There was room for two extra sailors. Together with another Fijian sailor Luke Qereqeretabua, I was one of those that got picked up to travel on the *Lachlan* to go to Christmas Island for the survey in preparation for the nuclear testing program.
>
> I was an engineer rating, so I worked in the boiler room until we got to Christmas Island. When we arrived, I was given the opportunity to go onto the island. Since I was the youngest on the motorboat, I was the first one to jump onto dry land and I was quite happy about that.[1]

Given his experience on the *Lachlan*, Paul was chosen to join the second FRNVR naval contingent posted to Christmas Island in 1957.[2] Over the next 15 months, he witnessed seven nuclear detonations during Operation Grapple:

---

1   This chapter is based on a series of interviews and discussions with Paul Ah Poy over 20 years, between 1997 and 2017. Unless otherwise noted, the direct quotes are drawn from an interview in Suva in November 2016. For further details about Paul's history, see Losena Salabula, Josua Namoce and Nic Maclellan: *Kirisimasi—Na Sotia kei na Lewe ni Mataivalu e Wai ni Viti e na vakatovotovo iyaragi nei Peritania mai Kirisimasi* (Pacific Concerns Resource Centre, Suva, 1999), pp. 25–28.
2   Statement of Paul Ah Poy's service history, dated 27 March 1998, in author's files.

8. THE SAILOR—PAUL AH POY

Twenty sailors and 40 soldiers in our draft flew out of Nadi on RAAF [Royal Australian Air Force] Dakota and Hastings aircraft, stopping overnight at Canton Island, then on to Christmas Island the next day. On arrival, we were all billeted at HMS *Resolution*, the naval establishment at the Port Camp, also known as Port London. The soldiers—all sappers—joined their colleagues who were engaged in the unloading of ships.

I was posted with three other ratings to the Landing Craft Squadron of the Royal Marines, to man a lighter engaged in ferrying cargo from ships to the port, where they were unloaded by soldiers or civilian labourers. We would go from the dock to the supply ship anchored out in the harbour. There would be soldiers and civilians on the ship to load the craft and we would take them back onshore. Mostly, it would take one whole day for a load or maybe two loads. We'd be transporting food, vehicles and some scientific stuff—we don't know what was in the boxes. Day in and day out, we had the weekend off and then started again on the Monday.

During my first six months on the island, I witnessed three hydrogen bomb tests. After my first six months, I was promoted as coxswain and they asked me if I'd like to go for R and R leave in Hawai'i or Fiji. I chose Fiji because my parents were still alive. I came back home in January 1958 on the RFA [Royal Fleet Auxiliary] tanker *Wave Master*. I was home for two weeks, then I flew back alone on a RAAF Dakota via Canton Island.

I stayed on Christmas Island for the whole period till the completion of the testing program. I was promoted to Leading Mechanic Engineer on arrival and posted back to the lighter *Prowler* as its coxswain. I witnessed another four bomb tests during my last six months of service on the island.

* * *

In the early days of Operation Grapple, most troops at Port Camp and Main Camp were living under canvas, using rudimentary sanitation and mess facilities. Task Force Commander Wilfred Oulton acknowledged the rough living conditions:

> The tented accommodation was fine although Spartan; the food was pretty bad, understandably so in the early days before cold storage became available; but the flies were appalling. There were innumerable dead land crabs everywhere, which supported a large fly population, and any gash left lying around the cook house or mess tents immediately brought a great increase in the nuisance.[3]

---

3 Wilfred Oulton: *Christmas Island Cracker—an account of the planning and execution of the British thermonuclear bomb tests 1957* (Thomas Harmsworth, London, 1987), p. 160.

The military's solution was to order an Auster aircraft from England, equipped with agricultural pesticide spraying equipment. The plane, known as *Flit* after the popular brand of insecticide, was used to douse the whole encampment and airfield every day with DDT. One British veteran recalled:

> We called the pilot 'Flight Sergeant Flit.' He was so bored with the job, that if he saw anyone out in the open, he used to dive-bomb them just for a distraction from his normal routine. A DDT soaking could have not done anyone any good.[4]

Paul Ah Poy vividly recalls the experience, worrying about the long-term health effects:

> During my time on Christmas Island, we had a problem with flies, I think because the population had to increase to many thousands of men. At one time, they got about 200 soldiers to spray the plantation among the tents and everything to try and get rid of the flies.
>
> You know, when you went to have your dinner, I'd look at my soup full of flies and I'd stand up and throw it away. The second day, still the same. The third day, I followed what the other troops were doing: take out all the flies, then drink your soup, otherwise you'd starve.
>
> So to solve the problem, they got a light plane, a propeller driven plane from the UK and it was to spray the island five days a week. When they spray the island, I mean everything on the island: truck, man, woman, children. I got sprayed by DDT five days a week. Most of us didn't know what was coming down, whether it was mist or light rain, but it was DDT—a banned substance right now. So apart from the nuclear weapon, the radiation, we got DDT added onto it.

Billie Burgess, one of two Women's Voluntary Service (WVS) volunteers providing social services on the island (see Chapter 10), also reported the drenching of her sister with DDT:

> As we are writing this, we are being drenched through the gauze windows of our bungalow with DDT spray. This is very necessary to keep down the breeding of the houseflies and often proves very amusing. The other day Mary was bringing a cup of tea round to the club room from the NAAFI

---

4   Letter to the author from P.D. Waltham, Hampshire, United Kingdom, 30 December 1998 (copy in author's files).

[Navy, Army and Air Force Institutes], when she was caught by an Auster which was flying overhead spraying the whole area with DDT. She was well sprayed and alas, the tea was ruined.[5]

Being dosed with DDT was not the only health hazard.[6] Limited protective gear was issued to some troops for the early tests (such as white cotton suits to reduce the risk of flash burns). Most veterans testified, however, that they never received protective gear, and served their term wearing standard army boots, shorts and shirts.

After the tests were relocated to Christmas Island in mid-1957, inhabitants of the island faced a number of pathways for the ingestion or inhalation of radioactive isotopes that might later contribute to illness. After each nuclear test, Fijian military personnel were involved in clean-up operations, such as disposing of the many birds that were maimed, blinded or killed by the nuclear explosions.

As Paul explains, the Fijians often ignored British regulations and caught seafood that may have been contaminated:

> We would spend the weekend fishing, catching lobsters, land crabs etc. Fresh drinking water we collected from the abandoned water tanks—probably contaminated by all the past tests. Most of the stones we stepped on turned into ashes.
>
> The poor sea birds flew into what was left of the trees or the side of buildings, as most were blind. At our base, we had a trawler which would go out daily to trawl for fish. All the fish they caught would be tested on a machine. If they were clean they go to the pot, the contaminated ones would be taken away.
>
> All our water was brought in by tanker from Hawai'i and then they shipped in evaporators from the United Kingdom. We Navy guys would run the evaporator converting seawater into freshwater. I can tell you, we were churning out tonnes of fresh water from seawater, but how about the radioactive material? It probably went into the tanks with the freshwater.

---

5   Billie Burgess: *WVS Club Christmas Island newsletter*, January 1957 (copy in author's files).
6   Unlike most medical authorities, the UK Government denies that constant spraying with DDT is bad for the health, even though the Ministry of Defence (MoD) has not undertaken any specific assessment of the risks associated with the use of DDT in nuclear testing. See statement by Secretary of State for Defence Derek Twigg, 'Nuclear Weapons: Testing', UK House of Commons, Hansard official report, 29 October 2007, col. 977W.

> I wasn't really bothered about it, because I told my colleagues 'don't drink any water, the water is no good for you'. Beer is cheap on the island, you pay four pennies for one can. Maybe that's why I'm still alive today.

The UK Government has long argued that most military personnel were located too far away from the actual detonations to be exposed to hazardous levels of radiation. Despite this, Paul Ah Poy and other military personnel were engaged in duties that increased the risk of exposure. On one occasion, he helped to dump drums of radiation-contaminated waste into the ocean:

> One clear sunny day, there wasn't much traffic in the port area. A huge truck arrived alongside our vessel. The normal stevedores did not load the special cargo into the *Prowler*, our lighter. Some Air Force personnel did the loading supervised by a Royal Navy Sub-Lieutenant. My three crew and I gave a hand and I happened to sit on one of the 44-gallon drums, after all 60 drums were loaded.
>
> All of a sudden a Marine Sergeant came and pushed me off the drum and we both fell down on the deck. I thought he was only playing. As we got up, he took me to one side and told me: 'Do you know what's your cargo, son?' I answered: 'No Sarg.' He told me: 'Since you are the Skipper of this tub, I'll let you in on what you are about to do. Don't ever sit or touch those drums, they contain nuclear waste. You will take it out to sea and dump them over the sides when we were about five miles west of the island.'
>
> The Navy officer came to me and said: 'What say, Cox'n, are we far enough?' I answered that we were beyond the four miles limit and it's time we head for home. He said: 'Right ho, boys!' The RAF boys and our crew started rolling the drums over the side and we returned to port.

* * *

After the three unsuccessful tests on Malden Island, operations were relocated to Christmas Island, for the Grapple X test of November 1957, the first truly thermonuclear detonation. The build-up for Grapple X involved 2,338 personnel (597 sailors from the Royal Navy [RN]; 625 soldiers from the British army; 1,009 RAF aircrew and 107 Atomic Weapons Research Establishment [AWRE] scientific and technical personnel).

8. THE SAILOR — PAUL AH POY

Grapple X brought new routines for the naval personnel. A preliminary duty was to move the Gilbertese labourers and their families from their homes onto ships of the Grapple flotilla (precautions that were abandoned for later tests during the Grapple Z series in 1958). Meanwhile, thousands of military personnel would be lined up, backs to the blast, as Paul details:

> On a normal test day, weather permitting, all Gilbertese civilians would be loaded on a Landing Craft Mechanised [LCM] and transported to a Landing Ship Tank [LST] anchored off the island. Its bow doors would open to let the loaded LCM to enter its flooded hold. They would remain there and watch movies until the test was completed.
>
> With us service men, it was a different story. We would all get up at 4 am and were told to have an early breakfast, because there was quite a few of us: 400 of us at the Port Camp and maybe about 3,000 up at the Main Camp. After breakfast we moved to the assembly area by 5.30.
>
> For some tests, we sailors would all board about eight LCM with motor running—50 men to a LCM. The loudspeakers in the port area would be issuing orders. We could hear the Valiant bomber jet engines being warmed up about 10 miles away at the airfield.
>
> The announcement would tell us that the bombers were taking off, that was the crucial time. If an accident might happen, we would all proceed full speed to sea towards the windward side of the crash area. I wouldn't like to think of what might happen, had there been an accident.
>
> We would then be ordered to disembark once the white-painted Valiants were in the air. First of all they'd call out our names to check that we were all there, all present. There would be no officers at all or any of the civilian scientists around at that time. We were told to sit down and wait for the time to be told to be ready. Sitting on the beach, there were 400 of us, soldiers, sailors and marines, and we would all sit down and then listen to the music from the loudspeakers. At about 7 am, we could clearly see two bombers in the sky about 10 miles away.

With loudspeakers broadcasting the communications between the command centre and the Valiant aircraft carrying the bomb, the waiting troops prepared for the moment of detonation. Even decades after the tests, the awesome power of the detonation still resonates in Paul's description:

I was afraid, really afraid. I shut my eyes and pressed my palms really tight into my eyes. Then they'd say 'get ready'. We were already very quiet and they'd count down from 10 to 1. When they got to 3, 2, 1, they'd say 'bomb gone' and then 'flash'.

At that time, some of us would open our eyes just slightly and we could see the bones through the palm of our hands. Then we close our eyes quickly again. We were all scared, and we'd feel the heat behind us. We were squirming, but were told 'keep still!' How can you keep still when you can feel the heat? It was just like someone holding a blowtorch just behind you. I was still squirming, then I feel the heat start to disappear, then a voice said 'shockwave' and oh boy, boom! There was a huge booming noise.

We were told 'open your eyes'. Then we could see the sand and the stone that went up in the air with the first shockwave. Before it came down again, the repeating shockwaves start to come in. They met the other shockwave and the stone and dust and pebble and sand went up while the top layer was coming down.

After the shockwave, we were told 'stop talking and stand up slowly'. We stood up slowly. 'Now turn around really slowly.' Some of us were scared to turn around, but I did follow the orders. Oh boy, you can look up skywards now. Look in the sky, there was no more sun. Instead there was a big round, like a full moon but quite huge, covering half of the sky.

To me it looked really beautiful. It looked golden, like looking at the moon. Then all of a sudden, it turned into a fireball and later into an ice cream cone, shaped like an ice cream cone with cream dripping down the side, then into a giant mushroom cloud.

Then two Canberra fighters would fly and scoop samples from the side of the mushroom and then keep on flying all the way to the UK to deliver the test samples within 24 hours. They were refuelled in the air by airborne tankers.

Paul explains that, at the time, the FRNVR sailors had limited knowledge of the potential hazards of radioactive fallout. The Fijian language even uses the term *kasigaga* (poisonous gas) rather than radiation:

We didn't know what was the meaning of radiation or nuclear testing or what not. I don't think that any place in the South Pacific at that time had a word for radiation or for nuclear weapons or atomic things like that. We don't know nothing at all.

8. THE SAILOR—PAUL AH POY

During the Grapple Y test in April 1958, 23 Fijian sailors were stationed at HMS *Resolution* at Port London. Nearly 60 years after the test, Paul clearly described his memories of the heat and blast, as the 3-megaton thermonuclear weapon exploded over the south-east corner of the atoll:

> I remembered vividly the month of April 1958. We were told that the next test would be the last of the dirty bombs and it was going to be a really big one. Oh boy, it really looked dirty, with its big black mushroom cloud before it turned white.
>
> At that time we could feel the wind start to blow and the clouds were really looking nasty, all black. Then the voice said 'it's going to rain, run for your life, run and take cover inside your tents!' Oh boy, we were not waiting for another order, we start to run. We ran for our tents and dove inside and we could hear the rain coming down. On Christmas Island it never rains, but that day it rained.
>
> We ran out, because we wanted to have a bath in fresh water and we opened our mouths to the sky. I took off my shirt, kept on my pants, shoes. Some only in underwear, some took off their underwear. Black rain was coming, it was really nasty when you look up to the sky, it was really black. When it was coming down, the rain didn't look like water from a tap, it looked quite different.
>
> They didn't tell us not to drink the water. I did—I opened my mouth and drank all the water I can before I went back inside. We stayed outside as long as we can because we were scared that someone might come and order us to go back into our tents.

* * *

Today, aged 81, Paul has a number of health problems that he attributes to exposure to radiation at Christmas Island. As well as the loss of hair and damage to his fingernails soon after the tests, Paul developed a rare skin disease. As detailed in Chapter 20, Paul's wives have suffered a number of miscarriages and his daughter Anne was born physically disabled. She died at the age of three-and-a-half. His son is unable to have children.

Paul Ah Poy at the Remembrance Day march, Nausori, Fiji, 11 November 2016
Source: Nic Maclellan.

He describes his health concerns, similar to those experienced by other Christmas Island veterans:

> When we went to Christmas Island we were all healthy, because we were medically checked out. But when we came back, we were not checked by a medical doctor. That's when things start to go wrong. I'm trying to get an answer as to why some of us got special clothing for the testing day and some of us not. I wasn't given any special clothing.
>
> Some tufts of my hair began to fall off and fingernails. My gums started bleeding and teeth got loose. I suffered from migraine headaches until I was about 35. I remembered while serving in the merchant navy, I woke up at about 3.00 in the morning and lost my memory for about one full minute. It was really frightening, for it happened about three times.
>
> One of my knee joints would just swell up whenever I bump something. My right wrist is troubling me up to this day. I have to wear dark glasses most of the time. A doctor in the United States removed 59 round growths from under my skin all over my body. It was tested and I was given the OK.

Others were not so lucky, suffering from leukaemia and other illnesses:

> One 26-year-old sailor, Alipate Loloma, died just three or four years after Christmas Island. The doctor told us he died from leukaemia of the blood—we don't even know what's the meaning of that, what was the meaning of nuclear at that time. He left four children behind. But when Ratu Penaia died, we knew because it was in the papers all the time, we knew what was the meaning of leukaemia.

Ratu Penaia was one of Fiji's leading statesmen: Governor General and then President of Fiji Ratu Sir Penaia Kanatabatu Ganilau (Tui Cakau, GCMG, KBE, KCVO, KStJ, DSO, MSD, ED). His life—and death—paralleled that of many other Christmas Island veterans.

9
The high chief— Ratu Penaia Ganilau

Ratu Penaia Ganilau and Fiji Royal Naval Volunteer Reserve (FRNVR) Commander Stan Brown prepare for the second Grapple test
Source: Courtesy Adi Sivo Ganilau.

Ratu Sir Penaia Ganilau, one of the most honoured figures in Fijian life, travelled briefly to the Line Islands in mid-1957 to visit the first contingent of Fijian sailors and witness a nuclear test. Today, Ratu Penaia's family continues to support Fiji's Christmas Island veterans, regarding their late father as one of the people adversely affected by the tests.

Ratu Penaia, born in 1918, was invested with the provincial title of *Roko Tui Cakaudrove* in September 1956. He was a political leader of note and one of the earliest Fijian graduates of the University of Oxford. As a company commander and later Commander of the Fijian battalion, he joined British counter-insurgency operations in Malaya in 1953 and was awarded a Distinguished Service Order (DSO) in 1956. He retired from the Royal Fiji Military Forces (RFMF) that year, with the rank of Lieutenant Colonel.[1]

Ratu Penaia's daughter Adi Sivo Ganilau says that his time in the army led to a lifelong commitment to 'supporting the troops':

> I do know that he was a proud soldier. There was a special place in his heart for the military. He cared very much about the welfare of his men. That's the father that I knew. Even after military service, he went back to check on the men. That's the kind of soldier he was—he'd rather be with the men where they were serving.
>
> Even later, when he was Deputy Prime Minister and President, he'd go out and visit them in the Middle East, Lebanon, Sinai or wherever. He had a very caring attitude towards people generally and the military was just special somehow.[2]

At the time of the Christmas Island tests, Ratu Penaia already held an authority that foreshadowed his later eminence. In later years, knighted as Ratu Sir Penaia Kanatabatu Ganilau (Tui Cakau, GCMG, KBE, KCVO, KStJ, DSO, MSD, ED), he was a government minister, Deputy Prime Minister and then Governor General of Fiji. He served as the Queen's representative in Fiji from 1983 until after Sitiveni Rabuka's 1987 military coup d'état, when he was appointed as the country's first president.[3]

---

1   Ratu Penaia's role in the Royal Fiji Military Forces (RFMF) deployment to Malaya is described in Manunivavalagi Dalituicama Korovulavula: *Vala Mai Malaya* (self-published, Suva, 2013).
2   Interview with Adi Lusiana Sivo Ganilau, Suva, Fiji, November 2016. Unless otherwise noted, direct quotations come from this interview.
3   Ganilau's role during the 1987 coups is detailed by the permanent secretary to the Governor General Peter Thomson: *Kava in the blood—a personal and political memoir from the heart of Fiji* (Tandem Press, Auckland, 1999), pp. 153–172. For contrasting views see: Eddie Dean and Stan Ritova: *Rabuka—no other way* (Marketing team international, Suva, 1988) and Brij V. Lal: *Islands of turmoil—Elections and politics in Fiji* (ANU E Press, Canberra, 2006), pp. 73ff.

9. THE HIGH CHIEF — RATU PENAIA GANILAU

He also held significant status in Fiji custom. In 1988, at Somosomo on the island of Taveuni, he was installed as *Tui Cakau*, serving in this high customary role until his death in 1993 (*Tui Cakau* is regarded as the most senior chief in the Tovata Confederacy, one of three in Fiji).

* * *

In late May and early June 1957, Ratu Penaia Ganilau travelled to Christmas Island to observe 'Orange Herald', the second Grapple test. He was accompanied by Fiji Royal Naval Volunteer Reserve (FRNVR) Commander Stan Brown, Lieutenant Charles Stinson and chaplain Reverend Osea Naisau.

For the 39 Fijian sailors deployed to support the testing program, morale was boosted by this visit from one of the highest chiefs in Fiji, as outlined in Ratu Penaia's biography:

> In 1957, forty Fijian naval ratings were invited by the Royal Navy to travel to Christmas Island to show the Navy 'how to live on a small Pacific Island' while atomic bomb tests were carried out. It was deemed appropriate that a Fijian chief should also be present on this momentous occasion in Pacific history, so Ratu Penaia was invited.
>
> The Fiji contingent sailed aboard two New Zealand frigates but transferred to HMS *Warrior* on arrival at Christmas Island. Ratu Penaia and Commander Stan Brown travelled up later and on their arrival Ratu Penaia was accorded a full Fijian ceremonial welcome aboard the *Warrior*, perhaps the first time that such a ceremony had taken place aboard a British warship.[4]

Grapple Task Force Commander Wilfred Oulton recalled the arrival of the two Fijian observers, five days before the 'Orange Herald' test:

> Colonel Penaia was a magnificent figure of a man, 6 feet 5 or more in height and built like the Rock of Gibraltar, smartly dressed in a British army tunic with the Fijian version of the kilt. He had an excellent Korean War [sic] record and looked the part. He and Bill Cook rapidly found a mutual interest in whiskey and the drinking thereof. This soon developed into a contest to see who could drink the most without weaving. In the end it was declared a draw![5]

---

4 Daryl Tarte: *Turaga—the Life and Times and Chiefly Authority of Ratu Sir Penaia Ganilau (GCMG, KCVO, KBE, DSO, KStJ, ED) in Fiji* (Fiji Times, Suva, 1993), p. 69.
5 Wilfred Oulton: *Christmas Island Cracker—an account of the planning and execution of the British thermonuclear bomb tests 1957* (Thomas Harmsworth, London, 1987), p. 341. Cook was the chief scientist on Christmas Island. Outlon was in error—Ganilau served in the Malayan emergency, not the Korean War.

Ratu Penaia's biographer Daryl Tarte describes how the Fijian chief was flown by helicopter to Malden Island, then transferred aboard a British naval vessel to witness the test on 31 May:

> On the day of the blast, 10,000 feet above Malden Island, some 35 miles distant, those aboard *Warrior* were dressed in white boiler suits, elbow length gloves and face masks. The *Warrior* lay with her starboard side to the blast and the men all faced to the port.
>
> Ratu Penaia recalls a hot blast on the back of his neck and when he looked around after the count there was a huge fiery sun pulsating with energy looking like a massive ice cream cone with its stalk planted on Malden Island. 'That's the end of the world', he thought. As a military man he saw it as the ultimate weapon and he prayed that no one would have to experience it in battle: 'It was too awesome to describe.'
>
> Later Brown and Ratu Penaia were taken ashore to Malden Island to check the radioactivity. They were given rubber boots to protect their feet but the Navy couldn't find a pair large enough for Ratu Penaia's feet. So he went without. 'It was rather frightening as bushes were still smouldering,' Brown comments.[6]

Official statements issued in London after the test argued that there had been no radioactive fallout, because the device was exploded high in the air. Despite this, the test actually did contaminate Malden Island with significant hotspots of fallout, which affected soldiers and scientific staff sent onto the island to gather equipment after the test.

Ernest Cox, an Assistant Trials Planning Officer from the Atomic Weapons Research Establishment (AWRE) was flown by helicopter from HMS *Warrior* to Malden Island after the test to retrieve scientific instruments. He soon noted that everything was not quite right:

> I said to my army helper 'What the hell is wrong and what the hell are we doing here?' We both had a strange feeling. We noticed no flies, no movement of lizards and no booby birds. We found several burnt and dead birds and, in the distance, we heard one of the three wild pigs—but we didn't dare approach too close to it. It was badly burnt and was going around in circles, blind. I said 'This bloody place is contaminated, and what the hell are we doing here?'[7]

---

6   Daryl Tarte: *Turaga*, op. cit., pp. 69–70.
7   Denys Blakeway and Sue Lloyd Roberts: *Fields of thunder—testing Britain's bomb* (George Allen and Unwin, London, 1985), pp. 156–157.

After two days on the island, Cox tried to shower off the dust:

> I had just taken my shorts off, when a chap came in with a monitor and said 'let me run it over you'. He did, and to his amazement, I had a reading of 3.80 Rs and another chap with me had a reading of 4.20 Rs. The Health Physics chap said 'what the hell could the rate have been yesterday?' We would have liked to have known! This was a contaminated area and we should have been issued with protective clothing—we didn't see any, not even a film badge.
>
> I was worried no more about that, but a few days after, I had another worry. Two thirds of my body was covered in blisters so thick you couldn't put a pin between them. It was horrible and frightening. The Medical Officer on HMS *Warrior* just stared at me and said: 'Bloody hell, I've never seen anything like this before'.[8]

Decades later, FRNVR sailor Amani Tuimalabe recalled stories about the visit of the high chief onto Malden Island soon after the Orange Herald detonation:

> Ratu Penaia, he went there on shore and he's got no shoes, no boots to fit him. So big! So he went bare feet there on the shore on Malden Island, but it's contaminated there from the tests. There was radiation there because that's the closest island to where the bomb dropped. Nobody lived there, only pigs or seagulls. So he came back from the island and his legs starts to itch and his leg swelled up. End up going to hospital but no cure for that.[9]

Commander Brown and Ganilau were flown back from Malden to Christmas Island where Ratu Penaia's feet were found to be 'very hot' and he had to be washed down. That night they were invited to the officer's mess to mark the occasion:

> It was a night of heavy drinking and Brown recalls having 'far too much.' He remembers Ratu Penaia coming to him in the early hours and saying 'they are trying to get me drunk.' But Ratu Penaia left most of them under the table and was up at daylight the next morning to catch the plane back to Nadi. Brown remembers feeling like death in the uncomfortable aircraft, but Ratu Penaia stretched out on the floor and slept all the way to Nadi.[10]

---

8   Quoted in Derek Robinson: *Just Testing* (Collins Harvill, London, 1985), pp. 44–45. Cox was evacuated to England for treatment.
9   Interview with Amani Tuimalabe, Suva, Fiji, November 2016.
10 Daryl Tarte: *Turaga—the Life and Times and Chiefly Authority of Ratu Sir Penaia Ganilau*, op. cit.

FRNVR sailor Amani Tuimalabe carries a memento of his service in Operation Grapple
Source: Nic Maclellan.

Shortly after returning home to Fiji, Ratu Penaia went to a fancy dress party at the Country Club on his home island of Taveuni, dressed in his anti-flash white overalls, gloves and mask. He shared with everyone the horror of the explosion.

9. *THE HIGH CHIEF* — RATU PENAIA GANILAU

***

As a young girl, Adi Sivo Ganilau understood little of her father's 1957 trip. But nearly six decades later, she recalls the overalls that he wore as protection against the flash of the nuclear detonation:

> He went there with Captain Brown to visit the men and just to find out how they were doing. All I remember is him getting prepared to go to Christmas Island. None of us knew where Christmas Island was, what he was going there for—I don't even know if my mother knew!

> But I do remember him coming back with that boiler suit outfit. We found out later from photographs that that was what he wore on Christmas Island. We didn't even know what the mission was, the bomb testing and all that, until much, much later.[11]

Ratu Penaia did not discuss the nuclear test with his children, according to his daughter:

> He never talked about it, never to any of us. I don't know whether it's a cultural thing, but they just kept quiet about it. I don't know whether he discussed it with my mother, but the children, definitely not. From what other people say, he was not able to wear shoes because his feet were too big. They couldn't find a pair of boots that fitted him, so who knows, maybe that's where the contamination came from.

Over the next three decades, Ratu Penaia was knighted and honoured, serving the Queen as Governor General of Fiji. His later years, however, were dogged by ill health. In the early 1990s, Ratu Sir Penaia suffered from Guillain-Barré syndrome, a rare auto-immune disease in which the body's immune system attacks the peripheral nervous system. Adi Sivo Ganilau recalls:

> He had some kind of syndrome, Guillain-Barré syndrome, with blisters around his neck. Well before that, I remember he also had tumours that were treated in Fiji and also he was said to have an enlarged heart. But much later at Government House, when he had the Guillain-Barré syndrome, that was quite crippling. That was really the thing that caused his hospitalisation in America.

---

11   Interview with Adi Sivo Ganilau, Suva, Fiji, November 2016.

> We kind of accepted that his health problems were probably due to Christmas Island. We read up a bit about the Christmas Island testing in the newspapers. We just put two and two together, saying 'okay, this is probably due to his exposure on Christmas Island', because all the illnesses came upon him one after the other at the end of his life.

Ratu Penaia died of leukaemia and sepsis on 15 December 1993 at the Walter Reed Army Medical Centre in Washington DC—the major US military hospital.[12]

With seven children in the family, Adi Sivo notes that her two younger brothers were also affected by health problems:

> My two youngest brothers were both born post–Christmas Island. They seem to be bigger than the rest of the children. I think after the youngest was born, my mother was advised not to have any more children. One thing I noticed with them as they grew older, they suffered just like other veterans with swelling in the legs. One of them particularly had some kind of skin disease that used to come on now and again and then disappear.

Supporting Fiji's nuclear veterans in a statement to the European Court of Human Rights, she reported:

> My two youngest brothers, who were born on 30 March 1958 and 8 August 1960 (after the Grapple tests), are sterile and to date they have no children.[13]

* * *

The tragedy of Ratu Penaia's death is marked by the fact that he was a committed monarchist and loyal to the United Kingdom, even as Fiji became a republic after the 1987 coup. He was appointed as a Knight Commander of the Royal Victorian Order (KCVO) in 1982 for 'his personal service to the Queen and in perpetuating the special relationship between Fiji and the throne'.[14]

---

12 'Penaia Ganilau, 75, Fiji Leader Who Became the First President', Obituary, *New York Times*, 17 December 1993.
13 Adi Lusiana Sivo Ganilau, written statement to the European Court of Human Rights, 1998, in author's files.
14 Daryl Tarte: 'Ratu Sir Penaia Ganilau' in *20th Century Fiji—people who shaped the nation* (University of the South Pacific, Suva, 2001), p. 177.

With their long history of service to the British Empire, the Ganilau family has never directly condemned the British authorities about the legacies of Christmas Island. Yet Ratu Penaia's children have clearly expressed their views through action.

Adi Sivo provided legal support to the Fiji Nuclear Veterans Association during their decade-long legal case in the United Kingdom (see Chapter 20), while Ratu Rabici Ganilau launched the book *Kirisimasi*, the first collection of testimony from Fiji's nuclear veterans, published in 1999 by the Pacific Concerns Resource Centre (PCRC). In his foreword to the book, Ratu Rabici stated:

> Pacific peoples have long expressed a desire to keep our region nuclear free. Fiji is proud to be the first country to ratify the Comprehensive Test Ban Treaty, to end nuclear testing in the atmosphere and underground. But we in the Pacific are still living with the radioactive legacies of decades of nuclear testing by Britain, France and the United States.
>
> Fiji's nuclear veterans have long sought recognition for their participation in the Christmas Island nuclear test program. This book as a contribution to the history of our nation, but I hope will assist the veterans to gain recognition for their service and, if need be, obtain compensation from the British government for any illnesses they have suffered as a result of exposure to nuclear radiation.[15]

For Adi Sivo, the cultural respect for leadership shown by ordinary Fijians means that many people will be measured in their public criticism of the British authorities. But she argues that leadership should also involve a reciprocal respect for those that follow:

> If you understand Fijian society, we look up to people who are in leadership positions. You want something done? We'll do it. But it works both ways and you've got to do the right thing by us. That's basically the underlying philosophy. In this case, going to Christmas Island, getting bombed and all that—now, please help us!

---

15 From the foreword to Losena Salabula, Josua Namoce and Nic Maclellan: *Kirisimasi—Na Sotia kei na Lewe ni Mataivalu e Wai ni Viti e na vakatovotovo iyaragi nei Peritania mai Kirisimasi* (Pacific Concerns Resource Centre, Suva, 1999), p. iii. After a long illness, Ratu Rabici died in 2011, leaving his wife Bernadette Rounds Ganilau and an adopted daughter.

As they view the Christmas Island mission in a cultural setting, Fijians look at issues of respect, reciprocity and honour, based on the cultural values of *ka vakaturaga* (chiefly system). For Adi Sivo Ganilau, the British Government's responsibilities to its former subjects have long been neglected:

> When approaching the Fiji Government (acting on behalf of Fiji's paramount chiefs), the British government (on behalf of Her Britannic Majesty, the Paramount Chief) would present traditional gifts (*tabua*, mats, pigs and *dalo*), inviting the Fijian servicemen to participate in Operation Grapple. This act in itself is a binding legal contract—there is precedence in Fijian jurisprudence.
>
> The Fijian servicemen then go out and do the dastardly deeds. When the mission is over and they return home, the British Government as the contracting party performs a *Qusi ni Loaloa* [literally 'wiping off the black paint', meaning war paint] to thank them for their services. This is compensation.
>
> Failure to perform such a ceremony would be unheard of and considered most *kaisi* [low-down, no class], especially coming from the upper echelons of the traditional hierarchy. That, in essence, is the Fijian cultural perspective on the Christmas Island bomb-testing mission.[16]

---

16   Personal communication to the author, May 2017.

10
The WVS ladies—
Mary and Billie Burgess

Mary (left) and Billie Burgess at the Ship Inn in Korea, 1954
Source: Australian War Memorial.

Apart from the wives and children living with the Gilbertese plantation workers on Christmas Island, the Grapple operation was a masculine affair, with thousands of men deployed from Britain to the central Pacific. In the early days of the military deployment, there were only two white women on Christmas Island: Mary and Billie Burgess.

For the first contingent of Royal Engineers redeployed from Korea to Christmas Island in 1956, construction of the military base was lonely and difficult work. In the build-up phase, UK troops worked hard, six days a week, to set up the camp and prepare wharves and port facilities. The central, urgent objective was to upgrade the Second World War airstrip on the island using concrete and tarmac, so it could land the larger jet aircraft used to drop the hydrogen bomb.

Lieutenant-Colonel Thomas Marquis, commander of the 28th Field Engineer Regiment of the Royal Engineers, reported:

> The men, aided by naval personnel and other small units of the Army, built 'boffin town' from prefabricated material. An air base, one-storey huts, a cinema, roads and power stations were built by the men, who worked round-the-clock shifts in six-day weeks.[1]

For the young British soldiers and sailors serving on Christmas Island in 1956, the adventure of travelling to a Pacific island soon turned to boredom. Marquis described life on a 'lonely island—a coral atoll, boasting little more than a few coconut palms. For entertainment, the builders of boffin town took to swimming, shark fishing, football, cricket and shell collecting'.[2]

Another thing lacking for the troops, month after month, was contact with women. Then the construction of a Navy, Army and Air Forces Institute (NAAFI) canteen was supplemented by a small club run by the Women's Voluntary Service (WVS), an operation initially staffed by Mary and Billie Burgess.

---

1   'Round the clock work building "Boffin Town"', *Dundee Evening Telegraph*, June 1957 (extracted in *Sapper Magazine*, June 1957).
2   Ibid.

10. *THE WVS LADIES* — MARY AND BILLIE BURGESS

The WVS was founded in 1938 to recruit women into Air Raid Precautions services during the Second World War.³ Over time, the WVS expanded to provide a range of services for British military personnel and their families, including the staffing of canteens, entertainment and support services, often in liaison with the official NAAFI in British garrisons or camps:

> The WVS is a civilian body, unpaid (apart from a very small expense allowance), and as the name implies, voluntary. It operates clubrooms for junior ranks and airmen and looks after the welfare of the troops. It also helps to maintain that thin veneer of civilisation, which we tend to discard in an all-male society.⁴

* * *

Originally from Bristol, the two sisters had worked with the WVS in Korea before arriving on Christmas Island. The WVS ran three centres at Inchon, which provided a home away from home for the British and Commonwealth troops deployed in Korea during allied military operations between 1950–53.⁵ The Burgess sisters staffed a centre known as Ship Inn, where soldiers could use the canteen, access books from the WVS Library, play records or board games, and gain some maternal sympathy as they tried to ignore the slaughter underway on the frontline.⁶

As British engineers were transported from Korea to Christmas Island aboard HMS *Devonshire*, Oulton reported that he was 'aghast' when the War Office insisted that two WVS women should accompany the troops:

> That's quite impossible! Motherly types they may be, but after months of no female companionship, I'm afraid the troops will see these ladies getting younger and more attractive every day and soon we'll have trouble. There's also the constant thought that one day we might have a really hairy emergency on our hands. Do we really have to have them?⁷

---

3   Today, the organisation continues in the UK as the Royal Voluntary Service (RVS). This chapter draws on material in the RVS archives, with thanks to RVS Deputy Archivist Jennifer Harrison.
4   'Bon voyage!', *Mid-Pacific News*, Vol. 3, No. 33, Thursday, 13 November 1958.
5   'With the WVS in Korea', letter to WVS headquarters in London, 31 August 1956.
6   Photos of Billie and Mary Burgess at the Ship Inn can be found in the collection of the Australian War Memorial, Canberra, ID numbers MELJ0196-0198, MELJ0209 and MELJ0196.
7   Wilfred Oulton: *Christmas Island Cracker—an account of the planning and execution of the British thermonuclear bomb tests 1957* (Thomas Harmsworth, London, 1987), p. 142.

Oulton was overruled and as the Royal Engineers redeployed from Korea, the WVS staff were sent to follow them. Travelling to Christmas Island aboard a Royal Air Force (RAF) flight, the Burgess sisters recorded their first impressions in a letter home to England:

> There below us lay the now famous Coral Island about which everyone is talking. Basking there in the brilliant tropical sunshine, looking every bit like the tropical isles one reads about in fairy tales. At last, travel-stained and a little weary, and covered in the inevitable dust, we reached the small green bungalow which was to be our home for as long as we were on the island.
>
> It had been constructed from disused huts left behind by the American Forces and is an absolute model of ingenuity. A large lounge, bedroom, small kitchen and toilet (including a shower—another memory of the Americans) are all decorated in a cool shade of cream and pale marine green. So hurried were the preparations for our arrival that the painters were literally leaving by the back door as we were coming in by the front.[8]

The Grapple Task Force had planned a NAAFI compound for the troops, but the facilities were not ready when the Burgess sisters arrived:

> Not only was our Centre not completed, but the NAAFI end of it was only in its primary stages. We cautiously asked when it was likely to be finished. They could not give us a definite date, but as soon as the canteen was finished they would be starting on our room. Here we were, with all our boxes and packing cases simply crying to be opened up. What were we to do?
>
> In the end we decided to open them one at a time and to take (when transport was available) all the more valuable articles back to our bungalow and store them on our veranda. Soon there came to light all the various treasures which WVS members had contributed. The sewing machine was the first to emerge, followed closely by the delightful kitchen utensils, some of which, unfortunately, we shall not be able to put to full use until our tiny kitchen is equipped with the small stove we are hoping will be installed.[9]

---

8   'Early days on Christmas Island', letter from Mary Burgess, published on Royal Voluntary Service Heritage blog, 1 February 2016.
9   Ibid.

10. *THE WVS LADIES* — MARY AND BILLIE BURGESS

In early December 1956, the two women began preparations to mark Christmas for the troops involved in constructing the camp and airstrip on Christmas Island:

> We had already approached the Army personnel with regard to a pantomime and, having found out that they were in the throes of producing a Christmas concert, we were determined to unpack next the boxes of costumes in order to help them. That afternoon we discussed with their producer what costumes would be required.
>
> They were putting on a little panto of The Christmas Carol as one of their acts in the show, and among the costumes mentioned was a long pair of lace edged pantaloons for Mrs. Cratchett and a frock coat for old Scrooge. Imagine our great surprise and delight when the first article out of the costume box was indeed a pair of unmentionables for Mrs. C. and not long after a frock coat was discovered for the old miser.[10]

Other WVS activities involved visits to the military hospital, providing magazines and games to the patients, with Mary Burgess reporting:

> We had a long natter with all the patients and they seemed very cheerful and quite delighted to see both us and the reading material. The chess sets and other games were also a great success.[11]

From December 1956, the WVS organised Christmas parties each year for the wives and children of the Gilbertese workforce:

> Girls in their party dresses, boys in their lava lava, all with gleaming faces, here and there were tiny children in grass skirts. Mothers with their offspring were all in their finery, some smoking pipes, which seemed to strike an odd note. Off we all set in a high spirits, everyone singing lustily their own native songs and popular English ones, even to 'she will be wearing khaki bloomers when she comes'.[12]

When he arrived on island, the Task Force Commander noted that the women 'were often to be seen cycling around the main camp, organising recreation for off-duty hours and were very highly regarded and appreciated by the men'.[13]

---

10   Ibid.
11   Ibid.
12   'Gilbertese children's party', typed report to WVS, December 1958.
13   Wilfred Oulton: *Christmas Island Cracker*, op. cit., p. 162.

The official handbook issued for new troops lauded the work of the WVS volunteers:

> The Misses Billie and Mary Burgess of the Women's Voluntary Services have brought a touch of home to the camp. They are to be found in the main camp NAAFI organising games, dancing, Highland dancing and concerts, and generally helping to make off-duty hours in the recreation room pleasant and free from boredom.[14]

Decades later, returned veterans described the two women as 'a couple of tough old birds who knew how to handle themselves':

> They oversaw much of the catering arrangements and acted as nurse, matron and surrogate Mum to many lonely serviceman stranded in the middle of nowhere for a year.[15]

The two sisters (aged in their mid-40s) won the hearts of the many troops in their teens and early 20s, away from home for the first time. Reflecting on the age difference, Royal Engineer Brian Tate noted that they were 'no NAAFI girls' but:

> They must have been about 90 at the time, I should think—but every day they looked marvellous. Always made you welcome. Yeah, I say they would 90 years old—they were about 25 years older than what we were! But a nice pair of women.[16]

While the Burgess sisters were on Christmas Island, the initial three Grapple tests were conducted on Malden Island, but one veteran recalled:

> They weren't bothered by the bombs, they took all that in their stride ... The only thing that bothered them was the frequency which their underwear disappeared from the washing line![17]

* * *

After a year's service, Mary and Billie Burgess left for Germany and other WVS volunteers arrived to continue WVS program. From September 1957, Freda and Elisabeth Hutchinson staffed the WVS clubrooms, as new troops deployed for the next round of tests on Christmas Island.

---

14 *Operation Grapple 1956–57*, Handbook for UK personnel, 1957.
15 'Does anyone know what happened to Mary and Billy?', *Fissionline*, No. 2, April 2013.
16 Derek Robinson: *Just Testing* (Collins Harvill, London, 1985), p. 37.
17 'Does anyone know what happened to Mary and Billy?', op. cit.

For the Grapple X test in November 1957 and subsequent tests on Christmas Island in 1958, WVS staff were required to evacuate their home on the day of the tests. During the Grapple Y test in April 1958, the two women joined Gilbertese labourers and their families below decks on board the HMS *Messina*.

They continued their work until 28 November 1958, when they left following the completion of the three Grapple Z tests. The task force newsletter farewelled them, noting that 'they must be the only British women to have seen six nuclear explosions'.[18]

The WVS had a rather prim program of activities, including ballroom dancing classes:

> In fact we have already enrolled the services of an instructor (a plumber who repaired our leaking tap, which, incidentally, is supplied with water from a converted petrol drum on the roof). A gold-medallist waiter is also among our ardent ballroom followers and he has volunteered to help us with these classes once they are under way.[19]

Given that most of the troops were working-class youth escaping post-war austerity in England and Scotland, they were often engaged in more mundane entertainment—fighting and drinking beer. Veterans' accounts provide plenty of evidence of rough-housing, practical jokes and drinking.

In the early years, there were two NAAFI bars on the island—a small one at Port London and a larger one at the Main Camp. The official handbook for Operation Grapple suggested the latter bar was more popular:

> A place to drink a nice cold beer or squash in the beer garden, pleasantly situated on the edge of the beach and listen to the pounding of the surf. Incidentally, the beer was specially canned for the operation, the lids being stamped 'Operation Grapple, Christmas Island' with the Grapple insignia.[20]

NZ sailor Gerry Wright—who joined the Navy in 1955 at age 16—recalled a more basic set-up than the tourist paradise presented in the official handbook:

---

18 'Bon voyage!', *Mid-Pacific News*, Vol. 3, No. 33, Thursday, 13 November 1958.
19 'Early days on Christmas Island', op. cit.
20 From chapter 8, 'Life on a desert island' in *Operation Grapple 1956–57*, Handbook for UK personnel, op. cit., p. 57.

The wet canteen was a large army-built shed with a bar of beer crates, tastefully arranged within a barbed wire compound. The beer was British, usually chilled, and supplied in cans. Can spanners (tin openers to the non-veteran) were specially made for Operation Grapple and had the Grapple emblem stamped on them. Seating was metal frame stacking chairs with some cane furniture outside. Over time, the cane chairs disappeared to other locations, including the ships, leaving just steel tables and metal chairs.

Those fortunate enough to find a table under an overhead fan could enjoy a gentle breeze. They were also in the best position at a later hour to throw an open beer can up into the fan, which would then be hurled off in any direction like a hand grenade, spraying everyone in its path with beer.[21]

The British officers and scientific staff had their own mess and bar, but generally ignored any mayhem at the Other Ranks venue. Wright recalls:

There was just one gate continuously manned by British military police. It was accepted that the troops needed somewhere to let their hair down, so anything within reason was fair game inside the compound. The military police were there to ensure major injuries were sent for attention and drunks slept it off before going back to their units. It was not uncommon for a sleeping drunk to be carried by his boisterous mates to the lagoon and thrown into the water.[22]

While participating in joint work activities, the Fijian military contingent faced racial restrictions common for the time. The Fijians were paid less than their British counterparts, and initially were restricted from buying beer. As with all soldiers, these regulations were soon ignored. The Fijians were popular with the British and NZ troops, as described by one Scottish veteran:

The Fijians were the most friendly bunch that you could ever meet and they were really easy to get along with. They weren't allowed any alcohol from the NAAFI, so we always bought them a couple of cases of beer and they, in turn, taught us how to catch crayfish and lobster. Sometimes they would come over to our tents and sing a few songs for us while one of them strummed a guitar.[23]

---

21   Gerry Wright: *We Were There* (Zenith Print, New Plymouth, n.d.), p. 56.
22   Ibid.
23   Ken McGinley and Eamonn P. O'Neill: *No Risk Involved—the Ken McGinley story—survivor of a nuclear experiment* (Mainstream Publishing, Edinburgh, 1991), p. 50.

Others recall the racial divide that was common at the time. Fiji Royal Naval Volunteer Reserve (FRNVR) sailor Amani Tuimalabe, who witnessed four nuclear tests and served on both the NZ warship HMNZS *Pukaki* and the British aircraft carrier HMS *Warrior*, noted:

> No problem with the New Zealanders, I liked them, but the British! They look down on us. Even now, it's still like that—English people, they discriminate. New Zealanders are all right, Australians are all right—they are close by, they are brothers—but the British, they're like that. Duty time, it's okay, but break time, they look down at us.[24]

Many Fijians in turn made firm friends amongst the Māori sailors from New Zealand and non-Anglo British troops. One returned Fijian sapper, Misaele Tikoenaliwalala, was known for the rest of his life as 'Jamaica', after making friends with a British West Indian soldier who holidayed in Fiji after his Christmas Island deployment.[25]

The rank and file soldiers and sailors seized every opportunity for rest and recreation on Christmas Island, given that daily work hours were often filled with mundane and routine tasks. The workload was different, however, for the RAF aircrew, whose task was to pilot the aircraft that would drop the bomb or fly through the resulting mushroom cloud, gathering radioactive samples that were vital evidence to determine the yield of the weapon.

24 Interview with Amani Tuimalabe, Suva, Fiji, November 2016.
25 Interview with his widow Miriama Tikoenaliwalala, Nausori, Fiji, November 2016.

11
The pilot—Geoffrey Dhenin

Geoffrey Dhenin (left) and crew before their flight to gather samples after the 1953 Totem 1 test
Source: Imperial War Museum.

The Royal Air Force (RAF) decided Britain's first operational atomic weapons, dubbed 'Blue Danube', were too small. The 1953 Totem tests in Australia had only shown an explosive yield of 8–10 kilotons, and military chiefs wanted more:

> A working party on the operational use of atomic weapons decided the Blue Danube was not powerful enough to destroy primary targets in the USSR, such as airfields or ports, with a single bomb. Therefore the working party stated 'the possession of a bomb in the 5 or 10-megaton range offers this possibility and would go a long way towards overcoming the need for improved terminal accuracy. Hydrogen bomb to give a yield of 5–10 megatons would weigh from 9,000–12,000 pounds and could be carried by the V-class bombers'.[1]

Military leaders thus proposed that Britain's main nuclear strike force should be larger Valiant bomber aircraft, which could reach distant targets. But before the development of a Valiant force to deliver the hydrogen bomb, aircrew used other planes during the Australian nuclear testing program between 1952 and 1957.

The first British atomic tests conducted on the Australian mainland were codenamed Totem 1 and Totem 2 in October 1953. The RAF, the Royal Australian Air Force (RAAF) and the US Air Force all deployed aircraft to Emu Field, in the desert of South Australia, to monitor the tests and collect samples of radioactivity from the mushroom cloud.

As the McClelland Royal Commission later reported, the RAAF deployed Lincoln aircraft because the Canberra planes requested by the British scientific team were not available:

> In the United Kingdom it was also decided that a Canberra aircraft should fly through the atomic cloud as soon as possible after the explosion to assess the aircraft's behaviour under such conditions and to gain information on types and levels of contamination.
>
> Australia was approached about providing such an aircraft but, with its Canberra production line not yet fully operational, the limited number of aircraft available to the RAAF and Australian commitments in

---

1   Andrew Brookes: *Valiant units of the Cold War*, Osprey combat aircraft, No. 95 (Osprey, Oxford, 2012).

South-East Asia, it was decided the request could not be met. The need to collect the information was given a very high priority and the British authorities decided to provide their own Canberra aircraft.[2]

***

The first time a Canberra bomber flew through a mushroom cloud to gather radiation samples was in October 1953, during Operation Totem. Commanded by RAF pilot Geoffrey Dhenin, the plane flew at 30,000 feet above the Australian desert north of Woomera for the Totem 1 test—the source of the black mist that reportedly blinded Yami Lester (Chapter 1).

After testing the level of radioactivity with sensors mounted on the wing, Dhenin made an initial pass through the mushroom cloud, followed by two more: one through the base and one through the top. On return to base, the aircraft was tested and found to be contaminated with radioactivity. Despite shielding on the aircraft, Dhenin and the two other crew members received high doses of gamma radiation.[3]

Britain's chief nuclear scientist William Penney told Dhenin that the aircrew had been exposed to radiation doses above the permitted level. Although they were scheduled to perform the same task for the Totem 2 test within a fortnight, the crew were withdrawn, with Penney telling Dhenin:

> Go home, boy. You have done enough. I cannot authorise such a thing a second time.[4]

Penney later brusquely dismissed the danger to the pilots, telling the 1984 Royal Commission:

> The fact that the crew of an RAF Canberra received significant doses of radiation as a result of their early passage through the cloud was reported to me. I did not regard it as very serious as it was a once in a lifetime dose.[5]

---

2   Government of Australia: *The Report of the Royal Commission into British Nuclear Tests in Australia* (Australian Government Publishing Service, Canberra, 1985), para. 6.5.39, p. 203.
3   The Royal Commission estimated their doses at 18, 19 and 21 R on their dosimeters (*Royal Commission*, op. cit., pp. 207–208).
4   'Air Marshal Sir Geoffrey Dhenin', obituary, *Daily Telegraph*, 11 May 2011.
5   William Penney: Statement to Royal Commission into the British Nuclear Tests, 1984. National Archives of Australia, NAA A6449, p. 2.

As they collected samples while flying through the mushroom clouds at Maralinga, the skin and engines of the RAAF Lincolns were contaminated with radioactivity. Thirty years later, Royal Commissioner James McClelland was critical of the lack of safety precautions from the British scientific team:

> Evidence confirms the appalling lack of foresight on the part of the British authorities, who did not perceive the need for special precautionary measures for air and ground crew during and after the Lincoln cloud sampling of Totem 1.[6]

In its final judgement, the Royal Commission found that the RAF aircrew received the highest recorded doses, greater than those recorded by RAAF Lincoln crews. The Royal Commission found that ground crew as well as pilots were affected:

> No special arrangements were made to ensure the radiation safety of aircrew in Lincolns prior to Totem 1. The RAAF was told at the time of Operation Hurricane that there would be no hazard to aircrew or ground staff from that operation … There was no attempt made to bring the RAAF aircrew within the framework of the regulations set down for the ground operations in the Emu area. As a result, no arrangements were made to provide any form of health control and, in consequence, no personal monitoring devices were provided.[7]

As preparations for Operation Grapple were underway in England in 1956, Penney and the RAF chiefs recognised that there was a need for significant changes in procedure. The hydrogen bomb tests, with greater explosive power, needed to allow the aircraft more time to get out of the impact range and avoid damage. After dropping a hydrogen bomb, a more powerful blast and heat would come from the weapon, with 10,000 times the explosive yield of the Totem atomic devices.

To practice the flying skills required to release a hydrogen bomb and escape before being hit by the massive blast wave, new Valiant aircraft were deployed with the RAF 49 Squadron, based at Wittering in England. Air Commodore Arthur Steele set up a detailed training program for the four teams of aircrew selected for Operation Grapple. By April 1956, the Valiant training program was supported by two new all-volunteer crews, led by Squadron leader Ted Flavell and Flight Lieutenant Bob Bates.

---

6   *Royal Commission*, op. cit., para. 6.5.124, p. 221.
7   *Royal Commission*, op. cit., para. 6.5.32, p. 202.

11. THE PILOT—GEOFFREY DHENIN

In September that year, Wing Commander Kenneth Hubbard took command of the 49 Squadron, with only months to prepare before the first test on Christmas Island. He has described the next two years as 'the most exciting and challenging task of my life'.[8]

By November, new Valiant bombers were delivered from the manufacturers Vickers, painted all-white to reflect the heat in the nuclear detonation. But there were numerous problems. On one trial run, an attempt to drop a dummy bomb weighing 10,000 pounds failed: the bomb did not release from the bomb rack during a trial run, but then—after the bomb bay doors had closed—fell out of the rack as the aircraft was returning to base. To compound the error, the dummy bomb fell to the ground when the bomb bay doors were opened on the airstrip!

The Valiant aircraft were flown to Christmas Island in early March 1957, where Air Commodore Steele continued the training program and a series of trials to familiarise the aircrew with the target on Malden Island.

The first Grapple test over Malden Island, codename 'Short Granite', was held on 15 May 1957. The Valiant bomber XT818 was piloted by Wing Commander Hubbard. The first bomb exploded with the yield of just 300 kilotons, to the disappointment of scientific staff who were expecting a megaton yield.

The work of pilots was hazardous, even beyond the dangers of dropping a hydrogen bomb. Following the Grapple 1 test, a Canberra aircraft crashed over Canada as it was urgently flying back to the United Kingdom with samples collected from the mushroom cloud. The day after the test, the Canberra was landing to refuel at Goose Bay, Newfoundland, but Pilot Officer J.S. Loomes and Flying Officer T.R. Montgomery were killed as the plane crashed in poor weather.

For the first test, the actual hydrogen bomb had been flown from England to Christmas Island on a Valiant aircraft, transiting through Canadian and US airspace with stopovers at Goose Bay, Newfoundland; Namao, Alberta; Offutt Air Force Base, Nebraska; Travis Air Force Base, California; and Hickam Air Force Base, Hawai'i.

---

8   Kenneth Hubbard and Michael Simmons: *Operation Grapple* (Ian Allen, London, 1985), republished more than 20 years later as *Dropping Britain's First H-Bomb—the story of Operation Grapple, 1957–8 (*Pen and Sword, Barnsley, 2008).

Given the failure of Grapple 1, the Atomic Weapons Research Establishment (AWRE) scientists had manufactured a larger device for the second Grapple test, using new techniques to trigger the detonation—a prototype of the warhead planned for the Blue Streak missile. A problem arose when the device, codenamed 'Orange Herald', was too large to fit into the bomb bay of a Valiant to be flown to the Pacific. Instead the device was disassembled and flown to Christmas Island in three separate loads on Hastings aircraft in May 1957.

As scientists and RAF crew tried to reassemble the components of the bomb, they found that two copper hemispheres used to surround the explosive sphere would not completely screw together. With the two bits of metal jammed tightly together, an RAF Warrant Officer told chief scientist Bill Cook: 'In my experience of this sort of engineering problem, sir, there's only one thing left to do—clout it!' Using a 7-pound copper-headed sledgehammer, he proceeded to thump the spheres to loosen the thread and allow them to be screwed into place![9]

* * *

With the completion of the three initial Grapple tests on Malden Island, RAF Canberra aircraft were again redeployed to South Australia for the resumption of atmospheric testing at Maralinga during Operation Antler. Following the three Antler atomic tests in September and early October 1957, five Canberra aircraft again flew back across the Pacific, to be used for the Grapple X and Y hydrogen bomb tests at Christmas Island.

En route, these planes landed at Nadi Airport in Fiji for maintenance and refuelling. British military authorities tried to hide the fact that the RAF aircraft were contaminated with radioactivity. A confidential memo from RAF Air Commodore W. P. Sutcliffe—the Commander of the Antler program in Australia—ordered crews of the RAF bombers not to tell local authorities in Fiji that their engines were radioactive. The memo noted that although the planes had been cleaned on the outside, their engines were still coated with radioactive material on the inside:

---

9   The full incident is described by Wilfred Oulton: *Christmas Island Cracker—an account of the planning and execution of the British thermonuclear bomb tests 1957* (Thomas Harmsworth, London, 1987), pp. 337–339.

11. THE PILOT—GEOFFREY DHENIN

Aircraft of the No. 76 Squadron flying to Christmas Island and stopping at Nandi and Canton may be radioactive internally ... There appears to be no regulations in force governing the transit of radioactive aircraft through international civil airports such as Nandi and Canton. The fact that an engine may be 'hot' should be concealed from the Nandi authorities unless they ask.[10]

The internal contamination of the aircraft posed a particular problem for ground crew from 76 Squadron, who were placed at greater risk as they serviced the engines. As occurred in Australia, the ground crew on Christmas Island were involved in the washing down the planes to remove surface radioactivity, but often operated with very basic equipment and no gear to monitor exposure rates. Bryan Young was one of the ground crew:

> We were cleaning off barrier paint above me and water came off the back of the wing. I was only wearing cotton whites so, of course it went straight through, and bearing in mind that it was contaminated water coming off, I wasn't a very happy person underneath. But we were all too busy at the time to do much about it. In the middle of decontamination, you can't just stop and say 'Oh God, I've got to go and shower all this lot off!' Work has to carry on.[11]

The number of aircrew and ground staff grew rapidly for the Grapple Y test in April and subsequent tests throughout 1958 (1,426 RAF personnel were deployed on Christmas Island throughout the year, the largest number at any time for Operation Grapple). With scientists preparing for the largest test of the whole operation, a new range of procedures were developed to cope with the larger blast.

On 28 April, the day of the test, Squadron Leader Robert 'Bob' Bates piloted the Valiant bomber XD825 carrying the hydrogen bomb (Bates later died of leukaemia). Five Canberra aircraft of 76 Squadron were also deployed: three planes circled the proposed drop zone while two others were sent downwind to track the mushroom cloud and collect

---

10   'Transient Canberras of No.76 Squadron—Nandi and Canton', Memorandum from Air Commodore W.P. Sutcliffe (Services Commander, Task Force 'Antler'), 13 October 1957, ATF/S.5014/Air, marked 'Confidential—UK eyes only'. See Rob Edwards: 'Plane deceit', *New Scientist*, 8 May 1999.
11   Interview on *Nationwide* program, BBC1 TV, 12 January 1983, cited in Denys Blakeway and Sue Lloyd Roberts: *Fields of thunder—testing Britain's bomb* (George Allen and Unwin, London, 1985), p. 169. Before leaving Christmas Island, Young reported skin problems and blinding headaches, with ongoing health issues after he returned home.

samples. Hundreds of troops were ordered onto landing craft offshore, standing room only, to prepare for evacuation out to see if the Valiant aircraft crashed on take-off.

Christmas Island veterans have long argued that the greatest radioactive fallout during Operation Grapple was created by this test, with an estimated yield of 2.8 megatons. As detailed in Chapter 17, the explosion was closer to sea level than expected. The detonation sucked up quantities of water and debris into the mushroom cloud, irradiating them in the process—fallout that spread over the naval flotilla and the Main Camp.

Flight Lieutenant Eric Denson captained Canberra WH980 and flew though the dispersing mushroom cloud of Grapple Y, 49 minutes after the detonation. Because of a fault on one of the dosimeters, Denson was ordered to keep the plane inside the cloud for six minutes; four minutes longer than the aircraft should have been inside. Denson and his crew are estimated to each have collected 13,000 rads (the equivalent of 6,500 full body X-rays).

After making several passes through the mushroom cloud, Denson's plane returned to the airstrip, but: 'when it landed and taxied to a halt at the far end of the runway near to the contamination pits, the Canberra sent every radiation counter crazy. His logbook showed he was in the air for one hour 55 minutes'.[12]

After the flight, Denson was told that his dosage exceeded the legal limit, excluding him from participation in further tests. His vomiting started almost immediately, and became so severe that he was forced to delay in Fiji for a further three days before returning to England.

For 18 years, Squadron Leader Denson suffered mentally and physically with breathing difficulties, acute sinusitis, mood swings, anxieties and depression.[13] In 1976, at the age of 44, Denson committed suicide, leaving wife Shirley and four children.

In 2002, Labour MP Siobhan McDonagh stood before the British House of Commons to call for justice for Eric Denson's family. She highlighted the ongoing secrecy over the medical records of service personnel, which could assist veterans' families with their pension claims:

---

12   Alan Rimmer: *Between Heaven and Hell* (E-book, lulu.com, 2012), p. 35.
13   For an interview with Shirley Denson, see ibid.

Great emphasis was placed on the imposition of strict orders of secrecy concerning any discussion of events going on in the south Pacific. Be that as it may, after Eric Denson's return in obvious ill health, no medical checks or follow-up—in fact, no duty of care of any reasonable kind— were provided that could have alerted him to the probable cause of his progressive medical problems. Significantly, no mention was made in his medical records of his activities in the south Pacific in 1958.[14]

For the final Grapple Z test on 11 September 1958, the Canberra sniffer aircraft was piloted by Christopher Donne. Ten minutes after detonation, Donne flew through the mushroom cloud at the highest possible level to gain samples of radioactivity for scientific staff on the ground. He later reported:

> I remember seeing this yellowy-brown thing ahead of me, stretching out almost as far as I could see, and I remember turning the aircraft and getting it straight and level and just scrambling up those last few feet and then approaching the cloud and hoping that I'd got a small part of it—we called it a 'cut'—from which, of course, we could work out when it was safe to send the other aircraft on … And then we hit it, and I can remember my navigator saying 'Bloody hell! Let's get out of here!' But, of course, we couldn't because there was no way I could turn the aircraft— the turbulence was causing me to concentrate very hard on flying it at all at that height.
>
> I can remember sort of glancing out of the side of my eyes to look at the instruments—the needles were pressed very firmly up against the stops … showing the very high levels of radiation, which were very much higher than we'd anticipated. I can remember the health physicist muttering in his beard something about it being very much hotter than he'd thought.[15]

After landing, the aircrew were decontaminated, with their heads shaved and fingernails clipped. Donne was informed that he must return to the United Kingdom and undergo blood testing. Decades later in 2013, Donne was still searching for information about the levels of radiation exposure for his crew, using Freedom of Information legislation.[16]

---

14 UK House of Commons, Hansard official report, 4 December 2002, Column 251WH.
15 Jane Resture: *About Christmas Island and bomb tests* (www.janesoceania.com/christmas_about/index.htm).
16 'Permitted radiation levels for aircrew flying through the clouds formed by the nuclear explosions at Christmas Island in the late 1950s', response by Ministry of Defence (MoD) to Christopher Donne, 29 November 2013 (www.whatdotheyknow.com/user/christopher_donne).

12

The Prime Minister—
Harold Macmillan

In early 1957, Harold Macmillan inherited a government in crisis. British, French and Israeli forces had invaded Egypt in October 1956, but were forced into an ignominious withdrawal by December—under American pressure—ending their unsuccessful military adventure.

The Suez crisis divided the Conservative government and, suffering from chronic depression, British Prime Minister Sir Anthony Eden fled to Jamaica in November. He spent weeks relaxing with his wife Clarissa at Goldeneye, the tropical retreat of novelist Ian Fleming, creator of the James Bond thrillers.[1] Eden's Personal Private Secretary Evelyn Shuckburgh noted his fragile mental state:

> A.E. has broken down and gone to Jamaica. This is the most extraordinary feature of the whole thing. Is he on his way out, has he had a nervous breakdown, is he mad? The captain leaves the sinking ship which he had steered personally onto the rocks.[2]

Eden was certainly 'on his way out'. Former Foreign Secretary and Chancellor of the Exchequer Harold Macmillan moved to replace the ailing leader and succeeded Eden as prime minister on 10 January 1957.

---

1   Matthew Parker: *Goldeneye: Where Bond Was Born* (Pegasus, 2015), pp. 210–218.
2   Evelyn Shuckburgh and John Charmley: *Descent to Suez, diaries 1951–56* (Littlehampton Book Services, 1986), p. 365, cited in Calder Walton: *Empire of Secrets—British intelligence, the Cold War and the twilight of Empire* (Harper Press, London, 2013).

British Prime Minister Harold Macmillan, 1957
Source: UK Government.

The new prime minister quickly moved to revitalise the crumbling British Empire. One of Macmillan's most significant decisions was to accept that Britain could no longer afford to garrison its vast network of colonies. His government initiated an 'audit of Empire' to look at the status of Britain's overseas dependencies. He also launched initiatives that led to the UK application to join the European Economic Community.

12. THE PRIME MINISTER — HAROLD MACMILLAN

Working with Minister for Defence Duncan Sandys, Macmillan began a defence review that ultimately transformed Britain's nuclear program and brought closer integration with US first strike nuclear war fighting strategies. The recognition that Britain's small atomic arsenal could do limited damage to the Soviet Union, while making the United Kingdom a key target for Russian nuclear counter-attack, only accelerated the push to develop a British thermonuclear weapon.

With the Conservative government buffeted by domestic and international criticism, its nuclear weapons program became an important symbol of British power and status. For this reason, there was a need to bury news of scientific difficulties and present the Grapple tests as a shining example of British technological prowess.

***

Later in life, Harold Macmillan's memoirs pointed to the importance of the first Grapple test:

> On 15 May came the successful explosion of the first British H-bomb.[3]

Following the first Grapple test on 15 May 1957, the newsletter released to British troops on Christmas Island proclaimed:

> Bomb gone! H-Bomb puts Britain on level terms … A flash, stark and blinding, high in the Pacific sky, signalled to the world today Britain's emergence as a top-ranking power in this nuclear age.[4]

The third Grapple test on 19 June, codenamed 'Purple Granite', was also hailed as a huge success. With a cricketing metaphor, the *Mid-Pacific News* reported: 'Hat trick—third drop successful'.[5]

From London, the UK Ministry of Supply issued an official statement noting: 'the tests have been so successful that nothing could be gained from continuing them'.[6]

---

3   Harold Macmillan: *Riding the Storm 1956–1959* (Harper and Row, New York, 1971), p. 296.
4   *Mid-Pacific News*, special souvenir edition, May 1957, p. 1.
5   'Britain continues nuclear tests—Hat trick', *Mid-Pacific News*, June 1957, p. 1.
6   Statement from the Ministry of Supply in London, reported in 'Britain Explodes Third H-Bomb in Pacific Tests', *Fiji Times*, 22 June 1957, p. 1.

Privately, however, scientists calculated that the objective of achieving a 1-megaton thermonuclear weapon had not been achieved, with yields between 0.2 to 0.7 megatons for the three blasts.[7] William Cook, the deputy chief scientist of the H-bomb development program, told Grapple Task Force Commander Wilfred Oulton:

> We haven't got it quite right. We shall have to do it all again, providing we can do so before the ban comes into force; so that means as soon as possible.[8]

In later years, some historians have argued that the public proclamation of success in May 1957 was a massive political bluff. They argue that London hoped to persuade the United States to review the 1946 McMahon Act and renew contact between scientists from the two countries, which had been broken by a series of British spy scandals.[9] Others have countered that the United States already knew about the limited yield from the tests, because US observers were present at the second UK test. They also note that Sir William Penney and other scientists were in regular contact with their US counterparts.[10]

Even today, British authorities are embarrassed that the first three tests did not reach megaton range. With extensive input from the Atomic Weapons Establishment, BBC TV broadcast a documentary in May 2017 that lauds the pluck and ingenuity of the British scientists that developed the hydrogen bomb. The documentary culminates triumphantly with the Grapple X test of November 1957, with the narrator proclaiming:

> The H-bomb had a yield of 1.8 megatons. For the scientists, it was a triumph ... the scientists had defied the odds and realised the politicians' dreams.[11]

---

7   Secrecy about the explosive power of the Malden Island tests was maintained for decades. The postscript to Wilfred Oulton's 1987 book about Operation Grapple incorrectly reports that seven of the nine tests reached megaton yield (*Christmas Island Cracker—an account of the planning and execution of the British thermonuclear bomb tests 1957* (Thomas Harmsworth, London, 1987), p. 403). In fact, only three of the nine Grapple tests, and none of the tests on Malden Island, were measured at megaton yield, as confirmed in the official history of the tests published by the Ministry of Defence (MoD) in 2001 (Lorna Arnold: *Britain and the H-bomb* (Palgrave Macmillan, London, 2001), Appendix 2, p. 236).
8   Wilfred Oulton: *Christmas Island Cracker*, op. cit., p. 356. Cook had served as chief of the Royal Navy's scientific service, but was appointed as William Penney's deputy in 1954.
9   Norman Dombey and Eric Grove: 'Britain's thermonuclear bluff', *London Review of Books*, 22 October 1992.
10   John Baylis: *Ambiguity and Deterrence—British Nuclear Strategy 1945–64* (Clarendon Press, Oxford, 1995), pp. 260–268.
11   *Britain's Nuclear Bomb: The inside story*, BBC TV documentary, broadcast 3 May 2017 (spoken by narrator at 56 minutes).

The film, however, never mentions that there were three previous tests at Malden Island in May and June 1957, all of which failed to reach the expected yield. With careful wording, the film even implies that Grapple X was conducted at Malden Island, rather than Christmas Island where thousands of troops were based! Shamefully, in an hour-long documentary, the BBC includes just one sentence to mention the decades-long controversy over nuclear safety for the troops during the tests.[12]

The official historian of Operation Grapple argues that, like the atomic tests in Australia, the three Malden Island tests were still a significant step in developing the hydrogen bomb:

> *Purple Granite* was fired on 19 June and operationally was a complete success, but the scientists at Christmas Island made a preliminary estimate of the yield at only 200 kilotons—even less than *Short Granite*. Grapple had been valuable; but undeniably disappointing as the American observers too were well aware ... Present policy was to move everything worth removing from Christmas Island after Operation Grapple. However, if facilities had to be rebuilt, a megaton trial could not be planned in less than about 18 months and if there was to be yet another trial at Christmas Island in 1959, a decision must be taken in 1957.[13]

At the time, the disappointing results meant there would need to be a quick decision by the British Government. As one Foreign Office historian has noted:

> The hallmark of British policy in 1957 was its great sense of urgency, designed to achieve as much as possible before any constraints on atmospheric nuclear tests could be agreed or were imposed. In fact, the thermonuclear program was conducted against the clock: the dates for the Christmas Island tests were set for political rather than technical reasons.[14]

Should they conduct another series of tests? While the government privately debated the options, Air Vice Marshall Oulton needed to know whether to maintain the large—and expensive—naval and military force in the Pacific.

---

12 'Since this [Hurricane] test and the others that followed, thousands of veterans have claimed they've suffered health problems as a result—claims which have not been accepted by successive governments.' BBC TV, op. cit., spoken by narrator at 42 minutes.
13 Lorna Arnold: *Britain and the H-bomb*, op. cit., pp. 147–148.
14 John R. Walker (Foreign and Commonwealth Office UK): *British nuclear weapons and the Test Ban 1954–73—Britain, the United States, Weapons Policies and Nuclear Testing, Tensions and Contradictions* (Ashgate, 2010), p. 21.

Rather than send a naval task force and thousands of men back to Malden Island—more than 600 kilometres from the base of operations—a cheaper option would be to test at Christmas Island. The decision to move from Malden to Christmas Island reduced the enormous logistic problems. But it brought the tests much closer to the military camp where thousands of British, New Zealand and Fijian personnel were stationed and to the village where the Gilbertese plantation workers were housed.

* * *

Even before the final test in the original Grapple series, the Ministry of Defence (MoD) was lobbying Minister of Supply Aubrey Jones to ensure that the Grapple Task Force would halt the planned decommissioning of the Christmas Island base. In an 11 June 1957 memo, eight days before the Purple Granite test, Minister for Defence Duncan Sandys wrote:

> I understand that instructions are being given to dismantle the test facilities on Christmas Island at the conclusion of the Grapple series. The new American disarmament proposals, which have been put by them to the Russians, might conceivably lead to a moratorium on nuclear tests as early as 1 July 1958. In these circumstances, we ought, if possible, to keep in being facilities for carrying out further tests at Christmas Island in the first half of next year. Please let me know whether this is practicable and what the financial and other implications would be. Meanwhile all action to dismantle these facilities should be suspended.[15]

Another letter from Jones to Prime Minister Harold Macmillan highlighted the cost of operations so far from England, as well as 'the uncertainty as to whether tests of this nature would continue, because of the difficulty of maintaining a care and maintenance force on an isolated island and because rough financial calculations showed that, unless tests were remounted at Christmas Island at intervals of less than three years, it would be as economical to evacuate the equipment, as to maintain it'.[16]

---

15   Memo from Minister for Defence Duncan Sandys to Minister of Supply Aubrey Jones, 11 June 1957. CO1036/282.
16   Memo from Minister of Supply Aubrey Jones to Prime Minister Harold Macmillan, marked 'Top secret/Atomic', 13 June 1957. CO1036/282.

Jones added that 'the Task Force Commander ought to have firm instructions. Without them, some 4,000 men will be idle in the area with a disastrous effect on morale, while great confusion will result from the disruption of transport arrangements'.[17]

Macmillan agreed that the military should halt the closure of the base, telling his ministers:

> The Task Force Commander should be asked to reverse his plans for withdrawing equipment and to arrange for a service of 200 to 250 to be kept on Christmas Island until replacements of a similar number arrive. No decision needs to be taken yet about the future program of tests, we will try to take this decision of our future program as soon as possible.[18]

The British Cabinet was panicked by the proposal for a moratorium on atmospheric nuclear testing by the two superpowers, the United States and Soviet Union. Despite (false) public claims that the three Malden tests had reached megaton range, ministers soon realised they would have to continue testing to develop an effective thermonuclear device.

On 22 June, just three days after the Purple Granite test, Cabinet ministers privately debated whether to announce a further series of tests. Some argued for a parliamentary statement to clarify the situation. But Prime Minister Macmillan privately expressed disdain for the need to make a formal statement to parliament about the future of the testing program. In a letter to Aubrey Jones, Macmillan noted:

> I have thought carefully over your suggestion for a statement, but I shall do my best to avoid it at present. Of all the Parliamentary techniques, I have always thought the ministerial statement the worst. A debate is one thing: you can put forward your own arguments and answer those of your opponents.

> The P. Q. [Parliamentary question] is another: you can always call it off after two or three supplementaries. But in a statement, you have all the disadvantages of exposing every flank at the same time, without the power to cover any of them effectively. Supplementary questions go on indefinitely and not stopped by the Speaker and yet you have no right to wind up the debate. I believe that ministers would do well to avoid statements wherever possible or to confine them to formal matters.[19]

---

17 Ibid.
18 Prime Minister's personal minute, serial no. M277/57, 15 June 1957. CO1036/282.
19 Prime Minister's personal minute, serial no. M291/57, 22 June 1957. CO1036/282.

Even though the naval task force had disbanded, the decision was made to continue with a 'maintenance party' on the island. Ministers were reluctant, however, to issue a public announcement of their decision, fearful that the opposition Labour Party would quickly argue this meant there would be a further series of nuclear tests. In response to his ministers' concerns, Macmillan wryly noted:

> To keep a fire engine is not a proof that you propose to commit the act of arson.[20]

British officials realised that the secret of further tests would not last long, given the number of British troops involved:

> This information is secret at the moment but some announcement will have to be made in the near future as will not be possible to conceal the change of plan after some of the service personnel on the island have been informed that they will be required to remain on the island to hand over to maintenance party which will be sent out from the UK later in the year.[21]

* * *

As well as deciding how much to tell the British public, the Macmillan Government was also torn between the need for secrecy and the need to consult with Commonwealth nations in the Pacific.

Macmillan's Secretary of State for Commonwealth Affairs Alec Douglas-Home (the Earl of Home) argued it was vital to keep Australia and New Zealand informed, especially if there was to be any parliamentary statement about the future of Christmas Island testing. In a letter to Minister of Supply Aubrey Jones, Lord Home stressed:

> Should there be any question of our making any statement which might reveal or even imply our future intentions as regard tests, we must consult them fully about it beforehand. Indeed I think that the sooner we are able to tell them fully and frankly our problem about future testing in the light of disarmament, the better it will be.[22]

---

20   Ibid., p. 2.
21   Memo from Mr Moreton to Prime Minister's Office, 19 June 1957. CO1036/282.
22   Letter from Alec Douglas-Home, Secretary for Commonwealth Relations, to Aubrey Jones, Minister of Supply, 22 June 1957. CO1036/282.

12. *THE PRIME MINISTER* – HAROLD MACMILLAN

Queen Elizabeth meets Commonwealth prime ministers, including Harold Macmillan of the United Kingdom (back row, to left of Queen), Jawaharlal Nehru of India (front, third from left) John Diefenbaker of Canada (fourth from right) and Robert Menzies of Australia (second from right)
Source: UK Government.

On 24 July, the decision to wind down operations after three tests was reversed. Macmillan told the Ministerial Committee on Atomic Energy that further tests would be required to allow the Atomic Weapons Research Establishment (AWRE) scientists to develop fusion, rather than fission, weapons.[23]

HMS *Warrior* and HMS *Salvictor* had already set sail for England, but other ships, including HMS *Narvik*, HMS *Messina* and RFA *Fort Rosalie*, were turned around and returned to Christmas Island. In early August, 400 troops of the 25th Field Engineer Regiment were flown via Honolulu to the Line Islands to replace the personnel of the 28th Field Engineers who had been working on Christmas Island since June 1956. By the end of August, the majority of personnel had been replaced with new troops.

---

23 Confidential annex, Minute 1, *Ministerial Committee on Atomic Energy*, Meeting 1, papers 1–2, 24 July 1957. UK National Archives Cabinet papers CAB 134/1328.

In preparation for the next test in November, Valiant aircraft began returning to the island on 11 October, with the Canberra 'sniffer' planes of 76 Squadron returning from Australia after participating in Operation Antler at Maralinga. The three atomic tests in South Australia (Tadje, Biak and Taranaki), held between 14 September and 9 October 1957, tested atomic triggers that could be used in a two-stage thermonuclear weapon, which was subsequently tested in Grapple X, Y and Z.

Even as the Grapple Task Force redeployed military and scientific personnel to Christmas Island, the UK Cabinet sought political and logistic support from the Australian, New Zealand and Canadian governments. Commonwealth Relations Office archives reveal personal correspondence between the prime ministers in London, Canberra, Wellington and Ottawa, showing that all three Commonwealth governments backed the UK plans and offered support from their armed forces. They all, however, pressed for secrecy to avoid adverse public reaction that could damage them politically.

In late July 1957, Macmillan met with Robert Menzies in London, who had been re-elected as Australian Prime Minister in January 1956. Macmillan briefed his Australian counterpart about the planned expansion of H-bomb testing, anxious to bolster Menzies' support for further operations in the desert of South Australia (previous British A-bomb testing at Maralinga had ended in October 1956, but the British were eager to use the desert test range again to develop atomic triggers for the thermonuclear weapons).

Australia was already well integrated into the weapons program. In 1956, the Menzies Government had signed a contract with the UK Atomic Energy Authority (UKAEA) to supply uranium for UK nuclear weapons development, using ore mined at Mary Kathleen in Queensland.

On 26 July 1957, Macmillan sent a personal message to New Zealand's Prime Minister Sidney Holland, seeking his support:

> I have spoken to Menzies, who is here, and he is very anxious that we should proceed and will give us all the help that we require from him. I may be questioned in Parliament before we rise, in which case I shall merely try to keep my hands free and say that until such time as there is an international agreement on tests we must be free to proceed, but I shall of course give no indication of our decision. No doubt in the course

of the next period there will be a certain leaking because of personnel involved, but I think we can ride this as long as none of us makes any definitive statement.[24]

In a detailed message the following day, Macmillan sought Holland's assistance for another series of tests later that year. He expressed concern that growing pressure for a Partial Test Ban Treaty in the United Nations might force a halt to the British testing program before the UK could finalise development of its megaton weapons:

> Even if a partial disarmament plan were to be agreed, there would certainly be a period before it could take effect, either as regards the suspension of tests or the cut-off of production of fissile material. Pressure may, however, grow for the suspension of tests as a measure isolated from a partial disarmament agreement and a resolution proposing this may well be introduced in the General Assembly of the United Nations during the forthcoming session.
>
> In that event, we should be in great difficulty with our public opinion and might be obliged to acquiesce. In order to forestall this risk therefore, we have decided to hold further megaton tests in the late autumn of this year. These tests would be in addition to the kiloton weapons trials we have already planned with the cooperation of the Australian government at Maralinga in September.
>
> We have a ready-made base for the megaton weapons trials at Christmas Island where the facilities established for Grapple are being maintained. It would obviously be out of the question for us to find another site and establish a new base in the time and therefore we propose to carry out the tests close to Christmas Island (instead of Malden Island as on the previous occasion).
>
> I hope therefore that you will feel able to agree that we might have reporting and measuring stations on your islands again. We should also be very grateful to have again the service of the Royal New Zealand Air Force (RNZAF) in collecting samples from outlying stations and of the Royal New Zealand Navy (RNZN) frigates as weather ships … I should therefore be very grateful if you could let me know quickly whether—as I much hope—you agree in principle to give us logistic support on the lines I have mentioned.[25]

---

24   Telegram no. 492 from Commonwealth Relations Office to UK High Commissioner in New Zealand, 10:45 PM, 26 July 1957. CO1036/282.
25   Telegram no. 493, marked 'Top secret and personal', from Commonwealth Relations Office, London, to UK High Commissioner in New Zealand and UK High Commissioner in Australia, 27 July 1957. CO1036/282.

Macmillan also acknowledged the growing concern in New Zealand about nuclear testing, and disquiet in NZ Pacific territories like Western Samoa (highlighted by the 1956 Samoan petition to the UN Trusteeship Council, calling for a halt to the British tests):

> I realise that the holding of a further series of nuclear tests in the Pacific may expose you to renewed pressure against the tests from a section of your public opinion. My colleagues and I greatly appreciate all the help you gave us in this respect over Operation Grapple and much hope that in the circumstances I have set out, we may count on your help once again.[26]

Holland's reply pledged that New Zealand would support further tests on Christmas Island with a naval deployment, as they had done at Malden Island. His reply also highlighted the concern of both UK and Commonwealth governments that there was growing international pressure for a nuclear test ban treaty:

> I fully understand reasons for United Kingdom's wishing to continue and complete Grapple in face of possible United Nations and popular pressure. I note also that Mr. Menzies, whom you were able to consult in London, is anxious that you should proceed and that he will give all possible help.
>
> For my own part I am quite willing to agree that New Zealand should give whatever assistance as possible on lines similar to that accorded for the tests. You may be assured that Air Vice Marshall Oulton will be given every facility to discuss his needs with service people here.
>
> I can appreciate that your present planning does not permit you to give me any precise idea of date of any tests, but I do hope that it would be possible on this occasion to keep me fully informed as to your intentions, especially in view of fact that they may very well coincide with date of the New Zealand general elections.[27]

Macmillan replied:

> I am very grateful for your most helpful personal message and for your willingness to assist us. You may rest assured that I shall keep you fully informed as to our intentions on dates as soon as possible to be precise.[28]

---

26 Ibid., p. 2.
27 Telegram no. 312, marked 'Top secret and personal', from UK High Commissioner in New Zealand to Commonwealth Relations Office, 2 August 1957. CO1036/282.
28 Telegram no. 525, marked 'Top Secret Cypher', from Commonwealth Relations Office to UK High Commissioner in New Zealand, 9 August 1957. CO1036/282.

12. THE PRIME MINISTER—HAROLD MACMILLAN

Macmillan advised Lord Carrington, the UK High Commissioner in Australia, that Menzies had indicated support for the expansion of the H-bomb program. A message from officials in London to Carrington in Canberra noted:

> You should know for your strictly personal and secret information that Prime Minister spoke and has subsequently written to Mr. Menzies on similar lines and requested same facilities in Australia as we had for Grapple. Mr. Menzies indicated that he would give all the help we require.[29]

Menzies had long been a supporter of the British nuclear program, personally approving atmospheric tests in Australia without seeking Cabinet or parliamentary approval. The telegram to the High Commissioner in Australia noted, possibly ironically: 'Presumably he will be informing Australian government.'[30]

Like Australia and New Zealand, Canada had joined the United Kingdom and United States in the 1947 UKUSA agreement, which opened the way for joint intelligence and surveillance operations between the five Anglophone nations.[31] Macmillan now turned to Canadian Prime Minister John Diefenbaker seeking support for the H-bomb program.

Less than two months after he was elected to office, Diefenbaker was personally approached by the British prime minister with a request to support the testing program. Macmillan asked his Canadian counterpart to allow overflights of Canada by RAF aircraft carrying the nuclear weapons from England to the Pacific. On 2 August, Diefenbaker wrote to Macmillan approving the flights:

> I appreciated receiving the personal message ... concerning your desire to have certain of your service aircraft overfly Canada and land at Goose Bay and Namao en route to and from nuclear tests to be held at Christmas Island in the late autumn. We would be glad to cooperate in the manner

---

29   Telegram no. 1058, marked 'Top secret and personal', from Commonwealth Relations Office, London, to UK High Commissioner, Canberra, 27 July 1957. CO1036/282.
30   Ibid.
31   Jeffrey T. Richelson and Desmond Ball: *The Ties That Bind—Intelligence Cooperation Between the UKUSA Countries—the United Kingdom, the United States of America, Canada, Australia and New Zealand* (George Allen and Unwin, Sydney, London and Boston, 1985); Nicky Hager: *Secret Power— New Zealand's Role in the International Spy Network* (Craig Potton Publishing, Nelson, 1996).

you suggest ... I assume that the same precautions in regard to safety will be followed as were followed in the earlier operations of the same nature, and it will not be necessary to give publicity to these flights over Canada.[32]

Uncertainty over the number of further tests on Christmas Island was causing problems for the Grapple Task Force, given they might have to return unused weapons to the United Kingdom if they were not fired. This was especially a diplomatic problem with Washington, as the warhead would have to transit through US air bases on the way home. The Atomic Weapons Trials Executive noted:

> There were indications that return by air might be unwelcome to the US government.[33]

Starting from August, there was massive investment in new infrastructure on Christmas Island. The wharves at Port London were rebuilt, while the main runway of Casady Field was resurfaced. New hangers and a control tower were built. The road from Port London village to the airfield was covered in asphalt. New huts with water and sanitation were built at Main Camp and Port Camp to replace some of the tents that housed the troops in 1956–57.

Despite the thousands of personnel involved, the fear that the next test would be another dud meant that the cult of secrecy was to be maintained:

> The Prime Minister has approved that there will be no observers at Grapple X and so informed the prime ministers of Canada, Australia and New Zealand.[34]

* * *

With preparations underway, the British Government could now decide on the timing of future tests. Throughout this period, as the Macmillan Government prevaricated over the public announcement of Grapple X, officials were pressing for a quick decision from government ministers:

---

32   Telegram no. 686 from UK High Commissioner in Canada to Commonwealth Relations Office, London, 2 August 1957. CO1036/282.
33   Atomic Weapons Trials Executive: *Operation Grapple X*, minutes of meeting held at St Giles Court, 11 September 1957, p. 3. CO1036/283.
34   Ibid.

It was agreed that this conflict between the desire for secrecy and the need to push the operation through should be put to the Prime Minister, together with some similar critical decisions. If he agreed to go ahead, delivery of the equipment and briefing of the people to operate it would be delayed till about 7 October.[35]

Ultimately, the next series of tests (Grapple X, Y and Z) were conducted with great urgency, driven by Cold War anxieties. Although the Pacific islands were marginal to the main Cold War fronts such as Germany or Korea, Soviet propagandists were ramping up criticism of British colonialism and the UK nuclear testing program:

> Carrying out of tests of nuclear weapons is contrary to the principles and objects of international trusteeship. Britain has spent millions of pounds on establishing her own proving ground for nuclear weapons on Christmas Island. The first British hydrogen bomb was exploded on this island in 1957. The British imperialists have established big airbases in Fiji. The British military command regards these islands as the strategic centre of the south-western part of the Pacific.[36]

The US and UK governments were panicked by the Soviet Union's launch of its first intercontinental ballistic missile in August 1957. This was followed by the successful launch of the Sputnik satellite on 4 October 1957—the first satellite capable of orbiting the earth. A preliminary assessment by the Eisenhower White House of this Soviet space triumph reported that:

> Soviet claims of scientific and technological superiority over the West and especially the United States have won greatly widened acceptance. Public opinion in friendly countries shows decided concern over the possibility that the balance of military power has shifted or may shift soon in favour of the USSR. The general credibility of Soviet propaganda has been greatly enhanced and American prestige and the American reaction, so sharply marked by concern, discomfiture and intense interest, has itself increased the disquiet of friendly countries and increase the impact of the satellite.[37]

---

35 File note, D.J. Derx, Colonial Office, 18 September 1957. CO1036/283.
36 J. A. Lebedev: 'Colonialism and the National Liberation Movement in Oceania', *The Peoples of Asia and Africa*, No. 5 (translated in 'Translations from the Soviet press', Colonial Office digest no. 399, p. 3). CO1036/859.
37 White House Office of the Staff Research Group: 'Reaction to the Soviet Satellite—A Preliminary Evaluation', 16 October 1957. Eisenhower Presidential Library, Box 35, Special Projects: *Sputnik, Missiles and Related Matters*; NAID #12082706.

Fears of Soviet technological advances were compounded by a major fire in October at the Windscale nuclear plant—the British reactor responsible for producing the super-heavy isotope tritium used in the thermonuclear weapons.[38]

Under pressure to act, the Grapple Task Force rushed to conduct the next nuclear test by November 1957—but relocated from Malden to Christmas Island, home to thousands of military personnel and Gilbertese islanders.

---

38 Lorna Arnold: *Windscale 1957—Anatomy of a Nuclear Accident* (St Martin's Press, New York, 1992), pp. 24–26.

13

The Foreign Officer—Gillian Brown

Churchill, Eisenhower and Macmillan—improving US–UK relations
Source: Ed Clark/Life.

Throughout Operation Grapple, the British Foreign Office had its work cut out to maintain diplomatic relations with countries around the Asia-Pacific region. There was widespread opposition to the nuclear testing program in Japan, India and many South-East Asian nations, as well as island territories closer to the test sites.

Britain's crucial ally the United States was also an uneasy partner. Despite close military-to-military cooperation, the US State Department was raising concerns over sovereignty in the Line Islands. Even with the decline of McCarthyism in the United States by the late 1950s, US Congressmen were still concerned about Soviet infiltration of the British Government, following the 1950 arrest of atom spy Klaus Fuchs and the 1951 defection to Moscow of Foreign Office diplomat Donald Maclean and MI5 agent Guy Burgess.[1]

With the Commonwealth Relations Office responsible for Australia, New Zealand and Canada, and the Colonial Office liaising with British colonies in the Pacific, much of the remaining day-to-day diplomatic legwork for the Foreign Office was undertaken by Gillian Gerda Brown.

Brown was one of the first female Foreign Office entrants recruited from elite universities. Born in 1923, she studied French and German at Somerville College, Oxford. Somerville is a non-denominational college established for women in 1879, which served as an important stepping stone into government for many women (Somerville graduates include the prime ministers Indira Gandhi and Margaret Thatcher).

Brown graduated from Oxford during the Second World War, just as the UK Foreign Office was opening its doors to more women. At age 21, she joined the Foreign Office Research Department in 1944, but soon transferred to the main career path in the Ministry. Even with the loss of older male staff to the military, it was an uncommon achievement. Women in the UK civil service often faced petty discrimination as well as structural limits on their careers in Whitehall (the Foreign Office maintained—until 1973—a policy that female officials must resign if they married, so a woman could not have a diplomatic post *and* a husband).[2]

As the wartime alliance with the Soviet Union broke down, Brown was posted to Hungary between 1952 and 1954, working as Second Secretary at the UK Embassy in Budapest. Her talents recognised, she returned to London and in 1956 became active in the Grapple committee, liaising

---
1   Ben McIntyre: *A Spy Among Friends: Kim Philby and the Great Betrayal* (Bloomsbury, London, 2014). It was only after the April 1958 Grapple Y test that the United States was willing to relax McMahon Act restrictions, with the signing of the 'Agreement on co-operation on the uses of Atomic Energy for Mutual Defence Purposes' in July 1958.
2   For the challenges facing female British diplomats, see Helen McCarthy: *Women of the World— The Rise of the Female Diplomat* (Bloomsbury, London, 2014).

with British embassies in Washington, Tokyo and Paris (experience that served her well for the next posting as First Secretary in the UK Embassy in Washington from 1959 to 1962).

As a young Foreign Officer, Brown represented her department at the first meeting of the Grapple committee, created to coordinate between government ministries and the armed services, each trying to protect its financial and institutional interests. Task Force Commander Wilfred Oulton described 'Miss Brown—Foreign Office' as 'a pleasant looking, quiet young woman in a brown woollen pullover and tweed skirt'.[3]

At these initial committee meetings, as the only woman representing a government ministry, Gillian Brown stood out from the crowd, sitting alongside a range of uniformed officers and be-suited officials: General Sir Frederick Morgan (controller of atomic weapons in the Ministry of Supply); Commodore Peter Gretton DSO, OBE, DSC (the Deputy Task Force Commander responsible for the naval squadron); and the 'portly, ruddy faced' Brigadier Ivor Jehu (Public Relations Officer for the Ministry of Supply).[4]

From mid-1956, a formal Atomic Weapons Trial Executive held regular monthly meetings at Castlewood House (the Ministry of Supply headquarters near St Giles Circus in London). The executive brought together representatives of all parties involved in the operation: headquarters staff of the Grapple Task Force; the Ministry of Supply (which was the lead ministry for the overall operation); Treasury; Foreign Office; Commonwealth Relations Office; Colonial Office; UK Atomic Energy Agency; Atomic Weapons Research Establishment; and the Admiralty, War Office and Air Ministry.

***

From the beginning, the project was shrouded in secrecy. Throughout the testing series, London sent a series of communications to British authorities in Tarawa, Suva, Honiara and other locations, setting out

---

3 Wilfred Oulton: *Christmas Island Cracker—an account of the planning and execution of the British thermonuclear bomb tests 1957* (Thomas Harmsworth, London, 1987), p. 75.
4 Ibid.

guidelines for secrecy and classification of communications. Different topics were given rankings ranging from 'confidential' to 'TOP SECRET/ Atomic', with documents, letters and telegrams to be coded accordingly.[5]

Any reference to the nature and purpose of the weapons test or the overall UK nuclear weapons program had the highest grade of 'TOP SECRET/ Atomic'. The same classification was given to any design details of the bomb, the efficiency of each test weapon or the expected and measured yield of each weapon (though this did not preclude a statement to the effect that test weapons will be in the 'megaton range').

'Top secret' classification was issued for the overall size, shape and weight of each test weapon and the likely areas and degree of contamination caused by the nuclear detonation. The very fact that further megaton trials were due to take place was given the same classification, as well as any details of the method and route transporting the weapons from the United Kingdom to the Pacific trial site.

The code word FIRED (Round fired successfully) was unclassified. However, another code word ORKIDS (Round fired, but yield very disappointing) was allocated for less successful operations and deemed 'Secret/UK eyes only'. In part, this secrecy was directed at the US military observers monitoring the operation, who were not to be told that the tests had not reached megaton yield. Other code words were allocated for plane crashes or accidents, including SNODOP (Accident—round lost—Christmas Island involved) and CHEVIT (Accident—round lost—Christmas Island not involved).[6]

After the initial distribution of code words covering all eventualities for the tests, the lists were amended to add one extra code: 'Round fired. Yield not obviously disappointing.'[7] This was an interesting addendum, given the explosive yield of the first three Grapple tests actually did disappoint the scientific staff, failing to reach a megaton yield, even as they were trumpeted by public relations officials as a great triumph.

---

5   'Operation Grapple X: security classifications', Telegram no. 483 from the Secretary of State for the Colonies to High Commissioner, Western Pacific Commission and Resident Commissioner, British Gilbert and Ellice Islands Colony, 4 September 1957. CO1036/282.
6   'Operation Grapple—list of code words', Appendices B and C to Grapex/57/P.3. CO1036/281.
7   Memo from Ministry of Supply, marked 'Secret/UK eyes only': Addendum to appendix C to Grapex (57)/P3, 'limited distribution' (number 18 of 25), 30 April 1957. CO1036/281.

Even after the tests began and were reported in the British and international media, a culture of secrecy permeated the British bureaucracy. For example, in the official Colonial Office reports about the British Gilbert and Ellice Islands Colony (GEIC) from 1956 onwards, there is no mention of the construction of the military base on Christmas Island, nor the testing of nuclear weapons![8]

In the GEIC itself, the first test on Malden Island on 15 May 1957 was not even mentioned in the *Headquarters Information Note* issued by the Office of the Resident Commissioner in Bairiki, Tarawa. Indeed, the first item in the newsletter issued a week after the test was a proclamation 'covering the double taxation agreement between the Colony and Norway, which was signed by his Excellency the High Commissioner on 20 May'![9]

Secrecy even extended to restricting written evidence of key decisions in London. Minutes of the Atomic Weapons Trial Executive were individually numbered and tightly restricted to a small circle of government representatives. But there were occasions where key decisions were not fully recorded. One example was noted in August 1957 by committee chair Eric Jackson (Director General, Atomic Weapons in the Ministry of Supply):

> For reasons familiar to the Executive, no minutes of the last meeting had been taken. The principal matter under discussion had been the site of the actual tests, i.e. Christmas (S.E tip) v Malden and the decision had gone in favour of the former.[10]

Even during the Cold War, at a time of concern about Soviet spying and popular opposition to nuclear testing, this culture of secrecy created practical difficulties. An ongoing problem was that overseas allies could not be told about the looming test program, the boundaries of the danger zone or the date of the actual test without a formal announcement from the government.

---

8   UK Colonial Office: *Gilbert and Ellice Islands Colony and the Central and Southern Line Islands— Report for the Years 1956 and 1957* (Her Majesty's Stationery Office, London, 1959) and *Report for the Years 1958 and 1959* (Her Majesty's Stationery Office, London, 1961).
9   *Headquarters Information Note*, No. 22, 23 May 1957. Office of the Resident Commissioner, Gilbert and Ellice Islands Colony, F 76/6/32 (1957). PAMBU document AU PMB 493.
10 Item 1, minutes of the August 1957 meeting, Atomic Weapons Trials Executive, St Giles Court, 14 August 1957. CO1036/282.

While the military focused on operational matters, a major concern for Foreign Office officials was to calm international opposition to the tests. They also sought to keep out the small number of civilians from other countries that might transit through Christmas Island or the danger zone.

* * *

Given the presence of US and Japanese business interests in the Line Islands, Gillian Brown lobbied the Colonial Office in late 1956 to impose restrictions on movement near Christmas Island:

> There are some legal complications involved in doing this, and we shall have to handle the matter rather carefully in order to avoid possible public complaint or even a claim for damages.[11]

The Colonial Office agreed to restrictions, noting:

> American civilians have no right to land on Christmas Island without visas, though American military aircraft and vessels could arrive simply by notifying us that they intend to do so. In view however of the close contact with the Americans, we agree with you that it is highly improbable that they would seek to embarrass us in this way during the tests.[12]

The date for public announcement of a danger zone around the Malden or Christmas test sites became a major battleground between different parts of the British Government. Internal correspondence between the Grapple Task Force, the Foreign Office and the Colonial Office highlights the tension between safety, security and political expediency. The military were eager for as much public notice as possible to keep aircraft and vessels far away from the Line Islands. In contrast, London-based officials sought to avoid any publicity that would exacerbate the growing international condemnation of the tests.

For security reasons, the Task Force Headquarters were reluctant to reveal the exact date of the tests, but officers deployed in the central Pacific were aware of the hazard that fishing boats might stray into the danger zone. At the same time, diplomats were well aware that early announcements

---

11   Letter from Gillian Brown, Foreign Office, to H.P. Hall, Colonial Office, 17 December 1956. CO1036/280.
12   Letter from H.P. Hall, Colonial Office to Gillian Brown, Foreign Office, 18 December 1956, p. 2. CO1036/280.

might strengthen the political opposition in neighbouring countries and territories—especially those like New Zealand and Fiji that were actively engaged in supporting the operation.

In January 1957, the Foreign Office proposed to close territorial waters around Christmas and Malden islands for the duration of the Grapple tests, but without giving any public notice of the closure. Foreign Office officials noted:

> I think we shall also need to be quite clear in our own minds about how far the Task Force Commander should go in persuading any intruders to leave the danger area if they are found on the high seas.[13]

The Grapple Task Force also wanted operational control of air and sea movements at Penrhyn, a northern atoll of the New Zealand territory of the Cook Islands. At an executive meeting for the testing program, the Commonwealth Relations Office representative 'had no doubt that the New Zealanders would agree to this so far as EENC movements were concerned but that they would not be willing to hand over control of the island or anything affecting the civil population'.[14]

However, the United States formally objected to this proposal, given that a number of the Line Islands—including Christmas—were subject to an ongoing dispute over sovereignty and control between the United States and United Kingdom.[15]

The British Embassy in Washington warned London that they would be breaching international law if they did not announce the closure of territorial waters, as the United States had done for its tests at Bikini and Enewetak atolls. On 9 January 1957, British Ambassador to the United States Sir Harold Caccia wrote:

> If we do not announce the closure of our territorial waters, we shall not be following any American precedent and the Americans will think that we are acting illegally. But they will not go out of their way to make trouble

---

13 Letter from J.C. Hainsworth, Foreign Office, to G.A.C. Witheridge, Ministry of Supply, 9 January 1957. CO1036/280.
14 Minutes of the January 1957 meeting, Atomic Weapons Trials Executive, St Giles Court, 9 January 1957, p. 2. CO1036/280.
15 For details of the dispute over sovereignty, which was not resolved until Kiribati gained independence in 1979, see W. David McIntyre: *Winding up the British Empire in the Pacific Islands*, Oxford History of the British Empire Companion Series (Oxford University Press, Oxford, 2014), pp. 323–324.

for us. Equally, they will not feel able to defend us, if our action makes any trouble for them. In these circumstances you will doubtless want to look again at the proposal to disregard what appears to be a requirement of international law.[16]

Foreign Office officials in turn complained about the US complaints:

> The US reaction to our idea of avoiding any public notice, though understandable, is rather tiresome. In order to avoid political comment and, more important, possible confusion in the minds of mariners and airmen about the true extent of the danger area, we would have much preferred to give no advance notice. Nevertheless, in view of the US warning, we consider that we may have to after all.[17]

The Foreign Office canvassed a variety of ways that they could technically meet their obligations for notification, but without actually informing pilots and sea captains who might infringe on the danger zone:

> Under international law, we are required to give the notification 'due publicity'. We do not think it necessary to send it out as a warning notice to mariners and airmen, particularly since—as the Task Force Commander has pointed out—these often go out in the form of wireless messages … An alternative is to circulate it to diplomatic missions here … This draws rather unwelcome attention to our action but seems a possible solution.[18]

The following month, the United Kingdom and United States went on to exchange formal diplomatic notes about Christmas Island and the proposed testing program. However, the British Government was reluctant to accept the US State Department proposal to publish the notes, arguing that:

> The US note now refers in paragraph 8 to safety precautions that we have not disclosed in public; secondly, publication would of course stimulate other governments to press for exchanges of notes on questions of compensation.[19]

---

16   Letter from Ambassador Sir Harold Caccia, British Embassy, Washington to P.H. Dean, Foreign Office, London, 9 January 1957. CO1036/280.
17   Letter from J.C. Hainsworth, Foreign Office to G.A.C. Witheridge, Ministry of Supply, 16 January 1957. CO1036/280.
18   Ibid.
19   Memo from H.C. Hainsworth, Foreign Office, London to J.C.A. Roper, British Embassy, Washington, 7 February 1957, ZE212/10/0. CO1036/281.

13. *THE FOREIGN OFFICER* — GILLIAN BROWN

* * *

By early 1957, the cult of secrecy amongst many British officials about the looming tests was already causing speculation and concern amongst the populations of inhabited islands across Polynesia.

In French Polynesia, for example, there was growing concern about the tests, even though the French dependency was located some distance from the proposed test site. Gillian Brown was in regular contact with the British consul in Papeete, Tahiti, as well as the UK Embassy in Paris, seeking to calm any public debate.

The Grapple Task Force were planning to establish a radiation-measuring station in Tahiti, to be operated by French officials. A second monitoring station was planned for Rangiroa atoll, 355 kilometres to the north-east, to be run by nuns from the local Catholic mission. However, because there was no suitable airfield in Tahiti or Rangiroa, Sunderland flying boats from the Royal New Zealand Air Force (RNZAF) base in Fiji were chosen to transport the necessary equipment. Later RNZAF visits to Tahiti were scheduled to collect samples after the tests for rapid transport back to England.

The regular RNZAF visits provoked speculation amongst local Maohi leaders in Tahiti. In early January 1957, the British consul in Papeete telegrammed London, asking for instructions on what to say about the testing program:

> Public and local legislative council anxious at rumours. Please reply whether permitted and how much to say.[20]

Brown consulted with colleagues in the Ministry of Supply, which was ultimately responsible for the operation, noting:

> The preparations for radiation monitoring [in Tahiti] are likely to attract increasing attention and if we show hesitance in revealing what they are, I suppose we might be wrongfully suspected of concealing dangers from the public.[21]

---

20 Telegram from British Consul, Papeete, to Gillian Brown, Foreign Office, London, 28 January 1957. CO1036/281.
21 Letter from Gillian Brown to D.H. Lovelock, Ministry of Supply, 30 January 1957. CO1036/281.

She also told the British Embassy in Paris:

> We still feel we should if possible avoid saying in public that radiation measurements are being taken ... this is a subject that is very open to misinterpretation by the public. We do not wish to create an entirely false anxiety. Perhaps you could explain matters to the French authorities.[22]

Radiation monitoring stations were mostly limited to British and Commonwealth territory for the first round of testing on Malden Island. For the November 1957 Grapple X test on Christmas Island, however, the system to monitor radiation was extended to locations controlled by the US military, such as Hawai'i and the Marshall Islands.[23] With the potential for local protests, Gillian Brown was initially reluctant to discuss the issue with US authorities, until just before the date of the test:

> Will it be possible to defer such discussion in the interests of secrecy, say until early October? Operational requirements must of course come first, but if, as seems likely, discussions would involve local meteorological and civil aeronautics officials at Honolulu, Kwajalein and Canton, who would not otherwise be aware of our intentions and who would not be accustomed to handling top-secret information, the risk of a leak would be increased.[24]

Similar concerns were evident in Tokyo, which continued to lobby for assurances over safety. In a letter to the Ministry of Supply, Brown noted:

> I think our main concern would be to reassure the Japanese about the possibility of fish or the sea being contaminated, without, of course, giving any assurance that we might later have cause to regret.[25]

A week before the first test on Malden Island, London-based officials were reluctant to reveal the actual date of the test to British colonial administrators in the Pacific:

> The Ministry of Supply have not agreed that the Governor of Fiji or the High Commissioner for the Western Pacific should be given advance warning of the actual timing of the tests ... Arrangements have been made

---

22   Letter from Gillian Brown to A. Duff, British Embassy, Paris, 6 February 1957. CO1036/281.
23   Letter from Squadron Leader Wilson to UK Foreign Office, London, 21 August 1957. GX/TS.3010/8/air. CO1036/282.
24   Letter from Gillian Brown, Foreign Office, London, to G.A.C. Witheridge, Ministry of Supply, 9 September 1957. CO1036/282.
25   Letter, marked 'Top secret/UK Eyes only', from Gillian Brown to D.H. Lovelock, Ministry of Supply, 30 January 1957. CO1036/281.

that, should there be an accident, the operational command will inform both the Governor of Fiji and the High Commissioner for the Western Pacific directly of this and of precautions which should be taken.[26]

Even after the later decision to continue the tests on Christmas Island, there was still a reluctance to share information with Colonial Office representatives in the Pacific. The Secretary of State for the Colonies noted that it was 'most important that information about our intentions should be kept secret as long as possible'.[27]

A Colonial Office file note marked 'secret' from August 1957 notes:

> So far we have told the High Commissioner for the Western Pacific little more than the planned time and place of the operation. Speed and secrecy have precluded us from telling him more before now.[28]

For safety of aircraft, the Resident Commissioner of the GEIC issued regulations to prevent planes overflying the test area. Following the first three tests on Malden Island, these safety regulations had expired on 1 August 1957. However, by early September, London was reluctant to inform the Resident Commissioner that he should renew the regulations preventing overflights:

> I think it might give rise to suspicion that there is something in the wind if they are renewed now, and I suggest we simply ask the High Commissioner to prepare the necessary regulations and hold them in readiness until we give the word.[29]

When Cabinet decided to continue with a further series of tests relocated to Christmas Island, British officials debated whether to inform other nations. In the diplomatic message sent to UK embassies in Washington, Tokyo and Paris a fortnight before the November 1957 Grapple X test, the Foreign Office stated:

> Please inform United States authorities … but it is not proposed to give advance notice to Japanese and French governments, as was done in January. French are not helping this time and the courtesy shown to the Japanese last time did us no good.[30]

---

26 File note by Mr Howard-Drake, 'Nuclear test in the Pacific', 9 May 1957. CO1036/282.
27 Telegram no. 359, marked 'Top Secret and personal', from the Secretary of State for the Colonies to acting High Commissioner, Western Pacific Commission, 2 August 1957. CO1036/282.
28 File note by D.J. Derx, Colonial Office, London, 5 August 1957. CO1036/282.
29 File note for draft correspondence from D.J. Derx, Colonial Office to the Ministry of Supply, 3 September 1957. CO1036/282.
30 Telegram no. 4413 from Foreign Office, London to UK Embassy, Washington; UK delegation, New York; UK Embassy, Tokyo; and UK Embassy, Paris, 24 October 1957. CO1036/287.

Secretary of State for Foreign Affairs Selwyn Lloyd delayed announcing the looming test until October at the United Nations, noting simply:

> These tests will begin in the near future. They will be held in the vicinity of Christmas Island and will take the form of explosions at high altitude of devices in the megaton range. A danger area will be declared at the appropriate time. The additional radioactive fallout from the tests will be negligible.[31]

For the troops deployed on Christmas Island, from Britain, New Zealand and Fiji, the threat was not 'negligible', despite the statements from bureaucrats in London. Limited protective gear and radiation dose badges were issued to some troops for the early tests (such as white cotton suits to reduce the risk of flash burns). Most veterans testified, however, that they never received such gear, and served their term wearing standard army boots, shorts and shirts (discussed in Chapter 18).

From oral testimony and archival research, there is evidence that the troops were placed in hazardous positions, which increased the risk of ingesting or inhaling radioactive isotopes from atmospheric tests like Grapple Y, which blew fallout across Christmas Island. The Fijians, for example, ignored British regulations and caught fish and crabs that may have been contaminated by fallout. Fijian military personnel were involved in clean-up operations after each nuclear test, including dumping contaminated materials offshore or disposing of thousands of birds that were maimed, blinded or killed by the nuclear explosions.

For naval personnel in the British and New Zealand warships deployed for Operation Grapple, there were further hazards as some ships manoeuvred through the post-testing danger zone. On land, too, the Gilbertese plantation workers and their families have also testified of their concerns, as six further tests were conducted above the south-east corner of Christmas Island.

---

31 Ibid.

14

The telegraphist—Roy Sefton

Like Paul Ah Poy, New Zealand sailor Roy Sefton joined the Navy as a young man to travel the world and seek broader horizons. At age 19, he was posted as a telegraphist and radio operator on the New Zealand frigate HMNZS *Pukaki*:

> This was my first ship and, after hearing the tales from all the old salts around the rum, I wanted to have experiences in exotic places like Hong Kong. Instead I ended up at Christmas Island.
>
> As a young man, I never imagined that I would eventually spend 40 years of my life campaigning for the rights of nuclear test veterans, including 22 of those years as Chairman of the New Zealand Nuclear Test Veterans Association.[1]

On 11 February 1957, with New Zealand Prime Minister Sidney Holland pledging support for Britain, the NZ Cabinet approved participation in Operation Grapple. HMNZS *Pukaki* and HMNZS *Rotoiti*—two frigates of the Royal New Zealand Navy (RNZN)—were to be sent between March and July 1957 to join the naval task force as weather ships.[2] The Royal New Zealand Air Force (RNZAF) would provide support for the radiation monitoring program and general transport duties.

---

1 Interview with Roy Sefton, Palmerston North, New Zealand, November 2015. Unless otherwise noted, direct quotes from Sefton come from this interview.
2 This chapter draws on the wonderfully comprehensive book by Gerry Wright: *We Were There—Operation Grapple* (Zenith Print, New Plymouth, n.d.) and a 1989 New Zealand Defence Force study (declassified in 1996) by John Crawford: *The involvement of the Royal New Zealand Navy in the British nuclear testing programmes of 1957 and 1958*, research paper for New Zealand Defence Force Headquarters, Wellington, New Zealand, 1989 (hereafter 'NZDF report').

Roy Sefton, aboard HMNZS *Pukaki*, 1957
Source: Courtesy Roy Sefton.

14. THE TELEGRAPHIST — ROY SEFTON

The presence of New Zealand ships in a British naval task force was regarded as normal procedure. Even with a small fleet, the RNZN had long worked in cooperation with the Royal Navy (RN). During the Second World War, more than 10,000 New Zealanders were trained at the HMNZS *Tamaki* base to serve aboard RN and RNZN vessels in every theatre of the war.[3] Six Loch-class frigates had been purchased from England in 1948, for a cost of £1.5 million, as the United Kingdom ran down the size of its wartime fleet.

At Christmas Island, two of these RNZN frigates joined the RN warships of the Grapple flotilla at Port London, a harbour inside the north-west arm of the island's lagoon (and, for later tests, at the opposite end of the island from ground zero). For naval personnel based on shore, the camp was redesignated as HMS *Resolution*.

Over the next two years, *Pukaki* was sent on four separate deployments to participate in all nine hydrogen bomb tests in 1957–58. *Rotoiti* was redeployed to the Far East in late 1957, after participating in the first three tests at Malden Island (May–June 1957) and the Grapple X test (November 1957). Over this period, 551 NZ sailors served on the two vessels.[4]

* * *

As a junior member of the *Pukaki*'s crew, Roy Sefton witnessed five nuclear tests:

> I did the first three tests and then returned to Auckland thinking it was all over. But no, the ship was sent back up to Christmas Island for Grapple X. We came back to New Zealand, but the same thing happened again and we were sent back for Grapple Y. After that there was a big shift and a lot of crew were taken off because they'd been there for a long time. I was one who was taken off, but there were some who stayed aboard and did all nine detonations.

---

3   Michael Wynd: 'From Participation to Protest: The Royal New Zealand Navy and Nuclear Testing 1957–1995', presentation to the biennial Sea Power Conference, Sea Power Centre, Sydney, Australia.
4   Only 3 per cent of the crew witnessed all nine tests, but 17 per cent witnessed at least one test. Data from Neal Pearce et al: *Mortality and cancer incidence in New Zealand participants in United Kingdom nuclear weapons tests in the Pacific*, Department of Community Health, Wellington School of Medicine, 7 March 1990.

Sefton recalled that, during the 1950s, conditions aboard the New Zealand naval vessels were pretty rugged by contemporary standards:

> Living on those ships, you really lived hard. When you're at sea, you are watch keeping or on shift work all the time. I was a telegraphist radio operator, so I saw very little outside the office. I went up to the radio shack, did my watch, slept, ate down below. In the evenings, you could go on deck for the beer issue, but I was too young at the time to draw a rum and beer ration.
>
> Our mess deck was very crowded and not everybody had a hammock, so some slept on the deck and others slept under the mess table on stretchers or things like that. You must remember we were in the tropics. A lot of guys, including myself, went down and got a stretcher from the stores and slept on the deck, because the heat down in the mess decks was too much. Those ships were built for the convoys to Russia in 1942 and they were not designed for the South Pacific.

For the first deployment, the two frigates left New Zealand on 14 March and travelled to Christmas Island via Fiji, collecting 39 Fiji Royal Naval Volunteer Reserve (FRNVR) sailors in Suva (see Chapter 7). The *Pukaki* sailed on directly to Christmas Island, while *Rotoiti* diverted via the Cook Islands.

On the day of the tests off Malden Island, the *Pukaki* and *Rotoiti* were tasked to monitor prevailing weather conditions and wind speeds, using meteorological balloons released at regular intervals and tracked by radar. In his study of the operation for the New Zealand Defence Force (NZDF), John Crawford has detailed the ships' key contribution:

> The main task of the New Zealand frigates was to be the collection of meteorological information, which was essential for the successful and safe conduct of the nuclear tests. The two weather ships would carry out patrols around the test site, during which they would regularly launch hydrogen filled balloons. The flight of these balloons, which were fitted with radar reflectors, was to be tracked by radar, and the information about wind patterns and other data was then to be passed to a meteorological centre on Christmas Island.[5]

For the first two tests, Short Granite and Orange Herald, the NZ frigates took up positions off Malden Island to monitor the airburst as the devices were dropped by Royal Air Force (RAF) Valiant aircraft. For both tests,

---

5 John Crawford: NZDF report, op. cit., p. 6.

Pukaki was stationed approximately 50 nautical miles from ocean surface 'zero point', where the bomb was targeted. *Rotoiti* was deployed further away, about 150 nautical miles from the area where the bomb was to detonate.

Interviewing Christmas Island veterans decades later, many are vague about dates and details. But they could all recall vivid impressions of the first time they viewed a nuclear explosion. Roy Sefton still has sharp memories of his first test, Short Granite:

> The most enduring impression I have of a detonation was the first one. I guess that was probably everyone's major impression. *Pukaki* and *Rotoiti* alternated as 'close-in' ship for each test, so *Pukaki*—the ship that I was on—was close in for Grapple 1.
>
> On the day of the test, us youngsters sat together at the communicators' blast station on the quarter deck. You were pretty much left to your own thoughts. It was a quiet, reflective time and none of us had any real idea of what we were going to see, including the ship's captain and all the officers. We've since learnt that even the scientists didn't know what would happen with Grapple 1, whether it would be a fizzer or a monstrous blast—a detonation of the size that they intended—because it was totally experimental.
>
> We sat there and then the bomber came out. They had direct radio contact with the ship and it was broadcast on the ship so you could hear the pilot. We were all sat down with our backs to the blast and you were required to put your hands over the goggles you were wearing and close your eyes. There was this horrific flash. You could see the bones of your hands. I remember there was silence from all these people on deck, and then all of a sudden, some good old naval language came out!

Following the detonation, the crew were ordered to stand up, turn around and face the blast.

> Photographs don't do it justice. Even though it was 80 miles away, it was amazing. It sort of bubbled, there were pinks and all these hot colours. After a period we watched it and the colour went out of the fireball. It took on that very white effect like a mushroom. The ship turned its bow towards the detonation and I thought 'bloody hell, why are we going there?'
>
> In those days, I didn't know what ionising radiation would do to me, but I remember looking around me instinctively, thinking 'is there anything getting at me?' I noticed one or two others doing the same thing and we caught each other's eyes. It wasn't saying anything but it was a look, you know, what the hell?

On the quarter deck of HMNZS *Pukaki* preparing for the Grapple 1 test, May 1957 (Roy Sefton is fourth from right)
Source: Courtesy Roy Sefton.

14. THE TELEGRAPHIST—ROY SEFTON

After the first test on 15 May, *Pukaki* passed within 6 nautical miles of the ocean surface 'zero point', as it returned towards the flagship HMS *Warrior* to hand over meteorological results and equipment.

For the third test on 19 June, the two frigates reversed their stations, with the *Pukaki* stationed further away. At the end of the three Malden Island tests, the frigates set sail on 25 June to return to New Zealand, arriving in mid-July. Questioned by the media, one Māori sailor described the bomb: 'Boy, she was a beaut!'[6]

* * *

After the initial three tests, it was clear that the devices had not reached the required yield as thermonuclear weapons. Given the failure to achieve a yield of 1 megaton, the British Government then decided to conduct further tests in late 1957 (see Chapter 12). As the light aircraft carrier and flagship HMS *Warrior* had already departed the Pacific, the decision to relocate the tests to Christmas Island allowed for command and control from the scientific bunker on the island.

With London debating whether to proceed, the New Zealand Government also discussed whether it should continue to provide naval support. Newly appointed Prime Minister Keith Holyoake finally confirmed that New Zealand ships would again deploy for the testing program until May 1958, telling the British Government:

> I am relieved to note that after this, you do not foresee need for further trials for at least 18 months and perhaps longer. You will, I am sure, appreciate logic of question which is increasingly being asked by average citizen in this part of the world—'why, if there is no danger from these tests, do the British and Americans not hold them near to home?'[7]

In October, the two frigates returned to Christmas Island in time to conduct weather monitoring for the Grapple X test, scheduled for 7 November. However, before the ships left port, there was no public announcement in New Zealand of the new deployment. It was a time of growing public opposition to the South Pacific tests and many members

---

6   'Hydrogen bomb "was a beaut"', *Auckland Herald*, 17 July 1957.
7   Barry Gustafson: *Kiwi Keith—a biography of Keith Holyoake* (Auckland University Press, Auckland, 2007). Holyoake had replaced Sidney Holland as leader of the governing National Party on 20 September 1957.

of the opposition Labour Party were calling for a nuclear test moratorium. With national elections looming on 30 November, Labour seemed likely to replace the governing National Party.[8]

Most sailors aboard the New Zealand frigates had little knowledge of the growing public debate over nuclear weapons—not just in New Zealand but across the Pacific region. Even so, despite being one of the younger members of the crew, Sefton had a personal interest in nuclear issues. As a radio operator, he also had the opportunity to hear news of what was going on in the outside world:

> As a youngster, I had a fascination with the bombings of Hiroshima and Nagasaki. So I had a little bit of knowledge and knew that the bomb could cause ongoing health problems. I was quite surprised to find that a number of people I served with at the time knew nothing about nuclear weapons, except that a big bomb had flattened a couple of cities.
>
> Leading up to the Christmas Island nuclear tests, we radio operators and signallers were handling communications coming into the ship, so we were aware of what was going on. Others on the ship never had a clue. Because of my position, I had a little knowledge of what we were going to do and what the possible consequences might be—and for myself, it did cause some nervousness.

As a junior member of the radio team, Sefton was required to improve his Morse code during his own spare time. As a training exercise, he used to listen to Press Association broadcasts in Morse to improve his capacity to record incoming messages from the fleet. But listening to the media reports and translating them from dots and dashes into English broadened his knowledge of how the world outside was viewing the tests:

> What I was getting from time to time was all these reports about protests against nuclear testing, which nobody else on the ship was getting. People in the UK were pushing prams to Aldermaston in protest, there were protests in New Zealand and I even received a newspaper clipping from my mother that the Japanese were intending to send a flotilla of protest yachts.

---

8   In a narrow victory, Labour leader Walter Nash won 41 seats to the National Party's 39, with Nash replacing Holyoake as Prime Minister on 12 December 1957. Despite rank and file party sentiment, the new Labour government did not end New Zealand's involvement in Operation Grapple, with the Royal New Zealand Navy (RNZN) continuing deployments for the remaining five tests in 1958.

14. *THE TELEGRAPHIST* — ROY SEFTON

You're sort of thinking to yourself: 'The outside world is protesting about the dangers of the stuff, so what the hell am I doing here?' I wasn't that naive that I believed all the stuff they told us about safety precautions was sufficient. The big giveaway was the instruction that you had to urgently get to shelter station if anything went wrong.

The frigates had been rigged with a system of hoses and spray heads to wash down the upper surfaces of the ship with seawater, as a crude device to prevent fallout from settling on the decks. For the early tests, sailors were issued with anti-flash gloves and hoods, white overalls (for officers) and tinted goggles. The NZ sailors also followed protocols issued for the British warships, with training in safety precautions well before D-day:

> The orders came from the United Kingdom that a skeleton crew was to run the ship below decks during the detonation, while the maximum number of crew was to be on deck to observe them. That raises the question in your mind—why? They practised what might arise if we encountered fallout. You had to get all the men that were on deck to shelter stations.
>
> You witnessed the detonation at what they called 'blast stations' and if we encountered radiation, the crew had to be moved very quickly from the deck to 'shelter stations'. The intensity of these training exercises became more frequent as we moved closer to the day. But they were terrible conditions, remembering it was nearly on the Equator. You might be down in the magazine with no ventilation, fully dressed with no skin showing. I believe one guy couldn't stand up to it and was taken off the ship and sent back to New Zealand.

The elaborate training and safety precautions taken for the Malden Island tests were not continued when Operation Grapple continued at Christmas Island. For Grapple X, for example, the crew abandoned much of the protective gear used in earlier tests, apart from goggles to lessen the flash of the detonation.

Even so, the megaton Grapple X test caused considerable damage from heat and blast, as reported by two US military observers at the test:

> The blast wave that hit the Joint Operations Centre at 23 to 27 miles distance broke practically all the quarter inch reinforced glass windows in the scientists air-conditioned building, as well as cracking the many windows that were left open …

The following day, Admiral Patrick took a trip to the South East point by helicopter and observed at a distance of 6 ½ to 10 miles from Ground Zero that timber and debris thrown up onto the beach were burning with a great deal of flame. On landing a point about 5 miles from point zero, birds were observed to have their feathers burnt off, to the extent that they could not fly. Dead fish were reported to have washed ashore.[9]

For the massive Grapple Y test on 28 April 1958, *Pukaki* was once again stationed about 80 nautical miles to the east of 'surface zero'. Engines were stopped to allow the maximum number of sailors to view the test, which had become so familiar that the crew wore no protective clothing.

Sefton recalls that over time, the NZ vessels had moved closer to the actual detonation point for each test:

> If you look at the positions of the ships, the distance from ground zero decreases with every test, until the ninth detonation when they were only 20 miles away. What also disappears is the protective clothing.
>
> I contrast conditions under the first test with those for Grapple Y, which was the biggest test that they did. It was the one known as 'the bomb that went wrong'. For the Grapple Y test, the ship was not closed down into damage control and as I stood on deck, I watched it in a pair of shorts and flip-flops. It was that casual, there was no 'blast stations'.
>
> After watching the blast, I remember I went down to my locker to get some coins to spend later at the ships canteen. But the blast wave from that detonation was the biggest that I've experienced. It gave me such a fright that the money flew out of my hand, as the ship rolled to starboard.

* * *

The British Government has long argued that the naval flotilla was located upwind from the tests at sufficient distance to protect crews from any radioactive fallout. But veterans have contested these claims, highlighting the way that after the tests, some ships passed near ground zero or under the path of the radioactive plume.

---

9   Brigadier General J.W. White (Deputy Chief of the Armed Forces Special Weapons Project, USAF) and Rear Admiral G. S. Patrick (Director, Atomic Energy Division, Office of the Chief of Naval Operations): *Report of United States observers of a nuclear test*, Atomic Energy Commission, AEC 663/13, 10 December 1957. Marshall Islands Nuclear Documentation Database (MINDD).

14. THE TELEGRAPHIST — ROY SEFTON

The day after Grapple Y, as it returned to Christmas Island, *Pukaki* passed directly through the surface zero point. During monitoring of sea water through the boiler room inlets, the crew were astonished to record significant radiation levels in the water—the first time radiation was monitored below deck. Radiation levels were soon found to be at lower levels than first thought, with human error causing the initial panic, according to then Able Seaman Gerry Wright:

> On Tuesday morning, *Pukaki* passed through ground zero on its way back to the London Roads. As it approached the area, Bernard Commons was sent down to the boiler room to monitor any radioactivity in the seawater. He quickly drew up a recording graph and began testing the seawater …
>
> Unfortunately, Bernard had made an error in the vertical axis of the graph by a multiple of 10. As the recording progressed, he realised his error, but had no time to recalculate the graph. The on-watch stoker Petty Officer, on being asked for more paper by Bernard, became terrified as the graph rocketed upwards. Bernard wondered if the Petty Officer ever believed him that he had made an error in drawing up the graph by slipping the decimal point one way, rather than they had run into an unexpected super high radiation level.[10]

Roy Sefton argues that, over time, there were many pathways for sailors to be affected by fallout, which rained from the clouds after some tests:

> We were always running short of fresh water, we couldn't condense it fast enough. On many occasions, the officer of the watch would spot a raincloud on the horizon. We would change course to go into it, so that we could shower and clean teeth and wash clothes in freshwater.
>
> I remember it well: we used to slant the awnings so the water ran off in great volumes and you could collect it in buckets. I believe that it was in those periods that radioactive contaminants entered our bodies either through inhalation or ingestion. There they stuck, pulsing away for 30 or 40 years.

The first of four Grapple Z tests, codename Pennant, was an atomic device suspended from barrage balloons 450 metres above the southeast point of Christmas Island. On 22 August 1958, *Pukaki* was closer to the action than scheduled, according to the NZ Defence Force study of the operation:

---

10   Gerry Wright: *We Were There*, op. cit., pp. 189–190. See also John Crawford's account of the incident in the NZDF report, op. cit., p. 52.

Because of a faulty star sight, the *Pukaki* was 28 nautical miles to the east of surface zero, five miles closer than the planned viewing position. All of the ship's company apart from six men required to man the wheelhouse, engine and boiler rooms were mustered on the deck. The crew faced away from the test site until 15 seconds after the blast before turning to see the fireball rise and the mushroom cloud form.[11]

In following years, Sefton began to suffer adverse health effects, which he now attributes to his involvement at Operation Grapple:

> At age 30, I was a Petty Officer and close to promotion as a Chief Petty Officer. I really wanted to stay in the Navy till I'd served my 20 years. But my health was deteriorating. At the time, I felt that if I'd signed on again, I wouldn't have lasted the distance.
>
> I'd stayed on in the Navy for 14 years and was suffering widespread joint and muscle pain, stiff necks and things like that. I also noticed that I was experiencing unexplained fatigue. I was having trouble staying awake during my times on watch, although with the job I had it was imperative to stay alert. If you'd slept on watch, you would have been demoted back the mess deck, so I left the Navy.
>
> My mistake was that I didn't look ahead. At the time, I wasn't thinking about war pensions or anything like that, so I didn't report my ailments to the Navy. In those days, unless the injury was pretty obvious, they'd give you a couple of paracetamol and tell you to return to duty.

* * *

In 1987, the Labour Government led by Prime Minister David Lange introduced the New Zealand Nuclear Free Zone, Disarmament and Arms Control Act to declare New Zealand's land, air and territorial sea as a nuclear-free zone.[12]

The same year, Auckland-based doctor Graham Gulbransen, a member of the International Physicians for the Prevention of Nuclear War, began to inquire into the health of the New Zealand Christmas Island veterans, sparking extensive debate in the media.[13] The public debate led to

---

11   John Crawford: NZDF report, op. cit., p. 54.
12   David Lange: *Nuclear Free: The New Zealand Way* (Penguin, Wellington, 1991).
13   'H-Bomb witnesses sought', *Dominion*, 21 July 1987; 'Sailor rubbishes Navy's claim of bomb test checks', *Evening Post*, 1 August 1987; 'Cancer check on Kiwi sailors at nuclear tests', *Evening Post*, 20 August 1987.

government responses, including a 1989 NZDF study by John Crawford and a 1990 medical study conducted by a team led by Associate Professor Neal Pearce of the Wellington School of Medicine.[14]

The 1990 Pearce study found an elevated level of leukaemia amongst the veterans and a supplementary report in 1996 noted:

> Although the numbers are very small, the leukaemia findings are of particular interest due to their consistency with a previously published large study of United Kingdom participants in the atmospheric nuclear weapons test program. It is concluded that some leukaemias and possibly some other haematological cancers, may have resulted from participation in a nuclear weapons test program. There is little evidence of an increased risk of cancers, other than haematological cancers, and there is no evidence of an increased risk for causes of death other than cancer in New Zealand participants in the test program.[15]

Many veterans were highly critical of government attempts to downplay potential health impacts, and the limited number of health conditions that they attributed to exposure to radiation.[16] On 2 July 1995, Roy Sefton and his wife Joan met with Christmas Island veteran Tere Tahi to found the New Zealand Nuclear Test Veterans Association (NZNTVA). The record of the founding meeting notes that:

> Several issues were discussed with the understanding that it was high time and association was established, as more and more of our veterans have journeyed to the heavens above … The question of compensation was spoken of light heartedly, with much emphasis being placed more on apology. Further discussions on this matter will need to be addressed after formation of the association.[17]

During the first NZNTVA conference in 1996, the sharing of stories meant that the poor health of the veterans and the impact on their families became dramatically clear. Former captain of HMNZS *Pukaki*,

---

14 John Crawford: NZDF report, op. cit.; Neal Pearce et al.: *Mortality and cancer incidence in New Zealand participants in United Kingdom nuclear weapons tests in the Pacific*, Department of Community Health, Wellington School of Medicine, 7 March 1990.

15 Associate Professor Neal Pearce: *Mortality and cancer incidence in New Zealand participants in United Kingdom nuclear weapons tests in the Pacific: supplementary report*, Department of Medicine, Wellington School of Medicine, June 1996.

16 See, for example, 'Why RIMPAC have been so scathing on the Pearce reports 1990-1996', *Prickley Heat*, November 1997, p10.

17 Minutes of the founding meeting of the New Zealand Nuclear Test Veterans Association (NZNTVA), signed by Roy Sefton and Tere Tahi (copy in author's files).

Commodore Richard Hale, OBE, RNZN Rtd (who witnessed the first three tests at Malden Island) became NZNTVA's patron. A campaign was immediately launched to secure pensions from the NZ Government and upgrade the pension grading for Operation Grapple veterans and their widows to War and Emergency status, which was achieved in 1998.

Roy Sefton QSM, Chair of the New Zealand Nuclear Test Veterans Association (NZNTVA)
Source: Nic Maclellan.

14. *THE TELEGRAPHIST*—ROY SEFTON

In the 1999 New Year's Honours list, Roy Sefton was honoured with the Queen's Service Medal for Public Service (QSM), for his part in obtaining War Disability Pensions and Surviving Spouses Pensions for NZ Grapple veterans and their widows. The QSM citation noted:

> He has worked tirelessly to gain recognition for the men whose health suffered as a result of their service on *HMNZS Pukaki* and *HMNZS Rotoiti* at Christmas Island during the nuclear testing of 1957 and 1958. Because of his commitment the men who served on *Pukaki* and *Rotoiti* were awarded full war pensions in March 1998.[18]

Over the next two decades, Roy Sefton and other members of the NZNTVA would continue to campaign for recognition of their service with Operation Grapple. As Chapter 20 will show, independent medical studies have documented significant genetic impacts for the New Zealand naval contingent. For troops based ashore, there were similar concerns.

---

18   *New Year Honours List 1999*, Department of the Prime Minister and Cabinet, New Zealand.

15

The soldiers—Isireli Qalo

English officers and soldiers from the Royal Fiji Military Forces (RFMF), Christmas Island, 1958
Source: Courtesy Mrs Loata Masi.

After the success of the November 1957 Grapple X test, with its yield of 1.8 megatons, the British Government decided to continue with Grapple Y and the Grapple Z series. To ensure that the remaining tests could be completed before a nuclear testing moratorium came into force, there was a major build-up of operations on Christmas Island throughout 1958.

The number of personnel surged in preparation for Grapple Y, with replacement British soldiers arriving aboard the troop ship TT *Dunera*. While the number of scientific and technical staff on the island remained steady at 114, British Army numbers doubled to 1,331 and the contingent of sailors increased to 851 during the year. The Royal Air Force (RAF) had the largest number of personnel deployed at any one time, with 1,426 aircrew serving on Christmas Island during 1958.[1]

Members of the Royal Fiji Military Forces (RFMF) were also sent to the island as a small part of this much larger deployment. Fijian soldiers who staffed the test sites from 1958 to 1960 worked as engineers, labourers and stevedores for the loading and unloading of ships. Later, after witnessing the tests, RFMF soldiers were also involved in clean-up operations, such as capturing and killing birds blinded by the nuclear detonation.

Today, the surviving Fijian military personnel are anxious about possible long-term effects from radiation exposure, for themselves and members of their family.

* * *

The idea to send soldiers as well as sailors from Fiji was driven by the colony's Governor Sir Ronald Garvey. Eager to promote employment opportunities for young Fijians, Garvey lobbied London in late 1957 to send a detachment of RFMF engineers and 20 Fiji Royal Naval Volunteer Reserve (FRNVR) ratings to Christmas Island:

> Fiji Military Forces would include 16 sappers with dock construction experience, two of whom hold road machinery licences and one a heavy bulldozer licence. Remainder of party capable, under supervision, of road construction or stevedore duties.[2]

The involvement of Fijians was not entirely welcomed by the Resident Commissioner of the British Gilbert and Ellice Islands Colony (GEIC), who was eager to promote employment opportunities for Gilbertese rather than people from other British colonies. From his headquarters in Tarawa, Commissioner Bernacchi saw the renewed military build-up on Christmas Island as an opportunity to improve revenues for the GEIC.

---

1 Data from 'Number of men involved in each operation, by service or employer', Table A4.1, Appendix 4 in Lorna Arnold: *Britain and the H-Bomb* (Palgrave Macmillan, London, 2001), p. 241.
2 Telegram no. 332 from Sir Ronald Garvey, Governor of Fiji, to Alan Lennox-Boyd, Secretary of State for the Colonies, 21 December 1957. CO1036/283.

He was overridden by his superior John Gutch, the Western Pacific Commissioner based in the British Solomon Islands Protectorate. Gutch recognised the logistic pressures that could limit the use of civilian labour and grudgingly endorsed the use of RFMF personnel:

> In view of (a) short term employment proposed (b) exceptional program of capital works now underway in Tarawa and British Phosphate Commission at Ocean Island (c) lack of civilian accommodation at Christmas Island, I have no objection to employing Fijian service (repeat service) personnel in this instance, and without prejudice to consideration of similar proposals in future.[3]

In the New Year, London quickly approved the deployment of Fijian soldiers and sailors, confirming that 'employment would be for three months in the first instance and that costs, including indemnity against claims for disability pensions etc. arising from any injuries would be a charge on United Kingdom funds'.[4]

On 20 January 1958, RFMF Captain Viliame Umu and Sergeant Isoa Vavaitamana led the initial contingent of Fijian soldiers to Christmas Island. The opportunity to leave Fiji for the first time was a huge adventure for most of the young men. One of the first Fijian soldiers deployed to Christmas Island was Private Isireli Qalo (RFMF 19333) from Naceva village on the island of Beqa:

> I was very young when I went to Christmas Island—many of us were young, some were kids. There were a number of us from the army infantry who were attached to the engineers from Samabula who went in one of the first trips to Christmas Island. We left the capital Suva and slept in Nadi before flying off in the plane to Canton Island where we stayed the night. The next day, we left Canton Island for Christmas Island.
>
> For our work on Christmas Island, they divided us into two groups. One group stayed at the Main Camp and was involved in construction work. I was one of those delegated to Port Camp. Those of us at Port Camp did stevedoring work—unloading cargo from Britain for Christmas Island.[5]

---

3   Telegram no. 649 from Sir John Gutch, Western Pacific Commissioner, to Alan Lennox-Boyd, Secretary of State for the Colonies, 24 December 1957. CO1036/283.
4   Telegram no. 5 from Alan Lennox-Boyd, Secretary of State for the Colonies to Sir Ronald Garvey, Governor of Fiji, 6 January 1958. CO1036/283. This is one among many statements from the British authorities that they would be responsible for death or injury to Fijian service personnel in the course of their duties.
5   Interview with Isireli Qalo, Suva, Fiji, 1998. Most interviews excerpted in this chapter were recorded in the Fijian language in 1998, and the translations come from the book *Kirisimasi—Na Sotia kei na Lewe ni Mataivalu e Wai ni Viti e na vakatovotovo iyaragi nei Peritania mai Kirisimasi* (Pacific Concerns Research Centre, Suva, 1999), with thanks to my co-authors Losena Tubanavau-Salabula and Josua Namoce.

Over time, successive deployments of Fijian troops lengthened to six and then 12 months. Josese Kalouvou (RFMF 19890) joined the army in 1958 as the RFMF expanded its recruitment of new troops. Under the command of Lieutenant Namosimalua Komaisavai, he was part of the next contingent to arrive in May 1958:

> After the Malayan campaign, we were the first recruits in the army—there were about 500 of us. After we went through our basic training, they picked 22 from my group of recruits and we were to go to Christmas Island for six months. We did construction work there, constructing buildings for the army.[6]

Isireli Qalo said that much of their work was routine, with little variation because of the isolation:

> It was a soldier's life on the island. We used to wake up every morning at 4 am. We got dressed, had our breakfast and then went for parade at 5.30 am. It was very hot on this island because it was near the middle of the earth [the Equator]. We worked every day and it was always hot. Contact between that place and home was very difficult.[7]

It was a major logistic exercise to feed the thousands of troops, but the kitchens were vital to keep up morale. The hardship rations issued to the original military contingents in 1956 had been replaced with more regular supplies of food, often shipped or flown from Hawai'i. Desalination plants provided fresh water supplies. Despite difficulties with refrigeration and a lack of fresh fruit or vegetables, the British Army ensured that the hard-working young men on the island were well fed with potatoes.

Private Eseroma Kuruwale (RFMF Engineers 18906) from Nakuruivau, Bau, Tailevu was flown to Christmas Island in May 1958. One of his fondest memories of the time was the food:

> Meals were served in the early morning until it was close to lunch time. It was the same with our evening meals. Supper went on until night time. For the Fijian soldier, it was up to his appetite. All the other British soldiers had only one serve. For the Fijian, it depended on his stomach—Fijian soldiers went twice or three times.[8]

---

6   Interview with Josese Kalouvou, Suva, Fiji, for *Kirisimasi*, op. cit., pp. 43–44.
7   Interview with Isireli Qalo, Suva, Fiji, for *Kirisimasi*, op. cit.
8   Interview with Eseroma Kuruwale, Suva, Fiji, for *Kirisimasi*, op. cit., pp. 54–55.

Mosese Koroi, who spent a year on the island in 1958–59, agreed that 'one thing good about being there was the food':

> We ate very well. Breakfast was being served from early mornings until 9.30 am and tea was at 10 o'clock. Lunch was served from 11.30 am onwards. Lunch was so good that there was no room for complaints. Relations between the soldiers from different countries were very good. Those of us in Main Camp numbered 1,000. One day, we would all eat at the same time. On other days, we would not know how many of us were there.
>
> We were always eating. We were very flattered with the service provided by those working in the kitchen. They were really good cooks and their service was really good. All we had to do was eat. Potatoes! There were plenty of potatoes. They used to bring our *dalo* [taro] from Hawai'i. One of us Fijian boys would be in the kitchen cooking this *dalo*.[9]

Despite this, the Fijians also supplemented the standard rations with seafood, caught from the surrounding lagoon and reef. Eseroma Kuruwale recalled that the soldiers often ignored official regulations that banned the consumption of fish following a nuclear test:

> When we Fijians were there, we used to go spear fishing along the shores. We ate the fish on the beach. During the time that the bomb was dropped, it wasn't allowed to eat fish, but you know, we Fijians always do it anyway. We were always yearning for fish. After a day or one week, we used to look for crayfish. We ate the crayfish which were very tasty. It was very easy to catch there. Not like in Fiji, where it is hard to find.[10]

* * *

From the 1950s to today, the British, NZ and Fijian veterans have faced penny-pinching by British officials, who often refuse to fund the commitments made by British political leaders. Files in the UK National Archives are full of correspondence between the Grapple Task Force, the Ministry of Supply in London, the commander of the RFMF and the Colonial Office, all seeking to shift responsibility for the employment of islander labour, the payment of pensions or the health care costs of military personnel who claim they were exposed to hazardous levels of radiation.

---

9   Interview with Mosese Koroi, Suva, Fiji, for *Kirisimasi*, op. cit., pp. 52–53.
10 Interview with Eseroma Kuruwale, Suva, Fiji, for *Kirisimasi*, op. cit.

As London and Suva discussed further deployment of troops to Christmas Island during 1958, every meeting included discussion over the payment of war pensions and gratuities for Fijian Navy and Army personnel who served on Christmas Island.[11]

British policy was clear. Fijian personnel serving on Christmas Island would receive disability pensions for illness or injury attributable to their involvement in Operation Grapple. Historic commitments made within the British Government to the colonial governor in Fiji are not legally binding with the independent Republic of Fiji. But the legal and administrative commitments made in the 1950s have a clear moral force, showing that the British authorities understood that they had an ongoing responsibility to address any injury or illness to the Fijian military personnel serving on Christmas Island, as well as to their families, widows and orphans.

While debating the best mechanism to pay the pensions, there is no doubt that London recognised its obligations to pay post-service pensions to the Fijian military personnel. This commitment is repeated in numerous letters and policy documents issued between government ministries:

> The Ministry of Supply has confirmed that the Ministry will indemnify the government of Fiji against claims for disability pensions or gratuities arising from injuries or sickness attributable to service by Fiji Military Forces on Christmas Island and to injuries received by Fiji Military Forces en route from Suvo [sic] to Christmas Island and vice versa. The rates and conditions applicable to such pensions or gratuities will be the same as those already agreed in respect of the Fiji Military Forces who served in Malaya.[12]

A 1958 letter from the Ministry of Supply to the War Office reconfirmed the commitment for disability pensions arising for injuries or sickness:

> Under the arrangements between us and the Fijian government, we have undertaken to indemnify the Fijian government against claims for disability pensions, et cetera, arising from injuries or sickness attributable

---

11 Correspondence is collated in the Colonial Office archive 'Proposal to Use Fijian Military Forces on Christmas Island', PAC 310/4/012. C01036/514. See, for example, 'Conclusions of a meeting held on Monday, 26 January 1959 at St Giles Court to decide the method of meeting claims for the employment of Fijian Naval and Army personnel at Christmas Island', Ministry of Supply minutes, 26 January 1959. DB/231/05. CO1036/514.
12 Telegram no. 315 from the Secretary of State for the Colonies to the Officer Administering the Government of Fiji, 4 July 1958. PAC 310/4/012. CO1036/514.

15. THE SOLDIERS — ISIRELI QALO

to service on Christmas Island or in transit. This we hope to do by payment of a lump sum in respect of each man, calculated by the government Actuary from information on the expectation of life on the individual and his rate of pension.[13]

A June 1958 letter from Ministry of Supply to the Government Actuary confirms that pensions would be paid to dependants as well as RFMF personnel, for both death and injury related to presence at the Christmas Island nuclear weapons base:

> The Ministry of Supply has undertaken to indemnify the government of Fiji against claims for pensions to which men of the Fiji Military Forces or their dependents may be entitled as a result of death or injury sustained by them during their service at the Nuclear Weapons Testing Base at Christmas Island in the Pacific.[14]

In response, the UK Government Actuary confirmed:

> This is a service which the Government Actuary would be prepared to undertake and I did not expect any substantial difficulty to arise in doing so. A substantial body of information regarding rates of mortality, et cetera, is already available to us from investigations made into the circumstances of pension schemes maintained for the benefit of government servants in overseas territories, including Fiji, or their widows and orphans.[15]

Despite this, Governor of Fiji was wary of lump sum payment, aware that it might be responsible for decades of funding for young men affected by illness or injury:

> If a monthly pension were paid, this government would be liable to meet the additional cost in the event of the pensioner outliving the period on which the actuarial calculation has been based.[16]

From the beginning, the armed forces tried to avoid responsibility. The British Admiralty and War Office attempted to shift responsibility for managing the payment of troops, leaving the administration to the Governor of Fiji. In an echo of contemporary debates about the

---

13   'Fijian forces at Christmas Island', Letter from G.M.P. Myers, Ministry of Supply, London, to Miss J.B. Payne, War Office, London, 29 October 1958. DB 231/05. CO1036/514.
14   Letter from G.M.P. Myers, Ministry of Supply, London, to C.E. Clarke, Government Actuary's Department, 5 June 1958. DB 231/05. CO1036/514.
15   Letters from Government Actuary's Department, London to G.M.P. Myers, Ministry of Supply, 13 June 1958. DB/231/05. CO1036/514.
16   'Fijians for Grapple', telegram from the Governor of Fiji to the Secretary of State for the Colonies, 23 August 1958. PAC 310/4/012. CO1036/514.

responsibility of the UK Government towards the government and people of Fiji, the Colonial Office condemned the parsimony of the armed services and Ministry of Defence (MoD) over the simple matter of meeting financial obligations to the Fijian service personnel:

> We are somewhat dismayed both at the complexity of the proposed arrangements and at the idea that the burden of operating them should fall principally on the government of Fiji. It must be remembered that these troops have been made available by Fiji at the request of Her Majesty's Government, in order to relieve the call on United Kingdom troops. It seems to us unfair to seek to impose upon the government of Fiji the complex arrangements now proposed for financing them.[17]

* * *

The issue of injury, illness or death was not academic. Isireli Qalo reported that the Fijian troops, like the Gilbertese workers, were often allocated dirty, difficult or dangerous tasks:

> I was involved in the unloading of the first bomb for Christmas Island. A cargo boat escorted by several warships brought the bomb to Port Camp. My job was to secure the unloading area and oversee the work of the Fijian boys.
>
> Those doing the unloading were organised into sections. There was only one white fellow who was allowed in the secured area with me, to oversee the unloading. We took this thing from the Navy and took it onto the island.[18]

Before travelling to the island, Qalo was not aware of the full scale of the operation, until he witnessed the Grapple Y test in April 1958:

> After some time there, we realised that we were doing work related to the tests. When it happened, I became afraid. We proceeded to the site where we were to sit during the tests. We were dressed in white clothes then moved away from the area where the bomb was to be tested. We had to press our eyes with our gloved hands until the explosion was complete.[19]

---

17 Letter from D.J. Derx, Colonial Office, London, to G.M.P. Myers, Ministry of Supply, London, 30 December 1958. PAC 310/4/012. CO1036/514.
18 Interview with Isireli Qalo, Suva, Fiji, for *Kirisimasi*, op. cit.
19 Ibid.

15. THE SOLDIERS — ISIRELI QALO

Decades later, the Fijian Christmas Island veterans have vivid memories of the day of the tests. As with the British troops, Fijian soldiers were lined up, backs to the blast, to prepare for a plane to drop the hydrogen bomb over the south-east corner of Christmas Island.

During his six months on the island, Josese Kalouvou witnessed two hydrogen bomb and one atomic bomb test:

> When they dropped the bombs, we were told to move far away and not to look at it. There used to be blasts. When it exploded everything below—trees and everything else—blew into the air. When the planes dropped this bomb you were not allowed to see it. If you saw it you would go blind. We wore protective clothing to protect our skin. Even with this clothing we could easily burn.[20]

Eseroma Kuruwale also recalled the routine:

> The usual practice was having lectures on the bomb, one or two days before it was tested. One English Major explained the difference between hydrogen and atomic bombs—their different strengths. He explained briefly that if it fell on Fiji, the whole island would be vaporised.
>
> Whenever the bomb was about to be tested, we used to be transported to the other side of Christmas Island at about 2 am in the early morning. We used to stay there until twilight, then we were transported back to the Main Camp in trucks. There we waited till daylight.
>
> At about 8 o'clock there was a plane in the air, which was used to forecast the weather. The bomb was dropped at 8 o'clock. There was a count from 10 to 1, then zero. At that time, you were to close your eyes. Don't try to force your eyes to see the light or it will be damaged.[21]

Anare Bakale (RFMF Engineer 10820) said that 'from the time I arrived there in '58 until my return, I continued to feel the effects of the bomb physically and mentally':

> At about 10.00 am before they exploded the bomb, our superior explained to us that the bomb would go off. We were advised that wherever we were working, we were to listen carefully to all instructions and follow whatever advice that came. When the instructions were given, we were asked to be on alert and be aware about our safety.

---

20 Interview with Josese Kalouvou, Suva, Fiji, for *Kirisimasi*, op. cit.
21 Interview with Eseroma Kuruwale, Suva, Fiji, for *Kirisimasi*, op. cit.

> A plane was flying, carrying this thing [the bomb]. We heard this plane flying and instructions were being regularly relayed. Instructions continued from about 10.00 am to 1.00 pm. I think they said the bomb was going to explode at 1.00 pm.
>
> They told us to close our eyes. If you opened your eyes, they will be injured forever. I swear that when I closed my eyes, I could still see the light from that thing. I also could feel the sound of this thing and it was the most terrible sound.[22]

Bakale recalled the enormous power of the hydrogen bomb, which destroyed vegetation in the south-east corner of the island:

> After two weeks, we went to see the site where this thing exploded. The whole place looked dry and black. Dead fish were floating in the sea. It was so horrifying. What if this explosion had hit us? I believe we would all have died.
>
> The island is all sand and all the plants that grew are those that grow on sandy soil. I did not see any trees similar to the ones we have here in Fiji, only plants that grew on sandy areas. The plants were very green, but when the fallout from the explosion reached these plants, they withered as if they had been watered with boiling water. Nothing was left. Everything from the stem to the leaves disappeared. Only the sand was left.[23]

---

22 Interview with Anare Bakale, Suva, Fiji, for *Kirisimasi*, op. cit., pp. 53–54.
23 Ibid.

16
The Banaban—Tekoti Rotan

As a member of the Fiji Royal Naval Volunteer Reserve (FRNVR 1133), Tekoti Rotan was based at Port Camp on Christmas Island in 1958. But Rotan used to sneak out of the military camp at night to meet with the Gilbertese labourers living in the nearby village:

> That village was an escape place for me. When I had time in the night, instead of going watching the film, I skipped out to the village and go and yarn with the people out there.[1]

Although he was serving in the Fiji Navy, Rotan was of Micronesian heritage. As one of the few military personnel to share a direct cultural connection with the Gilbertese workers on Christmas Island, Rotan bridged the gulf between soldiers and sailors from the South Pacific and civilian labourers from Micronesia.

In 1957–58, a fierce debate erupted between British officials over the best way to recruit more labourers to Christmas Island, now that the test site was being relocated from Malden Island. Some ministries pressed for increased numbers of disciplined Fijian military personnel, while the Gilbert and Ellice Islands Colony (GEIC) administration argued that more civilians should be recruited from overcrowded and underemployed communities in the Gilbert Islands.

---

1   Interview with Tekoti Rotan, Suva, Fiji, November 2016. Unless otherwise noted, direct quotes from Rotan are taken from this interview.

Tekoti Rotan in Suva, Fiji, November 2016
Source: Nic Maclellan.

One incident facing Tekoti Rotan puts a human face on this bureaucratic policy battle:

> The funny thing is, when we sailors went there, we had this cloth hat to protect us from the heat. I always bring my hat down to hide myself from the Gilbertese people. So when we Fijians went to work, they start complaining: 'What are these Fijians doing here? Now we've got a job, they're coming again!'
>
> They didn't know that I could hear them. Three days this kept on, then I said to myself, 'No, I'd better not do this, they'll get very angry at me.' So I went to them and shook their hand and said in i-Kiribati '*Kam na mauri*!' [Greetings]. Most were shocked and said 'you bugger!'

For Rotan, the cultural bond with the Gilbertese was a warm memory of his time on the island, as a 24-year-old, far from home:

> I was fortunate because some of them were relatives from my mother's side. My mother was from Kiribati and I was warned before I went to Christmas that 'you'll find some of your *kaivata* [countrymen] there'. So I said, 'good, what are their names?'

Gilbertese men living on Christmas Island had arrived on the island from the GEIC's western archipelago as plantation workers. They lived, together with their families, at the village near Port London—a total of about 260 men, women and children over the period of the operation. But with the plantation halting work during Operation Grapple, many were hired to support the British military effort with mundane tasks to improve conditions for the troops living under canvas. The islanders were initially deployed as general labourers, as laundry assistants and for 'sanitary duties (i.e. emptying Elsan toilets), a task of relatively short duration for which extra pay would be awarded'.[2]

Under the direction of Percy Roberts (a New Zealander employed as a colonial service District Officer), the Gilbertese workers were also deployed on the wharves. They assisted with unloading barges as new supplies arrived from England and were transported from ship to shore. One report to Western Pacific Commissioner John Gutch noted:

---

2   'Employment of local labour in Operation Grapple', note prepared by Task Force Grapple for discussions with his honour M.L. Bernacchi CMG OBE, Resident Commissioner Gilbert and Ellice Island Colony, 26 March 1958. Grapple archives GRA/S.102/36/ORG, Appendix A. Elsan was a popular brand of portable chemical toilets, widely used in the United Kingdom.

> The landing of large quantities of stores and equipment and the construction of a major airfield on Christmas Island was a difficult and arduous task and its completion in time would not have been possible without the outstanding help of the District Officer and the island labour force.[3]

* * *

Tekoti Rotan's travels from his home island to the Caroline Islands, the Gilbert Islands, Fiji and finally to Christmas Island reflect the many ways that resource extraction, military conflict, labour mobility and displacement have reshaped the lives of Pacific islanders.

Rotan was born on Banaba, known as Ocean Island to the GEIC colonial authorities. As with Nauru, the island of Banaba was rich with phosphate. It was the location of a major mining operation that eventually consumed two thirds of the island's land.[4]

Born in 1934, Rotan's childhood was disrupted by the Second World War, as Japanese forces advanced across Micronesia. Banaba was occupied by the Japanese military and the population dispersed, as Rotan recalled nearly 75 years later:

> During the war, my family and other members of the Banaban community were uprooted and taken away to the island of Kosrae in the Caroline Islands as prisoners of war. I spent the rest of the war years on Kosrae. As a prisoner of war, I was educated in the Japanese school on the island of Kosrae. At that time I could speak and write in Japanese.
>
> The British came back again and collected all the Banabans from Kosrae and Nauru and some of us went to Tarawa [main island and capital of the GEIC]. We were all gathered together in Tarawa and they tried to convince us that we must not go back to Banaba, because the land was not habitable for us.
>
> The British were trying to get rid of us from Banaba because we were blocking the mining work in our own villages. So the war provided them with the excuse. In 1945, my community was further uprooted and we were brought by the British government to be settled on the island of Rabi in Fiji. The reason was because our home land Banaba was considered unsuitable for resettlement as the result of phosphate mining.

---

3   Telegram from Secretary of State for the Colonies Alan Lennox-Boyd to Western Pacific Commissioner John Gutch, 17 April 1957. CO1036/281.
4   The history of phosphate, Banaba and Rabi is movingly recorded by Katerina Teaiwa: *Consuming Ocean Island—stories of people and phosphate from Banaba* (Indiana University Press, Bloomington, 2015).

16. THE BANABAN—TEKOTI ROTAN

The arrangement was alright, we'll come to Fiji for two years while you people prepare the island for us to go back. So we came—but when we came here to Fiji, it's not two years. We've been in Fiji ever since![5]

In the 1950s, as they prepared a contingent to join the British counter-insurgency campaign in Malaya, the Royal Fiji Military Forces (RFMF) promoted their proud record of service to Empire in Bougainville and Solomon Islands during the Second World War. Seeking employment and training, many young Fijian villagers were attracted to sign up, but the Banaban elders on Rabi discouraged recruitment:

> When we arrived in Rabi, there were less than 1,000 of us Banabans. Most of us were killed during the war and they were worried that our community would slowly be diminishing. So they said to our young men: 'None of you should volunteer to go to war. We want you to stay on the island. Produce! We want our community to grow.' So we stayed.
>
> For myself, however, I still remembered the suffering we had under the hands of the Japanese. I think I had anger in me. I said, I must go and join the army someday, because I want to protect. No such thing should happen again to our people. So I convinced my father: 'Let me go to Suva to continue my education.' I studied bookkeeping, because at that time at school, we were over age, and I could not progress further.
>
> That's the time that I heard of the recruitment for the Navy. The commanding officer happened to be a man who'd served in Kiribati, so he knows our people. So I went to see him and I joined. Then, because of the war, I failed my medical tests. They said I had TB—the aftermath of it was still there on my chest. Three months they gave me injections all the time. My body was stiff because of all the injections. Then when I went to the medical test, I passed, and that's how I joined the Navy.

While working at the Fiji naval headquarters at Lami in 1958, Rotan was intrigued when officers called for volunteers to go and help the British soldiers prepare Christmas Island for the testing program:

> Most of us were young men and said, 'That's exciting, we'll go', without realising! We knew there was a bomb there, but we were just going to prepare the island, construction work, build the road, that's all we know. We didn't know that we'd be there during the actual test.

---

5   For other childhood memories, see the speech by Tekoti Rotan to International Meeting, World Conference on A and H Bombs, Tokyo, August 2002.

> Because we were in the Navy, we were assigned to do stevedoring work on the wharf, carting building materials and foodstuffs from the big boat anchored outside. Because I was a Leading Seaman then, I was assigned a landing craft and one pontoon. We carry a big load from the ship, then I go up on the pontoon, take it out to the ship, load it up with goods or big machinery and bring it back to the shore.
>
> As I was in charge of one of the landing craft, I was warned that in case of emergency, they told me where to go, where to rush to the army camp and where to pick up those people and move away from the island. So then I start to realise that this is not a fun thing.

Rotan returned early to Fiji because his wife was suffering ill health during her pregnancy, but still lined up, back to the blast, for one test:

> Because I was there only for three months, I only witnessed one test. They told us to assemble on the beach. We had this broadcasting mike and as soon as the pilot takes off, we can hear everything, from their position on the air field and he's going up. When he's ready, he says, 'I'm ready now to release the bomb' and it's counting, 10 to 1, and then it goes.
>
> We were looking at the sea. They said, 'Turn around', and the first thing we notice that lightning! That lightning came, phew! If it lasted more than five seconds, we would have been dead. It was very painful. After that, I would look up and we would see this ball of black cloud up there and then the fire inside start drifting off from the island.

For Rotan, the scale of the nuclear detonation and the attendant risk of fallout raised the stakes beyond normal military duty:

> We were all young people. We'd all signed our death warrant when we joined the Navy, so we thought this is what we signed for. But that's the time we realised, you know, there was some danger in the work we were doing.

* * *

The status of the Gilbertese labourers on Christmas Island became a source of tension between the military command, different government departments in London and Colonial Office staff in the Pacific.

For the Colonial Office, seeking to improve revenues and living standards in the GEIC, the build-up of operations on Christmas Island created a great opportunity to provide waged employment for Gilbertese workers.

Despite penny-pinching in London, Operation Grapple provided a steady stream of funds that the GEIC Resident Commissioner would never otherwise see.

The military, however, were reluctant to be responsible for undisciplined civilian staff, plus women and children, who had their own housing and food needs. Before the tests began, Wilfred Oulton and the Grapple Task Force were also concerned about the presence of Gilbertese on Christmas Island when tests actually occurred. As the Malden Island tests were still being planned in early 1957, GEIC Resident Commissioner Michael Bernacchi was told:

> Task Force Commander has now decided that it will be impractical remove civilian labour temporaly [sic] from Christmas during actual time of tests and that there is no alternative but to evacuate civilian labour for two months from 1 May till 1 July. So far as possible, number of labourers on island should be reduced minimum before this period. Task Force will assist with transport and movement of food etc supplies. They would prefer to move labour as short distance as possible (e.g. to Fanning Island).[6]

As the test site was relocated from Malden to Christmas Island in mid-1957, the Western Pacific Commission was 'concerned about the reference to tests being close to Christmas Island, but no doubt the authorities are fully aware of the distribution of population in the area … Necessity to evacuate civilians from other islands should, I feel, be avoided'.[7]

Writing to officials in the Pacific, the Colonial Office in London confirmed that populated islands outside the prescribed danger area would take no extra precautions:

> I am assured that neither Fanning Island nor other inhabited islands in the area, apart from Christmas, will need to be evacuated for tests and that the test will carry no risk for inhabitants of these islands or any in the Colony. Civilian population on Christmas Island will be evacuated but not for any great length of time.[8]

---

6 Telegram from Secretary of State for the Colonies to Sir John Gutch, High Commissioner Western Pacific, and Resident Commissioner M.L. Bernacchi, Gilbert and Ellice Islands Colony, 10 January 1957. CO1036/280.
7 Telegram no. 418 from Western Pacific Commission to Secretary of State for the Colonies, 12 August 1957. CO1036/282.
8 Draft telegram from D.J. Derx, Colonial Office, London, to Assistant High Commissioner, Western Pacific Commission, n.d. CO1036/282.

Under pressure from the Colonial Office, the Grapple Task Force again debated the status of the Gilbertese islanders on Christmas Island:

> It is not intended to evacuate the civilian population of Christmas Island for any great length of time and our present plans are that on firing days, civilians will be embarked in a ship and sailed out of the immediate danger area. They will be landed again on Christmas Island as soon as the burst has taken place and there is no danger to human life.[9]

A September 1957 letter from the Secretary of State for the Colonies did, however, acknowledge there was a level of risk for people housed in vessels of the naval taskforce:

> Should an accident occur, either due to a crash on take-off by the bomber or surface burst instead of a high airburst, then there may be a risk to ships lying in the anchorage.[10]

For the people on the ground, however, these bureaucratic policy debates meant little. Tekoti Rotan explains that safety regulations issued from London had little meaning for the islanders. One example is the supposed ban on the consumption of fish that might be contaminated with fallout:

> The only warning we had before the test, was they warned the people: 'After the test, don't eat any fish!' But you know, I'm from Kiribati. I love raw fish and this is the only dangerous thing after the test. They said 'Don't!', but I ignored them.
>
> I went to the Kiribati people and said: 'Hey, raw fish, we're not supposed to eat the raw fish!' But they said, 'Oh, we've been eating it and nothing's happened.' That was the biggest mistake for them.

As the tests were relocated from Malden to Christmas Island, the Grapple Task Force was more open to the use of Pacific labour—Gilbertese or Fijian—given the time and cost involved in shipping British troops halfway round the globe. However, by mid-1957, there were just 76 Gilbertese workers, together with their families, stationed on Christmas Island. London then proposed to increase the labour force to more than 200 Gilbertese workers by the end of the year. This expanded

---

9   Letter from Group Captain F.M. Milligan, Headquarters Task Force Grapple, to G.A.C. Witheridge, Ministry of Supply, 9 August 1957. GX/TS. 3001/8/Air.
10 Letter from P. Rogers, Secretary of State for the Colonies, 20 September 1957, marked 'Top Secret'. CO1036/283.

labour force would serve for one year and then local administrators would need to continue providing employment for half this labour force in subsequent years.

Initially, 24 further Gilbertese labourers plus their families were to be sent to Christmas Island from Tarawa aboard the *Constantine* in September 1957. However, the request floundered for months, due to lack of transport and uncertainty about the availability of housing for the extra labourers on Christmas Island. The acting Resident Commissioner complained to London:

> District Officer has no labour reserves to draw from, other than those already at Christmas Island, and if more are required to bring numbers up to 90 by September, they will have to be specially recruited in the Gilbert and Ellice islands (not Phoenix, which proved unsatisfactory last occasion). This will involve chartering vessel immediately and with the *Tungaru* overhaul, the only possibility is the *Matapula*.
>
> This would prove serious embarrassment administratively and would be uneconomical for small numbers involved … Some indication of the length of time required, as taking Gilbertese away from home for long periods only leads to trouble. If families are to accompany, transport commitments would be trebled and could not be met with our resources without incurring delay and serious embarrassment, particularly in view of the Betio harbour project.[11]

Officials in London sent dozens of telegrams and letters to officials in Tarawa and Suva, trying to find appropriate shipping to relocate the labourers required for work at the Christmas Island base. The incessant demands from half a world away clearly angered the local officials, who felt—correctly—that the Grapple Task Force and UK officials were trying to conduct operations on the cheap, drawing resources from the colonial administration that would create long-term problems for the local economy.

---

11 Telegram no. 89 from Acting Resident Commissioner, Gilbert and Ellice Islands, to the Secretary of State for the Colonies, 25 August 1957. CO1036/282. On 25 May 1957, the UK Government announced that Michael Bernacchi, who had left Tarawa due to ill health, would end his posting. He was temporarily replaced by his deputy Frederick Pusinelli as Acting Resident Commissioner. However, Bernacchi later returned to his post and played an ongoing role in negotiating with Grapple Task Force over labour supply for the operation. *Headquarter Information Note*, No. 23, Extraordinary edition, 25 May 1957. Gilbert and Ellice Islands Colony. F76/6/32 (1957). PAMBU document AU PMB Doc 493.

The acting Resident Commissioner in Tarawa believed that London-based officials did not understand that Christmas Island was nearly 3,300 kilometres away from the colony's administrative headquarters in the Gilbert Islands. In August 1957, he wrote tersely:

> Although I am taking immediate action to comply with the Task Force request, I feel it my duty to stress the crippling effect which the diversion of the *Matapula* and *Tongaru* to Christmas Island will have on the economy and routine administration of this Colony, which cannot adequately be recompensed by simple reimbursement of expenditure. The Colony is dependent on these vessels for maintaining food supplies and collecting copra, neither of which can be neglected for any long period. I would therefore earnestly request reconsideration of outside assistance.[12]

* * *

The colonial administrators in Tarawa were anxious that the expansion of facilities on Christmas Island would have long-term, adverse economic implications. The new tasks allocated to the Gilbertese labourers would undercut the plantation economy and the revenues raised for the whole colony from copra in the Line Islands. These concerns were backed by the Western Pacific Commission in Honiara, which told London:

> Resident Commissioner points out that further tests will involve further interruption of copra production at Christmas Island. Over 12 months, crops now lying. Recent rain may result in increased percentage of germination and consequent loss of copra and of income to the plantation and revenue. Further delay in resuming plantation operation will involve further running down, extent of which is difficult to assess.
>
> While these factors can doubtless be included in the claims for compensation, assessment of this will have to be authorised. Meantime, plantation owes the government about £30,000. Two years ago, there was hope of settling the case but until plantation can resume full operation, liquidation of debts is postponed, which is detrimental to the Colony, which with diminishing copra revenue cannot carry the burden indefinitely. Resident Commissioner suggested there is case for settlement of compensation and also that Grapple might buy or lease land occupied, particularly the airfield.[13]

---

12   Telegram no. 99 from Resident Commissioner, Gilbert and Ellice Islands to the Secretary of State for the Colonies, 30 August 1957. CO1036/282.
13   Telegram no. 440 from acting High Commissioner, Western Pacific Commission, to the Secretary of State for the Colonies, 16 August 1957. CO1036/282.

As the government refused to tell him the date for the next test and how long the Grapple test series would continue, the Resident Commissioner proposed that the UK Government purchase the Christmas Island plantation:

> While I regard it as absolutely incumbent on the Colony to afford Grapple every assistance, I am becoming increasingly concerned over the long-term implications of these latest developments. It is appreciated that it is difficult at this stage for the planners to envisage how long Christmas Island is going to continue to be required for nuclear tests, but Grapple's stake there is becoming considerable with permanent airfield, including installations of more permanent character than hitherto, and it is hard to believe that they will not continue to require the island as base for some years to come.
>
> In the circumstances it is becoming virtually impossible to continue to regard Christmas Island as a normal economic commercial proposition. The plantation is heavily in debt at present, and whereas it was originally considered that if Grapple activity ceased in mid-1957, 12 months copra could be safely left on the ground and harvested afterwards, these latest developments might well result in the whole crop being lost.
>
> There is also the loss of revenue to the government in respect of export duty on copra of order of $14,000 per annum and this is most serious with the Colony on the threshold of critical financial period ... I am therefore coming increasingly to the conclusion that the logical solution of the problem is that the military to purchase Christmas Island from this government, with the Colony providing administration of labour and whatever other assistance is required.[14]

The archives reflect the ongoing battle between the more junior Colonial Office and the Ministry of Supply, Treasury and War Office. The Colonial Office was concerned that the War Office push to continue with further nuclear tests into 1958–59 would leave the colony in a financial hole, especially because the Ministry of Supply and Treasury were more focused on the military's needs:

> The Colonial Office has two main interests in these operations. The first is to ensure that the safety of the inhabitants of the Colony, and in particular the Gilbertese labour on Christmas, is not prejudiced by them ... The second point of interest is to ensure that the Colony

---

14 Telegram no. 92 from Resident Commissioner, Gilbert and Ellice Islands Colony, to Secretary of State for the Colonies, 25 August 1957. CO1036/282.

does not suffer financially from the operation ... With the extension of 'Grapple' activities beyond what was expected, the assessment and payment of compensation to the Colony for any loss incurred in respect to the coconut plantation on Christmas has been indefinitely delayed.[15]

Some London-based officials tried to smooth the waters, recognising that the local administration could face long-term financial damage:

> We really recognise here that if Grapple does continue on the island and its activities interfere with the plantation, we shall have to come to some better arrangement with the Ministry of Supply for reimbursing the Colony for revenues of which it is thereby deprived: the principle of 'once and for all' compensation at the end of the exercise will no longer work ... Any extra identifiable costs incurred by the Colony as a result of Grapple X will be reimbursed by Her Majesty's Government [HMG] and the principle of compensation for loss of plantation revenue is also accepted, again subject to HMG being convinced that there is a clear case.[16]

* * *

The inter-ministry debate came to a head in early 1958. The Grapple Task Force was eager to expand the labour force on Christmas Island, as they faced numerous logistic challenges to be ready for the April 1958 Grapple Y test.

The UK Government planned to issue instructions to make all the existing Gilbertese labour force available for work in support of military operations and also to increase the numbers. Islanders would be employed to undertake basic labouring jobs, in order to allow more British military personnel to undertake tasks directly related to the nuclear weapons program. Potential jobs for islander labour were identified as:

> General labours in technical wing, DDT mixing for Auster flight, galley fatigues, store pumping parties, sanitary squad, general labours in equipment section, camp fatigues, groundsmen ... stores (lifting and sorting), assistance to electricians, plumbers etc, sorting and erecting huts, stevedores and shore offloading party.[17]

---

15 File note, D.J. Derx, Colonial Office, 18 September 1957. CO1036/283.
16 Personal letter from P. Rogers to R.J. Minnett, 20 September 1957. CO1036/283.
17 'Requirement for Gilbertese Labour', Appendix C, briefing note for M.L. Bernacchi CMG OBE, Resident Commissioner, Gilbert and Ellice Islands Colony, March 1958. CO1036/514.

GEIC Resident Commissioner Michael Bernacchi was eager for more local labourers to be transported from the Gilbert Islands to Christmas Island to undertake these tasks. However, the British military preferred more disciplined Fijian troops instead, as they argued in a March 1958 briefing note to Bernacchi:

> Generally speaking, it has been found that Fijians work harder than Gilbertese. That this is so is probably not just a matter of temperament, but a combination of several factors such as a) Fijians have their own non-commissioned officers, b) they are a disciplined body, c) they are temporarily away from their homes and d) they live and work in units within the Task Force and are instilled with a spirit of competition. The Fijians have, amongst the unit sent to Christmas, more tradesmen than the Gilbertese.[18]

The debate came to a head when Bernacchi travelled from Tarawa to Christmas Island in March 1958 to meet with Royal Navy (RN) Captain J.G. ('Guy') Western, who was visiting the island from London as representative of the new Grapple Task Force Commander John Grandy. Bernacchi and Western met with District Officer Percy Roberts and other Grapple staff to thrash out the practicalities of bringing in extra Fijian or Gilbertese labour.

Colonial Office officials had drafted a briefing note for the Resident Commissioner to prepare for the meeting, which highlighted the cost to the GEIC of supporting Operation Grapple:

> The Colony's problem is purely an economic one and this has apparently still not been understood. The Colony is prepared, and only too willing, to give Grapple what help it can within the limits of its resources, always providing it is told clearly what is required, and can be given some warning. The Colony however is desperately poor and must be adequately compensated for its efforts and losses.[19]

Officials were wary of the War Office suggestion that Gilbertese labourers should be put under military discipline:

> The suggestion that the Colony should raise a Gilbertese military unit for employment at Christmas Island is impracticable. The administrative effort which it would entail would be beyond the Colony's present

---

18 'Employment of local labour in Operation Grapple', A note prepared by Task Force Grapple for discussions with His Honour M.L. Bernacchi CMG OBE, Resident Commissioner, Gilbert and Ellice Islands Colony, March 1958. CO1036/514.
19 'Grapple', Confidential Resident Commissioner's Brief, March 1958, p. 1. CO1036/514.

resources. The suggestion that the Task Force Commander might enlist the Gilbertese as locally enlisted personnel requires more careful consideration. What it comes down to is that they would be deprived of their families and provided with tent accommodation and military rations, but it would not overcome the problem of returning them to their families, say every 12 months.[20]

At the face-to-face meeting on Christmas Island, the military made an offer to add another 270 Gilbertese labourers to the workforce in coming years. In return, Bernacchi gave way in his opposition to the deployment of more Fijian soldiers. The minutes of the meeting record:

> The Resident Commissioner Gilbert and Ellice Islands had no objection to the employment of additional Fijian Military Forces by Task Force Grapple on Christmas Island, provided they did not replace or preclude the employment of Gilbertese labour. He agreed that the duties on which Fijian uniformed personnel were at present employed could not at present be undertaken by Gilbertese civilians.[21]

* * *

When the government finally agreed that the Grapple X test would be conducted in November 1957, the Colonial Office had pushed for renewed arrangements for moving the Gilbertese to safety:

> Because time is so short, it has been decided to carry out the November tests off the south east tip of Christmas Island: it would have taken too long to set up Malden again …
>
> The proposal is to remove the Gilbertese from Christmas Island before the bombing aircraft takes off and place them in a ship, in the Christmas anchorage, which has immediate notice to steam. They will remain in the ship until after the test when they will be returned to their village. Should an accident occur, either due to a crash on take-off by the bomber or surface burst instead of a high airburst, then there may be a risk to ships lying in the anchorage. This risk is not immediate and there will be ample time to direct the ships to move on to avoid the risk.[22]

---

20   Ibid., p. 2.
21   'Minutes of a meeting held in residence of District Officer Christmas Island on 24 March 1958', Headquarters Task Force Grapple, marked 'confidential', 25 March 1958, p. 4. C01036/514.
22   File note for draft correspondence from D.J. Derx, Colonial Office to acting High Commissioner, Western Pacific Commission. n.d. CO1036/282.

16. *THE BANABAN*—TEKOTI ROTAN

In the lead-up to the next test in April 1958, the pressure to increase the islander workforce created another problem. Looking after hundreds of additional Gilbertese would place pressure on the RN on the day of a nuclear test. Some Gilbertese workers and their families had been housed below decks during the Grapple X test, but larger numbers could not easily be accommodated aboard British warships.

At his March 1958 meeting with Commissioner Bernacchi, Captain Guy Western explained proposals to evacuate the existing Gilbertese workers and their families to neighbouring islands, or place them below decks in ships on the day of a nuclear test. In response:

> The Resident Commissioner stated that his view was that if it was safe for service personnel to stay on the island, it was safe enough for Gilbertese. At the time of the first operation, the High Commissioner had, however, sought assurances from the Colonial Office that there was no danger and these were not then forthcoming in sufficiently explicit terms.[23]

If Gilbertese workers were to be evacuated from the island aboard the naval task force 'it would in any case be necessary for women and children to be placed below decks in a ship, as the children could not be expected to carry out the safety drill'.[24]

The meeting then agreed to recruit extra Gilbertese workers, but noted that some Gilbertese men might be left in their village huts during forthcoming tests:

> The introduction of the full number of additional Gilbertese might be dependent upon the non-evacuation of male adults during tests. If agreed by the Task Force Commander, action would be initiated by the Task Force to give the High Commissioner a firmer assurance as to their safety.[25]

As we'll see in the next chapter, not all islanders were protected below decks when there was a 'surface burst instead of a high airburst' in April 1958.

---

23 'Employment of Gilbertese labour and Fijian military personnel at Christmas Island', minutes of a meeting held at Headquarters Task Force Grapple, 26 March 1958. GRA/S.102/36/ORG, pp. 1–2. C01036/514.
24 Ibid.
25 Ibid.

17

The mothers—Sui Kiritome

Sui Kiritome and her daughter Rakieti in Tarawa, Kiribati, 2004
Source: Nic Maclellan.

Suitupe Benan Kiritome arrived on Christmas Island from the capital Tarawa in early 1957. She was accompanying her husband, Kiritome Itaia, who was posted to work as head teacher for the children of the Gilbertese labourers on the island. Kiritome Itaia was soon used as an interpreter for the British military to help pass on instructions to the islanders. During her time on the island, Sui Kiritome gave birth to two children.

At the time of her arrival, however, the Grapple Task Force was debating whether to relocate the Gilbertese community already living on Christmas Island. The closest inhabited location was Fanning Island, known to the islanders as Tabuaeran, which hosted a Cable & Wireless communications station and copra plantation. After debate between the Task Force and the Gilbert and Ellice Islands Colony (GEIC) administration, nearly 60 Gilbertese workers and family members were relocated to Fanning in January 1957 aboard the GEIC's copra transport ship *Tungaru*, with a further 40 relocated in February on the MV *Tulgai*.[1]

By mid-March, just two months before the first test on Malden Island, the remaining Gilbertese community at Port London was made up of 44 males, 29 females and 56 children (including 18 toddlers and babies aged less than two years old). The Grapple Task Force then proposed:

> to remove all female and juvenile native population from Christmas Island for the duration of the tests and to reduce the male population to the minimum required to maintain administration and security … Those remaining will be the District Officer, clerks, wireless operators, three police, mechanics, office assistants, servants, dependents (total 32 persons). All agreeable to remain.[2]

By the end of April 1957, a fortnight before the first test on Malden Island, another 31 Gilbertese men, 26 women and 47 children were to be relocated to Fanning Island. They were followed by another three females and the remaining children a week before the test. Two alcoholic 'indulgers' were sent to Canton Island for the duration of the testing program.[3]

* * *

Following the initial three tests on Malden Island, the UK military began to relocate the testing site to Christmas Island. Once again, authorities were uncertain how to deal with the Gilbertese population living in the village at Port London, as Mrs Kiritome explained:

---

1 Telegram no. 84 from John Gutch, Western Pacific Commissioner to Secretary of State for the Colonies, 11 February 1957. CO1036/281.
2 'Evacuation of native population', Memo from Air Vice Marshall Wilfred Oulton, Headquarters Grapple Task Force, 29 March 1957, GRA/6/5/AIR, marked 'restricted'. CO1036/281.
3 Ibid.

17. THE MOTHERS—SUI KIRITOME

> I think it was sometime towards the end of 1957 when word came from the District Commissioner that, because of the nuclear test, all the local people on Kiritimati should be repatriated to Tarawa. We were then informed that all, except the teacher, wireless operator and constables, were to be taken to Fanning Island. So we went to Fanning during the first test.
>
> We were in Fanning for three months, and then we returned to Kiritimati. We were in Kiritimati for some time before everyone else returned from Tarawa. Then, sometime at the beginning of 1958, the second test took place [Grapple Y].[4]

Despite the policy to keep all women and children below decks, Sui Kiritome was on deck and exposed to the aftermath of the massive atmospheric test on 28 April 1958, codenamed Grapple Y. Christmas Island veterans have long argued that the greatest radioactive fallout during Operation Grapple was created by this two-stage thermonuclear device, which detonated with an estimated yield of 2.8 megatons.

Royal Engineer Ken McGinley had arrived on Christmas Island aboard TT *Dunera* just weeks before the Grapple Y test. He recalled the enormous impact of the bomb, and the subsequent winds and rainfall:

> This was the daddy of all bombs. There was something incredibly sinister about the shimmering line of energy, skimming over the ocean with amazing speed. I dived to the ground and as it hit, I felt an impact and a crack like lightning had hit close by. The huge fireball forming above me seemed to stretch from horizon to horizon. I knew straight away we were far closer than we should have been from a bomb that size. It was truly awesome; a great rolling, roiling, boiling mass of fire. Then a spout seemed to rise from the ground and the familiar mushroom cloud began to form.[5]

---

4   This section is based on an interview with Suitupe Benan Kiritome, 3 May 1998, with thanks to her daughter Rakieti and son-in-law Ueantabo Neemia-McKenzie. Unless otherwise noted, all direct quotes from Mrs Kiritome come from this interview, which is published in Losena Salabula, Josua Namoce and Nic Maclellan: *Kirisimasi—Na Sotia kei na Lewe ni Mataivalu e Wai ni Viti e na vakatovotovo iyaragi nei Peritania mai Kirisimasi* (Pacific Concerns Resource Centre, Suva, 1999), pp. 59–61.

5   For his eyewitness testimony and photos of damage to the camp, see Ken McGinley and Eamonn P. O'Neill: *No Risk Involved—the Ken McGinley story—survivor of a nuclear experiment* (Mainstream Publishing, Edinburgh, 1991), pp. 57–68.

The initial run to drop the bomb was aborted when reports of an approaching ship raised concern. An hour later, Squadron Leader Bob Bates released the bomb from his Valiant aircraft. The nuclear test was supposed to be an air burst at an altitude of 2,350 metres, high enough to avoid the irradiation of land and water that would generate extensive radioactive fallout.

Mushroom cloud from the Grapple Y test, 28 April 1958
Source: Alamy stock photos.

Despite later official denials, many contemporary reports state that the explosion was nearly a kilometre closer to sea level than expected. The detonation sucked up quantities of water and debris into the fireball and mushroom cloud, irradiating them in the process. Irradiated water and debris then fell back to ground, contaminating an area estimated at 80 to 160 kilometres.[6]

Twenty-three-year-old British soldier Archie Ross had arrived on Christmas Island on 4 November 1957, but his memories of the Grapple Y test remained with him years later:

> I still remember, as though it was yesterday, the stem of the mushroom cloud reaching down to the sea and the waves parting like that famous scene from the film the Ten Commandments when Moses causes the Red Sea to part. I remember seeing the water rushing up the spout, followed by all the mud and sand from the seabed, all being sucked up into the cloud like a giant vacuum cleaner.[7]

In an interview translated by her daughter Rakieti, Mrs Kiritome described the movements of the Gilbertese on the day:

> Just before the test, we were informed of the arrangements. We were told that the test would take place early in the morning around 5 or 6 am, and that we should be ready at the wharf for evacuation from the island. We were transported to the ships on landing craft. My husband, Kiritome, was the interpreter for the British officers. He assisted them during the evacuation of the island by ensuring that people take their allocated transport.
>
> Evacuation of Kiritimati began about 3 am when the roll call was taken. People were grouped on the basis of their home islands and a representative from each island group was responsible for ensuring that people from his island were all accounted for. We were told that no one should remain on the island. People made their way to the landing craft as their name was called. We were told before leaving our houses that we should take down things hanging on the walls, as well as ensuring that our pets and animals are kept away from the light.

---

6   For details, see analysis by former Ministry of Defence (MoD) official John Large, in Appendix X, Case of *McGinley and Egan v the United Kingdom*, European Court of Human Rights, Strasbourg, France, 9 June 1998. § 68, Reports of Judgments and Decisions 1998-III, pp. 3, 7.
7   Alan Rimmer: *Between Heaven and Hell* (E-book, lulu.com, 2012), p. 26. Archie Ross had significant health problems later in life, and his first child was born with deformities. See Derek Robinson: *Just testing* (Collins Harvill, London, 1985), p. 32. Ross died in 2016, after a long involvement in the British Nuclear Test Veterans Association (BNTVA).

> When we arrived on the ship, my husband was told to explain to the local people what was expected of them, and later, the progress of the test. A movie was shown, and sweets were shared around. When the countdown to the blast began, my husband told the people to put their hands to their ears to muffle the sound of the blast.

With UK naval personnel lining the decks to witness the rising mushroom cloud, the 24-year-old woman and her husband were invited to come on deck:

> Just after the blast, the captain came to my husband and invited us to accompany him to the deck to see what happened after the blast. We went up on deck and we saw everyone on deck wearing protective clothes, covering their head, faces and bodies. Some of them were studying the effects of the bomb with binoculars. We didn't wear protective clothing— we went on deck wearing our normal clothes.

> We were watching the black smoke or cloud from the blast which was drifting towards us. When it came overhead, I felt something like a light shower falling on me. I thought it was rain. My husband stood under a lifeboat so he was protected from the light shower … It was just like rain. I felt wetness on my head, my face and skin.

> When we got home later that day, we noticed that the door and glass windows in our house were broken. The concrete wall cracked, and our pet frigate bird was running around the house blind.

* * *

Given the yield of the test—the largest in the Grapple series—there should have been little surprise that fallout could reach the British naval task force, the military camp on Christmas Island and Port London village. Unlike Grapple X, which was conducted in the dry season, Grapple Y was undertaken in the wet season and the Grapple Task Force was well aware that rainfall over Christmas Island was more likely.

In preparations for fallout issued for the Grapple X test the previous November, Task Force Commander Oulton had acknowledged that 'there is a possibility of washout on Christmas Island itself':

> If active material were allowed to drift over Christmas Island and were deposited locally by heavy rain, the possibility of a very hazardous contamination level cannot be excluded. It must be a firm requirement

that no rain shall fall on Christmas Island until the activity up to rain level has drifted clear of the island, for example, say 1–3 hours after the explosion unless the winds are light.[8]

There is extensive evidence that authorities knew of the danger of rain for Grapple Y.[9] In the period leading up to the test, the commander of the bombing aircrew Group Captain Kenneth Hubbard noted 'difficult and uncomfortable weather conditions which made life unpleasant for all concerned'.[10] Several days before the detonation, the Commander of the Port Camp warned of a slight risk of rain on 28 April. On the day of the test, Group Captain Hubbard noted that:

> Squadron Leader Bob Bates and crew, flying Valiant XD825, although scheduled for take-off at 0800 hours local, were delayed due to an unacceptable degree of cloud cover on the day—not unexpected as the previous two days had produced heavy showers from the intertropical front.[11]

After he took off, the Valiant pilot announced that the target area was obscured by cumulus clouds which rose to 40,000 feet.

Mrs Kiritome's testimony of black mist is corroborated by other sources. Leading Aircraftman Robert Brown belonged to an Royal Air Force (RAF) unit responsible for fire protection at the Atomic Weapons Research Establishment (AWRE) installations on Christmas Island. He reported that 10 minutes after the detonation, he saw the sky over the Main Camp and the airfield was dark and overcast. About 20 minutes after the detonation, members of the RAF unit could see rain falling over both the camp and the airfield, with the RAF officer in charge stating: 'The poor chaps over there are catching it.'[12]

Returning to base 30 minutes after the detonation, Brown noticed a thin layer of black misty cloud at about 1,500 feet over Port London —where the Gilbertese workers lived.

---

8   'Fallout predictions at Grapple X', memorandum, Task Force Commander Wilfred Oulton, 8 November 1957.
9   See Annexes to *Suitupe Kiritome v United Kingdom*, European Court of Human Rights, Strasbourg, France, (49753/99), 1999.
10 Kenneth Hubbard and Michael Simmons: *Dropping Britain's First H-Bomb —the story of Operation Grapple 1957 – 8* (Pen and Sword, Barnsley, 2008), p. 169.
11 Ibid., p. 170. Unlike other witnesses, Hubbard's book makes no mention of rain or weather conditions after the test.
12 Statement by Robert Brown, in Annexes to *Suitupe Kiritome v. United Kingdom*, European Court of Human Rights.

For Sui Kiritome, the aftermath of her exposure was not immediately apparent, but she soon noticed effects:

> Some time after the test, something happened to my head and face. Every time when I combed my hair, I was losing strands of my hair and something like burns developed on my face, scalp and parts of my shoulder. My face was the worst affected because I was looking up at the black cloud from the blast which was directly above us when the light shower fell on my face. The rest of my body was not affected because of my clothes. It was not really that painful.
>
> When we returned to Tarawa, we went to see Dr Neete O'Connor. He treated me and he was surprised that nothing changed and that the burn mark on my face remained. The mark remains on my face till today. It has been on my face for the last 40 years or so now.

Sui Kiritome's first child Tabokai was born on Christmas Island in March 1957. When he was a few months old, a reddish rash developed around his neck. New Zealand official Percy Roberts arranged for the family to see a British medical doctor for treatment.

As she stood on the deck of the British warship for Grapple Y, Sui Kiritome was six months pregnant with her second child. Given 'the black cloud and smoke from the blast', Mrs Kiritome was anxious about possible health impacts when her daughter Rakieti was born on 24 July 1958:

> A strange thing happened during her birth. Blood came out from all cavities in her body —from her eyes, nose, ear … I was told by my husband that the doctor was very surprised to see what happened to the child.

* * *

As the Grapple series progressed, the Grapple Task Force abandoned more elaborate safety procedures for the islanders. For two of the smaller Grapple Z tests ('Pennant' on 22 August 1958 and 'Burgee' on 3 September 1958), the Gilbertese workers and their families 'were marshalled ashore in a safe place' even though officials acknowledged that anyone who deliberately or accidentally observed the initial flash of the nuclear test was 'likely to have their eyesight temporarily or permanently impaired'.[13]

---

13   Memo from Captain J.G.T. Weston, Headquarters Task Force Grapple, to H.P. Hall, Colonial Office, London, 5 November 1958. CO1036/284.

Taparu Kamabo, who lived on the island during 1958, reported that the blast of one test ripped off the doors and windows from his house. In a filmed interview, Kamabo explained:

> Some children during that time got eye problems. They find it hard to see properly ... [some islanders] were given a choice —they were given things to cover their ears and eyes with. But especially those with big families went onto the ships, because they find it hard to put on those things. They were really afraid and frightened, but what else could they do, so they just sit and accept whatever may come.[14]

Tonga Fou arrived on Christmas Island from Tarawa to work as a labourer in 1957. Interviewed on the island five decades later, he noted:

> It was a lot of fun—we worked with the soldiers, fishing together, playing together. In these days, we don't think about the bomb, because we enjoying ourselves ...
>
> But the question I say is why? Why the British tried their tests on Christmas Island, why they come this long distance? For one reason. One reason. To take a picture of the H-bomb. But why are they not thinking that human beings are staying on the island? We don't know, but my feeling is that there is radiation. When I think of the people who were there at the bomb, how they died, it was mostly women, suffering with bleeding.[15]

Makurita Baaro—the Ambassador to the United Nations for the Republic of Kiribati—has recalled childhood memories of the way that children on Christmas Island were affected:

> In 1963, I started school for the first time, and one of my classmates had no teeth. She never had teeth. Another boy in the same class had patchy white and brown skin and was forever teased for this. Both my classmates had something in common: they were born on Kiritimati where their parents were, when atmospheric tests were conducted between 1956 and 1962.[16]

---

14   Taparu Kamabo, speaking through an interpreter, in the 2012 documentary *Kiritimati— Between Sky and Ocean*.
15   Interview of Tonga Fou by Owen Sheers in 'Bomb Gone', *Granta*, No. 101, 1 August 2008.
16   Speech by Ambassador Makurita Baaro, Informal Meeting of the United Nations General Assembly to mark the 2015 Observance of the International Day against Nuclear Tests, UN Headquarters, New York, 10 September 2015.

In meetings sponsored by Pacific churches, i-Kiribati women living on Christmas Island at the time of the tests have reported effects on their children, such as Teamo Mikaere, whose son was visually impaired at birth.[17] Ambassador Baaro notes that, in later years, there was great uncertainty in her country about potential health effects:

> In Kiribati, no studies have been done on the effects of these nuclear tests on our people—we do not have the medical facilities nor the capacity to do this. I spoke to an elderly mother with two disabled children, born on Christmas Island in the late 1950s. Her accepting explanation, said with a smile, was 'they were our children born during the testing time on Christmas Island.' And that was it, for families, women and children alike were exposed to these tests.[18]

---

17 'Country report Kiribati' in Morvan Sidal (ed.): *The Legacy of Nuclear Testing*, report of a Pacific Conference of Churches (PCC) workshop, Kiribati, 7–9 February 2005.
18 Speech by Ambassador Makurita Baaro, op. cit.

18

The last soldiers—Josefa Vueti

Royal Fiji Military Forces (RFMF) soldiers deployed to Christmas Island, 1958
Source: Courtesy Mrs Loata Masi.

By mid-1958, the small Fijian contingent on Christmas Island amounted to two officers and 60 other ranks, of which 22 were construction engineers.

With the decision to continue testing on Christmas Island after the April 1958 Grapple Y test, the Governor of Fiji approved the deployment of further forces. In June 1958, the Royal Fiji Military Forces (RFMF) headquarters in Suva wrote to the Grapple Task Force confirming:

> The government of Fiji has approved in principle the employment of a maximum of 80 Fijian servicemen from the Fiji Military Forces and the FRNVR with Task Force Grapple until September 1960 … No difficulty is anticipated in meeting the Grapple requirement for 40 construction engineers from 1 January 1959 onwards. The provision of 20 other ranks of the FMF for stevedoring duties represents no problem.[1]

The Fijian contingent was just a small part of the general deployment for the final four Grapple tests. As with previous operations, there were a mix of service and civilian personnel deployed for Grapple Z, amounting to 4,375 men. With the new UK naval task force deployed offshore, there were 1,438 soldiers and 2,017 aircrew—the largest number for any of the test series in 1957–58. With 182 scientific and technical staff on the island, it was also the largest contingent of non-military personnel.[2]

The Grapple Z series involved four nuclear detonations at the south-east point of Christmas Island in August and September 1958: two atomic weapons tethered from balloons, and two airburst hydrogen bombs.

Despite a general wind down of operations after Grapple Z, with many British personnel heading home, the UK Government decided to maintain the facilities on Christmas Island, in case further tests were needed in 1959. To limit the cost of sending troops from England, a new Fijian contingent was deployed later in 1958 under the command of Lieutenant Etuate Nima Senibici. RFMF troops were to serve 6–12 month stints over the next two years.

* * *

---

1 'Employment of Fijians at Christmas Island', Letter from Headquarters, Royal Fiji Military Forces (RFMF), Suva, Fiji, to Headquarters, Grapple Task Force, London, 11 June 1958. G000/2. CO1036/514.

2 Data from 'Number of men involved in each operation, by service or employer', Table A4.1, Appendix 4 in Lorna Arnold: *Britain and the H-Bomb* (Palgrave Macmillan, London, 2001), p. 241. During the Grapple Z series, beyond the engineers deployed on land, 16 Fijians were attached to 269 Squadron involved in reconnaissance, meteorological patrol and air-sea rescue.

18. THE LAST SOLDIERS — JOSEFA VUETI

Josefa Vueti was just 20 years old when he served on Christmas Island in 1958–59. Hailing from the village of Natogadravu in the province of Tailevu, Vueti joined the army in 1956. He travelled to Christmas Island as a Private in the RFMF in late 1958, after the last bomb had been tested:

> I was told that I was to go to Christmas Island. However, I did not know what I was to do there. I was just told to go.
>
> In the weeks before we were to leave our trip was delayed because the bomb had just exploded. It was exactly a week after the bomb had exploded that we left for Christmas Island. I spent a whole year there. I was supposed to stay there for only six months but it was extended for another six.
>
> On Christmas Island, we worked. We stayed at the Main Camp, living in tents. We were to build the houses and to complete construction works. When the boats arrived, we used to go down to Port Camp to load and unload the boats and the equipment for work done at the island. My pay there every fortnight was one pound, one shilling.[3]

The main RFMF Engineers contingent was posted with varying British units to supplement their workforce. The Fijian soldiers were under 12 Independent Field Squadron from April 1958 to February 1959; under 36 Corps Engineer Regiment, Royal Engineers, from February 1959 to November 1959; and under 73 (Christmas Island) Squadron, Royal Engineers, from November 1959 to April 1960.

There was a gulf of experience and understanding between most Britons and the Pacific islanders. This is best symbolised by the UK Treasury officials that approved funding for uniforms and tools for the Fijian troops, but queried the proposed budgets for *dalo* (taro), *yaqona* (kava) and Fijian newspapers, which would provide small comfort and memories of home for the islanders sent to Christmas Island.

For example, a 1959 letter from the Ministry of Supply to the Governor of Fiji asks 'on what grounds it is considered that Fijian newspapers and supplies of kava should be provided at public expense?'[4]

---

3 Interview with Josefa Vueti, Suva, Fiji, 1998. Most interviews excerpted in this chapter were recorded in the Fijian language in 1998, and the translations come from the book *Kirisimasi— Na Sotia kei na Lewe ni Mataivalu e Wai ni Viti e na vakatovotovo iyaragi nei Peritania mai Kirisimasi* (Pacific Concerns Research Centre, Suva, 1999).
4 'Fijian troops at Christmas Island' Draft telegram to the Governor of Fiji, Annex A to Ministry of Supply letter to Donald J. Derx, Colonial Office, London, 29 January 1959. DB/231/05. CO1036/514.

As military operations wound down, these costing pressures grew even greater, with the troops forced to bear the consequences of London's parsimony. Despite the precedent set with the deployment of Fijian troops to Malaya, the Ministry of Supply disputed the cost of kava and newspapers proposed by the Governor of Fiji for Christmas Island, noting: 'We are withholding payment of this item and for supplies of *dalo* until some explanation is received'.[5]

For months, penny-pinching UK bureaucrats continued to quibble over funding for these supplies, finally noting:

> We have received a reply from Suva which we regard as generally satisfactory on these points, with the exception of the proposed man day rate for supplies of *yaqona*. The Commander FMF suggests that the amounts charged for supplies so far support a rate of one shilling, 5 pence per man per day, which he considers not excessive or unreasonable. On the scanty evidence we have here about consumption … we think that three quarters of a penny per man per day is nearer the mark … I should be grateful for a quick reply as I am holding up a further Fijian claim for payment.[6]

Josefa Vueti reflected on the differences between the Fijian troops and the remaining British force involved in maintaining the facilities:

> While at Christmas Island we did not go anywhere else. Fijian soldiers did not have any leave like the other soldiers. The Europeans went on leave after six months to Hawai'i. For us, if you were sent there for one year, it was for one year. You were never sent on leave to any other place. Even when we returned to Fiji, we still worked another week before going on leave.

> We were poorly paid compared to the British soldiers. The wages of the British soldiers were so high compared to us. The British soldiers gave us drinks—they made us drunk! Our overseas allowance at that time was two shillings a day. I deducted this two shillings for my mother, and took just one pound for myself. One pound a week—that's what I got drunk on. I had a white friend there who used to buy me drinks and got drunk every day. I had no money with me. When I came back I did not even buy anything, even clothes.[7]

---

5   Letter from G.M.P. Myers, Ministry of Supply, London to Donald Derx, Colonial Office, London, 11 May 1959. CO1036/514.
6   'Fijian troops at Christmas Island', letter from Ministry of Supply, London to Donald J. Derx, Colonial Office, London, 18 June 1959. CO1036/514.
7   Interview with Josefa Vueti, Suva, Fiji, for *Kirisimasi*, op. cit., pp. 44–47.

Niko Buke joined the RFMF in 1950. After a couple of years he was decommissioned, but was recalled in 1958 for service on Christmas Island. With other servicemen, he underwent five weeks of training at the RFMF barracks in Nasese. A carpenter by trade, he was drafted into the Engineers section for construction work, but did other odd jobs as well on Christmas Island.

> We were engineers and were sent to do construction work and also help in the clean-up operation. We also did some work on the runway on the island.
>
> Christmas Island was an island isolated from other places. You could not go anywhere else. The nearest island had i-Kiribati people living on it and we were not allowed to go there.
>
> We were never told about the conditions on Christmas Island—nothing about contamination or anything of the sort. We never tried to ask— this was the army, so you just followed orders. We also ended up doing stevedoring work, moving lots of heavy equipment from the ships and barges onto the island. We also loaded some materials onto the ships. There were a lot of metal and other heavy equipment around.[8]

Buke spent six months on the island. Even after the departure of the 4,000 troops who had served on the island in 1958, there was a lot of accumulated rubbish, with broken-down vehicles, drums of unused asphalt and other materiel. Niko Buke thought it was a long way from an island paradise:

> There was a lot of rubbish and metal debris on the island. The sea did not look good. We were told that the sea and the fish were contaminated. However, we Fijians did not care and went ahead catching fish and crabs. We got poisoned along with some of the white boys.
>
> The place was very hot, even during the nights. We used to take off our shirts to cool off, although they did not allow us to. The island had lots of coconut trees on it. However, the coconut trees did not look healthy. They were like the *drala* tree that we have here in Fiji. Some coconut trees were just stumps and others seemed deformed with extra trunks growing out of them.
>
> We always felt sick, although it was not noticeable. I got sick a lot when I was there.[9]

---

8   Interview with Niko Buke, Suva, Fiji, for *Kirisimasi*, op. cit., pp. 48–49.
9   Ibid.

Epeli Cama (RFMF Engineers 19318) was a Lance Corporal in the Engineers detachment. He had served on attachment with the NZ Army for a year, but on his return to Fiji was approached about serving on Christmas Island from 1959 to 1960. He left Fiji in a British oil tanker, *Tank Wave Master*, with RFMF Captain Viliame 'Bill' Masi and five others:

> I only knew about the work that we Fijian soldiers were to do when I reached the island. We were to do construction work for the British soldiers who were conducting nuclear tests on Christmas Island. But when I reached there, they had already completed the tests.
>
> This island was a reef covered by sand washed on it by the tide. There were coconut trees. It was a place where the sunshine was really hot. They supplied us with sunglasses to use during work because of the heat and sunshine. We wore hats and no shirts during work because of the sun.
>
> Our drinking, bathing and washing water was produced from processed seawater. The place also had a lot of flies. Everyday a plane would spray DDT over the camp to lessen the flies.[10]

Captain Viliame 'Bill' Masi and British officers inspect Fijian troops on Christmas Island
Source: Courtesy Mrs Loata Masi.

---

10   Interview with Epeli Cama, Suva, Fiji, for *Kirisimasi*, op. cit., pp. 55–57.

18. THE LAST SOLDIERS—JOSEFA VUETI

Emori Ligica (RFMF 19612) was another member of the Engineering contingent:

> We did construction work on Christmas Island where the British soldiers were camped for the tests. We went during the clean-up operation, but construction of buildings, roads and other work was still being done on Christmas Island.
>
> There were about a hundred Fijian soldiers there. Troops were exchanged every six months. We went and stayed there on different times. Those who were married spent six months there, before returning. We single young men usually spent between 10 to 11 months on Christmas Island.
>
> On Christmas Island we wore boots and trousers. We never wore any shirts because it was too hot there. There were no strict regulations about things on the island or along the beach. Since they had conducted nuclear tests there, they told us not to eat anything in the sea or on land. However, they just told us—there was no strict enforcement of regulations to stop us from eating anything from the sea. We Fijians used to eat a lot of fish. The place had a lot of *lairo* [land crabs]. This was what we usually ate during our break from work. We were always fishing and eating things from the beach.
>
> I knew that the military had all the power to stop us. They knew the many effects of the bombs. The fallout may have contained many types of harmful gases. They should have restricted us from eating from the sea, from eating the crabs or anything from inland like coconuts. These may have been contaminated, from the things emitted by the bombs during the tests.[11]

* * *

Two atomic explosions had damaged the terrain at ground zero on the south-east corner of the island: 'Pennant' and 'Burgee', which were tethered from balloons and fired during Grapple Z. These tests had the lowest yield of any of the nine Grapple tests, but also produced significant fallout, because they were conducted at lower levels, irradiating hundreds of tons of soil, plants and other debris, which were dispersed by the winds as fallout.

---

11 Interview with Emori Ligica, Suva, Fiji, for *Kirisimasi*, op. cit., pp. 50–52.

Like other soldiers, Emori Ligica took the opportunity to explore the island, including areas that were off limits:

> At one time, we went to the other part of the island. I asked some of those who were with me, which included some British soldiers, why this part of the island was burnt. The British soldiers said that this was the damage done by the hydrogen bombs that were dropped in this area. We thought that the same could happen to the lives of human beings. The trees were all destroyed. If this happened to the trees then all these different illness could happen to us.[12]

Epeli Cama was also concerned about the damage caused by the Grapple Z tests:

> I watched a film of the first test that was conducted on the side of the island they called South East Point. They showed this film only once. In the film, the navy ships were always ready to evacuate everyone (soldiers, navy and air force) in case of an accident.
>
> The side of the island called South East Point was burned. The heat from the explosion must have caused it. The film showed us how terrifying this test was. Some of the British soldiers said that South East Point got burnt because of the heat from the explosion. This means that Christmas Island and all living things in and around it had been contaminated by the tests.
>
> I believe if they clearly told us everything about the aim of Christmas Island (everything that happened including the poisonous gases from the tests, the environment, and the weather), most of the 300 of us would have refused to go.[13]

Malakai Niubasaga (RFMF Engineers 19765) travelled to Christmas Island in 1959.

> At one time a couple of European soldiers and one of my Fijian colleagues came and invited me to go to the island where the bomb had fallen. I asked the European gentlemen, why is this place like this? We saw that everything was burnt out and black. When I looked, it was so terrifying whatever happened there.
>
> It was so shocking since the bomb had fallen 60 miles away. They said that, that was how strong that bomb was. I was very amazed at how this happened. After that we returned and I kept on thinking about what happened there.[14]

---

12 Ibid.
13 Interview with Epeli Cama, Suva, Fiji, for *Kirisimasi*, op. cit.
14 Interview with Malakai Niubasaga, Suva, Fiji, for *Kirisimasi*, op. cit., pp. 57–58.

18. *THE LAST SOLDIERS* — JOSEFA VUETI

Osaia Colelala (RFMF Engineers 19679) echoed his fellow soldiers:

> I was one of those who went to Christmas Island in 1959 after the British nuclear bomb testing. It's true that I didn't experience the bomb's explosion, but I did see the destruction that it had made around Christmas Island. In my view, it was frightening for this thing to be exploding in the air—on the island nothing was alive.
>
> In the six months I was there, I saw a lot of frightening things. Every living thing on top of the island was poisoned, including the sea. We used to find dead fish on the shore, which had been poisoned by what came out of the weapon we'd been working on. It was this same sea water which we drank when it was recycled for drinking. Maybe this is why we have health problems since returning.
>
> When I came back, I got married. I had four children. One died. I think it was something to do with what our bodies experienced in that place.[15]

* * *

With the departure of most British troops at the end of testing in 1958, the Women's Voluntary Service (WVS) maintained a small operation until March 1960. By mid-1959, a new Navy, Army and Air Forces Institute (NAAFI) Fleet club at HMS *Resolution* had opened with a billiard room, table tennis, gift shop and bar complete with darts board and a snack bar.[16] Services provided to the remaining detachment included weekly visits to the hospital, arrangements for the development of photos or delivery of flowers to family members in the United Kingdom and organising variety shows.[17] The daily routine was disrupted by a short visit by the Duke of Edinburgh in April 1959, during a Pacific Tour.

At the end of 1959, it was announced that personnel would be reduced to 1,700 by the start of 1960 and just 300 by the following July. Epeli Cama recalled the British authorities decided the Fiji deployment should be wound up, with troops being transported back to Suva:

---

15 Interview with Osaia Colelala, Suva, Fiji, for *Kirisimasi*, op. cit., p. 57.
16 'WVS report for March and April 1959, Junior Ranks Club, Christmas Island', Report to WVS Headquarters, 1 May 1959.
17 'WVS report for January and February 1959, Junior Ranks Club, Christmas Island', Report to WVS Headquarters, February 1959.

> One hundred and five of us Fijian soldiers left Christmas Island for the last time in 1960. The directive came from the British that all Fijian soldiers were to leave after we had finished our work. I was a very sad farewell to the British troops when we returned to Fiji.
>
> It seemed that when we returned we were already contaminated. I left the army in 1960 and got married in 1962. My wife had a child before we got married. Up until today, I have not been able to have children. I have been to various medical people. The doctor declared that I could not have any children because of problems with my reproductive system.[18]

Returned soldier Niko Buke believes his service on Christmas Island affected his health after returning to Fiji, and that the British authorities have a responsibility to look after the ageing men who served Empire:

> We have to be compensated for suffering. We were working on this barren and isolated island in the middle of the sea. Now I am beginning to realise the bad effects of all this. We have to be compensated for all the health problems that we are suffering. This compensation is our right. We should be compensated because we never received the same amount of pay paid to British veterans. We were under the leadership of British officers.
>
> My wife and I never had any children. We married very young, yet this thing happened to us. We could not have children. We have two adopted children.
>
> Many of those who served together have passed away. There are not many of us around anymore. Those that died were not supposed to die. Those of us still around are lucky to alive. If I had known that we would face all these things, I would not have gone.[19]

Josefa Vueti agreed:

> We should be remembered, because we took Fiji's name there. We did not go of our own free will. We went as Fijian soldiers. I thank God for allowing this opening where this issue about those of us who went to Christmas Island is brought up. We should be remembered.[20]

---

18 Interview with Epeli Cama, Suva, Fiji, for *Kirisimasi*, op. cit.
19 Interview with Niko Buke, Suva, Fiji, for *Kirisimasi*, op. cit.
20 Interview with Josefa Vueti, Suva, Fiji, for *Kirisimasi*, op. cit.

19

The President—John F. Kennedy

Harold Macmillan (left) meets US President John F. Kennedy at Key West in Florida to plan US nuclear tests on Christmas Island
Source: US Government.

As he stood before the United Nations General Assembly in September 1961, US President John F. Kennedy said that 'general and complete disarmament must no longer be a slogan':

> Today, every inhabitant of this planet must contemplate the day when this planet may no longer be habitable. Every man, woman and child lives under a nuclear sword of Damocles, hanging by the slenderest of threads, capable of being cut at any moment by accident or miscalculation or by madness. The weapons of war must be abolished before they abolish us …
>
> To halt the spread of these terrible weapons, to halt the contamination of the air, to halt the spiralling nuclear arms race, we remain ready to seek new avenues of agreement. Our new Disarmament Program thus includes the following proposals: first, signing the test-ban treaty by all nations. This can be done now. Test ban negotiations need not and should not await general disarmament.[1]

Just three months later, Kennedy was negotiating with British Prime Minister Harold Macmillan to use Christmas Island for a new series of US nuclear tests.

In the early 1960s, renewed diplomatic tensions between the United States and Soviet Union meant the 1958 nuclear testing moratorium could not hold. In March 1961, Harold Macmillan had diverted from a Caribbean tour, flying from Trinidad to Key West in Florida to meet with John F. Kennedy. The two leaders debated strategic cooperation, including the possibility of joint action in the brewing political crisis in Laos—the precursor to the Vietnam War.[2]

Viewing Britain as a declining imperial power, the Kennedy administration saw the United States as the leader of the Western alliance and 'the free world'—attitudes that sparked US interventions in the Congo (with the murder of independence leader Patrice Lumumba), the Bay of Pigs fiasco in Cuba and deployment of US Special Forces in Indochina.[3] Macmillan in turn hoped for an Anglo-American partnership, where Washington would recognise the United Kingdom's role on the UN Security Council.

With France losing the Algerian War, it tried to improve its crumbling imperial power by commencing a nuclear testing program in its North African colony. The Gerboise Bleue test was held at Reggane in the Sahara

---

1   President John F. Kennedy: *Address before the General Assembly of the United Nations*, New York City, 25 September 1961.
2   Nick White: 'Macmillan, Kennedy and the Key West meeting: Its significance for the Laotian Civil War and Anglo-American relations', *Civil Wars*, Vol. 2 No. 2, 1999.
3   For critical discussion of JFK's role in the Indochinese wars, see Noam Chomsky: *Rethinking Camelot—JFK, the Vietnam War and US political culture* (Verso, London, 1993).

desert on 13 February 1960.[4] Trying to maintain its status as the key European nuclear power, Macmillan hoped to encourage the United States to quickly negotiate a total ban on atmospheric testing, but believed that US nuclear superiority over Russia would best be maintained by another round of US nuclear weapons tests before any ban.[5]

In the folly that would lead to the Cuban Missile Crisis in 1962— 10 days that almost destroyed the planet—the Kennedy administration had encouraged nuclear scientists and strategists to 'think the unthinkable' and develop policies to fight and win a nuclear war.[6] Despite his disarmament rhetoric, Kennedy had won the presidency with talk of a fictitious missile gap with the Soviet Union, and the new administration sought to bolster its nuclear forces.

For this reason, the United States offered the United Kingdom use of the Nevada test site for further British nuclear experimentation, but sought something in return. In December 1961, the two Western leaders held a meeting in Bermuda, this time to discuss the use of Britain's Christmas Island facilities for US nuclear testing. At the Bermuda conference, the architect of Britain's hydrogen bomb Sir William Penney chipped in to the discussion with musings on how many nuclear weapons it would take to destroy a country:

> If you're talking about Australia, it would take twelve. If you're talking about Britain, it would take five or six, but to be on the safe side, let's say seven or eight and I'll have another gin and tonic, if you would be so kind.[7]

* * *

---

4   For a comprehensive overview of French nuclear testing, see Bruno Barrillot: *Les essais nucléaires français 1960–1996* (CDRPC, Lyon, 1996) and *L'héritage de la bombe: Polynésie–Sahara 1960–2002* (CDRPC, Lyon, 2002).
5   Nigel Ashton: *Kennedy, Macmillan and the Cold War: The irony of interdependence* (Palgrave Macmillan, London, 2002), p. 154.
6   Kennedy-era strategic analyst Herman Kahn became notorious for his book *Thinking about the unthinkable* (Horizon Press, 1962), which promoted fantasies about the survivability of nuclear warfare. In earlier work at RAND Corporation, Kahn had critiqued the notion of Mutually Assured Destruction (MAD) and advocated first strike attacks to decapitate the Soviet leadership. See Herman Kahn: *The Nature and Feasibility of War and Deterrence* (RAND Corporation, Santa Monica, 1960). Combined with traits from Nazi rocket scientist Werner Von Braun and 'father of the hydrogen bomb' Edward Teller, Kahn's personality was used as a model for Doctor Strangelove, the scientist at the heart of Stanley Kubrick's astounding satire of the nuclear era.
7   Arthur M. Schlesinger Jr: *A Thousand Days: John F. Kennedy in the White House* (Houghton-Mifflin, Boston, 2002 reprint), p. 491.

After the completion of the 1957–58 Grapple atmospheric tests, most British troops were redeployed back to England—but some British and Fijian military forces were maintained on the island. As leaders debated the test moratorium, the airstrip and infrastructure on Christmas Island were maintained, under a joint arrangement between London and Washington.

Despite a long personal letter to Kennedy and similar missives to the Russian leader Nikita Khrushchev in early 1962, Macmillan could not revive the stalled talks for a Partial Test Ban Treaty in Geneva. He then acceded to proposals from the US military for the United States to conduct the further series of nuclear tests at Christmas Island and Johnston Atoll, codenamed Operation Dominic.

On 8 February, Macmillan announced that 'the facilities at Christmas Island' would be made available to the United States:

> It is the joint view of the US and UK governments that the existing state of nuclear development would justify the West in making such further series of nuclear tests as may be necessary for purely military reasons.[8]

The agreement between the UK and US governments allowed the US military to carry out nuclear weapons testing no more than 25 miles and no less than 5 miles from Christmas Island.[9] Britain traded the use of facilities at the Christmas Island base in return for access to the US testing ground in the Nevada desert in order to test British nuclear weapons underground. The UK also negotiated access to data from the Dominic test series.

Under a program known as Operation Brigadoon, the British Government also agreed to provide 300 personnel to support the US operation on Christmas Island, including British army troops and Royal Air Force (RAF) aircrew.[10]

---

8   Quoted in Adam Roberts: *Nuclear Testing and the Arms Race* (Peace News, Oxford, March 1962), p. 4.
9   'Nuclear Test Veterans', Mr Llew Smith MP, UK House of Commons, Hansard official report, 4 February 1998, col. 1006.
10 'Atomic tests on Christmas Island: Brigadoon 1961–1962', DEF 37/15/6 Part A, UK National Archives, Dominion Office file DO 164/20. See also UK National Archives, Ministry of Defence Registered Files (General Series) prior to 1964: files DEFE 7/2364–2370.

The first phase of the US program (Operation Dominic I) was conducted in a rush. Between 25 April to 11 July, 24 atmospheric nuclear tests were conducted at Christmas Island, with weapons dropped from US aircraft. The tests ranged in yield from the appropriately named 'Petit' at 2.2 kilotons to the massive 'Pamlico' at 3.8 megatons.[11]

During Operation Dominic, the US Navy also tested submarine-launched missiles armed with nuclear warheads in the ocean east of Christmas Island as well as off the West Coast USA.

On 4 May 1958 under Operation Frigate Bird—the symbol of Christmas Island—the ballistic missile submarine USS *Ethan Allen* (SSBN 608) launched a Polaris missile towards Christmas Island from 806 kilometres east of the island: 'The warhead exploded as planned 500 miles short of the island but within the Christmas Island danger zone.'[12]

The successful test provided significant proof of the capacity for a missile-launched airburst, and opened the way for Britain to purchase Polaris missiles from the United States.[13] A week later, in Operation Swordfish, the submarine fired a rocket-launched antisubmarine ASROC nuclear depth charge.

In October, five more airdrops were detonated in the vicinity of Johnston Island, a US possession located between the Marshall Islands and Hawai'i. Johnston (known to the indigenous Kanaka Maoli people as Kalama) was claimed for the Kingdom of Hawai'i in July 1858, with the support of King Kamehameha. With the US takeover of Hawai'i in 1898, Johnston effectively became a US possession, even though the Territory of Hawai'i continued to claim jurisdiction over both Kalama Island and neighbouring Sand Island well into the 20th century.

Johnston Atoll had first been used for two US nuclear tests during Operation Hardtack in 1958. This testing program involved nuclear tests on Bikini and Enewetak atolls in the Marshall Islands, but from 22 April

---

11 Full details of all 24 tests are available in 'Operation Dominic 1', US Defense Threat Reduction Agency (USDTRA) Fact Sheet, May 2015. 'Petit' means 'small' in French.
12 Barton C. Hacker: *Elements of Controversy* (University of California Press, Berkeley, 1994), p. 216.
13 Under the December 1962 Nassau Agreement, the United Kingdom purchased US Polaris A-3 ballistic missiles for its four Resolution-class submarines, which served as Britain's nuclear strike force between 1968 and 1996. Today, the Royal Navy (RN) relies on US Trident missiles aboard its basllistic missile submarines.

to 19 August 1958, administration of Johnston Atoll was assigned to the Commander of Joint Task Force 7 for the duration of the test series. Two rocket launches from Johnston codenamed Teak (31 July) and Orange (11 August) both involved 3.8-megaton explosions from nuclear warheads on rockets launched from Johnston Atoll. After the tests were completed, the island reverted back to the command of the US Air Force.

* * *

During the later Dominic series in 1962, there were five successful attempts to loft rockets into the atmosphere from Johnston Island to create high-altitude air bursts: Starfish Prime (8 July), Checkmate (19 October), Bluegill Triple Prime (25 October), Kingfish (1 November) and Tightrope (3 November).

These rocket-launched tests, collectively designated Operation Fishbowl, were designed to study the effects of nuclear detonations as defensive weapons against incoming ballistic missiles. The 1.4-megaton high-level explosion from Starfish Prime lit the sky from Australia to Hawai'i, causing an enormous electromagnetic pulse that put out streetlights in Honolulu, 1,300 kilometres away. The blast pumped radiation into the Van Allen belts, capable of destroying or seriously degrading the orbit of seven satellites.

But not all tests were achieved without error. These operations were preceded by a number of aborted nuclear missile launches from Johnston, including three that caused plutonium contamination on the island that still lingers today.

The first failed test 'Bluegill' on 2 June 1962 was aborted when radar lost track of the Thor missile carrying the nuclear warhead. Range safety officers ordered the missile and warhead to be destroyed.

The next 'Starfish' test on 19 June led to massive contamination of Johnston Atoll. The launch of a Thor missile carrying a nuclear warhead was aborted a minute into its flight, and a self-destruct order blew the missile apart at about 30,000 feet. Large pieces of radioactive debris (including pieces of the booster rocket, engine, re-entry vehicle and missile parts) fell back to the island.

In 2000, the impact of this test was assessed by the US Defense Threat Reduction Agency (USDTRA), which conducted the *Johnston Atoll Radiological Survey* (JARS):

> More debris landed in the surrounding waters and on adjacent Sand Island, where residual plutonium from the test device was found. A large collection of alpha contaminated scrap was isolated during the initial clean-up ... It is likely that some portion of the plutonium was pulverised and consequently dispersed in the winds occurring between the destruct altitude and the ground and thus did not contribute to contamination at JA. It is however also likely that residual plutonium, in addition to that recovered from Sand Island, fell into the waters of JA.[14]

The test codenamed Bluegill Prime in July caused the most serious contamination. After a malfunction on the launch pad, officials destroyed the rocket by remote control after ignition but before the rocket had lifted off. The explosion of the Thor missile scattered debris in all directions:

> Plutonium material, mixed with the flaming fuel, drained into trench cables and was carried away in the smoke from several fires. This resulted in a deposition of alpha contamination on the launch pad complex that represented a major contamination problem. Contaminated debris was scattered throughout the wire-enclosed pad area and neighbouring areas. Metal revetment buildings were highly contaminated with alpha activity.
>
> Burning fuel flowing through cable trenches caused contamination on the interior of the revetments and all equipment contained therein. Fuel, which spilled and flowed over the compacted coral surrounding the launch mount and revetments, resulted in highly contaminated areas. Prevailing winds at the time of the destruction caused general contamination of all areas downwind of the launch mount.[15]

In an effort to continue with the testing program, US troops were sent in to do a rapid clean-up. The troops scrubbed down the revetments and launch pad, carted away debris and removed the top layer of coral around the contaminated launch pad. The plutonium-contaminated rubbish was dumped in the lagoon, polluting the surrounding marine environment. The JARS study politely notes:

---

14 USDTRA: *Johnston Atoll Radiological Survey* (JARS), 6 January 2000, pp. 1–18.
15 Ibid., pp. 1-119–1-121.

> Sea-disposal of radioactive waste for control of the radiological hazard was then considered expedient and proper … there was no effort made to analyse the magnitude and extent of the radiological hazard resulting from the destruction of a nuclear device on a launch complex.[16]

At the time of the Bluegill Prime disaster, the top-fill around the launch pad was scraped by a bulldozer and grader. It was then dumped into the lagoon to make a ramp, so the rest of the debris could be loaded onto landing craft to be dumped out into the ocean. An estimated 10 per cent of the plutonium from the test device was in the fill used to make the ramp. Then the ramp was covered during later dredging to extend the island (the lagoon was dredged in 1963–64 and used to expand Johnston Island from 220 acres to 625 acres).

The JARS study notes that:

> Much of these [contaminated] sediments may have been incorporated back into the islands in the 1964 dredging and filling work, and thus much of the plutonium contamination from Bluegill Prime may have been redeposited on the island. Any contamination not redeposited on the island through dredge and fill still contaminates the lagoon.[17]

The major Bluegill Prime disaster seriously affected the health of US Naval Air Force personnel who were present at Johnston Island. Crewmember Michael Thomas notes that the flight crew and ground support staff were trapped on the island following the destruction of the nuclear warhead.[18] In later years, the Squadron members of 'VP-6' present during that episode suffered an 85 per cent casualty rate of illness and cancers: non-Hodgkin's lymphoma was the biggest killer followed by thyroid cancer, throat cancer, oesophageal cancer, kidney cancer, multiple myeloma, and various skin cancers. Nearly 30 per cent of the crew experienced reproductive problems, with their wives suffering stillbirth and deformities in babies.[19]

On 15 October the same year, another test misfired. In the Bluegill Double Prime test, the rocket was destroyed at a height of 109,000 feet after it malfunctioned 90 seconds into the flight. US Defence Department officials confirm that when the rocket was destroyed, it contributed to the radioactive pollution on the island.

---

16   Ibid., p. 1-121.
17   Ibid., pp. 1-122–1-123.
18   Letter to the author from Michael Thomas, 28 November 2000. Thomas served at Johnston Atoll in 1962 as a member of US Naval Air Force, Navy Patrol Squadron Six, Flight Crew One.
19   Ibid.

With the completion of Operation Dominic at Christmas Island and two series of atmospheric and underground tests at the Nevada test site (Operation Storax and Operation Dominic II), the United States revived negotiations with the Soviet Union for a test ban treaty. On 5 August 1963, the United States, United Kingdom and Soviet Union signed the *Treaty Banning Nuclear Weapons Tests in the Atmosphere, in Outer Space and Underwater*—with underground testing still permitted, the agreement became known as the Partial Test Ban Treaty.

As with all Pacific nuclear test sites, the end of nuclear testing has not ended the nuclear hazard for the peoples of the Pacific. From 1963 to 1970, Johnston Atoll was maintained as a testing site in a state of 'readiness to test', in case the US President decided to breach the Partial Test Ban Treaty.

More than 550 drums of contaminated material were dumped in the ocean off Johnston in 1964–65. Since then, US defence authorities have surveyed the island in a series of studies, and collected 45,000 tonnes of soil contaminated with radioactive isotopes. Plutonium pollution was heaviest near the old rocket launching site, in the lagoon offshore the launch pad and near Sand Island. The contaminated soil was dug up and collected on the north of the island, in a fenced area covering 24 acres.

In the aftermath of the Partial Test Ban Treaty, Christmas Island lost its value for the US and British military. Plans for a permanent US satellite tracking base on the island failed to materialise and, in September 1963, the last US forces left the island. British forces did an initial clean-up, dumped unwanted material into the ocean and packed their bags. Tons of rusting vehicles, batteries, drums of unused asphalt and other toxic wastes were simply abandoned on the island.

On 29 June 1964, the Royal Navy (RN) owered its flag at the HMS *Resolution* base at Port London. Britain's military presence on Christmas Island was ended.

Johnston was used by the US military until 2000 and the island was expanded many times in size through dredging and reconstruction. Beyond the 1962 nuclear tests, Johnston Atoll was used to store chemical weapons from Okinawa after 1970 and drums of Agent Orange defoliant from the Vietnam War in 1972. Throughout the 1990s, the island was also the site for the Johnston Atoll Chemical Agents Disposal System, an incineration plant for chemical weapons removed from Okinawa and Germany following the end of the Cold War.[20]

* * *

As the British Gilbert and Ellice Islands Colony (GEIC) moved towards independence in 1978–79, researchers around the Pacific were concerned that an independent Kiribati would inherit environmental problems from the UK and US nuclear testing programs.

An unpublished research study from the University of South Pacific in 1978 found that 'there appears to be cause for concern about risk and radiological hazard on Christmas Island'.[21] Fifteen years later, the South Pacific Regional Environment Program (SPREP) called for further studies on possible radiological hazards on Kiritimati:

> i-Kiribati continue to work farm, fish and reside there, despite the fact that any ill effects of their stay on Kiritimati will probably not show up for years or generations. It is thus seen as critical to have Kiritimati Island reassessed for radioactive contamination in light of the increasing evidence based on the cancer levels in the Marshall Islands.[22]

Funded by a £9.1-million contract from the UK Ministry of Defence (MoD), a team from Safety and Ecology Corporation Ltd (SEC) was deployed in 2005 for a clean-up operation on Christmas Island.[23] SEC sought to remove more than 23,000 cubic metres of military material, but this focused on rusting equipment, oil drums, waste asphalt, asbestos and toxic chemicals left behind four decades earlier. Toxic or otherwise hazardous waste, including radioactive material, was transported back to the United Kingdom for disposal.[24]

---

20   Nic Maclellan: 'Radiation on Johnston Atoll—cleaning up the Cold War', *Pacific News Bulletin*, August 2000.
21   D. Medford: *Illustrative calculations on the radiological surveillance of Christmas Island*. Centre for Applied Studies in Development (University of the South Pacific, Suva, 1978), p. 5.
22   Randy Thaman and Ueantabo Neemia-Mackenzie: *Kiribati country report for United Nations Conference on Environment and Development (UNCED)*, South Pacific Regional Environment Program (SPREP), Apia, June 1992, p. 56.
23   Iain Laing: 'Green team booked to clean up island', *The Journal*, 22 March 2005.
24   'Christmas Island: Radioactive Waste', Under-Secretary of State for Defence Andrew Robathan, UK House of Commons, Hansard Written Answers for 17 February 2011.

The operation involved extensive negotiation with local communities, given some equipment had been repurposed for housing and pig pens.[25] Despite this attempted clean-up, comprehensive surveys of possible radiological contamination on the south-east corner of the island were not conducted.

A decade later, speaking at a ceremony at the UN headquarters in New York to mark the 2015 International Day against Nuclear Tests, Kiribati ambassador to the United Nations Makurita Baaro said:

> In Kiribati, when the tests ended, much of the equipment used for the testing were dumped in the ocean or just left behind. In seeking to have a study done on assessing the safety of Kiritimati from radiation, an offer was quickly made for a clean-up of the island, more than 30 years after the tests, by one of the testing countries. Kiritimati was deemed clean. The question is: is it really clean?
>
> With this history in mind, our region collectively has been most vocal about nuclear issues. In fact, the very establishment of the Pacific Islands Forum, the annual gathering of our Pacific leaders, emanated from the frustration of not being able to discuss nuclear issues, deemed political by the metropolitan powers who were members within the South Pacific Commission at that time and also the testers of the nuclear weapons.[26]

Operation Dominic highlighted the hypocrisy of Britain's refusal to acknowledge the health problems faced by military personnel after their service on Christmas Island during Operation Grapple. The United States would provide compensation to its troops from Operation Dominic for the same illnesses found amongst British veterans that would not by compensated by the UK Government.

---

25 'From a mere clean-up contract to changing lives —engaging the local stakeholders during the remediation of Christmas Island, Pacific Ocean' presentation by Dr J.P. Steadman, Safety and Ecology Corporation Ltd, to WM 2006 conference, 26 February–2 March 2006, Tucson Arizona. The WM Waste Management Symposia are annual conferences 'for discussing and seeking safe, environmentally responsible, technically sound and cost effective solutions to the management and disposition of radioactive wastes and the decommissioning of nuclear facilities to enhance the transparency and credibility of the global radioactive waste industry'. *WM Symposia*: www.wmsym.org/aboutwms.
26 Speech by Ambassador Makurita Baaro, Informal Meeting of the United Nations General Assembly to mark the 2015 Observance of the International Day against Nuclear Tests, UN Headquarters New York, 10 September 2015.

The issue is best shown by the case of Roy Prescott, one of the Royal Engineers on Christmas Island. As part of Operation Brigadoon, Prescott was seconded to the US Government to support the 1962 Dominic testing program. Decades later, Prescott was diagnosed with lung cancer. In July 2006, he was granted US$75,000 compensation from the US Government, under the US Radiation Exposure Compensation Act.[27] However, earlier that very year, the UK MoD had refused compensation, arguing that there was no proof his cancer was caused by exposure to ionising radiation.

Just weeks before he died, Prescott spoke out from his sickbed, calling on Prime Minister Tony Blair to change British policy and shift the burden of proof required to access pensions and compensation:

> I am a casualty of the Cold War and whilst I am pleased that I am receiving compensation and recognition from the US government, it really galls me lying here—a critically ill man—that the British Government continues to fail in its duty of care towards me and thousands of other nuclear test veterans by denying that we were exposed to radiation during service.
>
> In light of the overwhelming evidence and research in the US which has led to this compensation payment, I call on the Prime Minister to admit that mistakes have been made, to apologise for the pain and suffering inflicted on the nuclear test veterans and their families, and to order a full public inquiry into the whole nuclear test veteran issue.
>
> I would like to see the automatic award of War Pensions to any nuclear test veteran suffering from one of the 19 recognised diseases under the US *Radiation Exposure Compensation Act*.[28]

In 2010, the widow of pilot Derek Spackman became the second family member to receive US$75,000 compensation from the US Government, having been twice refused a war pension by the United Kingdom. Spackman was one of the 15 aircrew of Canberra bombers who participated in the 1954 Aconite program, collecting samples of radioactivity after US nuclear tests in the Marshall Islands. For this hazardous duty, Spackman was

---

27   The US legislation works on a presumptive list that recognises lung cancer as one of many diseases that can be caused by radiation released in the tests.
28   Rob Evans: 'US compensation for British nuclear test veteran', *The Guardian*, 26 July 2006; 'Nuclear test veteran gets U.S. payout', *Daily Mail*, 25 July 2006.

19. *THE PRESIDENT*—JOHN F. KENNEDY

awarded a Queen's Commendation for Distinguished Service in 1957. He was diagnosed with aggressive cancer of the pharynx in 2000 and, despite treatment, died five months later.[29]

For the survivors of US and British nuclear testing in the Pacific, the debate over the economic, social and environmental impact has not ended. From medical research to court battles, from NGO activity to parliamentary debates, the story of Christmas Island continues into the 21st century.

---

29 Rob Evans: 'Widow of British nuclear test veteran awarded $75,000 by US', *Observer*, 21 October 2010.

Interlude—Contested illnesses

Many nuclear survivors across the Pacific—from Marshall Islands and Kiribati to Tahiti and Fiji—suffer from what medical anthropologists describe as 'contested illnesses'.[1] They fear that their illness is related to their involvement in state-sponsored nuclear testing, but often cannot get official recognition of their concerns. They suffer without mainstream medical support or state legitimation. Their quest for recognition and understanding, in the face of unrelenting official denial of any problem, can be a huge drain on time, finances and emotion, and can rip families apart.

NZ researcher Dr Catherine Trundle has documented the challenges for Christmas Island veterans who have ongoing health problems but lack solid medical proof and political validation of the connection to their service in a nuclear test site:

> Contested illnesses linked to environmental causes such as low dose radiation or chemical exposure test the efficacy of science and medicine, because the causal pathways between toxins and health outcomes are complex and little understood; they are not adequately revealed by clinical and epidemiological models and techniques, which struggle to map low dose exposure and response relationships.[2]

In Kiribati and Fiji, the cohort of islander participants is too small for proper epidemiological studies that could determine whether the incidence of certain illnesses is greater than one would expect in the general population. Beyond this, the ageing survivors in developing island states have limited access to accurate information, financial resources or documentation that could support their claims.

---

1   Dr Catherine Trundle and Brydie Isobel Scott: 'Elusive Genes: Nuclear Test Veterans' Experiences of Genetic Citizenship and Biomedical Refusal', *Medical Anthropology: Cross Cultural Studies in Health and Illness*, Vol. 32, No. 6, 2013, p. 503. DOI: 10.1080/01459740.2012.757606.
2   Ibid., p. 503.

The first megaton hydrogen bomb test—Grapple X, November 1957
Source: Royal Air Force (Created by UK Government, available through Creative commons at: commons.wikimedia.org/wiki/File:OperationGrappleXmasIslandHbomb.jpg).

Despite these limitations, popular memory and personal testimony still raise many concerns. As one example of this process, consider the bizarre story of a small contingent of English women and children who made a fleeting visit to Christmas Island in early 1958. The women's subsequent concerns for the children's health were dismissed by doctors.

With the decision to extend the test series following the first test on Christmas Island in November 1957, a sudden decision was taken to rotate home much of the original contingent of British service personnel. In turn, more than 1,000 relief troops were carried to Christmas Island aboard the troop ship TT *Dunera* to continue operations in 1958.

There was also a special treat for some of the troops who remained on Christmas Island, after their lengthy service in difficult conditions throughout 1956–57: the military authorities agreed that some families of troops remaining on the island could travel aboard the *Dunera*. The wives and children would be allowed a brief visit onshore during the few days the troop ship unloaded, before returning to England. In the end, 30 wives and 31 children were taken aboard the *Dunera* for the round-trip to the Pacific, paying £25 for the privilege. Sadie Midford, who travelled with her three-year-old son and six-month-old baby daughter, was one of the women to make the journey. Years later, she recalled the day of their arrival on Christmas Island:

> There were a couple of ladies from the Women's Voluntary Service waiting for us and we all had a big party. Tony, my husband, didn't recognise me at first because I'd had a new hairdo and I hadn't seen him for over a year. The children loved it. We were only on the island two or three days and they played in the sand or swam in the lagoon the whole time. Our three-year-old played in the water for hours.[3]

The joy of the visit soon began to dissipate on the return trip, however, especially when six-month-old Valerie suddenly began to lose her hair. Sadie Midford reported:

> I noticed she had developed a bald spot as we sailed home on the boat. At first it was only small, about the size of a sixpence, and I didn't think much about it. But over the months, it gradually got bigger and bigger until it was about the size of the palm of my hand, I took her to a doctor who said he had no idea what was causing it. He asked me if I had changed their diet, things like that, but I said I hadn't.
>
> Then I told him about my trip to Christmas Island and he didn't believe me. He said: 'Are you seriously asking me to believe that the government sent children to an H-bomb testing zone?' I said they most certainly had, but he still wouldn't believe me and sent me away.[4]

---

3   Quoted in Alan Rimmer: *Between Heaven and Hell* (E-book, lulu.com, 2012), p. 20.
4   Ibid.

Fifty years later, Valerie Chir (née Midford) reported that she faced significant health problems.[5]

Dorothy Cannaby, who also travelled aboard the *Dunera* to visit her husband Maurice on Christmas Island, died in 2002 from breast cancer. After returning to England, Dorothy suffered six miscarriages before having three children, all of whom had birth defects. Maurice Cannaby attributes her health problems to their time on Christmas Island.[6]

* * *

The veterans' concerns about intergenerational effects have been rejected by the British authorities. However, publicity over these illnesses led to a December 2002 parliamentary debate on the Christmas Island tests in the UK House of Commons. During the debate, the UK Under-Secretary of State for Defence Dr Lewis Moonie argued:

> There is no current scientific or medical evidence to show that the health problems, or other physical problems, suffered by the children or grandchildren of test veterans could be attributed to the veterans' participation in the test programme.[7]

The same debate exists in New Zealand, with one academic critic of the nuclear veterans arguing that 'no connection has been demonstrated in any studies anywhere between parental exposure to radiation and the appearance of abnormalities in the children'.[8]

However, this official position is sharply contested by other medical researchers, who point to more contemporary studies on genetic impacts. As nuclear weapons researcher Dr Tilman Ruff has noted, the notion that there is a 'safe' levels of exposure to radiation is increasingly contested:

---

5 'At 31, I had to have part of my cervix removed because of pre-cancerous cells.' Susie Boniface: 'Babies were exposed to lethal radiation after being sent to nuke-blasted Christmas Island', *Sunday Mirror* (UK), 9 March 2008.
6 Susie Boniface: 'My wife visited and later had 6 miscarriages & died of cancer', *Sunday Mirror* (UK), 9 March 2008.
7 Parliamentary Under-Secretary of State for Defence Dr Lewis Moonie, UK House of Commons, Hansard official report, 4 December 2002, col. 262WH.
8 Professor Ron Smith: 'The ill children of nuclear test veterans—victims of just unlucky?', *NZ International Review*, Vol. 24, No. 2, 1999, p. 22.

INTERLUDE — CONTESTED ILLNESSES

> Any and all levels of ionising radiation exposure, including doses too low to cause any short-term effects or symptoms, are associated with increased risks of long-term genetic damage, chronic disease and increases in almost all types of cancer, proportional to the dose. Radiation both increases the chance of developing cancer and brings earlier its onset. These excess risks persist for the lifetime of those exposed. It has been conclusively established that there is no dose of radiation below which there is no incremental health risk—all radiation exposure adds to long-term health risks.[9]

With the UK Ministry of Defence (MoD) denying that few if any troops were exposed to hazardous levels of radiation, surviving veterans and their families are still deeply concerned about unexplained health problems, especially related to fertility.

Over the decades, as information about potential hazards from radiation became more widely discussed, the families of returned Christmas Island veterans began to worry. As Dr Catherine Trundle has argued:

> [With] hereditary illnesses, contained within family lineages or the result of chance mutations within specific genes, emotions of blame and guilt are muted or enacted largely within the family sphere. By contrast, test veterans claim that their illnesses are genetically transmitted, but of a recent environmental and social origin. Attributed to radiation exposure, their illnesses thus link damaged bodies directly to the moral culpability of the State.[10]

In research and interviews for this book, I came across numerous anecdotes from veterans, their widows and children, which testify to a range of problems with reproductive health, from miscarriages and sterility to deformities in children.

Susitino Lasagavibau, who witnessed three tests off Malden Island in 1957, suffered from skin ailments in later years. He expressed uncertainty about whether his military service had contributed to the death of his child:

---

9   Tilman Ruff: 'The humanitarian impact and implications of nuclear test explosions in the Pacific region', *International Review of the Red Cross*, Vol. 97, No. 899, 2015, pp. 775–813. For broader international standards, see Committee to Assess Health Risks from Exposure to Low Levels of Ionizing Radiation: *Health Risks from Exposure to Low Levels of Ionizing Radiation: Biological Effects of Ionizing Radiation VII* (BEIR VII) (National Academies Press, Washington, 2006).
10   Dr Catherine Trundle and Brydie Isobel Scott: 'Elusive Genes', op. cit. See also Catherine Trundle: 'Biopolitical endpoints: Diagnosing a deserving British nuclear test veteran', *Social Science and Medicine*, Vol. 73, Issue 6, September 2011, pp. 882–888.

I returned, married and had children. My third child died. I cannot explain it. The child was very healthy, but just died suddenly. There was no clear medical explanation. I cannot really blame the tests because I am not a doctor or expert. Some sicknesses which I never used to suffer from are affecting me now.[11]

Paul Ah Poy has faced concerns beyond his own health problems, with tragedy striking his children:

Despite us being told not to marry, we thought it was just a big joke. I did get married with my first wife and we stayed together for about 13 years. We didn't have any children, she kept on losing them when she got pregnant. After three months, she went to the doctor and she came back home and said 'I cannot carry a baby for more than three months', about three times.

When I was away at sea, she decided to leave me, so I only thought it was fair for her to go. I thought that was all quite normal, but later on I thought it was from the nuclear testing program, it was from my DNA that I was carrying.

Then I got married again and after one year, my beautiful son was born. I was happy and thought it could go back to normal. Then my son started to have problems with his arms, legs and face. The skin started to swell up and go down again, swell up one day and the next day, go down again. I took him to the doctor and the doctor couldn't do anything. Then he grew up and he's okay. He's okay and will be 37.

But at 27 years of age he went to the doctor. The doctor did complete tests, because he wanted to know if he could have children, because he had a girlfriend. The doctor told him: 'Son, sorry, you cannot have children.' So this was one of the things that happened to most of our children. Quite a few of us guys don't have children, and it is sad really when we come to the age when we want to see our grandchildren, but we don't have grandchildren.

I had a daughter Anne, but she lived only for three-and-a-half years. One day she was sitting on the floor, she just lay down and went to sleep and didn't wake up again. When she started to have breathing problems,

---

11   Interview with Susitino Lasagavibau, Suva, Fiji. See Losena Salabula, Josua Namoce and Nic Maclellan: *Kirisimasi—Na Sotia kei na Lewe ni Mataivalu e Wai ni Viti e na vakatovotovo iyaragi nei Peritania mai Kirisimasi* (Pacific Concerns Resource Centre, Suva, 1999), pp. 34–35.

> I used to take around to all the doctors in Suva. I was tired from carrying her round from doctor to doctor, but they all said there is nothing wrong with your daughter, until the day she died.
>
> Now I have another son and he seems okay, maybe, probably. Probably I may have grandchildren but I don't know, I really don't know what life will be like.[12]

Tekoti Rotan is also concerned that his time on Christmas Island could have affected his family's health as well as his own:

> One of my daughters, she gave birth and the grandson was born with a twisted foot. According to the news that we read, that is part of the symptom of radiation. The children can be born with defects, one of my grandson's born that way.[13]

Viliame Cagilaba echoed the concerns of other Fijian sailors who participated in the first naval contingent to the Malden Island tests. When he returned to Fiji after witnessing three tests in May and June 1957, he suffered from a range of maladies:

> Headaches became a normal thing for me. When I had these headaches, I was not able to look at the light. I also could not stand the heat. The headaches would go on for weeks. From 1957 until 1984, I suffered from this illness. After that it went away. I also suffered dental problems. My teeth kept falling out. My gums never bled. Sometimes while moving my tongue around my mouth one tooth would fall out with no bleeding at all. The remaining teeth were then pulled out. I now wear a full set of false teeth. I also would suffer body aches. Sometimes I would go off balance when trying to stand up.[14]

His main concern, however, was for his younger son who also suffered from jaw and gum problems, and was unable to play sport because of back problems and breathing difficulties:

> During our training, they told us these gamma rays can damage one's reproductive system if one was exposed to it. They told us about the bomb —that even if it does not affect you, it could have some effect on your children, grandchildren or future descendants.[15]

---

12 Interview with Paul Ah Poy, Suva, Fiji, November 2016.
13 Interview with Tekoti Rotan, Suva, Fiji, November 2016.
14 Interview with Viliame Cagilaba, Suva, Fiji, 1998, for *Kirisimasi*, op. cit., pp. 29–32.
15 Ibid.

Sainimili Nukurama is the widow of Filimoni Nukurama (RFMF 19825), who served on Christmas Island with the RFMF Engineers:

> My husband said that they had gone to Christmas Island for the nuclear bomb tests. After his service in the army we got married and then we decided to have children. However, in the six month of my pregnancy I had a miscarriage and the baby was aborted. After one year, I became pregnant again. I also lost this one. The third one I lost after three months. After this third one, I could not have children again.
>
> My husband later told me that he believed all these problems were linked to his service on Christmas Island. He kept on telling me this all the time.[16]

Similar concerns over lingering health impacts were expressed by Cagimudre Lewenilovo, wife of the late Ratu Yavalanavanua Epeli Lewenilovo, who served on Christmas Island as an engineer (RFMF 18866):

> My husband and I used to talk about their service on Christmas Island. One thing he told me was that in Fiji he was in the Army band. However, some members of the band were included in the Army engineers section to construct buildings at the test area. They were going to Christmas Island without any knowledge about the bomb.
>
> One thing that I usually noticed with my husband was that he always suffered from diarrhoea. He also suffered from occasional and severe stomach ache. He told me once that sometime in 1963 before we were married, he was admitted to CWM hospital [in Suva] suffering from severe diarrhoea during which he passed out. It happened to him several times during our marriage. Whenever it happened he had to stay in bed, and sometimes we had to take him outside to lie down. I always thought that he suffered from normal diarrhoea. However, I later knew that it must be related to his service on Christmas Island during the nuclear tests.
>
> Moreover, every day after work he experienced body pain. We used to massage his body every day. That was part of our normal life. He could not eat cold food. When he went to drink *yaqona* [kava], his food was warmed up before he ate. His health was of concern to us all the time. I also noticed that his hair was falling off and thinning out very fast. Some foods he could not eat. When he ate tinned fish that was cooked, his body used to be riddled with boils.

---

16 Interview with Sainimili Nukurama, Suva, Fiji, 1998, for *Kirisimasi*, op. cit., p. 62.

These are some of the things that happened to us when we were together. We had only two children. The two children are six years apart in age. The younger of the two is a girl. I had one miscarriage round about 1973. After the miscarriage, I could not have any more children.[17]

A common theme has been the fears of ageing men about the future health of their grandchildren, or the lack of children and grandchildren to care for them in old age. For this reason, a 2006 study led by Professor Al Rowland, indicating that there have been genetic impacts amongst the NZ sailors deployed to Christmas Island, has resonated across the veterans' community.

---

17 Interview with Cagimudre Lewenilovo, Suva, Fiji, 1998, for *Kirisimasi*, op. cit., pp. 63–64.

20

The research scientist— Al Rowland

Elliston Rowland wanted to be a concert pianist, but ended up as a geneticist.

Sitting at the piano at his home in Palmerston North, on New Zealand's North Island, Rowland said:

> I was reasonably good on the piano, but when it came to performing before the public, I was incredibly nervous. After an early concert, I collapsed in a complete sweat. So I gave it away and focused on my other great love: science![1]

The son of a railway worker, Rowland went on to become a scientific researcher and geneticist. Known as Al rather than the formal Elliston, he studied at Victoria University in Wellington, New Zealand, for his undergraduate and doctoral studies. Together with wife Alison, Rowland then travelled to Kenya in 1977 to lecture at the University of Nairobi. After four years in Africa, they returned to New Zealand in 1982 and Rowland commenced work as a lecturer and researcher at Massey University in Palmerston North.[2] His field of interest soon moved to genetic research:

---

1   Interview with Al Rowland, Palmerston North, New Zealand, 27–28 November 2015. Unless otherwise noted, direct quotes from Rowland in this chapter come from this interview.
2   The chapter draws on information from an unpublished manuscript by Al Rowland: 'British atomic bomb testing: An unintended legacy', December 2014 (copy in author's files).

Although my first interest was in plant genetics, I switched to human genetics early on. I had a research career looking at genetic damage, looking at any harm to the chromosomes as a consequence of exposure in the environment to various chemicals or various agents. But it was only an approach by Roy Sefton of the New Zealand Nuclear Test Veterans Association that set me on the path to look at the legacies of radiation exposure during Operation Grapple.

Al Rowland ONZM
Source: Nic Maclellan.

20. THE RESEARCH SCIENTIST—AL ROWLAND

Having witnessed five tests as a crew member of the HMNZS *Pukaki*, Sefton joined other New Zealand Nuclear Test Veterans Association (NZNTVA) members to lobby government ministers for financial support to investigate the health problems facing the veterans.

During the term of the Bolger National Party Government, Deputy Prime Minister Winston Peters had pledged a financial grant to the veterans. However, Peters was removed from office in 1998 before the NZNTVA could access the funding, which was then refused by the new National Party Prime Minister Jenny Shipley. Before the 1999 elections, the opposition Labour Party under Helen Clark had agreed to honour the $200,000 funding grant to the Operation Grapple veterans. However, after new elections, the incoming Labour Government was concerned that the grant might be used entirely on legal fees for a case against the UK Government.

With a further election looming, Sefton said that the veterans association tried again:

> In the run up to that election, we approached every party and lobbied to have this promise that was previously made by government to be paid. It doesn't matter whether you are National, Labour or whatever, it was a political promise.
>
> I had been for some time very interested in research because I considered that epidemiological studies are so open to misinterpretation depending on which side of the fence you're on. I remember the day when I was speaking to the chief adviser of the Minister of Veterans Affairs Mark Burton. I said, 'Look, I'm thinking about research. What say from a grant of $200,000, we put $100,000 into research and the rest into other areas?'
>
> It was only a matter of an hour or so and she came back to me and said, 'Subject to a meeting with the minister, the answer is yes.'[3]

Together with the president and senior advisory officer of the Returned Services Association, the veterans soon met the minister and, on 27 April 2002, NZNTVA held a well-attended conference to sign an agreement on the use of the funding. Later, Minister Burton presented a cheque for $200,000 to NZNTVA. For Roy Sefton, this opened the way to find scientific support:

---

3   Interview with Roy Sefton, Palmerston North, New Zealand, November 2015.

The thing is, I don't think they ever thought we would come up with someone like Al Rowland! Originally I had been looking to have the research done in the United Kingdom, on a research model that Saint Andrews University had undertaken. But I went up to Al Rowland and said, 'How much of this could you do?' I was scientifically naive at that time and wasn't sure whether it could be done here in New Zealand.[4]

Al Rowland wasn't interested in the legal aspects of the veterans' campaign, but said he was open to conducting a genetic study:

Roy Sefton had first approached Dundee University and St Andrews University in Scotland—they are among the top universities in the world looking at genetic damage in humans as a consequence of exposure to radiation. He wanted Dundee University to do a study of the New Zealand nuclear test veterans who took part in Operation Grapple. However, the British universities couldn't get ethics approval to do the study, so instead Roy approached me to ask whether I would be able to do the research.

At first, I was reluctant to do that, because the nuclear tests had taken place nearly 50 years previously. However, I talked to scientific colleagues, including Professor John Podd at Massey University who is a neuropsychologist with extensive experience in studying human populations. For basically humanitarian reasons, we decided that the alternative—to do nothing—was not good enough. So even though it was a bit like looking for a needle in a haystack, we thought that it was worth taking a look.

* * *

The proposed New Zealand study would follow other medical research into British Christmas Island veterans, which had been underway for many years. In 1983, following numerous parliamentary questions about veterans' health, the UK Government commissioned a survey by the National Radiological Protection Board (NRPB) of 22,000 men involved in the Australian and Kiribati tests. The survey studied official documents for causes of death and detailed the incidence of cancer for the cohort, using the National Health Service Cancer Register.

---

4   Ibid.

The NRPB report, issued in November 1988, stated that there was no excess mortality either from all causes or from all cancers, except for a significantly higher level of deaths from leukaemia and multiple myeloma among the test participants compared to the control group. The NRPB report concluded:

> There may well have been small hazards of leukaemia and multiple myeloma associated with participation in the program, but their existence is certainly not proven and further research is desirable.[5]

The NRPB carried out two more surveys in 1993[6] and 2003,[7] without reaching conclusions significantly different from the 1988 report (although the 1993 study reported a possible small increase in the risk of leukaemia in the first 25 years following exposure).

Based on the 1993 NRPB study, the UK Ministry of Defence (MoD) adopted a policy that pensions for War Disablement would only be granted for those veterans suffering specific leukaemia within 25 years of exposure. However, in a shameful subterfuge to avoid further liability, UK ministers have stated that the adoption of this policy 'is not an acknowledgment that those present at the sites were exposed to harmful levels of ionising radiation. The accepted service link is purely presence at the test sites'— as if leukaemia was caused simply by visiting a Pacific atoll![8]

---

5   S.C. Darby et al.: *Mortality and cancer incidence in UK participants in UK atmospheric nuclear weapon tests and experimental programmes*. NRPB-R214. (Her Majesty's Stationery Office, London, 1988). See also S.C. Darby et al.: 'A summary of mortality and incidence of cancer in men from the United Kingdom who participated in the United Kingdom's atmospheric nuclear weapon tests and experimental programmes', *British Medical Journal*, No. 296, 1988, pp. 332–338.
6   S.C. Darby et al.: *Mortality and cancer incidence 1952–1990 in UK participants in the UK atmospheric nuclear weapon tests and experimental programmes*. NRPB-R 266 (Her Majesty's Stationery Office, London, 1993); S.C. Darby et al.: 'Further follow-up of mortality and incidence of cancer in men from the United Kingdom who participated in the United Kingdom's atmospheric nuclear weapon tests and experimental programmes', *British Medical Journal*, No. 307, 1993, pp. 1530–1535.
7   C.R. Muirhead et al.: *Mortality and cancer incidence 1952–1998 in UK participants in the UK atmospheric nuclear weapons tests and experimental programmes*, NRPB-W27 (Her Majesty's Stationery Office, London, 2003); C.R. Muirhead et al.: 'Follow up of mortality and incidence of cancer 1952–1998 in men from the United Kingdom who participated in the United Kingdom's atmospheric nuclear weapon tests and experimental programmes', *Occupational and Environmental Medicine*, No. 60, 2003, pp. 165–172.
8   Parliamentary Under-Secretary of State for Defence Dr Lewis Moonie, UK House of Commons, Hansard official report, 4 December 2002, col. 264WH.

The NRPB reports have been used for nearly two decades as a shield by UK politicians, whenever challenged about health impacts.[9] However, the methodology, data and conclusions of the NRPB reports were widely criticised by British veterans and their legal and scientific advisers. At the time the reports were published, the British Nuclear Test Veterans Association (BNTVA) was angered the NRPB only looked at deceased but not living veterans, who continue to report a range of health concerns.

The same debates occurred in Australia, where government studies were launched into radiation exposure and veterans' health following the 2002 Clarke Review into war pensions.[10] These two studies—on dosimetry and on mortality and illness of veterans from Monte Bello, Emu Field and Maralinga—were also sharply challenged by Australian participants of the British atomic tests.[11]

In 1999, a study by Sue Rabbitt Roff of Dundee University reported an excess of multiple myeloma among a group of 2,500 test veterans. With 45 reported cases of multiple myeloma (when the UK average is three per 100,000), this was twice the rate reported by the NRPB. Thirty per cent of the men in the sample had already died, and of these 'two thirds of them died from cancers that are pensionable in the United States as presumptively radiogenic among nuclear veterans'.[12]

As part of this research, retired nurse Ruth Mackenzie gathered information from 235 NZ sailors, including 97 who had died. Of 443 reported conceptions, there were 99 miscarriages, 16 stillbirths and two were aborted. Two died soon after birth because of severe deformities and 25 others in early childhood.[13]

---

9   See, for example, 'Christmas Island Nuclear Tests', statement by John Spellar, Secretary of State for Defence, UK House of Commons, Hansard Written Answers for 20 January 1999, col. 462.
10   Michael Carter et al.: *Australian participants in British nuclear tests in Australia*, Vol. 1: Dosimetry (Department of Veterans' Affairs, Canberra, May 2006); Richard Gun et al.: *Australian participants in British nuclear tests in Australia*, Vol. 2: Mortality and cancer incidence (Department of Veterans' Affairs, Canberra, May 2006).
11   See, for example, Jack Lonergan: *An analysis of the studies conducted to assess the impact of the British Nuclear Tests at Monte Bello, Emu Field and Maralinga on Australian participants* (copy in author's files); and John P. (Jack) Lonergan: *Submission to the Senate Standing Committee on Foreign Affairs, Defence and Trade: Inquiry into the Provisions of the Australian Participants in British Nuclear Tests (Treatment) Bill*, 27 October 2006.
12   Sue Rabbitt Roff: 'Mortality and morbidity among children and grandchildren of members of the British Nuclear Tests Veterans Association and the New Zealand Nuclear Tests Veterans Association and their children', *Medicine, Conflict and Survival*, Vol. 15, No. 3, 1999, pp. 1–51. See also 'Nuclear test veterans' survey prompts official inquiry', *The Lancet*, Vol. 353, 23 January 1998. The study was based on a self-selected cohort of 2,200 British, 238 New Zealand and 62 Fijian veterans.
13   Matthew Dearnaley: 'Nuclear veterans target Britain—claim for children's birth defects', *New Zealand Herald*, 9 April 1998.

20. THE RESEARCH SCIENTIST—AL ROWLAND

HMNZS *Pukaki* proceeds towards the mushroom cloud after Grapple 1 test at Malden Island, May 1957
Source: Roy Sefton.

* * *

Given the debate over evidence, causation and 'contested illnesses', Al Rowland and his colleagues at the Institute of Molecular Biosciences at Massey University were aware they were walking into a political, as well as medical, battlefield. They decided to proceed, however, to conduct independent research on blood samples taken from a selected group of the NZ sailors who witnessed the British tests from HMNZS *Pukaki* and *Rotoiti*:

> I made it very clear to the veterans that I was separate to them, and this was a completely independent university study. I said that I may not find anything about long-term genetic damage, but they said that they just wanted the study done.
>
> It took a year to obtain ethics approval, because in those days we had to approach six different hospital ethics committees throughout the North Island, where most of the veterans were living. We eventually obtained ethics approval and also *iwi* approval [the necessary authorisation from the indigenous Māori].
>
> John Podd persuaded me that this must be done as a case-control study, where you have to select a matched control group. Because of his experience in this area, he agreed to select the study participants.

Given that there were only 551 NZ sailors involved in Operation Grapple, and many of them were unable to participate in the study, it was vital to establish a group of control subjects (a separate matched group of people who resemble as closely as possible the group of veterans at the heart of the study, except for one key variable—the veterans witnessed the nuclear explosions and the control group did not). Rowland said that the control group required a rigorous selection process:

> John set up his research team with Judy Blakey—a Master's graduate who played a key role in gathering information about each veteran and control volunteer. We first obtained a list of veterans' names from the Department of Veterans Affairs in Wellington. This was a fundamentally important step—it was crucial that an authorised list of names and addresses was obtained from the department rather than rely on self-referral from the veterans themselves.
>
> We then sent out a letter of invitation to all the nuclear test veterans from the list provided by Veterans' Affairs, inviting them to participate in the study. After we sent out a letter of invitation to all the nuclear test veterans, Judy interviewed every one of them, but then John's group

had to select the matched control group. Using protocols that had been established in other radiation studies overseas, we developed a very extensive questionnaire, which we presented to all prospective candidates.

John's team then proceeded to select a matched control group. They had to be matched for age, cigarette smoking, alcohol consumption and exposure to paints or solvents—all possible confounding factors that could affect the interpretation of the results, should a difference be found. We also rejected any prospective participant who had received or was receiving chemotherapy, as they could possess damaged chromosomes.

In the end, we obtained a very well matched control group, which was critical. The Returned Services Association was particularly helpful in this respect in offering to put up posters and hand our flyers in a number of clubs. Because of the healthy soldier effect, we chose ex-policemen or ex-army personnel—but not airmen or ex-naval personnel, given the controversy surrounding possible radioactive contamination of the ships.

The decision not to include former Royal New Zealand Navy (RNZN) personnel in the control group would later be questioned. The researchers would not accept former RNZN men for the control group because of the possibility of residual radiation on the Grapple frigates, which may have affected personnel who trained on or visited the Grapple ships in Auckland between nuclear tests, or later crewed the ships.

The elaborate matching of the control group with the veterans was a critical step in the process. It was also crucial for the researchers to operate without knowing whether blood samples came from one of the veterans or one of the control group. Samples taken from study participants were taken directly to Massey University's Health Clinic, and were given a new code so that the research team could not identify any participant.

The NZ Department of Veterans' Affairs was initially very helpful and even provided funding for one of the assays conducted by the university researchers (the sister chromatid exchange assay). But even with the NZ Government grant of $100,000, some of the tests were very expensive, and the team considered dropping one of the assays in the cytogenetic analysis.

Roy Sefton said the NZNTVA would step up to make up the shortfall:

> I advised Al Roland that the risk of dropping a possible ground-breaking assay could be disastrous, and NZNTVA would attempt to fundraise the amount required. The commitment of the NZNTVA members was such

that many made personal donations. Others, often old and sick, stood in the streets in winter selling raffle tickets, or were involved in other fundraising activities. We raised the $78,000 required.

As we could not use government funding above the agreed $100,000, NZNTVA has actually raised in excess of $110,000 to cover additional costs to ensure the research was carried out in full.[14]

In consultation with experts such as Dr Peter Bryant of Saint Andrews University, the research team settled on five assays.[15] Rowland explained that, using blood drawn from the veterans as well as the matched control group, his research team conducted a range of tests to look at potential damage to chromosomes:

> We went on to perform a series of five or six tests looking at various aspects of the genetic machinery, because radiation can affect different things. It can affect the chromosomes themselves in terms of breakages. It can affect the DNA repair system. You can look at fractionation of DNA—so we looked at all these different aspects
>
> There were techniques we hadn't previously used in my lab such as multicoloured fluorescence in situ hybridisation or mFISH. Peter Bryant from St Andrews University offered to train a senior technician from my laboratory, Liz Nickless, in the technique. He was very helpful, opening up his lab so she could study in Scotland. Liz brought back the technology to a lab and it was the first application of mFISH in New Zealand.
>
> I could not have wished for a more dedicated genetics research team, including Elizabeth Nickless, Mohammed Wahab, Chad Johnson and Ruth Wrenn. Each of them was assigned a separate assay to perform and I am forever grateful to them for the contribution they made, as without their meticulous individual efforts the study could not have been done.
>
> At a conference held in Papeete in 2006, I also had the good fortune to meet a brilliant scientist, Professor Claude Parmentier from the Institut Gustave-Roussy in Paris. He examined our findings in considerable detail and offered to calculate a dosage reconstruction from our data, ably supported by another of his colleagues, Radhia M'Kacher. This gave extra weight to our findings.

---

14   Interview with Roy Sefton, Palmerston North, New Zealand, November 2015.
15   For the technically minded, these included mFISH (multicolour fluorescent in situ hybridisation), G2 assay, micronucleus assay, COMET assay and sister chromatid exchange. Two of the assays, the G2 assay and the micronucleus (MN) assay, show no difference between the veterans and the matched controls, which suggests that DNA repair mechanisms in the veterans are not deficient.

When radiation hits the chromosomes inside cells, the chromosomes can break and recombine with each other—a process known as a 'chromosome translocation'. These translocations are a well-known consequence of radiation exposure. Although Rowland's team applied a range of tests, mFISH is the main assay used internationally for detecting damage to chromosomes caused by radiation exposure.

The mFISH technique involves 'painting' each chromosome a different colour, which can make breaks and rearrangements between chromosomes clearly visible. By showing whether translocations have occurred, the team could then count the number of translocations for each subject. Later, comparing the results for both the veterans and the controls allowed the team to determine whether there was any statistical difference.

After Rowland's team had finished their study, they discovered that the mFISH assay, in particular, showed a highly significant difference. Their research paper noted:

> The difference between the veterans and the matched controls with this particular assay is highly significant. The total translocation frequency is three times higher in the veterans as a group than the control group, the latter showing normal background frequencies for men of this age. This result is indicative of the veterans having incurred long-term genetic damage as a consequence of performing their duties relating to Operation Grapple.[16]

Rowland and his team were surprised that the mFISH tests showed such clear results:

> In the end, we found an alarming result. If you are looking at a person in their 60s or 70s for genetic translocations, you would expect to find about nine or 10 translocations per 1,000 cells. This is the normal background frequency. As a group, the veterans averaged 29 translocations per 1,000 cells. To compare, that is comparable to what was discovered in workers involved in the clean-up of Chernobyl, meaning there was severe genetic damage. Scientists do not often engage in hyperbole but without exaggeration, this result is extraordinary.

---

16   Al Rowland: 'British atomic bomb testing: An unintended legacy', December 2014 (copy in author's files).

The results are indicative of the veterans as a group having incurred long-term genetic damage as a consequence of performing their duties during Operation Grapple. In their published research study, the team reported:

> A careful comparison of the veterans and the controls for possible confounding factors, together with a close analysis of the scientific literature in related studies, leads us to a probable defining cause for the chromosome anomalies observed. Ionising radiation is known to be a potent inducer of chromosome translocations. We submit the view that the cause of the elevated translocation frequencies observed in the veterans is most likely attributable to radiation exposure.
>
> We hold the view that the genetic damage was caused by exposure to harmful radiation, probably through ingestion of ionising particles during the course of the veterans' participation in the series of bomb blasts known as Operation Grapple.[17]

* * *

NZNTVA's Roy Sefton believes the results of the independent study had enormous implications beyond New Zealand:

> We were mindful that genetic research identifying radiation damage in the NZ Operation Grapple veterans would make a strong case for compensation from the UK Government and also strengthen the pension claims by ex-Commonwealth nuclear test veterans and widows. Certainly the Massey University finding of genetic damage in NZ Operation Grapple veterans was a key factor in the decision of the London legal firm, Rosenblatt Solicitors, to go on with the class action for the UK, NZ, and Fijian compensation claimants against the UK Government.[18]

---

17   M.A. Wahab, F.M. Nickless, M. Najar, R. Kacher, C. Parmentier, J.V. Podd, R.E. Rowland: 'Elevated chromosome translocation frequencies in New Zealand nuclear test veterans', *Cytogenetic and Genome Research*, Vol. 12, No. 2, 2008, pp. 79–87. DOI: 10.1159/000125832.
18   Interview with Roy Sefton, Palmerston North, New Zealand, November 2015.

Public release of the results caused a firestorm in the media across Australia, New Zealand and the United Kingdom, boosting the momentum in the long-running class action before the British courts.[19] One British MP told the UK House of Commons that the Massey University study 'has opened up a hornet's nest that cannot be denied in further research'.[20]

NZ Prime Minister Helen Clark responded that the research was of 'great interest' and her government would study it further:

> By today's standards obviously it's simply extraordinary that people were ordered to stand on the deck of a frigate and witness an atmospheric test ... We now need to consider the research and in the interim we encourage any nuclear test veteran who has a disability that they believe is attributable to or aggravated by their service to apply for a War Disablement Pension.[21]

A year later, Roy Sefton and the NZNTVA were dismayed at ongoing delays. As the research was published in a peer-reviewed journal in June 2008, Sefton told the media that the association expected the government to act now rather than wait for the outcome of the long-running court case in England (which would drag on until 2014):

> When the results first became public last year, the Government promised to respond when the study had been peer-reviewed and published. Well, now they have to stop sitting on their hands and do something.[22]

Even after the study was peer-reviewed, it caused ripples in the scientific community in Britain —hardly surprising, given the results reopened the debate that authorities had tried to close through repeated invocation of the NRPB studies. Rowland was well aware that research by colonials would not be warmly received by some in London:

---

19   See, for example, Hamish Stuart: 'Study finds nuclear veterans suffered genetic damage', *New Zealand Herald*, 14 May 2007; 'Nuclear blast veterans have genetic damage —Massey study', *Radio New Zealand*, 15 May 2007; Ean Higgins: 'Nuclear veterans plan class action', *The Australian*, 15 May 2007; 'Nuke tests caused NZ genetic damage: report', ABC News Online, 14 May 2007; 'Boost for N-test veterans' case', *BBC News Online*, 15 May 2007. 'Nuclear test veterans to push for legal action', *ABC News Online*, 15 May 2007.
20   Dr Ian Gibson MP, UK House of Commons, Hansard official report, 22 October 2008, col. 419.
21   'Nuclear test study could help sailors' lawsuit—lawyer', *NZ Herald*, 15 May 2007.
22   Ruth Hill: 'Study backs nuclear test veterans' claims', *The Dominion Post* (NZ), 16 June 2008.

When the paper was published, it wasn't welcomed with open arms by all the scientific community. Some researchers like Peter Bryant spoke glowingly, but it was too much for a handful, especially in Britain and Australia. It struck me that their disagreements were on flimsy grounds scientifically and had more to do with the organisation they worked for.

I felt secure in our findings knowing that the paper we published, in the top chromosome journal in Europe, had been scrutinised by world experts and peer-reviewed by top scientists in this field. I was particularly heartened by the comments made by Dr David Brenner, who is unquestionably one of the top scientists in this field.

Brenner, the Director of the Columbia University Center for Radiological Research and Higgins Professor of Radiation Biophysics, was called as an expert witness in the long-running court case by veterans (a legal battle described in the next chapter). Before the court, Brenner stressed that the NZ research study had provided evidence of a statistically significant difference between the veterans and the control group:

> In my opinion, the Rowland mFISH study provides extremely strong evidence that the nuclear test veterans have a statistically increased burden of chromosome aberrations, compared to the controls. The measured aberration rates in the matched control group were what one would expect for individuals of their age—indicating that the methodology, precision and accuracy of the 2008 Rowland mFISH study was appropriate ...
>
> The excess chromosome aberrations measured by Rowland and colleagues provide evidence that the individuals have, in the past, been exposed to ionising radiation, over and above natural background (in particular a median estimated dose of around 150 mSv, with the highest dose estimate being 431 mSv).[23]

UK Government critics of the Rowland report acknowledge the evidence of increased chromosomal translocations, but argue that this does not necessarily mean that there will be adverse health effects as a result. In contrast, Dr Brenner's written report to the UK court highlights the increased risk to health over the life of the nuclear survivor:

> There is independent evidence from large-scale epidemiological studies— in particular Japanese atomic bomb survivors, but also nuclear workers— that individuals exposed to radiation doses in this range have an increased

---

23   Dr David Brenner, submission to the High Court of Justice, Queen's Bench Division, London, 6 November 2008. *AB and Others versus Ministry of Defence* [2009] EWHC 1225 (QB).

lifetime risk of both cancer incidence and cancer mortality. For example, atomic bomb survivors exposed in 1945 in the dose range from 5 to 150 mSv (and followed up for many decades) show statistically-significant increased risks of both cancer incidence and cancer mortality. Atomic bomb survivors who received high doses have proportionately lifetime cancer risks.

What is well established is that for solid tumours, the latency period is long, ranging from about ten years to at least fifty years. More precisely, the increased relative risk of cancer produced by a radiation exposure is generally maintained throughout the lifetime of the exposed individual … Thus the radiation-induced damage can remain latent in stem cells for many years until the damaged stem cell or one of its progeny starts to divide inappropriately as a result of the damage.[24]

Al Rowland retired from Massey University in 2009. Two years later, he was invested as an Officer of the New Zealand Order of Merit (ONZM), 'for services to genetic research'.[25]

Despite the publication of the Massey University research in a peer-reviewed journal, the NZ Government was reluctant to accept the political and financial implications. Al Rowland was soon to discover that the NZ bureaucracy would move to distort his findings:

Immediately after our paper was published, I received a phone call from the Secretary of New Zealand Veterans' Affairs to say that they did not accept any research conducted on the New Zealand nuclear test veterans that had not been previously approved by his office. I was astounded, especially seeing the funding and approval for the research had come from the New Zealand Cabinet. I could sense a 'Yes Minister' scenario working here. The powers-that-be were clearly disturbed by our findings.

In 2009, the NZ Government established an expert panel of six academics to review the research. After commissioning further reviews of the Massey University study, the initial report of the Ministerial Advisory Group on Veterans Health was forwarded to Minister of Veterans Affairs Judith Collins in December 2010, with the panel's chair confirming:

---

24 Ibid. For evidence of chromosomal translocations in a Japanese survivor of the Hiroshima bombing, and the onset of multiple cancers 50 years after his exposure in 1945, see Mitsuo Kodama: *Hibakusha: A-Bomb survivor* (Shift Project, Hiroshima, 2016), pp. 43–57.
25 *Queen's Birthday Honours list*, 2011, www.dpmc.govt.nz/publications/queens-birthday-honours-list-2011.

> The mFISH study did demonstrate an increased number of stable translocations. From these results it is reasonable to conclude that the nuclear test veterans were exposed to ionising radiation, but it is not possible to determine the exposure dose ... The Massey University mFISH study results do provide evidence that the nuclear test veterans were exposed to ionising radiation.[26]

For Rowland, the findings of the panel were a confirmation that the NZ nuclear veterans had incurred long-term genetic damage as a consequence of performing their duties during Operation Grapple, and also that this was attributed to radiation exposure:

> One could say this was a considerable achievement. One might also reasonably assume that the minister would go along with her expert panel's findings—but no. The veterans were waiting expectantly for a public acknowledgement from the government. Instead, after three years, a new document headed 'Executive Summary' was released in 2013.

This May 2013 summary document—only released to the veterans in 2017—now serves as the NZ Government's official position, even though the report is unsigned and has no public acknowledgement of the author. It argues against the core findings of the original research, concluding:

> The causality for statistically significant elevated frequencies of some chromosomal anomalies in exposed veterans, which may indicate long-term damage, could not be attributed to radiation alone; the health consequence or seriousness of these chromosomal changes are not certain, and enhanced medical surveillance of veterans' children was not supported.

Even today, Rowland is angered by the process and revision of the original findings of the panel:

> I find details of this 2013 document concerning our mFISH study quite staggering. It blatantly contradicts the 2010 conclusions of the Ministerial Advisory Group. To state that 'there is not enough evidence to attribute causality to radiation exposure alone' cuts right across the conclusions of international experts.

---

26 Letter from Professor John Campbell, Chair, Ministerial Advisory Group on Veterans Health to Minister of Veterans Affairs Judith Collins, 23 December 2010: www.veteransaffairs.mil.nz/assets/Veterans-Affairs-site-assets/Research/32.pdf.

The 2013 document is full of confusion and glaring inaccuracies. For example, the document erroneously states that the participants were self-selected, which they definitely were not. The 2013 document also questions why ex-naval personnel were not recruited for the study, ignoring the controversy over the possibility that the New Zealand boats were contaminated.

I accept that one can pick holes in any study, but the criticisms voiced in the 2013 government document fly in the face not only of international experts who are fully qualified in this area, but also their own expert panel. It illustrates what the New Zealand nuclear test veterans have had to suffer from officialdom for many years. In summary—the truth is too uncomfortable for them, yet searching for the truth is what science is all about.

The most damning comment made in the 2013 document is that the government does not support any case for the veterans' offspring to be studied. Even if the government could not bring itself to admit that the cause may be attributed to radiation exposure, they seem to accept that the veterans had incurred long-term genetic damage while performing their duties during Operation Grapple. So why not study their offspring? On scientific grounds as well as moral grounds this refusal is a miscarriage of justice.

For the veterans, this latest roadblock is extremely worrying. NZNTVA chair Roy Sefton has written in a submission to the NZ Government:

> The ageing veterans have no interest in any further research on themselves. Government is aware that the prime concern is now with the genetic make-up of their off-spring and possible trans-generational damage. The veterans wish their children to be genetically researched.[27]

* * *

The Massey University study only involved NZ sailors, although the initial contingent of 39 Fijian naval reserves had travelled aboard the NZ frigates to Christmas Island. The Fijians served aboard British vessels off Malden Island for the first three Grapple tests. For this reason, Al Rowland's

---

27 New Zealand Nuclear Test Veterans Association (NZNTVA): 'An in depth report on the exposed and control groups used in the Massey University research on veterans of Operation Grapple', submission to the Minister of Veterans Affairs, April 2017.

research was still highly regarded by members of the Fiji Nuclear Veterans Association, who were concerned that the same genetic anomalies might affect their members.

Because the surviving group of Fijian veterans is so small and the men in their 80s suffer from a range of ailments, it is not possible to conduct a scientifically valid genetic study using the techniques used for the NZ sailors on *Pukaki* and *Rotoiti*. But the research provided new impetus in the veterans' legal fight for compensation, described in the next chapter.

For Al Rowland, now living in retirement, his involvement in the research study was important:

> On a personal note, I find it fulfilling, albeit sad for the veterans. A reputable document is now on record which shows that the New Zealand nuclear test veterans' claims over the years that 'something' had happened to them as a result of their participation in Operation Grapple was not a figment of their imagination. They have incurred a lifetime legacy of genetic damage simply from following orders, in the name of protecting our country.
>
> The evidence from our study points strongly in the direction that the New Zealand nuclear test veterans were exposed to radiation which resulted, as a group, in long-term genetic damage. Our conclusions were that the high frequency of chromosome translocations was caused probably through ingestion of ionising particles because all the New Zealand frigates that participated in the program sailed either through ground zero immediately after the blast or were within close proximity and thus may have encountered fallout from blowback or contaminated rain.

The NZ research sparked renewed debate in the United Kingdom, prompting a response from the newly elected Conservative government led by Prime Minister David Cameron. In 2010, in response to ongoing pressure from veterans, the UK MoD commissioned an independent expert group to conduct a health needs audit to identify the health experiences, concerns and health and social care needs of British nuclear test veterans.[28]

---

28   Rebecca Miles, et al.: *British Nuclear Test Veterans Health Needs Audit Commissioned by the UK Ministry of Defence* (Miles and Green Associates, October 2011).

The report—the first research commissioned by the UK Government since the NRPB studies—found 83 per cent of veterans have developed between two and nine serious long-term illnesses since their service on Christmas Island, with some suffering more than 10 illnesses.

Another 2014 study reported there were 'significant excess levels of miscarriages, stillbirths, infant mortality and congenital illnesses in the British veterans' children relative both to control children and expected numbers'.[29]

For the NZ researchers, the publication of their results would feed into ongoing legal battles. The publication of the study came in the middle of a decade-long class action brought by UK, NZ and Fijian veterans, as they fought from the lower courts to the full bench of the UK Supreme Court and the European Court of Human Rights.

---

29   Christopher Busby and Mireille Escande de Messieres: 'Miscarriages and Congenital Conditions in Offspring of Veterans of the British Nuclear Atmospheric Test Programme', *Epidemiology*, Vol. 4, No. 4, 2014. DOI: dx.doi.org/10.4172/2161-1165.1000172.

21

The litigant—Pita Rokoratu

The Royal Courts of Justice on G.E. Street, The Strand, London
Source: Anthony M. (via Flickr). Available at: commons.wikimedia.org/wiki/File:Royal_courts_of_justice.jpg.

Nearly 40 years after he left the Navy, Able Seaman Pita Rokoratu (FRNVR 1196) would travel to London to testify in court. In a decade-long case—ultimately unsuccessful—Christmas Island veterans from three countries sought to use legal channels to seek civil damages from the British Government. For Rokoratu, the veterans' claims were about Britain's moral, as well as legal, responsibility:

> I can say that Britain murdered us. All the illnesses are affecting my children and grandchildren. Britain should do something to thank us. It has achieved its aims. It now has a great deal of power. It has an obligation to those who risked or gave their lives.
>
> It's true that we Fijians are always up to any challenge. Colonial days are over now. We have a time of enlightenment. Something should certainly be done. We Fijians are always embarrassed about claiming for compensation. However, since we are now living in a time of new attitudes, it is right to claim for compensation.[1]

Rokoratu's participation in the class action had its roots at the time of Operation Grapple, when he witnessed three hydrogen bomb tests at Christmas Island between August 1958 and August 1959:

> I was in the Fiji navy from 1956 up until 1960. In November 1957 we were told that they wanted some navy servicemen to replace some who were already serving there on Christmas Island. Our job was to transport equipment, supplies and material shipped from Britain from the ships to the island, as there was no wharf for the big ships there.
>
> Before going to Christmas Island, we knew that they were conducting the tests there. But they did not tell us any details of the tests or the possible effects. We were only informed about it after the first test. They told us that there was a chance of something going wrong with the plane that was carrying the bomb. If they found that we had been exposed to radiation, we would not have returned to Fiji. It was better that we stayed on Christmas Island. That was the time we realised what we were facing.

Returning from his Christmas Island deployment, Rokoratu spent four years with the survey section of the Fiji Government's marine department before joining the prison service, where he worked for the next 20 years.

---

1   Interview with Pita Rokoratu, recorded in the Fijian language in Suva in 1998. The translation comes from the book *Kirisimasi—Na Sotia kei na Lewe ni Mataivalu e Wai ni Viti e na vakatovotovo iyaragi nei Peritania mai Kirisimasi* (Pacific Concerns Research Centre, Suva, 1999), pp. 40–42. Unless otherwise noted, direct quotations come from this interview.

In the 1990s, as Fiji's Christmas Island naval veterans began to organise, Rokoratu joined the Fiji Nuclear Veterans Association. As they shared stories of their lives and families, many realised that they had common health concerns:

> As the years went by working in the Prison's Department, I was getting tired easily. I noticed that I was suffering from illnesses, which never used to affect me. I used to play rugby before. Now my body was always tired. Certain parts of my body began swelling. My eyes were not as good as before. I asked to resign five years before I was to retire because of my health.

After blood tests, he was initially diagnosed with aplastic anaemia, a rare disorder that occurs when there is damage to the bone marrow and the body stops producing enough new blood cells. This illness can be caused by exposure to radiation, toxic chemicals or certain viruses. He also suffered from leucopoenia, a diminished white blood cell count, which decreases a person's ability to fight infection and disease. From 1965, he lived with extensive lipomatous growth all over his body. His only two sons are afflicted with the same skin condition.

Like many veterans, Rokoratu believed that his health problems were related to his participation in the British nuclear test program. On Christmas Island, Rokoratu was not provided with any protective clothing or radiation measuring devices when he witnessed the Grapple Z tests.

> There was one army doctor on Christmas Island, but he never made inquiries about our health. After that, we continued with our normal work … Those of us in that group were all very young. Before going abroad, we only had the normal medical checks, but we did not have any medical tests after returning. We came back and were discharged at the army camp. At that time there was no pension scheme after returning.

* * *

As the Fiji Nuclear Veterans Association slowly built links with their British and New Zealand counterparts, the Fijians decided to join in the legal battles for compensation that had begun in Britain.

An initial case lodged by Melvyn Pearce in 1985 reached the UK High Court in 1988, where the UK Ministry of Defence (MoD) denied liability and sought to rely on immunity from suit under the *Crown Proceedings Act 1947*. Initially, Pearce won a significant victory, establishing that the ministry could not rely on the immunity of the Crown from suit.[2] However, soon afterwards, his claim was discontinued. Melvyn Pearce faced apparently insurmountable hurdles in his legal challenges against the UK Government, which continue to constrain legal action by many survivors of Britain's nuclear testing program.

First, some cancers and illnesses are only evident years or decades after the event, meaning most veterans often miss the deadline to lodge compensation cases under various statutes of limitation that bar late legal actions.

Second, many surviving veterans lack the detailed documentation required to show any direct exposure to radiation, or even to prove their physical location on the day of the tests. Even if radiation dosimeters were worn at the time, the data was not recorded or was subsequently lost or discarded.

Third, there is the fundamental difficulty of demonstrating a causal link between exposure to radiation and the disease or condition affecting the veteran. Some illnesses and cancers that can be attributed to exposure to ionising radiation can also be caused by inherited genetic factors or other exposure to toxins, chemicals or smoking.

Fourth, proving the connection between Christmas Island service and later illness is legally complex and expensive, but the burden of proof is placed on the shoulders of the veterans, not the British State. In the final words of their ruling in 2010, the UK Court of Appeal judges noted that reversing the responsibility of proof onto the MoD would change the legal terrain:

> We cannot say that any of these claimants who have, so far, not been awarded pensions will succeed in their attempts to do so, but their chances of success must be far greater with the MOD having to prove the absence of causation than they ever were while the claimants had to establish it.[3]

---

2   *Pearce v. Secretary of State for Defence* [1988] AC 755.
3   *Ministry of Defence versus AB and Others*, UK Court of Appeal (Civil division) [2010] EWCA Civ 1317, Case No: B3/2009/2205, para. 305.

21. THE LITIGANT—PITA ROKORATU

Finally, lawyers for the UK MoD have argued that the long delay in lodging cases before the courts '"fatally and irrevocably eroded the cogency of the evidence" because many of the senior civilian and military figures whom the defendant would wish to call are now dead or so old that they cannot be expected to remember events with clarity'.[4]

There are many examples of crucial data on radiation exposure being lost or destroyed. The UK MoD does not hold records of exposure rates for Fijian personnel. In his history of the NZ Grapple deployment, veteran Gerry Wright reports that data for the New Zealand sailors from HMNZS *Pukaki* and HMNZS *Rotoiti* is unavailable, even though personnel were issued with film badges for the early Grapple tests:

> Everyone's personal radiation detection badges were marked, packaged and transferred to the carrier *Warrior*. Because of the volatility of the chemicals used in testing these films, it was considered unwise to have them read at sea. It is understood that on *Warrior's* return to the United Kingdom, the films were apparently classified as 'used' and accordingly destroyed.[5]

In a letter to the author, British veteran Dave Whyte outlined the failure of the UK authorities to accurately record evidence that could be used in claims for war pensions or compensation. Whyte served on Christmas Island during 1958, witnessing Grapple Y and the four tests during the Grapple Z series. He was involved in clean-up operations after Grapple Z Pennant (22 August) and Burgee (23 September):

> I was ordered into the highly radioactive area known as ground zero two hours after detonation of two atomic bombs to clear up the debris. I was not supplied with any protective clothing or the respirator automatically supplied to the civilian AWRE [Atomic Weapons Research Establishment] workers, but was supplied with a radiation film badge (for gamma radiation) and a Quartz Fibre Electroscope (QFE) dosimeter (for beta radiation).
>
> When I delivered my truck to the decontamination centre, I noticed a civilian AWRE worker dressed in full protective clothing and wearing a respirator jump into the truck and drive it away to empty it. Inside the centre, they took my radiation film badge and placed it, along with others, in a box, My QFE dosimeter was read and recorded and recharged for the next user. I was recorded as receiving 5R per hour [46.6 mSv].

---

4   *Ministry of Defence versus AB and Others* [2010] UK Court of Appeal, para. 39.
5   Gerry Wright: *We Were There—Operation Grapple* (Zenith Print, New Plymouth, n.d.), p. 128.

> My truck was returned, emptied of the cargo, but was not decontaminated. At that time, it didn't mean anything to me, as I knew nothing about radiation. So I used my vehicle to transport friends to the Main Camp and the port area for the cinema and NAAFI [Navy, Army and Air Forces Institute] facilities.[6]

Whyte is critical of suggestions by the MoD that all data during the nuclear testing was meticulously recorded:

> Years later, when I wanted to claim a war pension, I decided to find out the dose of radiation I received. I discovered that my radiation film badges had mysteriously disappeared and no records had been made regarding the radiation levels on the dosimeters. I had a blood count taken prior to Grapple Z commencing and another taken after the completion of Grapple Z. The earlier blood count is in my service records, but no trace can be found of the latter one.[7]

The failure of the British Government to conduct medical studies both before and after the tests reinforces the difficulty of documenting the changes in the veterans' health. In an interview, Fijian veteran Emori Ligica noted:

> We were all medically examined and were healthy when we left for Christmas Island. When we returned, we were never medically checked.[8]

Despite the difficulty of legal challenges, surviving veterans and their families still believe that the British Government has a case to answer. Veterans aged in their 80s as well as their children continue to testify of the illness, trauma and heartache that plague them to this day. For 20 years, the nuclear veterans have unsuccessfully lodged a series of court cases and appeals in the United Kingdom and European Court of Human Rights, seeking damages under civil law for the illnesses they attribute to their service on Christmas and Malden islands.[9]

* * *

---

6 Letter to the author from Dave Whyte, 4 February 2015 (copy in author's files).
7 Ibid.
8 Interview with Emori Ligaca, Suva, Fiji, 1998, for *Kirisimasi*, op. cit., p. 151.
9 A useful summary of the UK litigation can be found in Patsy Richards: 'Nuclear Test Veterans—compensation', House of Commons Library, standard note SNSC-05145, 31 January 2013.

As founding chair of the British Nuclear Test Veterans Association (BNTVA), Scottish veteran Ken McGinley would launch one of the first cases against the British Government. In 1997, McGinley and Ken Egan lodged a case before the European Court of Human Rights in Strasbourg, which recognised the merits of their claims but sent them back to the United Kingdom to use all relevant avenues of appeal.[10] Another unsuccessful case before the European Court involved a young girl suffering from leukaemia that she attributed to her father's service on Christmas Island.[11]

In 2002, several veterans obtained legal aid in England and instructed Alexander Harris and Clarke Willmott (two different firms of solicitors) to bring claims for damages. As a legal adviser to the Fijian Nuclear Veterans Association, Adi Sivo Ganilau provided support to the British law firms to gather information in Fiji about the effects on the Christmas Island veterans and their families:

> When they sent their two paralegals down to collect data, we went around Fiji where the families were. We got to see some of the children who'd been affected—it's quite tragic. Many of them have horror stories to tell. I wouldn't wish it on anybody else.[12]

The associations of British, New Zealand and Fijian veterans soon agreed to proceed with a joint action before the British courts, rather than a series of individual claims.

On 23 December 2004, a group of 1,011 claimants lodged a case against the UK MoD.[13] The group comprised mainly British service personnel, but also Fijian and NZ veterans, as well as a few civilians and the families of veterans that had died. From the larger group, 10 test cases were chosen, with Pita Rokoratu representing the Fijian contingent. Adi Sivo notes:

---

10 Judgment, *Case of McGinley and Egan v. the United Kingdom*, European Court of Human Rights, Strasbourg, France, 9 June 1998. § 68, Reports of Judgments and Decisions 1998-III (10/1997/794/995-996).
11 *L.C.B. v. the United Kingdom*, 9 June 1998, European Court of Human Rights, Strasbourg, France. § 35, Reports of Judgments and Decisions 1998-III.
12 Interview with Adi Lusiana Sivo Ganilau, Suva, Fiji, November 2016.
13 *AB and Others versus Ministry of Defence* [2009] EWHC 1225 (QB). A list of 707 survivors of the group is included as an appendix in their 2014 case before the European Court of Human Rights: *Jean Ethel Sinfield and Others against the United Kingdom*, European Court of Human Rights (Fourth Section), Application no. 61332/12, 18 February 2014.

> Both sides had to pick 10 veterans and Pita Rokoratu happened to be one of the 10 for the plaintiffs. We did some preparatory work here in Fiji. They needed some more information, so we prepared statements. Then our lawyers in England allowed us to accompany him to London.
>
> Pita was pretty good when he was put on the stand. I suppose we had gone over his statement repeatedly, so by the time he got onto the stand, he was quite confident in the way he was cross-examined by the other side.[14]

The UK MoD used a technical argument that the case should be struck out because of the long delay since the nuclear tests were conducted. The MoD argued that the claims were 'time-barred', meaning a case must be lodged within three years of the event or 'the date of knowledge (if later) of the person injured' (a difficult barrier, as many of the veterans' illnesses were only apparent decades after their service on Christmas Island). The veterans' lawyers, instructed by the legal solicitors Rosenblatt, argued in part that the new scientific study by Professor Al Rowland reaffirmed the veterans' longstanding claim that they were exposed to radiation during the tests.

During argument, the MoD accepted that a small number of cases existed where military personnel, especially pilots were exposed to 'prompt high dose' radiation (because of their close proximity to the mushroom cloud of one or more of the nuclear tests). They claimed, however, that only 159 men of the nearly 20,000 people who were present in Australia and Kiribati died as a result of radiation exposure. The veterans' associations challenged this number, arguing that many more people faced delayed low dose exposure (for example, through the ingestion of radionuclides from fallout while swimming in contaminated waters or eating contaminated fish).

A fatal problem for the veterans was that they lacked the documentary evidence of exposure rates for military personnel to prove the higher levels that anecdotal evidence has highlighted (the required data can be found in nine volumes of records—dubbed the Blue Books—that the MoD still refuses to release).

---

14 Interview with Adi Lusiana Sivo Ganilau, Suva, Fiji, November 2016.

On 5 June 2009, High Court judge Mr Justice Foskett ruled that the 10 test cases out of 1,011 claims could proceed to full trial, a major step forward in the bid to claim damages under civil law. Foskett effectively decided to use his discretion and 'disapply' the time limit barring the case, ruling that the veterans could sue the government:

> All things being equal, a veteran who believes that he has an illness, injury or disability attributable to his presence at the tests whose case is supported by apparently reputable scientific and medical evidence, should be entitled to his day in court.[15]

Five years into the case, the courts had not considered the core issues raised by the veterans, but were bogged down in technical arguments. Fifty-nine of the veterans had died since the claim was lodged, and more were ailing. For the legal team that prepared the case, lawyer Ian Rosenblatt welcomed Foskett's ruling:

> We are very disappointed that both the Government and the Ministry of Defence (MoD) have chosen to make our clients keep on fighting for so many years. We now hope that the MoD will accept the need to help these people and make a swift and adequate offer of compensation. So far, this case has cost the tax payer around £10 million. This sum could have provided more than £10,000 in interim compensation to each and every one of the veterans who have been affected by the MoD's irresponsible actions.[16]

However, the MoD continued to resist pleas for a negotiated settlement. It soon appealed against the High Court ruling, on limitation issues and Justice Foskett's refusal to strike out or summarily dismiss the claims. After hearings, the Court of Appeal gave judgment on 19 November 2010. Lady Justice Smith, Lord Justice Leveson and Sir Mark Waller considered, and overruled, Foskett's decision.[17] Their ruling found that nine out of the 10 cases were statute-barred and could not proceed. Just one case, by Bert Sinfield, had been brought in time.[18] As it rejected Pita Rokoratu's

---

15 'Nuclear veterans win right to sue', *BBC News*, 5 June 2009. In his technical ruling, Foskett exercised the section 33 discretionary power under the *Limitation Act 1980* to disapply the limitation period.
16 'Rosenblatt Secures Victory for Nuclear Veterans', media release, Rosenblatt Solicitors, 5 June 2009.
17 *Ministry of Defence versus AB and Others*, UK Court of Appeal [2010]. The Court of Appeal upheld the trial judge's refusal to strike out the case, but on different grounds. Available at: www.bailii.org/ew/cases/EWCA/Civ/2010/1317.html.
18 Sinfield joined the case late in the day, after being diagnosed with non-Hodgkin's lymphoma in October 2005, which meant he was not time-barred. He died in February 2007, with his widow participating in the case in his stead.

action, the Court of Appeal ruled that the Fijian veteran could not prove causation or, on balance of probabilities, have his illness attributed to radiation exposure.[19]

The court decided that nine out of 10 of the test cases were rejected because of the difficulty of proving causation after more than 50 years had passed:

> We think that the judge has significantly and wrongly underestimated the claimants' difficulties on causation and is therefore unlikely to have given appropriate weight to that when applying the broad merits test. We think also that he has demonstrated an incorrect willingness to give weight to the claimants' contention that if their cases are not allowed to proceed, there will be a perceived injustice.[20]

The three appeal judges, however, recognised the political and moral significance of their ruling for the veterans:

> We recognise that these decisions will come as a great disappointment to the claimants and their advisers. We readily acknowledge the strength of feeling and conviction held by many of the claimants that they have been damaged by the Ministry of Defence in the service of their country.
>
> The problem is that the common law of this country requires that, before damages can be awarded, a claimant must prove not only that the defendant has breached its duty of care but also that that breach of duty has, on the balance of probabilities, caused the injury of which the claimant complains.[21]

On 28 July 2011, the UK Supreme Court agreed to consider an appeal from the nine unsuccessful claimants against the Court of Appeal decision, once again defeating MoD attempts to have the case thrown out. Neil Sampson of Rosenblatt Solicitors led a legal team before the Supreme Court, but the MoD deployed a larger team, with two Queen's Counsel and 15 barristers.

After hearings were held from 14 to 17 November 2011, the Supreme Court gave judgment on 14 March 2012.[22] The higher court overturned the Court of Appeal ruling that nine out of 10 lead cases in the action

---

19 *Ministry of Defence versus AB and Others* [2010] UK Court of Appeal, paras 286–298.
20 Ibid., para. 157.
21 Ibid., para. 303.
22 *Ministry of Defence versus AB and Others* [2012] UK Supreme Court, UKSC 9.

had been brought beyond the legal time limit.[23] The veterans' hopes were raised once again—before the Ministry again dashed them to the ground with another appeal to the full bench of the court.

The final blow came in a 14 March 2012 ruling in the full Supreme Court, with a narrow 4–3 verdict overturning the June 2009 Foskett ruling. The majority ruled the veterans' case 'had no prospect for success'. Tragically, Pita Rokoratu died of a heart attack, just days before the Supreme Court ruling on his test case. Ken McGinley of the BNTVA paid tribute, saying:

> Pita was a gentle giant. I'm glad his suffering is over and he passed away before learning of this final kick in the teeth. He volunteered to go to Christmas Island, and he deserved so much better than we gave him.[24]

Following the Supreme Court decision, the government confirmed in the House of Lords that it would not take action in response to the common law claims:

> The Ministry of Defence has no plans to pay common law compensation. On 14 March 2012, the Supreme Court ruled in favour of Ministry of Defence on all lead cases that claims by nuclear test veterans were time-barred, and further declined to allow the claims to proceed under the statutory discretion. In handing down judgment, all seven justices recognised that the veterans would face great difficulty proving a causal link between illnesses suffered and attendance at the tests.[25]

In a final blow, in December 2016 the War Pensions Tribunal rejected an appeal case seeking pension rights.[26] Applications from British veterans were rejected, even though Justice Blake accepted evidence from the veterans that had previously been rejected by the MoD (such as evidence of rainfall over Christmas Island after the Grapple Y test).[27]

* * *

---

23 'British nuclear test veterans take cancer claims to supreme court', *Guardian* (UK) Thursday 28 July 2011. For Sampson's perspective on the case, see Frank Walker: *Maralinga* (Hachette, Sydney, 2014), pp. 269–272.
24 Susie Boniface: 'Nuclear test veteran dies after years of suffering as MoD throw out his court claim', *Daily Mirror*, 12 March 2012.
25 UK House of Lords, Hansard official report, 26 November 2012, col. WA2.
26 *Abdale and Others versus Secretary of State*, War Pensions and Armed Forces Compensation Chamber, Royal Courts of Justice, London, 16 December 2016.
27 Ibid., paras 194–201, pp. 57–59.

The government's cult of secrecy, so evident in the 1950s, has lingered into the 21st century. In the House of Commons, the UK Government refused to reveal details of negotiations for a potential settlement between the veterans and the MoD that Justice Foskett had encouraged to avoid drawn-out litigation. Secretary of State for Defence Robathan stated:

> In accordance with the wishes of Mr Justice Foskett of the High Court, discussions were held between representatives of the Ministry of Defence and the Claimants involved in the Atomic Veterans group litigation. I am unable to publish the terms of the discussions because these were and remain subject to a confidentiality agreement between the parties.[28]

In a final attempt, Jean Sinfield—widow of the serviceman whose case had been allowed to proceed—took her case to the European Court of Human Rights.[29] Her case alleged breaches of the European Convention of Human Rights, given that there has been no public investigation into the causes of death of the deceased nuclear veterans. She also claimed that neither legal aid nor any other source of funding was made available to allow the veterans to pursue their case, despite its size, complexity and importance. The European Court, however, ruled against the claim.

The veterans' associations in the South Pacific, who had spent a decade in fruitless litigation, were demoralised by the UK Government's refusal to act. Then the son of Chief Petty Officer Ratu Inoke Bainimarama— the leader of the first naval contingent—decided that the Fijian veterans should wait no more.

In January 2015, Rear Admiral (retired) and Prime Minister of Fiji Voreqe Bainimarama stood before the veterans and their families to state that his government would provide a financial grant to the surviving veterans and the families of those who had died:

> We need to erase this blight on our history. We need to lift the burden on our collective conscience. There is a saying that justice delayed is justice denied. And these men have been denied justice long enough.[30]

---

28 UK House of Commons, Hansard official report, 17 July 2012, col. 769W.
29 *Jean Ethel Sinfield and Others against the United Kingdom*, European Court of Human Rights (Fourth Section), Application no. 61332/12, 18 February 2014.
30 Prime Minister Voreqe Bainimarama: 'Speech at the first pay out to veterans of Operation Grapple', media release, Office of the Prime Minister, Suva, Fiji, 30 January 2015.

22
The Rear Admiral— Josaia Voreqe Bainimarama

Josaia Voreqe Bainimarama, former Republic of Fiji Military Forces (RFMF) Commander and current Prime Minister of Fiji
Source: Islands Business.

They gathered slowly at the Suva Civic Centre, in the heart of the Fijian capital. On 30 January 2015, Fiji's surviving Christmas Island veterans, their friends, families and supporters came together for a long-awaited ceremony.

Standing before the crowded hall, Prime Minister Voreqe Bainimarama announced that his newly elected government would provide a financial grant to the surviving veterans and to the families of those who have died:

> Fiji is not prepared to wait for Britain to do the right thing. We owe it to these men to help them now, not wait for the British politicians and bureaucrats. So today, I have the great honour to award these survivors a modest token of what we can afford to finally acknowledge the great injustice that was done to them almost six decades ago.

> You may ask: why is Fiji taking responsibility for something that is the fault of Britain? My answer is this: Too much time has passed. The ranks of these survivors are rapidly thinning. Too many men—our fellow Fijians—have gone to their graves without justice. Those who remain deserve justice and Fiji as a nation is determined for them to finally get it.[1]

For Bainimarama, the debt owed was personal. As a Chief Petty Officer, his father Inoke led the first contingent of 39 Fiji Royal Naval Volunteer Reserve (FRNVR) sailors to Christmas Island. The younger Bainimarama had also served in the Fiji Navy, rising to the rank of Rear Admiral before taking power in a military coup in 2006. After eight years of governing by decree, the September 2014 national elections had brought Bainimarama to the office of prime minister.[2]

Speaking to the ceremony, he was blunt about the long delay to recognising the veterans' needs:

> We need to erase this blight on our history. We need to lift the burden on our collective conscience. There is a saying that justice delayed is justice denied. And these men have been denied justice long enough.

> To them I say: We salute you for following your orders at the time, the orders of a colonial power pursuing its own agenda in the world. You are living testament to our determination to never again allow our pristine Pacific environment to be violated by outside powers in such a destructive and terrible manner.[3]

---

1 Prime Minister Voreqe Bainimarama: 'Speech at the first payout to veterans of Operation Grapple', media release, Office of the Prime Minister, Suva, Fiji, 30 January 2015.
2 For background to the 2006 coup, see Jon Fraenkel and Stewart Firth: *From election to coup—the 2006 campaign and its aftermath* (ANU E Press, Canberra, 2007).
3 Prime Minister Voreqe Bainimarama: 'Speech at the first payout to veterans of Operation Grapple', op. cit.

22. THE REAR ADMIRAL – JOSAIA VOREQE BAINIMARAMA

The road to the ceremony was long and arduous, involving campaigns by veterans and their supporters, networking with other nuclear survivors and telling truth to power.

* * *

Britain's obligation to the Fijians serving in the British armed forces during the 1950s is clearly set out in the Colonial Office archives. At the time Fijian soldiers were recruited for service on Christmas Island in 1958, the Secretary of State for the Colonies guaranteed the Governor of Fiji that the UK Government would undertake the costs, including indemnity claims for disability pensions arising from any injuries, as a charge on UK funds. Over the next six months, there was extensive correspondence between the Ministry of Supply, Treasury, the Government Actuary and other officials to clarify this indemnity.[4]

On 27 June 1958, the Ministry of Supply told the Colonial Office that 'we had received Treasury agreement to … our undertaking to indemnify the Fijian government against claims for disability pensions or gratuities'.[5]

Ministry of Supply officials confirmed information had been passed to the Governor in Fiji that:

> The Ministry of Supply has undertaken to indemnify the Government of Fiji against claims for pensions to which men of the Fijian Military Forces or their dependants may become entitled to as a result of death or injury sustained by them during their service on the Nuclear Weapons Testing Base at Christmas Island in the Pacific.[6]

Decades later, Paul Ah Poy and other young men who supported God, Queen and Empire have become bitter about the British Government's refusal to recognise their role, let alone provide even token compensation.

Given the diversity of participants in Britain's testing program in Australia and Kiribati, there has often been confusion or disharmony amongst the veterans, as an ageing cohort of men tries to decide the best way to approach

---

4   Collated in UK National Archives file PAC.310/4/012. CO1036/514.
5   Outward telegram from the Secretary of State for the Colonies to Sir Ronald Garvey, Fiji, 'Priority/confidential number 5', 6 January 1958, (marked 'Confidential'). CO1036/514.
6   Letter from G.M.P. Myers, Ministry of Supply, to D.J. Derx, Colonial Office, London, 17 June 1958. CO1036/514.

government and assert their rights. The main coordinating group in each country has seen disgruntled or eccentric members breaking away to form their own sub-groups.[7]

In all countries, nuclear veterans have been critical of the Returned Services association or league, arguing that the official body has failed to actively support their calls for pensions and compensation.[8] For example, Fiji's Christmas Island veterans feel that some other returned service personnel saw Operation Grapple as a peacetime operation, without the danger—or valour—of armed conflict. Added to this, veterans of the Grapple contingent returning to Fiji were initially not eligible for Fiji's Aftercare Fund, a pension scheme for personnel who served in overseas armed conflicts.

Tekoti Rotan notes that the Christmas Island veterans' campaign has sometimes been met with criticism from other members of Fiji's Returned Services Association:

> They ask 'why are you asking for more money now?'. It's because we suffered. You died on the spot but for us, no. Our children are affected and that's the big difference between your task and our task. That is why we are complaining, because we need support. So now they're slowly realising it.[9]

The problems of distance, time and official secrecy hamper the efforts of elderly and often sick men. From the 1980s, some Fijian soldiers tried to gain information from London, with limited success. In December 1989, former Republic of Fiji Military Forces (RFMF) warrant officer Jiovesa Ramacake wrote to the British Ministry of Defence (MoD) listing the military personnel who had served on Christmas Island and seeking information on pension schemes:

---

7   In New Zealand, for example, the late Trevor Humphrey established RIMPAC as a separate group, publishing the newsletter *Prickley Heat* between 1996 and his death a decade later. For a collation of documents, see Trevor Humphrey: *A pixie in a mushroom patch* (self-published, Wanganui, 1996), copy of newsletter and book in the University of Hawai'i at Manoa library.
8   See, for example, the critique of the New Zealand Returned Services Association (NZRSA) published in *Prickley Heat*, Vol. 3, No. 4, August 1999 after the NZRSA backed the government's position on war pensions. See also 'NZRSA offers minister support with A-Test survey', *NZRSA Review*, Vol. 58, No. 5, October 1987.
9   Interview with Tekoti Rotan, Suva, Fiji, November 2016.

> There is a rumour amongst us ex-servicemen who had served as human guinea pigs during the hydrogen and atomic bomb tests that were held on Christmas Island in 1958, that there is some compensation for us. However we cannot be certain, for we all have retired from the service and such news are hard to come by. Should it be true then I would be most grateful if you would supply me with all the available information.[10]

A short reply from the MoD noted:

> I have to say that there is no special compensation scheme. However, if you or your fellow colleagues believe that you are suffering from ill health, disease or illness that could be attributable to negligence on behalf of the Ministry of Defence, then it is open to you to make a claim in common law.[11]

In the mid-1990s, Fiji's Christmas Island veterans began to share stories and organise amongst themselves. Paul Ah Poy, the current President of the Fiji Nuclear Veterans Association, was one of the early organisers:

> We still didn't know what was wrong with us until Losena Salabula of the Pacific Concerns Resource Centre [PCRC] put an ad in the paper and on the radio for all the veterans to go up to [the PCRC office in] Toorak and get together. So we all went up there and started to talk about our family. Then we knew that something was really wrong.

> When Ratu Inoke Bainimarama formed the association for the nuclear veterans returned from Christmas Island, only us sailors from the Naval Association joined up. There wasn't very many of us so I suggested 'what about the others, the soldiers?' So he thought it was a good idea and then we all got together.

> Unfortunately, he died a few years later on, so we asked Ratu Jone Tabaiwalu to be the leader. We chose him as our president, but he didn't last long. He was our leader for another three years but he died. We had an election and I was elected as President of our association, which I am still, right now.[12]

***

---

10 'British hydrogen and atomic bomb tests—Christmas Island 1958', letter from J.N. Ramacake, Nausori, Fiji to UK Ministry of Defence, 20 December 1989 (copy in author's files).
11 Letter from S. McIntosh, Ministry of Defence, London to J.N. Ramacake, Nausori, 11 January 1990; letter from Peter Smart, UK ambassador to Fiji, to Sailosi Kepa, Minister for Justice and Attorney General, 5 February 1990 (copies in author's files).
12 Interview with Paul Ah Poy, Suva, Fiji, November 2016.

From the mid-1990s, the New Zealand Nuclear Test Veterans Association (NZNTVA) also began campaigning, pressing for war pensions from New Zealand and compensation from the United Kingdom, fundraising for the Massey University genetic research and liaising with veterans associations in Australia, Fiji, Britain and France.[13]

As well as supporting Grapple veterans, the NZNTVA began working with NZ sailors deployed on HMNZS *Otago* and HMNZS *Canterbury* to waters off French Polynesia in July 1973 to protest against French nuclear weapons testing at Moruroa and Fangataufa atolls.[14] The NZ Government was undecided whether the Moruroa veterans had been affected by radiation, but NZNTVA argued that any war pension recognition and other gains made by the Operation Grapple veterans should also apply to veterans deployed to French Polynesia.

On 30 March 1998, the NZ Government announced that Operation Grapple veterans would be eligible for the highest war pension available to New Zealand returned serviceman.[15] In June that year, NZ Prime Minister Jenny Shipley also announced that compensation would be made to the children of Operation Grapple veterans who had been affected genetically through their parents' exposure to radiation.

Important steps, but for NZNTVA's Roy Sefton, there's still a way to go:

> In New Zealand, you get a war pension because of your service and any health outcomes that may be due to it. But a pension is not compensation. If we were to be granted compensation by the British Government, it wouldn't affect our war pension from the New Zealand Government. However, we were advised that the NZ Government would not pay both a pension and compensation. This made obtaining compensation from the UK Government all the more important for NZNTVA.
>
> We applied to get the American system of presumptive lists of illnesses here in New Zealand. There are a whole lot of conditions listed, and if you've got one, at least you get a pension for that. You're looking at more

---

13 A full run-down of activities is detailed in Roy Sefton: 'NZNTV Association', *Navy Times*, September 2002, p. 11.
14 Gerry Wright: *Mururoa Protest* (Zenith Print, New Plymouth, n.d.). The NZ Moruroa veterans went on to establish their own network, and were eventually given War and Emergency status, qualification for the New Zealand Special Service Medal (Nuclear Testing) and included in the Nuclear Presumptive List.
15 Office of the Deputy Prime Minister and Treasurer: 'Peters delivers on promise to nuclear test veterans', media release, 30 March 1998. See also Cathy Bell: 'H-bomb tests crews win pension', *Dominion*, 31 March 1998.

than 20 cancers where, if you've got one and you've got your doctor to confirm it, then almost in return a pension comes back. It's the same if you're a widow and your husband has died from a declared illness.

Our government eventually announced presumptive lists for all theatres of war and emergencies that NZ forces had been involved in. NZ nuclear test veterans or their widows, on medical certification, automatically qualify for a pension for 26 listed health conditions. Additionally, government now offers assistance to children who suffer five specified health conditions.

The Department of Veterans Affairs in New Zealand were happy to accept this system because it cut down the waiting list. Beyond this, however, there are a number of conditions that aren't recognised by the establishment as being related to radiation—a common one is heart disease and frequently the government tries to get around recognising that as a problem.[16]

New Zealand nuclear veterans receive the New Zealand Special Service Medal (Nuclear Testing)
Source: Courtesy Roy Sefton.

To address the issue of recognition for service, NZNTVA pressed the NZ Government to issue a medal for those who had served at Operation Grapple and the 1973 French Polynesia deployment. The New Zealand

---

16 Interview with Roy Sefton, Palmerston North, New Zealand, November 2015.

Special Service Medal (Nuclear Testing) was approved by Queen Elizabeth in 2002, to be awarded to all NZ nuclear test veterans. More than 700 NZ personnel have been granted the medal since that time, recognising 'the service of those personnel who were part of an official New Zealand Government presence at an atmospheric nuclear test between 1956 and 1973'.[17]

* * *

In Fiji, veterans had a longer struggle for recognition and financial support. The issue of access to the After-Care Fund would only be rectified by government legislation four decades after veterans returned from Christmas Island.

The publication of the book *Kirisimasi* by the Pacific Concerns Resource Centre (PCRC) in June 1999 sparked widespread public interest and spurred government action.[18] The newly elected Coalition Government under Labour Prime Minister Mahendra Chaudhry quickly agreed to address the longstanding problem that participation in the British nuclear testing program was seen as a peacetime operation, ineligible for support from Fiji's military pension scheme. On 16 July 1999, the Fiji Minister of Finance declared that Operation Grapple was an 'active operation', opening the way for changes to war pensions' legislation.

That year, Paul Ah Poy also travelled to England to lobby UK parliamentarians. On 20 October 1999, he stood alongside members of the British Nuclear Test Veterans Association (BNTVA) in the British House of Commons at a meeting with MPs, and stated:

> I have journeyed far from the other side of the world to bring to you the testimony of what is left of the men and family of the Fijian soldiers and sailors and i-Kiribati … We should be remembered, because we took Fiji's name there, we went as Fiji soldiers. I thank God for this opening, where the issue about us who went to Christmas Island is brought up. We should be remembered.[19]

---

17 *The New Zealand Special Service Medal (Nuclear Testing)*, New Zealand Defence Force (NZDF) website at: medals.nzdf.mil.nz/category/f5/f5.html.
18 Excerpts and photos from the book were widely published in the Fiji media: 'Tavo na italanoa ni vakalutu gasaukuro', *Nai Lalakai*, 24 June 1999; 'Blast from the past—lest we forget' *Fiji Daily Post*, 26 June 1999, pp. 20–21.
19 Speech by Paul Ah Poy, UK House of Commons, London, 20 October 1999. Copy in author's files.

On 1 December 1999, the House of Representatives in Fiji finally debated amendments to the After-Care Fund Act, which would allow all military personnel who served in Operation Grapple to access Fiji's returned services pension scheme.[20] As Home Affairs Minister Joji Uluinakauvadra noted:

> Unlike our veterans of the Second World War and the Malayan campaign, our servicemen who served in Operation Grapple do not have access to the Fiji servicemen After-Care Fund … Whilst there is no readily available data on those who were affected by nuclear radiation in Operation Grapple, it is however necessary to put in place mechanisms which can assist those who may be affected. At present none exist.[21]

During the debate, politician after politician from both sides of the aisle rose to condemn the British Government's failure to act. Opposition leader Ratu Inoke Kubuabola—who in 2017 serves as Defence Minister in the Bainimarama Government—stated:

> These men and women were put to unnecessary and unwarranted risk and as you know, nuclear testing is an evil which we have never supported of our own free will. This exercise was taken in the interests of our colonial masters and we were used as guinea pigs … It is only now that we are being told of the damaging effects, traumatic effects, physical as well as psychological of participation in such exercises. In this spirit, the British were supposed to be our trustees. They were obliged to do, according to the Deed of Cession, a treaty of contracts to safeguard not just our rights and interests, but our persons as well, which included our health.
>
> I believe, Mister Speaker, the British were negligent in this instant, extremely negligent, for the well-being of our service personnel and we must fulfil our obligations to our people. At the same time, this is a case where the British must fulfil their responsibilities. They should be asked to compensate the ex-servicemen involved, as well as families, that is the wives and children of those who were taken to Malden Island and Christmas Island.[22]

---

20 'House passes bill to cater for Christmas Island veterans', *Fiji Sun*, 14 December 1999; 'Bill for former soldiers passed', *Fiji Times*, 14 December 1999; 'Fiji soldiers guinea pigs in nuclear testing', *Fiji Sun*, 14 December 1999.
21 Debate over Fiji Servicemen's After-Care Fund (Amendment) Bill 1999, Daily Hansard, House of Representatives, Parliament of Fiji, Wednesday, 1 December 1999, p. 1933.
22 Debate over Fiji Servicemen's After-Care Fund (Amendment) Bill 1999, Daily Hansard, House of Representatives, Parliament of Fiji, Wednesday, 1 December 1999, pp. 1936–1937.

In the subsequent Senate debate, MP John Ali affirmed:

> Our soldiers had done their part. They have done their service to their colonial masters. What equity has the colonial masters done? What have they done for our ex-servicemen? Nothing, sir. They are only prepared to go to the international forums and point a finger at other countries as terrorists. But is it not terrorism to use innocent people as guinea pigs and leave them on the road?[23]

The bill finally passed the Fiji Senate on 13 December 1999.[24] This opened the way for Grapple veterans, for the first time, to apply for a monthly allowance of F$94 for welfare, medical care, supply of surgical appliances and loans for the education of their children.[25]

This small step by the Fiji Government was not matched by the British Government. Even though they served the British Empire when Fiji was under colonial rule, Fijians today are not included in the class of service personnel eligible for a British war pension, unless they currently serve in the British Armed Forces.[26]

After the amendment of the After-Care Fund legislation, the Chaudhry Government made commitments to carry the veterans' claims before the UK Government. However, this pledge was soon overtaken by events. After the May 2000 coup in Fiji, Chaudhry and members of his Coalition Government were held hostage for nearly two months, then removed from office.[27]

---

23 Senator Ali, Debate over Fiji Servicemen's After-Care Fund (Amendment) Bill 1999, Daily Hansard, Senate, Parliament of Fiji, Wednesday, 1 December 1999, p. 1933.
24 An Act to Amend the Fiji Servicemen's After-Care Fund Act, Act no. 41 of 1999 replaced the term 'war service' with 'campaign service', including the Malayan campaign and Operation Grapple within the remit of the Act.
25 Frederica Delailomaloma: 'Bill for former soldiers passed', *Fiji Times*, 14 December 1999; Reggie Dutt: 'Fiji soldiers guinea pigs in nuclear testing', *Fiji Sun*, 14 December 1999; 'Bill to benefit ex-servicemen', *Daily Post*, 14 December 1999.
26 UK Pension Service Order of 1983, part 2, schedule 4. As of 19 November 2002, only 30 war pensions being paid to UK nuclear test veterans were associated with their participation in nuclear tests—16 to nuclear test veterans themselves and the remainder to their widows. Data from 'Minutes of Evidence', UK Select Committee on Defence, *Legacy Issues for the Armed Forces Pension Scheme: Compensation for nuclear test veterans*, March 2003.
27 On the 2000 coup, see Robbie Robertson and William Sutherland: *Government by the gun—the unfinished business of Fiji's 2000 coup* (Pluto Press, Annandale, 2001); Brij V. Lal and Michael Pretes (eds) *Coup—reflections on political crisis in Fiji* (Pandanus Books, Canberra, 2001).

With support from PCRC, the veterans continued to carry their case to international audiences and connect with other nuclear survivors. In two trips to meet with Japanese antinuclear activists in 2002 and 2003, Tekoti Rotan tied the Fijian experience to that of Japanese *hibakusha* (nuclear survivors):

> We stand in solidarity with you as we know what you had suffered as a result of the bombing in World War Two. We consider the bombing of Hiroshima on August 6 and Nagasaki on 9 August 1945 to be an atrocity to the human race because it involved the mass killing of women and children. We support our joint call for compensation for the suffering endured … For a long time you and me had relied too much on what the scientist and our political leader said to us. But what did we find? It only brings trouble, poverty, and death to us.[28]

In Kiribati, the descendants of Christmas Island residents have not organised in the same way as the Fijian military personnel, but Catholic and Protestant denominations have continued to highlight the nuclear legacy.

In 2005, a regional ecumenical meeting was organised by the Pacific Conference of Churches (PCC) in Tarawa. It brought together nuclear survivors from Kiribati, Marshall Islands, Tahiti, Fiji and Australia to review the legacies of five decades of nuclear testing in Oceania. Reverend Baranite Kirata of the Kiribati Protestant Church, which hosted the meeting, proclaimed:

> The message of the Lord is clear: you shall not kill and you shall love thy neighbour as yourself. These commandments were ignored by those who tested weapons of mass destruction in the Pacific. The people of the Pacific continue to seek the truth in relation to the health and environmental impacts of nuclear testing.[29]

Paul Ah Poy also travelled to Tahiti to meet survivors of French nuclear testing. In 2006, he participated in activities commemorating the 40th anniversary of the first French nuclear test on Moruroa Atoll. The meeting was organised by *Moruroa e Tatou*, the association of former

---

28 Speech by Tekoti Rotan to International Meeting, World Conference on A and H Bombs, Tokyo, August 2002.
29 Media release from Pacific Conference of Churches (PCC) workshop, Tarawa, Kiribati, 7–9 February 2005.

Maohi workers who staffed the French nuclear test sites at Moruroa and Fangataufa atolls, during France's 193 atmospheric and underground tests in the South Pacific.

As Fiji returned to parliamentary rule after the 2000 Speight coup, PCRC's Losena Salabula was elected to parliament as a minister in the subsequent government led by Prime Minister Laisenia Qarase. The incoming leader also pledged support for the veterans:

> As the colonial power that had absolute authority over the Fiji islands, Britain had the great responsibility. It was responsible for the health and welfare of the people that were taken there. I think most important of all, if there were to be any tests, they should have ensured that there was absolutely no way that the health and safety of those people was going to be compromised.
>
> Now the evidence that is before us would suggest that there were in fact real dangers to these people. I would go as far as to say that Britain did not take sufficient caution to safeguard the health and security of our people. They have only said they have no responsibility whatsoever ... So that's the stand that Britain has been taking, which is most unfair and very unfortunate. I think the very least is to start talking to the Fijian Government and other governments that were affected, even if only to determine whether there is a case or not. That would be a very good start.[30]

However, before negotiations between Fiji and the United Kingdom could start, Qarase was overthrown in another military coup in December 2006, led by then Commodore Voreqe Bainimarama.[31] It took another eight long years of organising and lobbying, and the return to parliamentary rule after September 2014 elections, for the veterans' long campaign to bear fruit.

---

30   Interview with Prime Minister Laisenia Qarase, 'Nuclear fallout', *Dateline*, SBS TV, July 2003 (Transcript on *Journeyman Films* at www.journeyman.tv/film_documents/1700/transcript/).
31   Jon Fraenkel, Stewart Firth and Brij V. Lal: *The 2006 military takeover in Fiji—a coup to end all coups?* (ANU E Press, Canberra, 2009).

At a ceremony on 30 January 2015, 26 surviving Christmas Island veterans were each presented with a cheque for F$9,865 (around US$4,700).[32] After receiving his award, 80-year-old Jone Velivai said:

> I have waited for more than 60 years for this day. I am thankful that I could live to witness this.[33]

After years of struggle, the leaders of the Fiji Nuclear Veterans Association were overwhelmed with emotion. Tekoti Rotan explained:

> I notice that when we ask for meetings, very few people turn up, because they don't have the money for their fares. But that day, oh! That city hall, we were swollen, the veterans and their family members, everyone was excited. They say, now we are being recognised that we suffer.
>
> We were grateful to the present Prime Minister because his father was also involved in the operation. It's very generous of him to do it like that and he's trying to make the British wake up. Fiji shouldn't be doing this, but he is doing it to make the British people know that they should do something.[34]

The Bainimarama Government stressed that this grant was not compensation for death, injury or illness, which is still the responsibility of the UK Government. Instead, then Minister for Defence, National Security and Immigration Timoci Natuva stressed the grant was:

> a one off payment as medical assistance, in recognition of the various ailments these veterans had suffered over the years since 1960, after their exposure to nuclear radiation during the tests at Christmas Islands … The payment is to help compensate some of the medical costs that had been borne by the veterans and families over the years and is not a form of compensation, as there is an ongoing legal case between the Veterans Association and the British Government.[35]

---

32   Those who were presented their payment on 30 January 2015 included Maciu Suguturaga, Tomasi Vasuca, Maleli Naigulevu, Wame Turaga, Peniame Silatole, Jona Vakaotia, Jone Varivai, Tekoti Rotan, Nacanieli Seru, Levaci Nawaqa, Emori Ligaca, Saiasi Tagayawa, Tevita Batikaciwa, Silivakadua Rakaria, Rt Kamarusi Kini, Josefa Ifa, Paul Ah Poy, Amani Tuimalabe, Anare Bakele, Ropate Voreqe, Ilimotama Baka, Rt Busa Rusiate, Qalo Isireli Nairevurevu, Vatimi Lagicere, Niko Buke, and Naibuka Naicegulevu.
33   Litia Cava: 'Veterans Salute Govt', *Fiji Sun*, 1 February 2015; See also Mere Naleba: 'Payout for nuclear veterans', *Fiji Times*, 30 January 2015.
34   Interview with Tekoti Rotan, Suva, Fiji, November 2016.
35   'Government to disburse funds to veterans of Christmas Islands Operation Grapple', Fiji Ministry of Defence media release, 29 January 2015.

In its 2015 budget, the Fiji Government allocated F$2.95 million to the MoD to cover the payouts to the veterans, their widows and children. To calm the fears of government ministers about the size of the payout, officials presented a formula calculating each payment as '50 cents a day'. In fact, the total sum was calculated at a rate of 50 cents for 365 days—backdated for 54 years![36]

Over the next year, a Task Force involving the MoD, RFMF and Fiji Nuclear Veterans Association travelled the country to distribute the remaining funds to veterans who were too ill or aged to travel to Suva. As Paul Ah Poy travelled with the government delegation, he was often overwhelmed with sadness:

> I was deeply touched when I had to go and meet the families. I had to go and travel all over the island to hand over the cheque and interview the children, the grandchildren. With the Defence group, they were quite happy just doing their work. But for me, it was different, because I was involved with the testing program. Each evening I had to go home, thinking of the little children. Why did they have to suffer?[37]

For the ageing veterans, often living in rural villages and peri-urban settlements, the financial grant provided funding to fix their houses, support their children or pay off health bills. Isaia Seruvatu Baro, for example, said his payment would be put towards longstanding medical problems:

> I would like to thank the Fijian Government for recognition of our service. This money will surely assist me in buying my hearing aid and payment towards my eye surgery.[38]

While the Fijian and NZ veterans have welcomed the financial support and recognition of their own government, they still direct responsibility home to the government and people of the United Kingdom. For Tekoti Rotan, the responsibility still lies in London:

> We feel sorry, because we looked up to the British government as our father, we believed in them and we hope that they will be honest with us and look after us … We asked the British to be honest and to fulfil their commitment to us, because our people are suffering, especially the women.

---

36 Personal communication from Ministry of Defence official, Suva, May 2016.
37 Interview with Paul Ah Poy, Suva, Fiji, November 2016.
38 Tevita Vuibau: 'Joy for war veteran exposed to nuke test', *Fiji Times*, 22 February 2015.

We are concerned with the widows, young women left behind with three, five kids because their husband died prematurely. Tough job, tough job. They're the ones who suffer more than us. We men are all right, but the women bring up children, feed them, clothe them. We are fortunate that the Fiji Government is providing free bus fare and free education. Without this the women will suffer or die, that's the worry of how to bring up their families.[39]

* * *

In 2015, the UK Chancellor announced a grant of £25 million for an Aged Veterans Fund to 'alleviate suffering and increase wellbeing' of UK military personnel. The fund began operations in April 2016 and a Nuclear Community Charity Fund (NCCF) received approval to launch five projects benefiting nuclear veterans. The decision, however, to transform the BNTVA from a campaigning organisation to a charity reliant on government funding has caused significant debate, with criticism that some senior executives are receiving high levels of pay and have conflicts of interest with their members' needs.[40]

The Aged Veterans Fund is for all UK military personnel, not just nuclear veterans, but is being promoted in a way that absolves the UK Government of future responsibility for compensation for the nuclear testing program in Australia and Kiribati. It undercuts the call by Fijian and NZ veterans for recognition and compensation, as the NCCF does not cover overseas veterans. MP John Baron, who serves as NCCF Chair, told the UK House of Commons:

> I stress that our proposals are different … because the £25 million would be distributed on the basis of need, not entitlement. That is why it is important to stress the *ex gratia* nature of the payment. There is no admission of liability; no admission of guilt.[41]

Many surviving Christmas Island veterans and their families believe the UK Government is still avoiding its responsibility and denying their rights. Reflecting on Britain's colonial ties to Australia, New Zealand, Kiribati and Fiji, Paul Ah Poy states:

---

39   Interview with Tekoti Rotan, Suva, Fiji, November 2016.
40   'Charity bosses cash in', *Fissionline*, No. 44, May 2016. The glossy propaganda newsletter *Campaign* produced by the new BNTVA charity since 2012 is in sharp contrast to the small typed publications produced by most veterans' organisations. Copies of *Fissionline*, compiled by journalist Alan Rimmer, can be found online at: issuu.com/search?q=Fissionline.
41   John Baron MP, UK House of Commons, Hansard official report, 29 October 2013, col. 233WH.

> Every time there was an emergency, our people would answer the call of our Queen. The troops would come back with a big parade, with medals and flags flying and the band would be playing. But with us Christmas Island veterans, we all sneaked home like a thief in the night. There was no medal and no band and we were told 'don't talk about it!' We still remember we were healthy and young and we came back with a legacy that will be with us until the end of time.
>
> To the government of Great Britain, the people of Great Britain, we would like to say, please, do what is right. We have done our duty to our Queen and our country. We can only wait and see, hopefully, that you will do something.[42]

As he stood before the Christmas Island veterans in 2015 to remember 50 years of US, British and French nuclear testing across Oceania, Voreqe Bainimarama gave voice to sentiments that resonate across the islands region:

> As one, the Pacific nations stand and say: 'Never again.' Just as we implore the industrialised nations now to stand with us in the battle against rising sea levels caused by the carbon emissions they cause, we also implore them to join us in our commitment to make the Pacific nuclear free.
>
> At the height of the Cold War, there were up to 70,000 nuclear weapons in the hands of the Great Powers. Through successive treaties and agreements, this has now been whittled down to around 16,000 weapons. But it is still enough to destroy our planet and the world we live in many times over.
>
> It is a form of madness that we in the Pacific—the ocean that takes its name from the word 'peace'—find incomprehensible. This is why we will always be on the side of those nations pressing for the dismantling of the world's nuclear arsenals.[43]

In 2017, the 60th anniversary of the Grapple tests, non-nuclear states finalised the text of the Treaty on the Prohibition of Nuclear Weapons, which opened for signature on 20 September 2017. As we remember the legacies of Christmas Island and other test sites, the new treaty is a vital step in the ongoing challenge to create a world free of nuclear weapons.

---

42 Interview with Paul Ah Poy, Suva, Fiji, November 2016.
43 Prime Minister Voreqe Bainimarama: 'Speech at the first payout to veterans of Operation Grapple', media release, Office of the Prime Minister, Suva, Fiji, 30 January 2015.

Aftermath

After the Second World War, **Sir Winston Churchill** served again as prime minister between the general election of October 1951 and his resignation in April 1955. On 15 January 1965, he suffered a stroke and died in London on the morning of 24 January 1965, at the age of 90.

Yankunytjatjara elder **Yami Lester** OAM died in Alice Springs on 21 July 2017, aged 75. The previous month, his daughter Karina had travelled to the United Nations to lobby 120 nations negotiating the new Treaty for the Prohibition of Nuclear Weapons. She presented a petition from indigenous groups around Oceania, and the treaty preamble now recognises 'the disproportionate impact of nuclear weapon activities on indigenous peoples'. The treaty, opened for signature on 20 September 2017, includes specific articles calling on state parties to support nuclear survivors.

Rinok Riklon and **Lemeyo Abon** both live in Majuro, Republic of the Marshall Islands, and continue to speak about the legacies of the Bravo test. Still 'floating like a coconut in the sea', they have not returned to live on their home island of Rongelap.

Matashichi Oishi, crew member of the *Daigo Fukuryu Maru* (*No. 5 Lucky Dragon*), is still an active campaigner against nuclear weapons. In March 2014, he joined Marshallese survivors in Majuro to mark the 60th anniversary of the Bravo test. In late 2016, aged 83, he was campaigning for a 2-ton carved stone to be placed as a memorial to the Bravo test on the site of the Tsukiji fish market in Tokyo.

Wilfrid Oulton was replaced as Commander, Joint Task Force 'Grapple', by John Grandy in 1958. Oulton returned to the Royal Air Force (RAF) Coastal Command Headquarters before retiring from the Air Force. From

1982 until his death, he served as Chairman of Medsales Executive Ltd. He died in Lymington, Hampshire, on 31 October 1997. His three sons all served in the Royal Air Force and Royal Canadian Air Force.

Businessman **James Burns** died on 5 August 1969 at Bowral, New South Wales. He was survived by two children, with son David succeeding him as chairman of Burns Philp & Co.

Harold Steele died on 16 April 1979, at age 85. His obituary highlighted his quest to sail into the Grapple danger zone, noting: 'Can we call it a wasted journey? There were those who said emphatically that it could never have produced positive results; but a man was willing to give his all in a frightening gesture for the cause he believed in.'[1]

'Supermac', otherwise known as Maurice **Harold Macmillan**, 1st Earl of Stockton, OM, PC, FRS, served as Prime Minister of the United Kingdom until 19 October 1963. He died on 29 December 1986.

After her service with the Grapple Task Force, **Gillian Brown** continued a distinguished career with the Foreign and Commonwealth Office (FCO), rising to Assistant Under-Secretary of State in 1978. She was made a Dame in 1981. Brown was just the second woman to reach Ambassadorial level in the FCO, serving as UK Ambassador to Norway between 1981–83. She died at Ravenstonedale, Cumbria, on 21 April 1999.

After working as a merchant seaman, **Paul Ah Poy** retired to live in Suva, Fiji. He still serves as President of the Fiji Nuclear Veterans Association, and has travelled to Britain, Japan and French Polynesia to support other nuclear survivors.

Adi Sivo Ganilau, daughter of the late Governor General **Ratu Sir Penaia Ganilau**, is active supporting the widows and children of Fiji's Christmas Island veterans.

Following his contribution to Operation Totem, pilot **Geoffrey Dhenin** rose to the rank of Air Vice Marshall in the RAF, and served as Director-General of RAF Medical Services in 1974–78. He lived until the age of 93; he died on 6 May 2011. After years of ill health, Operation Grapple pilot **Eric Denson** committed suicide in 1996, leaving a wife and four children.

---

1   Muriel Ricketts: 'Harold Steele', obituary, *The Friend*, Vol. 137, 18 May 1979, p. 476.

Sir William Penney—chief scientist for the British nuclear tests in Australia and Kiribati—died in 1991 at the age of 82, suffering from liver cancer.

Roy Sefton is still active, campaigning for the rights of the New Zealand naval personnel from the *Pukaki* and *Rotoiti* who grappled with the bomb. Ill health has hampered his love of music and painting and he no longer plays the drums.

Upon his return from Christmas Island in 1959, **Tekoti Rotan** returned to Rabi and joined the Fiji Civil Service. After serving as the representative for Rabi in the parliament of the Republic of Kiribati from 1992 to 1994, Rotan was installed as chairman of the Rabi Island Council of Elders in 1996. He lives today in Suva, Fiji, and continues as a committee member for the Fiji Nuclear Veterans Association.

Professor Al Rowland retired from Massey University in 2009 and lives with wife Allison in Palmerston North, New Zealand. Two years after retiring, on the Queen's Birthday Honours list, he was invested as an Officer of the New Zealand Order of Merit (ONZM) 'for services to genetic research'.

Pita Rokoratu died of a heart attack in March 2012, just days before the Supreme Court ruling on his test case, which refused to allow the case to proceed.

Ratu Inoke Rewaqari Bainimarama of mataqali Nadamanu from Bau, Tailevu, served as the founding President of the Christmas Island Nuclear Veterans Association until his death.

His son Josaia Voreqe Bainimarama enlisted with the Fiji Navy on 26 July 1975, rising to Commander of the Fiji Military Forces in 1999. Voreqe 'Frank' Bainimarama led a military coup against the Qarase Government in December 2006. His regime ruled by decree until elections in 2014, when his FijiFirst Party won an overwhelming majority in the parliament. Today, **Rear Admiral (retired) Josaia Voreqe Bainimarama** serves as elected Prime Minister and Foreign Minister of Fiji.

Acknowledgements

History is made through collective action and many people played their part—often unrecognised—during the Grapple nuclear tests. The writing of this book was also a collective effort, though my name is on the front cover.

While living in Fiji in the late 1990s, I co-authored *Kirisimasi*, a short history of the Fijian soldiers and sailors who witnessed the British H-bomb tests. That book is long out of print, but with the 60th anniversary of the tests in 2017–18, the idea of reprinting the book was transformed into plans for a wider history, which would capture the diverse regional responses to the nuclear tests.

This book therefore draws on research and interviews conducted for *Kirisimasi* during the late 1990s, and I must thank my co-authors Losena Salabula and Josua Namoce Mudreilagi for their blessing to proceed. I also acknowledge other colleagues from the Pacific Concerns Resource Centre who collaborated in this work, especially our director Lopeti Senituli, Ema Tagicakibau, Tupou Vere, Hilda Lini, Ellen Whelan, Stanley Simpson, Siteri Kalouniviti, Feiloakitau Kaho Tevi, Marie-Pierre Hazera, Patrina Dumaru, Peter Emberson, Fipe Tuitobou, Sophie Naisau, Arieta Tirikula and many others.

For *Grappling with the Bomb*, new interviews and archival research were undertaken in Fiji, Australia, New Zealand, Japan, the Marshall Islands and Kiribati. Given the decades since the tests, I acknowledge the insight of Karen Ishizuka in her history *Serve the People*, who stressed the importance of 'our endeavour to document our history before too many of us leave this earth or forget how to tie our shoes'.

My greatest debt is to the military veterans, lawyers and journalists around the Pacific who work with nuclear survivors and maintain the struggle for recognition, clean-up and compensation. For interviews and advice,

I must thank Paul Ah Poy and the members of the Fiji Nuclear Veterans Association; Roy Sefton of the New Zealand Nuclear Test Veterans Association; Roland Oldham and members of *Moruroa e Tatou* in Tahiti; Abacca Anjain-Maddison, Giff Johnson, Bill Graham and many others in the Marshall Islands.

Thanks to the many survivors, scientists and campaigners who shared their stories for this book, including Paul Ah Poy, Rinok Riklon, Lemeyo Abon, Amani and Avelina Tuimalabe, Tekoti Rotan, Adi Sivo Ganilau, Levani Nawaqa, Roy Sefton and Al Rowland. I'm sorry I've only been able to weave fragments of their vivid memories into this text. I must also thank Torika Bolatagici, Joji Nabalarua and Larry Thomas for permission to use extracts of interviews gathered as we worked on the forthcoming documentary *Kirisimasi*.

A tragedy of modern times is that governments refuse to properly fund archives and libraries, despite their importance for our understanding of both the past and the present. I acknowledge the generous assistance of staff from the University of the South Pacific, National Library of Australia, National Archives of Australia, State Library of Victoria, Australian War Memorial and The Australian National University. Special thanks to Kylie Moloney of the Pacific Manuscripts Bureau (PAMBU) for advice and contacts.

My search for information on Harold Steele received valuable assistance from Jennifer Milligan (Senior Library Assistant, Library of the Religious Society of Friends, London). I owe an enormous debt to Jennifer Hunt (Deputy Archivist, Royal Voluntary Service Archive and Heritage Collection, Oxford), who found a box containing Women's Voluntary Service reports from Mary and Billie Burgess that had lain untouched for many years. Hiroshi Taka and Akira Kawasaki provided copies and translations of Japanese statements and newsletters from the 1950s. The Nuclear Claims Tribunal in Majuro and websites managed by Glenn Alcalay and Alex Wellerstein provide a treasure trove of documents and interviews on the Marshall Islands. Bruce Sowter went beyond the call of duty to search for articles about Christmas Island in ancient editions of the *Fiji Times*. John Waddingham designed the maps, superbly setting Christmas Island in its regional context.

ACKNOWLEDGEMENTS

This book draws on my reporting as a journalist in the Pacific, as a correspondent for *Islands Business* magazine in Fiji, as a former broadcaster with Radio Australia and a writer for other regional media. I owe thanks to editors Samisoni Pareti, Netani Rika and the late Laisa Taga of *Islands Business*, as well as Peter Browne of *Inside Story*.

Early versions of some chapters were presented at seminars and conferences, including a paper to the 2015 Labour History conference in Melbourne, published as 'Grappling with the Bomb: Opposition to Pacific nuclear testing in the 1950s', *Proceedings of the 14th Biennial Labour History Conference* (Melbourne: Australian Society for the Study of Labour History, 2015). Thanks to editors Phillip Deery and Julie Kimber.

The chapter on Bravo was much improved by insights gleaned from 'The Marshall Islands nuclear legacy—charting a course towards justice', a conference held in Majuro on 1 March 2017 (the anniversary of the Bravo test). Thank you to the Government of the Republic of the Marshall Islands and Bill Graham (former public advocate for the Nuclear Claims Tribunal) for the invitation to participate. I wish I was a poet like Kathy Jetnil-Kijiner, whose performance poem 'History Project' says everything you need to know about US testing in the Marshall Islands.

Comparisons between US, French and UK malfeasance were road-tested with students at the University of Melbourne, the University of the South Pacific, the University of Nagasaki and the Center for Pacific Island Studies at the University of Hawai'i at Manoa, with support from Richard Tanter (Australia), Sandra Tarte and Robert Nicole (Fiji), Tatsujiro Suzuki (Japan) and Terrence Wesley-Smith and Jerry Finin (Hawai'i).

I was guided through the intricacies of ionising radiation and reproductive health by Dr Tilman Ruff and Dr Peter Karamoskos, public representative on the Radiation Health Committee of Australian Radiation Protection and Nuclear Safety Agency (ARPANSA) and a member of the ARPANSA Nuclear Safety Committee. All remaining errors are mine, not theirs.

It's a daunting task for a journalist to try to write history (so many footnotes), but Pacific historian Stewart Firth encouraged me to submit the text to ANU Press and editor Emily Hazlewood took on this project with enthusiasm. The rigour and expert support of copyeditor Beth Battrick of Teaspoon Consulting made all this intelligible.

Thanks to Daryl Tarte, for extracts from his biography of Ratu Sir Penaia Ganilau, and to Adi Sivo Ganilau, for sharing memories and photos of her father.

Special thanks to Sandra and Nikolai Tarte, for decades of hospitality in Suva, and Tea Hirshon for a view of the ocean in Tahiti.

Sadly, too many of the people who first inspired me to report on the health and environmental legacies of nuclear testing are gone: Amelia Rokotuivuna and Ruth Lechte of Fiji, Grace Molisa of Vanuatu, Darlene Keju of the Marshall Islands, Nui Ben Teriitehau and Marie-Therese Danielsson of Te Ao Maohi (French Polynesia), Dr Bill Williams of Australia and Teresia Teaiwa, daughter of Fiji and Kiribati and scholar of masculinity, militarism and Methodism, who long ago reminded me that war is not just about boys and their toys. The death of John Taroanui Doom on Christmas Day 2016 and of Bruno Barrillot in March 2017 deprives us of two eloquent champions for nuclear survivors in the Pacific.

So many others have helped along the way, sharing their knowledge of nukes, Pacific history, Quaker and Catholic protest or the many legacies of nuclear sacrifice zones: Abacca Anjain-Maddison, Ambassador Tony de Brum, Maire and Tamara Bopp du Pont, Patrina Dumaru, Stewart Firth, Greg Fry, Bill Graham, Vanessa Griffen, Michael Hamel-Green, Dimity Hawkins, RMI President Dr Hilda C. Heine, Dale Hess, Unutea Hirshon, Giff Johnston, Senator Kenneth Kedi, Vito Maamaatua, Wes Morgan, Vijay Naidu, Wadan Narsey, Ueantabo Neemia-McKenzie, Fran Newell, Robert and Raijeli Nicole, Val Noone, Roland Oldham, Sitiveni Ratuva, Tilman Ruff, Joan Shears, Suliana Siwatibau, Clare Slatter, Sister Margaret Sullivan, Dave Sweeney, Bev Symonds, Richard Tanter, Sandra Tarte, Katerina Teaiwa, Oscar Manutahi Temaru, Gabi Tetiarahi, Sue Wareham, Ellen Whelan and Tim Wright. Apologies to all those I've forgotten.

Apologies as well to Aroha and passing visitors who were earbashed about thermonuclear death and British perfidy at the breakfast table. Above all, as always, this is for Nancy.

Nic Maclellan
Melbourne, Australia, 2017

Bibliography

Operation Grapple

Arnold, Lorna: *Britain and the H-Bomb* (Palgrave Macmillan, London, 2001). doi.org/10.1057/9780230599772

Blakeway, Denys and Sue Lloyd Roberts: *Fields of thunder—testing Britain's bomb* (George Allen and Unwin, London, 1985).

Crawford, John: *The involvement of the Royal New Zealand Navy in the British nuclear testing programmes of 1957 and 1958*, research paper for New Zealand Defence Force Headquarters, Wellington, New Zealand, 1989 (declassified 1996).

Hubbard, Kenneth and Michael Simmons: *Operation Grapple* (Ian Allen, London, 1985).

Hubbard, Kenneth and Michael Simmons: *Dropping Britain's First H-Bomb—the story of Operation Grapple, 1957–58* (Pen and Sword, Barnsley, 2008).

Humphrey, Trevor: *A pixie in a mushroom patch* (self-published, Wanganui, 1996).

McGinley, Ken and Eamonn P. O'Neill: *No Risk Involved—the Ken McGinley story—survivor of a nuclear experiment* (Mainstream Publishing, Edinburgh, 1991).

Oulton, Wilfred: *Christmas Island Cracker—an account of the planning and execution of the British thermonuclear bomb tests 1957* (Thomas Harmsworth, London, 1987).

Priestley, Rebecca: *Mad on radium—New Zealand in the atomic age* (Auckland University Press, Auckland, 2013).

Rimmer, Alan: *Between Heaven and Hell* (E-book, lulu.com, 2012).

Robinson, Derek: *Just testing* (Collins Harvill, London, 1985).

Salabula, Losena, Josua Namoce and Nic Maclellan: *Kirisimasi—Na Sotia kei na Lewe ni Mataivalu e Wai ni Viti e na vakatovotovo iyaragi nei Peritania mai Kirisimasi* [Fijian troops at Britain's Christmas Island nuclear tests] (Pacific Concerns Resource Centre, Suva, 1999).

Smith, Joan: *Clouds of Deceit—the deadly legacy of Britain's bomb tests* (Faber and Faber, London, 1985).

Trundle, Catherine: 'Searching for Culpability in the Archives: Commonwealth Nuclear Test Veterans' Claims for Compensation', *History and Anthropology*, Vol. 22, No. 4, 2011, pp. 497–512. doi.org /10.1080/02757206.2011.626773

Wright, Gerry: *We Were There—Operation Grapple* (Zenith Print, New Plymouth, n.d.).

Wynd, Michael: 'From Participation to Protest: The Royal New Zealand Navy and Nuclear Testing 1957–1995', presentation to the biennial Sea Power Conference, Sea Power Centre, Sydney, Australia.

British atomic testing in Australia

Arnold, Lorna: *A Very Special Relationship—British Atomic Weapons Trials in Australia* (Her Majesty's Stationery Office, London, 1987).

Attwood, Bain: *Rights for Aborigines* (Allen and Unwin, 2003).

Barwick, Garfield: 'Statement in the House of Representatives on the ratification by the Australian government of the Nuclear Test Ban Treaty, by the Minister for External Affairs Sir Garfield Barwick on 15 August 1963', in *Nuclear Testing, Select Documents on International Affairs*, No. 2 (Department of External Affairs, Canberra, 1963).

Carter, Barbara: 'The peace movements in the 1950s' in Ann Curthoys and John Merritt: *Better Dead than Red—Australia's first Cold War 1945–59* (Allen and Unwin, Sydney, 1986).

Cross, Roger: *Fallout—Hedley Marston and the British bomb tests in Australia* (Wakefield Press, 2001).

Cross, Roger and Avon Hudson: *Beyond Belief—the British bomb tests, Australia's veterans speak out* (Wakefield Press, Kent Town, 2005).

Curthoys, Anne and Joy Damousi (eds): *What did you do in the Cold War, Daddy? Personal stories from a troubled time* (NewSouth Publishing, Sydney, 2014).

Government of Australia: *The Report of the Royal Commission into British Nuclear Tests in Australia* (Australian Government Publishing Service, Canberra, 1985).

Jordan, Doug: *Conflict in the Unions—the Communist Party of Australia, politics and the trade union movement, 1945–60* (Resistance Books, Sydney, 2013).

Lester, Yami: *Yami—the autobiography of Yami Lester* (IAD Press, Alice Springs, 1993).

Mattingley, Christobel: *Maralinga's long shadow—Yvonne's story* (Allen and Unwin, Sydney, 2016).

Mattingley, Christobel with Yalata and Oak Valley communities: *Maralinga—the Anangu story* (Allen and Unwin, Sydney, 2009).

Milliken, Robert: *No Conceivable Injury—the story of Britain and Australia's atomic cover-up* (Penguin, Ringwood, 1986).

Mittman, Jan Dirk (ed.): *Black Mist, Black Country* (Burrinja, Upwey, 2016).

Parkinson, Alan: *Maralinga—Australia's nuclear waste cover up* (ABC Books, Sydney, 2007).

Penney, William: Statement to Royal Commission into the British Nuclear Tests, 1984. National Archives of Australia, NAA A6449.

Symonds, J.L.: *A History of British Atomic Tests in Australia* (Australian Government Publishing Service, Canberra, 1985).

Tame, Adrian and Rob Robotham: *Maralinga: British A-bomb, Australian Legacy* (Fontana/Collins, Melbourne, 1982).

Tynan, Elizabeth: *Atomic thunder—the Maralinga Story* (NewSouth Publishing, Sydney, 2016).

Walker, Frank: *Maralinga* (Hachette, Sydney, 2014).

Watt, Alf: *Rocket Range Threatens Australia* (Australian Communist Party South Australian State Committee, Adelaide, 1947).

Wilson, Deborah: *Different white people—radical activism for aboriginal rights 1946–72* (UWA Publishing, Perth, 2015).

British nuclear and strategic policy

Arnold, Lorna: *Windscale 1957—Anatomy of a Nuclear Accident* (Palgrave Macmillan, London, 1992).

Ashton, Nigel: *Kennedy, Macmillan and the Cold War: The irony of interdependence* (Palgrave Macmillan, London, 2002). doi.org/ 10.1057/9780230800014

Ball, S.J.: 'Military Nuclear Relations between the United States and Great Britain under the Terms of the McMahon Act, 1946–1958', *The Historical Journal*, Vol. 38, No. 2, 1995.

Baylis, John: *Ambiguity and Deterrence—British Nuclear Strategy 1945–64* (Clarendon Press, Oxford, 1995). doi.org/10.1093/ acprof:oso/9780198280125.001.0001

Brixey-Williams, Sebastian: 'UK revokes ICJ jurisdiction over its nuclear weapons', *BASIC* (British American Security Information Council), 27 March 2017.

Brookes, Andrew: *Valiant units of the Cold War*, Osprey combat aircraft, No. 95 (Osprey, Oxford, 2012).

Colville, John: *The Fringes of Power: 10 Downing Street Diaries 1939–1955* (W.W. Norton & Co, London, 1985).

Dombey, Norman and Eric Grove: 'Britain's thermonuclear bluff', *London Review of Books*, 22 October 1992.

Farmelo, Graham: *Churchill's Bomb—a hidden history of science, war and politics* (Faber and Faber, London, 2013).

Gilbert, Martin: *Winston S. Churchill, Volume VIII: Never Despair 1945–6* (Heinemann, London, 1988).

Gowing, Margaret: *Independence and deterrence*, Volume 1 (Macmillan, London, 1974).

International Court of Justice: *Declarations Recognising the Jurisdiction of the Court as Compulsory, United Kingdom of Great Britain and Northern Island*, 27 February 2017.

Macmillan, Harold: *Riding the Storm 1956–1959* (Harper and Row, New York, 1971).

McCarthy, Helen: *Women of the World—The Rise of the Female Diplomat* (Bloomsbury, London, 2014).

McIntyre, Ben: *A Spy Among Friends: Kim Philby and the Great Betrayal* (Bloomsbury, London, 2014).

Rosenberg, Jonathan: 'Before the bomb and after: Winston Churchill and the use of force', in John Lewis Gaddis (ed.): *Cold War statesman confront the bomb: nuclear diplomacy since 1945* (Oxford University Press, 1999). doi.org/10.1093/0198294689.003.0008

Walker, John: *British nuclear weapons and the Test Ban 1954–73: Britain, the United States, Weapons Policies and Nuclear Testing, Tensions and Contradictions* (Ashgate, 2010). doi.org/10.1080/10736700.2012.655090

Walker, John: 'Potential Proliferation pointers from the past: Lessons from the British Nuclear Weapons Program, 1952–69', *The Nonproliferation Review*, Vol. 19, No. 1, 2012, pp. 109–123.

Walton, Calder: *Empire of secrets—British intelligence, the Cold War and the twilight of Empire* (Harper Press, London, 2013).

Walton, Calder and Christopher Andrew: 'Still the missing dimension: British intelligence and the historiography of British decolonisation', in Patrick Major and Christopher Moran (eds): *Spooked—Britain, Empire and intelligence since 1945* (Cambridge Scholars Publishing, Cambridge, 2009).

White, Nick: 'Macmillan, Kennedy and the Key West meeting: Its significance for the Laotian Civil War and Anglo-American relations', *Civil Wars*, Vol. 2, No. 2, 1999. doi.org/10.1080/13698249908402406

British peace movement

Anon.: 'From Operation Gandhi to the Direct Action Committee Against Nuclear War (DAC)', *Non-Violent Resistance*, 22 March 2015.

Bone, Andrew (ed.): *Détente or destruction 1955–57, collected papers of Bertrand Russell*, Volume 29 (Routledge, New York, 2005).

Brown, Michael and John May: *The Greenpeace Story* (Dorling Kindersley, London and New York, 1991).

Direct Action Committee (DAC): *Policy Statement*, 10 April 1958.

Olive, Win: *Voyage of the Pacific Peacemaker* (Wild & Woolley, Glebe, 1999).

Ricketts, Muriel: 'Harold Steele', obituary, *The Friend*, Vol. 137, 18 May 1979, p. 476.

Roberts, Adam: *Nuclear Testing and the Arms Race* (Peace News, Oxford, March 1962).

Taylor, Richard: *Against the bomb—the British peace movement, 1958–1965* (Clarendon, Oxford, 1988).

Walter, Nicolas: 'Direct action and the new pacifism', *Anarchy: A Journal of Anarchist Ideas*, no. 13, Freedom Press, March 1962.

Wittner, Lawrence: *Resisting the bomb—a history of the world disarmament movement, 1954–70*, Volume 2 (Stanford University Press, 1997).

US nuclear testing in the Pacific

Barker, Holly: *Bravo for the Marshallese—regaining control in a post-nuclear, post-colonial world* (Wadsworth, Belmont, 2004).

Bigelow, Albert: *The Voyage of the Golden Rule* (Doubleday & Company, Garden City, NY, 1959).

Bordnera, Autumn, Danielle Crosswell, Ainsley Katz, Jill Shah, Catherine Zhang, Ivana Nikolic-Hughes, Emlyn Hughes and Malvin Ruderman: 'Measurement of background gamma radiation in the northern Marshall Islands', *Proceedings of the National Academy of Sciences of the United States of America* (PNAS), Vol. 113, No. 25, 2016, pp. 6833–6838. doi.org/10.1073/pnas.1605535113

Cronkite, E.P., Robert A. Conard and V.P. Bond: 'Historical events associated with fallout from Bravo shot—Operation Castle and 25 years of medical findings', *Journal of Health Physics*, Vol. 73, No. 1, 1997, pp. 176–186. doi.org/10.1097/00004032-199707000-00014

Georgescu Calin: *Mission to the Marshall Islands (27–30 March 2012) and the United States of America (24–27 April 2012)*, UN Special Rapporteur on the implications for human rights of the environmentally sound management and disposal of hazardous substances and wastes, UN Human Rights Council, Twenty-first session, 3 September 2012, A/HRC/21/48/Add.1.

Johnson, Giff: *Nuclear past, unclear future* (Micronitor, Majuro, 2009).

Johnson, Giff: *Don't Ever Whisper—Darlene Keju: Pacific Health Pioneer, Champion for Nuclear Survivors* (CreateSpace Independent Publishing, 2013).

Johnston, Barbara Rose and Holly Barker: *Consequential Damages of Nuclear War—the Rongelap report* (Left Coast Press, 2008).

Kunkle, Thomas and Byron Ristvet: *Castle Bravo: Fifty years of legend and lore*, US Defense Threat Reduction Agency, DSTRIAC SR-12-001, January 2013.

Niedenthal, Jack: *For the good of mankind—a history of the people of Bikini and their islands* (Micronitor, Majuro, 2001).

Petition from the Marshallese People Concerning the Pacific Islands: 'Complaint regarding explosions of lethal weapons within our home islands to United Nations Trusteeship Council, 20 April 1954', circulated as UN Trusteeship Council document T/PET.10/28, 6 May 1954.

'Radioactive Debris from Operation Castle—islands of the mid-Pacific', memorandum, US Atomic Energy Commission, 18 January 1955.

Reynolds, Earle: *The Forbidden Voyage* (David McKay Company, New York, 1961).

Robie, David: *Eyes of Fire—the Last Voyage of the Rainbow Warrior* (Little Island Books, Auckland, 2015).

Smith, Gary: *Micronesia—decolonisation and US military interests in the Trust Territory of the Pacific Islands* (Peace Research Centre, The Australian National University, 1991).

Weisgall, Jonathan: *Operation Crossroads—the atomic tests at Bikini Atoll* (Naval Institute Press, Annapolis, 1994).

US nuclear policy

Alperovitz, Gar: *The Decision to Use the Atomic Bomb and the Architecture of an American Myth* (Vintage, 1996).

Chomsky, Noam: *Rethinking Camelot—JFK, the Vietnam War and US political culture* (Verso, London, 1993).

Goodman, Michael: *Spying on the Nuclear Bear: Anglo-American Intelligence and the Soviet Bomb, Stanford Nuclear Age series* (Stanford University Press, 2007).

Hacker, Barton: *Elements of Controversy* (University of California Press, Berkeley, 1994).

Kahn, Herman: *The Nature and Feasibility of War and Deterrence* (RAND Corporation, Santa Monica, 1960).

Kahn, Herman: *Thinking about the unthinkable* (Horizon Press, 1962).

Northrup, Doyle and Donald H. Rock: 'The detection of Joe 1', *Studies in Intelligence*, Central Intelligence Agency (CIA), Vol. 10, Fall 1966 (declassified by the CIA in September 1995).

Rabbitt Roff, Sue: 'Project sunshine and the slippery slope: The ethics of tissue sampling for strontium-90', *Medicine, Conflict and Survival*, Vol. 18, Issue 3, 2002, pp. 299–310. doi.org/10.1080/13623690208409637

Schlesinger, Arthur M. Jr: *A Thousand Days: John F. Kennedy in the White House* (Houghton-Mifflin, Boston, 2002 reprint).

French nuclear testing

Barrillot, Bruno: *Les essais nucléaires français 1960–1996* [The French nuclear tests 1960–1996] (CDRPC, Lyon, 1996).

Barrillot, Bruno: *L'héritage de la bombe: Polynésie—Sahara 1960–2002* [The legacy of the bomb: French Polynesia—Sahara 1960–2002] (CDRPC, Lyon, 2002).

Danielsson, Marie-Thérèse and Bengt: *Moruroa mon amour* [Moruroa, my love] (Stock, Paris, 1974).

Danielsson, Marie-Thérèse and Bengt: *Poisoned reign* (Penguin, Ringwood, 1986).

Maclellan, Nic (ed.): *No Te Parau Tia, No Te Parau Mau, No Te Tiamaraa— for justice, truth and independence* (Pacific Concerns Resource Centre, Suva, 1999).

Maclellan, Nic and Jean Chesneaux: *After Moruroa—France in the South Pacific* (Ocean Press, New York and Melbourne, 1998).

Stone, David: 'The awesome glow in the sky: the Cook Islands and the French nuclear tests', *Journal of Pacific History*, Vol. 2, Issue 1, 1967, pp. 154–155. doi.org/10.1080/00223346708572108

Van der Vlies, Pieter and Han Seur: *Moruroa and Us* (CDRPC, Lyon, 1997).

Wright, Gerry: *Mururoa Protest* (Zenith Print, New Plymouth, n.d.).

Soviet nuclear testing

Kabdrakhmanov, Kanat: *Odinochestvo—dom bez sten, dusha bez doma— Transtsedentalnoe kocheve, konets puti; 470 bomb v serdtse Kazakhstana* [470 Bombs in the Heart of Kazakhstan], (Kazakhstan, Almaty, 1994).

Kassenova, Togzhan: 'Banning nuclear testing: Lessons from the Semipalatinsk nuclear testing site', *The Nonproliferation Review*, Vol. 23, no. 3–4, 2016, pp. 329–344. doi.org/10.1080/10736700.2016.1264136

Lebedev, J.A.: 'Colonialism and the National Liberation Movement in Oceania', *The Peoples of Asia and Africa*, No. 5 (translated in 'Translations from the Soviet press', Colonial Office digest no. 399, p. 3).

Maclellan, Nic: 'Tikhookeanisky region v yaderny vek: istoriya, problemy, perspective' [The nuclear age in the Pacific: history, problems, perspectives], *Yaderny Kontrol*, Moscow, Vol. 8, No. 1, January–February 2002.

Shilkov, A.M.: 'The National Liberation Movements in Oceania', pamphlet from *All-Union Society for the Dissemination of Political and Scientific Knowledge* (translated in 'Translations from the Soviet press', Colonial Office digest no. 365, p. 10).

Japan and nuclear testing

Dower, John: *Embracing defeat—Japan in the wake of World War Two* (W.W. Norton, New York, 1999).

Gensuikyo: *No More Hiroshimas, the news of the Japan Council against A and H-bombs*, Vol. 4, No. 9, 30 May 1957.

Kodama, Mitsuo: *Hibakusha—A-Bomb survivor* (Shift Project, Tokyo, 2014).

McCormack, Gavan and Hank Nelson: *The Burma-Thailand Railway* (Allen and Unwin, Sydney, 1993).

Oishi, Matashichi: *The day the sun rose in the west—Bikini, the Lucky Dragon and I* (University of Hawaii Press, Honolulu, 2011), translated from Japanese by Richard H. Minear.

Tanaka, Yuki: *Hidden Horrors—Japanese war crimes in World War II* (Westview Press, Colorado, 1996).

Tanaka, Yuki: *Japan's comfort women—Sexual slavery and prostitution during World War Two and the US Occupation* (Routledge, London, 2002).

Health impacts of nuclear testing

Anon.: 'Nuclear test veterans' survey prompts official inquiry', *The Lancet*, Vol. 353, 23 January 1998.

Busby, Christopher and Mireille Escande de Messieres: 'Miscarriages and Congenital Conditions in Offspring of Veterans of the British Nuclear Atmospheric Test Programme', *Epidemiology*, Vol. 4, no. 4, 2014.

Carter, Michael et al.: *Australian participants in British nuclear tests in Australia*, Vol. 1: Dosimetry (Department of Veterans' Affairs, Canberra, May 2006).

Committee to Assess Health Risks from Exposure to Low Levels of Ionizing Radiation: *Health Risks from Exposure to Low Levels of Ionizing Radiation: Biological Effects of Ionizing Radiation VII* (BEIR VII) (National Academies Press, Washington, 2006).

Conard, Robert et al.: *March 1957 medical survey of Rongelap and Utirik people three years after exposure to radioactive fallout* (Brookhaven National Laboratories, Upton New York, 1958).

Conard, Robert, V.P. Bond, J.S. Robertson and E.A. Weden: *Operation Castle Project 4.1a, medical examination of Rongelap people six months after exposure to fallout* (Department of Energy, Washington, March 1954).

Darby, S.C. et al.: 'A summary of mortality and incidence of cancer in men from the United Kingdom who participated in the United Kingdom's atmospheric nuclear weapon tests and experimental programmes', *British Medical Journal*, No. 296, 1988, pp. 332–338.

Darby, S.C. et al.: *Mortality and cancer incidence in UK participants in UK atmospheric nuclear weapon tests and experimental programmes.* NRPB-R214. (Her Majesty's Stationery Office, London, 1988).

Darby, S.C. et al.: 'Further follow-up of mortality and incidence of cancer in men from the United Kingdom who participated in the United Kingdom's atmospheric nuclear weapon tests and experimental programmes', *British Medical Journal*, No. 307, 1993, pp. 1530–1535.

Darby, S.C. et al.: *Mortality and cancer incidence 1952–1990 in UK participants in the UK atmospheric nuclear weapon tests and experimental programmes.* NRPB-R 266 (Her Majesty's Stationery Office, London, 1993).

Eisenbud, Merril: 'Human radiation studies, remembering the early years', United States Department of Energy, Office of Human Radiation Experiments, DOE/EH-0456, May 1995.

Gun, Richard et al.: *Australian participants in British nuclear tests in Australia*, Vol. 2: Mortality and cancer incidence (Department of Veterans' Affairs, Canberra, May 2006).

Humphreys, Trevor: 'Why RIMPAC have been so scathing on the Pearce reports 1990–1996', *Prickley Heat*, November 1997.

Lonergan, Jack: *An analysis of the studies conducted to assess the impact of the British Nuclear Tests at Monte Bello, Emu Field and Maralinga on Australian participants* (copy in author's files).

Lonergan, Jack: *Submission to the Senate Standing Committee on Foreign Affairs, Defence and Trade: Inquiry into the Provisions of the Australian Participants in British Nuclear Tests (Treatment) Bill*, 27 October 2006.

Miles, Rebecca et al.: *British Nuclear Test Veterans Health Needs Audit Commissioned by the UK Ministry of Defence* (Miles and Green Associates, October 2011).

Muirhead C.R. et al.: 'Follow up of mortality and incidence of cancer 1952-1998 in men from the United Kingdom who participated in the United Kingdom's atmospheric nuclear weapon tests and experimental programmes', *Occupational and Environmental Medicine*, No. 60, 2003, pp. 165–172.

Muirhead C.R. et al.: *Mortality and cancer incidence 1952–1998 in UK participants in the UK atmospheric nuclear weapons tests and experimental programmes*, NRPB-W27 (Her Majesty's Stationery Office, London, 2003).

Pearce, Neal et al.: *Mortality and cancer incidence in New Zealand participants in United Kingdom nuclear weapons tests in the Pacific*, Department of Community Health, Wellington School of Medicine, 7 March 1990.

Pearce, Neal: *Mortality and cancer incidence in New Zealand participants in United Kingdom nuclear weapons tests in the Pacific: supplementary report*, Department of Medicine, Wellington School of Medicine, June 1996.

Rabbitt Roff, Sue: 'Mortality and morbidity among children and grandchildren of members of the British Nuclear Tests Veterans Association and the New Zealand Nuclear Tests Veterans Association and their children', *Medicine, Conflict and Survival,* Vol. 15, No. 3, 1999, pp. 1–51.

RAND Corporation: *Project Sunshine—worldwide effects of Atomic Weapons* (RAND, Santa Monica, 6 August 1953).

Ruff, Tilman: 'The humanitarian impact and implications of nuclear test explosions in the Pacific region', *International Review of the Red Cross*, Vol. 97, No. 899, 2015, pp. 775–813. doi.org/10.1017/S1816383116000163

Ruff, Tilman: 'Health implications of ionising radiation', in Peter van Ness and Mel Gurtov (eds): *Learning from Fukushima: Nuclear power in East Asia* (ANU Press, Canberra, 2017).

Sidal, Morvan (ed.): *The Legacy of Nuclear Testing*—report of a Pacific Conference of Churches (PCC) workshop, Kiribati, 7–9 February 2005.

Smith, Ron: 'The ill children of nuclear test veterans—victims of just unlucky?', *NZ International Review*, Vol. 24, No. 2, 1999.

Trundle, Catherine: 'Biopolitical endpoints: Diagnosing a deserving British nuclear test veteran', *Social Science and Medicine*, Vol. 73, Issue 6, September 2011, pp. 882–888.

Trundle, Catherine and Brydie Isobel Scott: 'Elusive Genes: Nuclear Test Veterans' Experiences of Genetic Citizenship and Biomedical Refusal', *Medical Anthropology: Cross Cultural Studies in Health and Illness*, Vol. 32, No. 6, 2013. doi.org/10.1016/j.socscimed.2011.05.034

Wahab, M.A., F.M. Nickless, M. Najar, R. Kacher, C. Parmentier, J.V. Podd, R.E. Rowland: 'Elevated chromosome translocation frequencies in New Zealand nuclear test veterans', *Cytogenetic and Genome Research*, Vol. 12, No. 2, 2008, pp. 79–87. doi.org/10.1159/000125832

Environmental impacts of nuclear testing

Firth, Stewart: *Nuclear Playground* (Allen and Unwin, Sydney, 1987).

Maclellan, Nic: 'Radiation on Johnston Atoll—cleaning up the Cold War', *Pacific News Bulletin*, August 2000.

Medford, D: *Illustrative calculations on the radiological surveillance of Christmas Island*, Centre for Applied Studies in Development (University of the South Pacific, Suva, 1978).

Steadman, J.P.: 'From a mere clean-up contract to changing lives—engaging the local stakeholders during the remediation of Christmas Island, Pacific Ocean', Safety and Ecology Corporation Ltd, presentation to WM 2006 conference, 26 February–2 March 2006, Tucson Arizona.

Thaman, Randy and Uentabo Neemia-Mackenzie: *Kiribati country report for United Nations Conference on Environment and Development (UNCED)*, South Pacific Regional Environment Program (SPREP), Apia, June 1992.

Cultural responses to nuclear testing

Barrell, Tony and Rick Tanaka: *Higher then Heaven—Japan, war and everything* (Private Guy International, 1995).

Broderick, Michael (ed.): *Hibakusha Cinema: Hiroshima, Nagasaki and the Nuclear Image in Japanese Film* (2nd printing Routledge, London, 2014; Japanese language edition: Gendai Shokan, Tokyo, 1999).

DeLoughrey, Elizabeth: 'Solar Metaphors: "No Ordinary Sun"', *Ka mate ka ora: A New Zealand journal of poetry and poetics*, Issue 6, September 2008.

Haigh, Gideon: 'Shute the messenger—How the end of the world came to Melbourne', *The Monthly*, June 2007.

Jetnil-Kijiner, Kathy: *Iep Jaltok—Poems from a Marshallese Daughter* (University of Arizona Press, Phoenix, 2017).

Maclellan, Nic: 'Young Pacific islanders are not climate change victims—they're fighting', *The Guardian*, 22 September 2014.

Shute, Nevil: *On the Beach* (Heinemman, Sydney, 1957).

Teaiwa, Teresia: 'Bad coconuts' (featuring Teresia Teaiwa, H. Doug Matsuoka and Richard Hamasaki) in *Terenesia*, spoken word recording by Teresia Teaiwa and Sia Fiegel.

Teaiwa, Teresia: 'bikinis and other s/pacific n/oceans', *The Contemporary Pacific*, Vol. 6, no. 1, 1994.

Tuwhare, Hone: *No Ordinary Sun* (Blackwood and Janet Paul, Auckland, 1964).

Fiji military, governance and politics

Dean, Eddie and Stan Ritova: *Rabuka—no other way* (Marketing team international, Suva, 1988).

Fraenkel, Jon and Stewart Firth: *From election to coup—the 2006 campaign and its aftermath* (ANU E Press, Canberra, 2007).

Fraenkel, Jon, Stewart Firth and Brij V. Lal: *The 2006 military takeover in Fiji—a coup to end all coups?* (ANU E Press, Canberra, 2009).

Halapua, Winston: *Tradition, lotu and militarism in Fiji* (Fiji Institute of Applied Studies, Lautoka, 2003).

Korovulavula, Manunivavalagi: *Vala Mai Malaya* (self-published, 2013).

Lal, Brij V.: *Broken waves—a history of the Fiji islands in the 20th century*, Pacific Islands Monograph Series, No. 11 (University of Hawaii Press, Honolulu, 1992).

Lal, Brij V.: *Islands of turmoil—Elections and politics in Fiji* (ANU E Press, Canberra, 2006).

Lal, Brij V. and Michael Pretes (eds): *Coup—reflections on political crisis in Fiji* (Pandanus Books, Canberra, 2001).

Maclellan, Nic: 'From Fiji to Fallujah: the war in Iraq and the privatisation of Pacific security', *Pacific Journalism Review*, Vol. 12, No. 2, September 2006.

Robertson, Robbie and William Sutherland: *Government by the gun—the unfinished business of Fiji's 2000 coup* (Pluto Press, Annandale, 2001).

Tarte, Daryl: *Turaga—the Life and Times and Chiefly Authority of Ratu Sir Penaia Ganilau (GCMG, KCVO, KBE, DSO, K St. J, ED)* (Fiji Times, Suva, 1993).

Tarte, Daryl: 'Ratu Sir Penaia Ganilau', in Stewart Firth and Daryl Tarte (eds): *20th Century Fiji—people who shaped the nation* (University of the South Pacific, Suva, 2001).

Teaiwa, Teresia: 'Articulated Cultures: Militarism and Masculinities in Fiji during the mid-1990s', *Fijian Studies: A Journal of Contemporary Fiji*, Vol. 3, Issue 2, 2005.

Teaiwa, Teresia: 'What Makes Fiji Women Soldiers? Context, Context, Context', *Intersections: Gender and Sexuality in Asia and the Pacific*, Issue 37, March 2015.

Thomson, Peter: *Kava in the blood—a personal and political memoir from the heart of Fiji* (Tandem Press, Auckland, 1999).

Pacific islands governance and politics

Bailey, Eric: *The Christmas Island Story* (Stacey International, London, 1977).

Buckley, Ken: 'Burns, James (1881–1969)', *Australian Dictionary of Biography*, Vol. 13 (Melbourne University Press, 1993).

Buckley, Ken and Kris Klugman: *The Australian presence in the Pacific—Burns Philp 1914–1946* (George Allen and Unwin, Sydney, 1983).

Gustafson, Barry: *Kiwi Keith—a biography of Keith Holyoake* (Auckland University Press, Auckland, 2007).

Hager, Nicky: *Secret Power—New Zealand's Role in the International Spy Network* (Craig Potton Publishing, Nelson, 1996).

Kinnersley, Des: 'Life on a remote Telegraph Cable Station in the early 1960s', *Overseas Telecommunications Veterans Association newsletter*, Vol. 7, Issue 1, June 2002, pp. 93–95.

Lange, David: *Nuclear Free: The New Zealand Way* (Penguin, Wellington, 1991).

Laracy, Hugh (ed.): *Tuvalu—a history* (Institute of Pacific Studies, Suva, 1983).

McIntyre, W. David: 'The Partition of the Gilbert and Ellice Islands', *Island Studies Journal*, Vol. 7, No. 1, 2012, pp. 135–146.

McIntyre, W. David: *Winding up the British Empire in the Pacific Islands*, Oxford History of the British Empire Companion Series (Oxford University Press, Oxford, 2014). doi.org/10.1093/acprof:oso/9780198702436.001.0001

Richelson, Jeffrey and Desmond Ball: *The Ties That Bind—Intelligence Cooperation Between the UKUSA Countries—the United Kingdom, the United States of America, Canada, Australia and New Zealand* (George Allen and Unwin, Sydney, London and Boston, 1985).

Teaiwa, Katerina: *Consuming Ocean Island—stories of people and phosphate from Banaba* (Indiana University Press, Bloomington, 2015).

Van Trease, Howard (ed.): *Atoll politics—the Republic of Kiribati* (Institute of Pacific Studies, Suva, 1993).

Newspaper and magazine articles

Anon.: 'Air Marshal Sir Geoffrey Dhenin', obituary, *Daily Telegraph*, 11 May 2011.

Anon.: 'Bill for former soldiers passed', *Fiji Times*, 14 December 1999.

Anon.: 'Bill to benefit ex-servicemen', *Daily Post*, 14 December 1999.

Anon.: 'Blast from the past—lest we forget', *Fiji Daily Post*, 26 June 1999.

Anon.: 'Bomb gone! H-Bomb puts Britain on level terms', *The Mid-Pacific News*, special souvenir edition, 15 May 1957.

Anon.: 'Bomb tests', *Fiji Times*, 4 April 1957.

Anon.: 'Bon voyage!', *Mid-Pacific News*, Vol. 3, No. 33, Thursday, 13 November 1958.

Anon.: 'Boost for N-test veterans' case', *BBC News Online*, 15 May 2007.

Anon.: 'Britain continues nuclear tests—Hat trick', *Mid-Pacific News*, June 1957, p. 1.

Anon.: 'Britain explodes Third H-Bomb in Pacific Tests', *Fiji Times*, 22 June 1957, p. 1.

Anon.: 'British nuclear test veterans take cancer claims to supreme court', *Guardian* (UK), 29 July 2011.

Anon.: 'Cancer check on Kiwi sailors at nuclear tests', *Evening Post*, 20 August 1987.

Anon.: 'Does anyone know what happened to Mary and Billy?', *Fissionline*, No. 2, April 2013.

Anon.: 'Fiji soldiers guinea pigs in nuclear testing', *Fiji Sun*, 14 December 1999.

Anon.: 'H-bomb tests alarm Japan', *Birmingham Post*, 9 May 1957.

Anon.: 'H-bomb tests—North, South, East or West of Christmas Island?', *Pacific Islands Monthly*, Volume XXVII, No. 5, December 1956, p. 55.

Anon.: 'H-Bomb witnesses sought', *Dominion*, 21 July 1987.

Anon.: 'House passes bill to cater for Christmas Island veterans', *Fiji Sun*, 14 December 1999.

Anon.: 'Hydrogen bomb "was a beaut"', *Auckland Herald*, 17 July 1957.

Anon.: 'Malvern couple refused visas for "suicide" plan', *Birmingham Post*, 27 March 1957.

Anon.: 'Maralinga's afterlife', *The Age*, 11 May 2003.

Anon.: 'Marshall Islanders urgent pleas—end A-bomb tests', *The Times* (London), 15 May 1954.

Anon.: 'Nuclear blast veterans have genetic damage—Massey study', *Radio New Zealand*, 15 May 2007.

Anon.: 'Nuclear test study could help sailors' lawsuit—lawyer', *NZ Herald*, 15 May 2007.

Anon.: 'Nuclear test veteran gets U.S. payout', *Daily Mail*, 25 July 2006.

Anon.: 'Nuclear test veterans to push for legal action', *ABC News Online*, 15 May 2007.

Anon.: 'Nuke tests caused NZ genetic damage: report', *ABC News Online*, 14 May 2007.

Anon.: 'NZRSA offers minister support with A-Test survey', *NZRSA Review*, Vol. 58, No. 5, October 1987.

Anon.: 'Our H-bomb tests will be "so small"', *News Chronicle*, 28 March 1957.

Anon.: 'Pacifist seeks to demonstrate against H-tests', *Florence Times* (US), 16 May 1957.

Anon.: 'Penaia Ganilau, 75, Fiji Leader Who Became the First President', Obituary, *New York Times*, 17 December 1993.

Anon.: 'Prepared to die on a Pacific atoll—pacifist's H-bomb protest', *The Scotsman*, 9 May 1957.

Anon.: 'Preparing for H-blast', *Daily Telegraph*, 20 December 1956.

Anon.: 'Round the clock work building "Boffin Town"', *Dundee Evening Telegraph*, June 1957.

Anon.: 'Sailor rubbishes Navy's claim of bomb test checks', *Evening Post*, 1 August 1987.

Anon.: 'Tavo na italanoa ni vakalutu gasaukuro', *Nai Lalakai*, 24 June 1999.

Anon.: 'Tokyo H-bomb protest', *Fiji Times*, 31 May 1957, p. 1.

Anon.: 'UN will not stop Pacific H-bomb test', *Fiji Times*, 23 July 1956, p. 1.

Anon.: 'We will risk our lives to prove the bomb is evil', *Sunday Pictorial*, 24 March 1957.

Anon.: 'Will sail to H-test area', *Daily Worker*, 19 March 1957.

Bell, Cathy: 'H-bomb tests crews win pension', *Dominion*, 31 March 1998.

Bird, Kai and Martin J. Sherwin: 'The Myths of Hiroshima', *LA Times*, 5 August 2005.

Boniface, Susie: 'Babies were exposed to lethal radiation after being sent to nuke-blasted Christmas Island', *Sunday Mirror* (UK), 9 March 2008.

Boniface, Susie: 'My wife visited and later had 6 miscarriages & died of cancer', *Sunday Mirror* (UK), 9 March 2008.

Boniface, Susie: 'Nuclear test veteran dies after years of suffering as MoD throw out his court claim', *Daily Mirror*, 12 March 2012.

Cava, Litia: 'Veterans Salute Govt', *Fiji Sun*, 1 February 2015.

Dearnaley, Matthew: 'Nuclear veterans target Britain—claim for children's birth defects', *New Zealand Herald*, 9 April 1998.

Delailomaloma, Frederica: 'Bill for former soldiers passed', *Fiji Times*, 14 December 1999.

Dutt, Reggie: 'Fiji soldiers guinea pigs in nuclear testing', *Fiji Sun*, 14 December 1999.

Edwards, Rob: 'Plane deceit', *New Scientist*, 8 May 1999.

Evans, Rob: 'US compensation for British nuclear test veteran', *The Guardian*, 26 July 2006.

Evans, Rob: 'Widow of British nuclear test veteran awarded $75,000 by US', *Observer*, 21 October 2010.

Higgins, Ean: 'Nuclear veterans plan class action', *The Australian*, 15 May 2007.

Hill, Ruth: 'Study backs nuclear test veterans' claims', *The Dominion Post* (NZ), 16 June 2008.

Laing, Iain: 'Green team booked to clean up island', *The Journal*, 22 March 2005.

Leigh, David and Paul Lashmar: 'Revealed at last: the deadly secrets of Britain's A-Bombs', *The Observer*, 24 March 1985.

Naleba, Mere: 'Payout for nuclear veterans', *Fiji Times*, 30 January 2015.

Narsey, Wadan: 'Raw deal for nuke test Guinea Pigs', *Sunday Times* (Fiji), 13 June 1999.

Rimmer, Alan: 'Charity bosses cash in', *Fissionline*, No. 44, May 2016.

Schreiber, Mark: 'Lucky Dragon's lethal catch', *The Japan Times*, 18 March 2012.

Sefton, Roy: 'NZNTV Association', *Navy Times*, September 2002, p. 11.

Sheers, Owen: 'Bomb Gone', *Granta*, No. 101, 1 August 2008.

Stuart, Hamish: 'Study finds nuclear veterans suffered genetic damage', *New Zealand Herald*, 14 May 2007.

Tetsuya Okahata: 'Protests against nuclear tests', *Chugoku Shimbun* (Hiroshima), 25 June 1995.

Vuibau, Tevita: 'Joy for war veteran exposed to nuke test', *Fiji Times*, 22 February 2015.

Waugh, Bill: 'Creation of the N-petition', *Associated Press*, 29 May 1954.

Government reports and factsheets

Australian Radiation Protection and Nuclear Safety Agency: *Australian Strontium-90 Testing program 1957–78* (ARPANSA, Sydney, n.d.).

Brigadier General J.W. White and Rear Admiral G.S. Patrick: *Report of United States observers of a nuclear test*, Atomic Energy Commission, AEC 663/13, 10 December 1957.

Proceedings of the Legislative Council of the Cook Islands, paper number 3, 1956.

Redfern Inquiry into human tissue analysis in UK nuclear facilities (Her Majesty's Stationery Office, London, 10 November 2010), Vol. 1.

Richards, Patsy: 'Nuclear Test Veterans—compensation', House of Commons Library, standard note SNSC-05145, 31 January 2013.

UK Colonial Office: *Gilbert and Ellice Islands Colony and the Central and Southern Line Islands—Report for the Years 1956 and 1957* (Her Majesty's Stationery Office, London, 1959).

UK Colonial Office: *Gilbert and Ellice Islands Colony and the Central and Southern Line Islands—Report for the Years 1958 and 1959* (Her Majesty's Stationery Office, London, 1961).

UK Ministry of Defence: 'UK atmospheric nuclear weapons tests: UK programme', Factsheet 5, June 2008.

UK Ministry of Defence: *Operation Grapple 1956–57*, Handbook for UK personnel, 1957.

UNESCO: *Bikini Atoll Nuclear Test Site*, World Heritage List.

US Atomic Energy Commission (AEC): *Minutes of the Advisory Committee on Biology and Medicine*, 13–14 January 1956 (AEC, New York, 1956).

US Defense Threat Reduction Agency (USDTRA): 'Operation Castle', Fact Sheet, May 2015.

US Defense Threat Reduction Agency (USDTRA): 'Operation Hardtack', Fact Sheet, May 2015.

US Defense Threat Reduction Agency (USDTRA): 'Operation Ivy', Fact Sheet, May 2015.

US Defense Threat Reduction Agency (USDTRA): 'Operation Dominic 1', Fact Sheet, May 2015.

US Defense Threat Reduction Agency (USDTRA): *Johnston Atoll Radiological Survey* (JARS), 6 January 2000.

Hansard reports, United Kingdom

'Hydrogen bomb tests Pacific (representation)', Hansard, UK House of Commons, 20 May 1954.

'Christmas Island Nuclear Tests', statement by John Spellar, Secretary of State for Defence, UK House of Commons, Hansard Written Answers for 20 January 1999, col. 462.

'Christmas Island: Radioactive Waste', Under Secretary of State for Defence Andrew Robathan, UK House of Commons, Hansard Written Answers for 17 February 2011.

'Nuclear Test Veterans', Mr Llew Smith MP, UK House of Commons, Hansard official report, 4 February 1998, col. 1006.

'Nuclear Test Veterans', Statement by Secretary of Defence John Spellar MP, UK House of Commons, Hansard official report, 4 February 1998, col. 1009.

Question to Prime Minister Harold Macmillan, UK House of Commons, Hansard official report, 16 April 1957.

Speech by Prime Minister Sir Winston Churchill, UK House of Commons, Hansard official report, 1 March 1955.

Statement by Dr Ian Gibson MP, UK House of Commons, Hansard official report, 22 October 2008, col. 419.

Statement by John Baron MP, UK House of Commons, Hansard official report, 29 October 2013, col. 233WH.

Statement by Parliamentary Under-Secretary of State for Defence Dr Lewis Moonie, UK House of Commons, Hansard, 4 December 2002, col. 262WH.

Statement by Prime Minister Harold Macmillan UK House of Commons Hansard official report, 5 March 1957, Vol. 566, col. 178.

Statement by Siobhan McDonagh MP, UK House of Commons, Hansard official report, 4 December 2002, col. 251WH.

Statement by Under-Secretary for the Ministry of Defence Derek Twigg, UK House of Commons Hansard official report, 29 October 2007, col. 979W.

UK Select Committee on Defence: *Legacy Issues for the Armed Forces Pension Scheme: Compensation for nuclear test veterans*, March 2003.

Hansard reports, Fiji

Debate over Fiji Servicemen's After-Care Fund (Amendment) Bill 1999, Daily Hansard, House of Representatives, Parliament of Fiji, Wednesday, 1 December 1999.

Debate over Fiji Servicemen's After-Care Fund (Amendment) Bill 1999, Daily Hansard, Senate, Parliament of Fiji, Wednesday, 1 December 1999.

Court cases

AB and Others versus Ministry of Defence [2009] EWHC 1225 (QB).

Abdale and Others versus Secretary of State, War Pensions and Armed Forces Compensation Chamber, Royal Courts of Justice, London, 16 December 2016.

Case of McGinley and Egan v. the United Kingdom, European Court of Human Rights, Strasbourg, France, 9 June 1998. § 68, Reports of Judgments and Decisions 1998-III (10/1997/794/995-996).

Jean Ethel Sinfield and Others against the United Kingdom, European Court of Human Rights (Fourth Section), Application no. 61332/12, 18 February 2014.

L.C.B. v. the United Kingdom, 9 June 1998, European Court of Human Rights, Strasbourg, France, § 35, Reports of Judgments and Decisions 1998-III.

Ministry of Defence versus AB and Others [2012] UK Supreme Court, UKSC 9.

Ministry of Defence versus AB and Others, UK Court of Appeal (Civil division) [2010] EWCA Civ 1317, Case No: B3/2009/2205.

Pearce v. Secretary of State for Defence [1988] AC 755.

Suitupe Kiritome v. United Kingdom, European Court of Human Rights, Strasbourg, France, (49753/99), 1999.

Archives and databases

AA: Atomic Atolls

www.atomicatolls.org

EISEN: Eisenhower Presidential Library

www.eisenhower.archives.gov

NAID #12082706: 'Sputnik, Missiles and Related Matters' Box 35, Special Projects.

MINDD: Marshall Islands Nuclear Documentation Database

data.nuclearsecrecy.com/mindd

PAMBU: Pacific Manuscripts Bureau

AU PMB Doc 493. Office of the Resident Commissioner *Headquarters Information Note*, Gilbert and Ellice Islands Colony. Series 1956–60.

SIHE: Solomon Islands Historical Encyclopaedia 1893–1978

www.solomonencyclopaedia.net

UK National Archives

discovery.nationalarchives.gov.uk

CO1035: Colonial Office Intelligence and Security Department (ISD):

- CO1035/48: 'Organisation of Intelligence Services in the Colonies: Fiji', 1 January 1956–31 December 1957.
- CO1035/107: 'Report on organisation of intelligence in Fiji', reports by Security Intelligence Advisers, January–December 1956.
- CO1035/113: 'Deportation of UK subjects or protected persons from colonial territories'.

CO1036: Pacific and Indian Ocean Department of the Colonial Office and Commonwealth Office (PAC Series):

- CO1036/236: 'US Hydrogen Bomb experiments—West Pacific'.
- CO1036/237: 'US Hydrogen Bomb experiments—West Pacific (Part II)'.
- CO1036/238: 'Financial arrangements Operation Grapple'.
- CO1036/280: 'Nuclear tests in the Pacific—Operation Grapple'.
- CO1036/281: 'Nuclear test in the Pacific (1)'.
- CO1036/282: 'Nuclear test in the Pacific (II)'.
- CO1036/283: 'Nuclear test in the Pacific'.
- CO1036/284: 'Nuclear test in the Pacific'.

- CO1036/513: 'Protests against the H-bomb tests in the Pacific'.
- C01036/514: 'Proposal to Use Fijian Military Forces on Christmas Island'.
- CO1036/859: 'Communism—Pacific'.
- CO1036/860: 'Australian and New Zealand interest in communism in the Pacific'.

DEF: Ministry of Defence Registered Files (General Series):

- DEFE 13/1012 Atomic weapons trials 1955–1957: 'Atomic weapons trials and training—Joint Operations', memorandum by Group Captain S.W.B. Menault, Royal Air Force, 29 November 1955. CMS.2680/55/DD Ops.
- DEF 37/15/6 Part A: 'Atomic tests on Christmas Island: Brigadoon 1961–1962'.

DEFE 5, COS Committee, Memoranda 1947–1970

- 'Chief of Staff Committee—Atomic Weapons Trials: Reports by the Defence Research Policy Committee', memorandum, 20 May 1953, UK National Archives CO53/257.

Unpublished documents, letters and reports

'British hydrogen and atomic bomb tests—Christmas Island 1958', letter from J.N. Ramacake, Nausori, Fiji to UK Ministry of Defence, 20 December 1989.

'Gilbertese children's party', typed report to Women's Voluntary Service, December 1958.

'Irati Wanti', Statement by the women of Kupa Piti Kungka Tjuta, South Australia, n.d.

'Rosenblatt Secures Victory for Nuclear Veterans', media release, Rosenblatt Solicitors, 5 June 2009.

'With the WVS in Korea', letter to Women's Voluntary Service Headquarters in London, 31 August 1956.

'WVS report for January and February 1959, Junior Ranks Club, Christmas Island', Report to Women's Voluntary Service Headquarters, February 1959.

'WVS report for March and April 1959, Junior Ranks Club, Christmas Island', Report to Women's Voluntary Service Headquarters, 1 May 1959.

Al Rowland: 'British atomic bomb testing: An unintended legacy', December 2014.

Billie Burgess: WVS Club Christmas Island newsletter, January 1957.

Letter from Peter Smart, UK ambassador to Fiji, to Sailosi Kepa, Minister for Justice and Attorney General, 5 February 1990.

Letter from S. McIntosh, Ministry of Defence, London to J.N. Ramacake, Nausori, 11 January 1990.

Ministry of Fijian Affairs: 'Names of naval personnel of the Fiji Royal Naval Volunteer Reserve who served ashore at Christmas Island from 23/12/57 to 23/2/58 before being transferred to Singapore to take MV Ramarama back to Fiji', Appendix 2, 23 March 1990.

Ministry of Fijian Affairs: 'Names of Fiji naval personnel who took part in the British nuclear testing at Christmas Island, in 1957 aboard HMS Warrior', 23 March 1990.

Minutes of the founding meeting of the New Zealand Nuclear Test Veterans Association (NZNTVA), signed by Roy Sefton and Tere Tahi.

Prime Minister Voreqe Bainimarama: 'Speech at the first pay out to veterans of Operation Grapple', media release, Office of the Prime Minister, Suva, Fiji, 30 January 2015.

Speech by Ambassador Makurita Baaro, Informal Meeting of the United Nations General Assembly to mark the 2015 Observance of the International Day against Nuclear Tests, UN Headquarters, New York, 10 September 2015.

Speech by Paul Ah Poy, UK House of Commons, London, 20 October 1999.

Speech by Tekoti Rotan to International Meeting, World Conference on A and H Bombs, Tokyo, August 2002.

Index

Abon, Lemeyo, 39, 40, 53–54, 339
Ah Poy, Paul, 135–145, 333, 336–338, 340
   background, 136
   DDT spraying, 138
   exposure to radiation, 138, 142–143
   Fiji Nuclear Veterans Association, 327
   health problems, 143–145, 286–287
   legal action, 330
   Operation Grapple, 136–138, 141–142
Āllokḷap, 24
anti-colonial sentiment, 68
antinuclear movement, 4–5, 338, 339. *see also* nuclear disarmament; Nuclear Non-Proliferation Treaty; nuclear testing moratorium; peace movement
   activism, 103
   in Britain, 91, 93–94
   calls for moratorium on tests, 44, 73, 182, 183, 221
   churches, 102
   cultural expression, 59, 60–61
   Emergency Committee for Direct Action against Nuclear War, 94, 102
   in Japan, 59, 62–68
   Marshall Islanders petition, 44–46, 52
   nuclear-free Pacific, 16, 338
   protest rallies, 63, 99, 102
   test ban treaty, 188
Arnold, Lorna, 9–10
atomic testing
   survivors, 4
Attlee, Clement, 20–23
Australia. *see also* McClelland, James 'Diamond Jim'; Menzies, Robert
   as nuclear testing location, 23–24, 26–32, 186 (*see also* Lester, Yami; Maralinga)
   public opinion, 34
   sample collection, 168, 172
   studies into effects, 296
   Royal Commission into British nuclear testing, 28, 36, 169–170

Baaro, Makurita, 255–256, 277
Bainimarama, Ratu Inoke, 6, 125–134, 327, 341
Bainimarama, Voreqe, 323–325, 334–335, 338, 341
   treatment of veterans, 322
Bakale, Anare, 229–230
Banaba (Ocean Island), 50, 71, 234
Bates, Bob, 170, 173, 250
Beale, Howard, 83–84
Bernacchi, Michael, 15–16, 48–50, 74, 222–223
Bevin, Ernest, 22–23

Bikini Atoll, 22, 40–41, 43–54, 56, 116
  UNESCO world heritage site, 54
Brenner, David, 304
Britain
  attitudes to Japan, 67–68
  Colonial Office, 15, 50, 241–242, 325
    evacuation of Gilbertese people, 244
    lack of reports on Gilbert and Ellice Islands Colony (GEIC), 197
    restrictions on movement near Christmas Island, 198
    secrecy, 203
  colonial ties to the Pacific region, 337–338
  diplomatic relations with Japan, 62–68, 87, 90, 101, 202
  diplomatic relations with Pacific region, 193
  diplomatic relations with United States, 84–89, 200
  Foreign Office, 15, 95, 181, 193–195, 198–200
  government, 14–16, 46–47, 48–51
  intelligence agencies, 92–93, 96–97
    infiltration, 194
    MI5, 91, 194
  media, 66, 180–181, 197
  Ministry of Defence (MoD), 314–322, 326–327
  Ministry of Supply, 225–228, 259, 325
  National Radiological Protection Board (NRPB), 294–296
  Pacific occupation, 70–72
  Quebec Agreement, 20
  relationship with Fiji, 225–228
  relationship with New Zealand, 206
  responses to antinuclear activists, 96–99
British military, 10, 73–75, 222. *see also* Royal Air Force (RAF)
  Aged Veterans Fund, 337
  Navy, Army and Air Forces Institute (NAAFI) services, 158, 160
  officers, 164
  Royal Engineers, 73–74, 158
  support for United States nuclear tests, 270
  war pensions, 332
  wives and children's visit to Christmas Island, 283–284
British Nuclear Test Veterans Association (BNTVA), 317–321, 330, 337
British secrecy, 8–10, 105–123, 184, 193–204
  codes, 195–196
  Freedom of Information laws, 175
  impact, 241, 322
  to minimise public outcry, 75–76, 78
  refusal to release records, 318
British testing programs, 1–4. *see also* Grapple Task Force; Operation Grapple; Oulton, Wilfred
  Aconite, 47, 48, 278
  bureaucracy, 259–260
  codes, 195–196
  declarations of success, 179–181, 196
  failure to keep records, 315–316
  fears of moratorium, 183
  flight procedures, 170–171, 173
  legal liability, 117, 295–296
  personnel, 105–123
  precautions, 3, 116–117, 170
  renewal, 185, 203–204, 211
  safety standards, 112–119
  studies into veterans' health, 294–296, 308–309, 316

INDEX

Task Force Commander, 69–80, 183
urgency, 185–192
use of Fijian personnel, 204, 243, 257–266 (*see also* Fiji; Fiji Royal Naval Volunteer Reserve (FRNVR))
   cultural differences, 259–260
   lack of records kept, 133–134
   responsibility for, 155, 156, 325–327, 331–332
Brown, Gillian, 193–195, 198, 201–202, 340
Brown, Stan, 126, 129, 132, 149
Buke, Niko, 261, 266
Burgess, Mary and Billie, 157–162
   background, 159
   DDT spraying, 138–139
   morale boosting, 161–162
   praise for, 162
Burns Philp & Company, 72, 81–90
Burns, James, 81–84, 340

Cagilaba, Viliame, 127–134, 287
Cama, Epeli, 262–266
Christmas Island, 36, 70–72, 74–80. *see also* Gilbert and Ellice Islands Colony (GEIC)
   absent from Colonial Office reports, 197
   DDT spraying, 138–139, 262
   decision to test on, 181–182
   drinking, 163–164
   facilities, 158–160, 190, 224, 239
   food, 224–225
   labourers debate, 231–234, 236–245
   living conditions, 137
   possibility of unused weapons, 190
   recreation, 163–165
   relocation to, 192
   safety procedures, 213
   troops, 163–165, 204, 221–230
   replacement, 185
   risks to, 118–119, 134
   United States presence, 269–275
   weather monitoring, 211
   wives and children's visit, 282–284
Churchill, Winston, 2, 19–37, 43–44, 339
   support of nuclear development, 26, 32–34
Clark, Helen, 293, 303
Cold War, 110, 191–192, 197, 268
   Cuban Missile Crisis, 269
   McCarthyism, 194
compensation claims, 313–316, 319
   challenges of proof, 314
compensation schemes, 8, 47, 277–279, 337
   grants, 322
   pensions, 218–219, 302–303, 321
      British avoidance of, 295–296, 313–316
      to Fijian personnel, 225–228, 325–331
Colelala, Osaia, 265
Coleman-Haseldine, Sue, 31
Conard, Robert, 51–52
contested illnesses, 281–289
Cook Islands, 15, 35–36, 76–78, 113, 121, 199, 208

Denson, Eric, 174–175, 340
Dhenin, Geoffrey, 167–175, 340
Diefenbaker, John, 189–190
diplomacy
   British diplomatic relations with Japan, 62–68, 87, 90, 101, 202
   British diplomatic relations with Pacific region, 193, 198–199
   British diplomatic relations with United States, 84–89, 200

Direct Action Committee Against Nuclear War (DAC), 102–103
Dodds-Parker, Douglas, 46

Eden, Anthony, 2, 35, 177
Edwards, Yvonne, 31
Eisenbud, Meril, 41–42, 52
Eisenhower, Dwight D., 24, 33, 43, 191
Elugelap. *see* Āllokḷap
environmental impacts of nuclear testing, 53, 143, 204, 230, 261–263
    contamination, 250–254, 263–265, 273–274
    rain, 215, 249, 252–253
    seawater contamination, 202
    wildlife, 133, 139–140, 150–151, 214
fallout, 41, 64
    contamination, 204 (*see also* environmental impacts of nuclear testing)
    definition, xx
    precautions, 4
    spread, 42, 57, 213, 214–216
    tracking, 47–48
Fiji
    government response to Christmas Island veterans, 330–332, 334–336
    participants in tests, 127–134, 135–145, 147–156, 221–230, 257–266
    respect for authority, 155–156
    Royal Fiji Military Forces (RFMF), 221–230, 235, 257–266
    support for veterans, 323–325, 336
Fiji Nuclear Veterans Association, 136, 308, 313, 335, 340
Fiji Royal Naval Volunteer Reserve (FRNVR), 16, 125–136, 222, 324

film badges, 107, 130, 204, 315–316
    lost, 314
France
    testing programs, 1, 268–269, 328
    Greenpeace, 6, 103
    Moruroa, 5, 333–334
Freedom of Information laws, 175
French Polynesia. *see* Tahiti

Ganilau, Adi Sivo, 148, 153–156, 317–318
Ganilau, Ratu Penaia, 147–156, 340
    background, 148
    Guillain-Barré syndrome, 153
    leukaemia, 154
    observation of Orange Herald test, 149–151
    service to Britain, 154–155, 156
    Tui Cakau, 149
Garvey, Ronald, 16, 97, 122, 222
genetic research, 298–302
Georgescu, Calin, 53
Gilbert and Ellice Islands Colony (GEIC), 48–50, 71. *see also* Christmas Island; Kiribati
    copra industry, 240–242
    independence, 276
    relocation of Gilbertese people, 141, 237, 239–240, 245, 248–249
Gilbertese islanders, 231–234, 236–245, 247–256
    employment by British, 222, 228
    exposure to radiation, 182
    housing, 3
    ignored in official history of tests, 12–13
    as labourers on Operation Grapple, 15–16
    as plantation workers, 71–72, 74, 76
    witness to nuclear tests, 1, 10

wives and children of Operation Grapple personnel, 158, 161–163
Godzilla movies, 59
Grapple Task Force, 73–75, 79, 121–122, 225, 237. *see also* Operation Grapple
Greenpeace, 6, 103
Gutch, John, 15–16, 223, 233–234

health impacts of nuclear testing, 151, 174–175, 216–217, 274, 296. *see also* film badges
anaemia, 313
awareness, 212
British and US responses to, 277–279
British denialism, 284–285, 294–296, 304
British responsibility for, 225–228, 266, 312, 336–337
cancer, 31, 217, 278–279, 284, 294–296
challenges of proof, 319–321
children, 254–256, 283–284, 285–287, 313, 328
debate over, 281–289
eyesight, 28–29, 145, 256
genetic damage, 298–302, 304–306
government responses, 217
hair, 40, 145, 254, 283
human experimentation, 110
infertility, 143, 154, 266, 286
leukaemia, 145, 154, 217
miscarriage, 143, 284, 286, 288–289
poisoning, 133
presumptive lists of illnesses, 8, 296, 328–329
Project Sunshine, 114–115
protective equipment, 130–131, 150, 152–153, *210,* 213–214

shortage of, 139, 204, 313
protective measures, 249
research into, 51–54
skin, 143, 145, 313
studies, 108, 217, 281, 291–309, 308–309
teeth, 287
veterans as guinea pigs, 108–110, 327, 331
Heine, Dwight, 44–45
Heine, Hilda, 43
Hiroshima bombing, 21, 58–59, 62, 212
HMNZS *Lachlan*, 35, 136
HMNZS *Pukaki*, 126, 165, 205–219, 297, 315,
HMNZS *Rotoiti*, 126, 205, 315
HMS *Warrior*, 73, 126–134, 185, 211
Holland, Sidney, 35–36, 187–188, 205
Holyoake, Keith, 211

India, 95–96
Intelligence and Security Department (ISD), 11, 93, 98

Japan
antinuclear sentiment, 58–59, 62–68
diplomatic relations with Britain, 62–68
impact of Bravo test, 55–58
nuclear survivors (*hibakusha*), 62, 333
peace activism, 99
response to British testing, 15, 62–68
response to United States testing, 55–58
Second World War, 234
surrender, 21
vessels, 89–90, 101–102

Jehu, Ivor, 78–79
Jetnil-Kijiner, Kathy, 61, 345
Johnston Atoll, 271–272, 275–276
justice. *see also* compensation schemes; legal action
    challenges of proof, 314
    contested illnesses, 281–289

Kennedy, John F., 267–270
Kiribati, 1, 333. *see also* Christmas Island
    radioactive hazards, 276
Kiritome, Sui, 247–248, 251–254
Kolikata, Peni, 132–133
Kubuabola, Inoke, 331

Lange, David, 216
legal action
    against Britain, 16, 155, 303, 311–322
    burden of proof, 314
    European Court of Human Rights, 316, 317, 322
    immunity of the Crown, 314
    joint action by veterans' associations, 317–321
    against United States, 42
Lester, Yami, 28–29, 339
Line Islands, 71–72, 82, 148, 198
Ligica, Emori, 263–264, 316
Lloyd, Selwyn, 111
Lucky Dragon fishing boat (*Daigo Fukuryu Maru*), 55–58, 62, 90, 339

MacDonald, Alex, 98
Macmillan, Harold, 105, 268, 270, 340
    audit of empire, 178
    nuclear testing program, 182–190
    relationships with Commonwealth prime ministers, 186–190
    succeeding Eden as prime minister, 177–179
Malden Island, 36, 75, 172, 197, 207
    relocation to Christmas Island, 192, 248
    safety procedures, 213
Manhattan project, 20, 110
Maralinga, 28, 30–32, 34–36, 170, 186–187
Marshall Islands, 39–54, 339
McClelland, James 'Diamond Jim,' 28, 36
McGinley, Ken, 249, 317, 321
media, 78–80, 100, 212–213, 303
    reporting on tests, 76–77
Menzies, Robert, 7, 23, 26–27, 186–187, 189
Mororua Atoll, 333–334

Nagasaki bombing, 21, 58–59, 212
Nehru, Jawaharlal, 44, 96, 99
New Caledonia, 119–120
New Zealand, 35–36, 187–188, 199, 284. *see also* Clark, Helen; Cook Islands; Holland, Sidney; Holyoake, Keith
    Christmas Island veterans, 216–219, 296, 298–299
    response to study, 305–307
    government response to veterans, 293, 328–330
    navy
        conditions on vessels, 208
        participation in Operation Grapple, 205–218
        vessels, 205–207, 208
    New Zealand Special Service Medal (Nuclear Testing), 330
    nuclear-free zone, 216
    opposition to nuclear testing, 211–212
    Polynesian administration, 76
    public response to nuclear testing, 15

New Zealand Nuclear Test Veterans Association (NZNTVA), 205, 217–219, 328–330
nuclear disarmament, 33, 182, 267–268. *see also* antinuclear movement
World Conference against A and H Bombs, 62
Nuclear Free and Independent Pacific (NFIP), 4–5
Nuclear Non-Proliferation Treaty, 16
nuclear power accidents
Daichi Fukushima, 16
Windscale nuclear plant, 192
nuclear secrecy, 23–25, 34
nuclear testing disasters, 272–275
nuclear testing moratorium, 14
nuclear tests
definitions, xix–xxi
detonation, 129–131, 136–137, 149–151, 174, 249–252
procedure, 141–143
witnesses, 213–214
Rokoratu, Pita, 312
Rotan, Tekoti, 236
Royal Fiji Military Forces, 222, 228–230
Sefton, Roy, 207, 208–211
nuclear waste disposal, 16, 31, 32, 140
clean-up programs, 53, 204, 222, 276–277, 315–316
dumping, 273–274

Oishi, Matashichi, 55–58, 339
Operation Grapple, 1–4, 70. *see also* Grapple Task Force
beer, 163
danger area, 106, 113–114, 116–119, 197–200
exposure to radiation, 7–8
failure to keep records, 315–316
flight zone, 203
impact on Gilbert and Ellice Islands Colony economy, 240–242, 243
perception of, 326, 330
personnel, 140–141
safety precautions, 105–123
tests
Burgee, 254, 263, 315
Grapple X, 140–142, 180–181, 190–191, 202–203, 213
Grapple Y, 143, 173–174, 214, 221–222, 249–254
Grapple Z, 141, 254, 258, 263–265, 316
Orange Herald test, 149–151, 172, 208
Pennant, 215–216
Purple Granite, 179, 181
Short Granite, 171, 208, 209–211
veterans, 6, 174, 328–330
Oulton, Wilfred, 69–80, 118, 339–340
on Christmas Island facilities, 137, 159
radiation monitoring stations, 121

Pacific Concerns Resource Centre (PCRC), 4, 155, 327, 330, 343
Pacific Conference of Churches (PCC), 4, 333
Pacific islanders, 7
Pacific islands. *see also* entries under individual islands
ban on vessels, 89–90
debate on sovereignty, 84–86, 88, 199–200
shipping routes, 86–87, 113
Parkinson, Alan, 32
Partial Test Ban Treaty, 37, 187, 275
peace movement, 59, 62. *see also* antinuclear movement

activism, 91–103
  Australian Peace Committee, 66
  in Japan, 100–101
  Peace Pledge Union, 94–95
Penney, William, 25–26, 34, 169, 269, 341
phosphate mining, 49–51, 71, 87, 234
plutonium, 32, 272–275
pollution. *see* environmental impacts of nuclear testing
Pouvanaa a Oopa, 7
Prescott, Roy, 278
presumptive lists of illnesses, 8, 296, 328–329
Project 4.1, 8, 25, 51–52
Project Sunshine, 114–115
protective equipment for nuclear testing, 130–131, 150, 152–153, 210, 213–214
  shortage of, 139, 204, 313

Qalo, Isireli, 223–224, 228

Rabbitt Roff, Sue, 296
racism, 7–8, 52, 113–114, 164–165
radiation, 105–123. *see also* film badges
  contamination, 143, 150–151, 196, 263, 272–275
  planes, 172–173
  decontamination, 315–316
  definition, xx
  exposure, 140, 209, 306
    British minimisation claims, 7, 204, 214–216
    pilots, 169–170
    planes, 173, 175
  health effects of, xxi, 51–54
  impact on indigenous peoples, 40, 51–54, 78
  monitoring, 119–123, 134, 201–202
  radiation poisoning, 57–58, 133
  safe threshold of, xxi, 111–112, 174, 284–285
  samples, 129, 165, 168–170, 174–175
Rarotonga treaty, 4–5
Returned Services leagues, 326
Riklon, Rinok, 39–40, 339
Rokoratu, Pita, 311–313, 319–320, 321, 341
Rotan, Tekoti, 231–236, 238, 287, 341
  involvement in veterans' campaign, 326, 333
Rowland, Elliston 'Al,' 291–309, 318, 341
  background, 291–293
  Officer of the New Zealand Order of Merit, 305
Royal Air Force (RAF), 167–175, 222
  nuclear equipment, 172
  Valiant bombers, 170–171
Royal New Zealand Air Force (RNZAF), 15, 36, 121, 187, 201
Ruff, Tilman, 112, 284

Salabula, Losena, 5, 327, 334
Second World War, 20–21, 67, 83. *see also* Hiroshima bombing; Manhattan project; Nagasaki bombing
secrecy of British government, 8–10, 105–123, 184, 193–204
  codes, 195–196
  Freedom of Information laws, 175
  impact, 241, 322
  to minimise public outcry, 75–76, 78
  refusal to release records, 318
Sefton, Roy, 205–216, 328–329, 341
  New Zealand Nuclear Test Veterans Association (NZNTVA), 218–219, 293–294, 299–300, 302–303, 307

South Pacific Air Lines (SPAL), 85–89
South Pacific Nuclear Free Zone, 5
Soviet Union
  Cold War, 191–192
  infiltration of British Government, 194
  Sputnik satellite, 191
  tensions with United States, 268
  testing programs, 23, 24–25
Spackman, Derek, 278–279
Steele, Harold, 91–92, 94–103, 340
Stockholm Peace Appeal, 7
strontium-90, 114–116
survivors, 10, 39–54, 209–211, 277–279. *see also* Bainimarama, Ratu Inoke
  of Australian nuclear testing, 28–31
  personal accounts, 127–134

Tahiti, 201–202, 333–334
Teaiwa, Teresia, 60–61, 346
thermonuclear weapons, 179–181, 211
  definition, xx
  Polaris missiles, 271
Tong Ting Hai, 77
Treaty on the Prohibition of Nuclear Weapons, 338, 339
Trundle, Catherine, 9, 281, 285
Truman, Harry, 21
Trust Territory of the Pacific Islands (TTPI), 42
Tuimalabe, Amani, 151–152, 165
Tuwhare, Hone, 60

United Nations Educational, Scientific and Cultural Organization (UNESCO), 54
United Nations General Assembly, 16
United Nations Trusteeship Council, 44–46, 52, 76, 188

United States
  atomic weapons, 21, 40, 58
  Cuban Missile Crisis, 269
  debate on sovereignty in Pacific, 84–86, 88, 199–200
  interventions, 268
  McMahon Act, 22–23, 119, 180
  monitoring nuclear tests of other countries, 119, 196
  nuclear secrecy, 22
  Quebec Agreement, 20
  Radiation Exposure Compensation Act, 278
  tensions with Soviet Union, 268
United States testing programs, 2, 11, 20, 22–24
  Bluegill Prime, 273–274
  Bravo test, 40–41, 43–54
    cultural response, 60–61
  Christmas Island, 269–275
  compensation for veterans, 277–279, 296
  criticism, 44–46
  disasters, 272–274
  Operation Castle, 41, 43
  Operation Dominic, 271, 272
  Operation Fishbowl, 272
  Operation Frigate Bird, 271
  Operation Hardtack, 41, 52, 103, 271
  Operation Swordfish, 271
uranium mining, 4, 16, 186

veterans, 325–327
Vueti, Josefa, 259–260, 266

War Pensions Tribunal, 321
Western Samoa, 76, 119–121, 188
Whyte, Dave, 315–316
Women's Voluntary Service (WVS), 157–165, 265